"*Anyone who is interested in preventing our collective conscio~~~~*
sleepwalking to extinction should read this ho~~~ ~~
practrical treatice, [...] a wonderful book
could indeed hope for a more peaceful, ,
joyful world."

Author and pi(

... transtormation

"*A profound, insightful, extensively researched, sensitive and much needed essay which provides a precious roadmap for traveling together towards a better world*"

Matthieu Ricard,
Author of Altruism: How Compassion Can
Change Ourselves and the World.

"*Thomas Legrand's book lucidly offers the new directions that are urgent to overcome the globalization of ignorance and indifference, and build the future that the next generations deserve*"

Federico Mayor,
Former Director-General of UNESCO

"*In his book, Thomas really addresses how we have, in today's societies, to redefine this element of culture. The book impacted me and could be also a very good instrument.*"

Mr. Miguel Ángel Moratinos,
High Representative,
United Nations Alliance of Civilizations

"*This book can open many hearts, many spirits, of many people so I hope it will come in the hands of politicians. Thomas has done an important work for all of us to be able to regenerate. Now is time to collectively engage and follow it through.*"

Violeta Bulc,
former European Commissioner for Transport,
Curator of Ecocivilisation

"*We desperately need to see a marriage of science and wisdom. Thomas Legrand has made a good case for it. It is a wonderful, ground-breaking and timely book*"

Satish Kumar,
Author, Editor and Activist,
Founder of the Schumacher College

"A tour de force. It is a very practical handbook. It will help me in my role in taking mindfulness to decision-makers and politicians around the world. That reconnection of wisdom and science is what we need."

Chris Ruane,
Former Bristish Member of Parliament,
founder of the Mindfulness All-Party Parliamentary Group

"Thomas Legrand is a thought leader whose time in the development field allowed him insights into how development needs to evolve toward more consciousness. This book is vital and pioneering to help us all start thinking through how this critical journey can happen. I encourage all development practitioners to read it to help guide their future work"

Andrew Bovarnick,
Global Head Food and Agricultural
Commodity Systems, UNDP

"Rarely has a book captivated me so much. I could hardly let go of it. Thomas has managed to brilliantly bring together the wisdom traditions, the latest social neuroscience, ecology and philosophical approaches - not just theoretically, but in a very practical way. It creates a deep insight into how we can really change our system, our society towards a new development paradigm"

Liane Stephan,
Managing Director and Founder of Awaris gmbh and
Co-Founder of the Inner Green Deal Initiative

"A masterpiece. Only a person like Thomas with a comprehensive knowledge of the sciences, a great deal of practical experience in ecological and human sustainability, intimate experiences with many religions and a deep involvement in spirituality and commitment to humanity, and a skillful ability as an author could create a book as valuable and timely as this. "

D. Paul Schafer,
Director, World Culture Project

"A great book. Thich Nhat Hanh will be proud !"

Kees Klomp,
Author and Professor of Applied Science

POLITICS
of
Being

POLITICS
of
Being

WISDOM and SCIENCE for
a New Development Paradigm

Thomas Legrand

Ocean of Wisdom Press

Politics of Being: Wisdom and Science for a New Development Paradigm

Published by Ocean of Wisdom Press

Library of Congress Control Number: 2021937957

ISBN (paperback): 9782957758302
eISBN: 9782957758319

To the Earth Wisdom,
and all its cultural representations;
to those who have sown it...

To my daughters, Sonia and Océanne;
to all the children of Mother Earth,
and those yet to come

Contents

III. An Agenda for Action

IV. The Politics of Being in Practice

Acknowledgments

MANY GOOD CONDITIONS have made this book possible.

I am, first and foremost, grateful to my wife Emelina Corrales for sharing this dream and helping create the conditions for this book to manifest. Having discussed with her at great length nearly all the ideas that are in this book, I think she deserves to be considered the cocreator of the *Politics of Being*.

I thank my spiritual teachers who have shown me the way and inspired this work, in particular, "Thay" (Zen Master Thich Nhat Hanh) and the Plum Village community for its support on the path.

I thank my parents for the education they have provided me and their caring support in my projects, as crazy as they may seem.

I am grateful to Jadzia Tedeshi, who helped me edit the first manuscript for this book and drastically improved the language. Being able to discuss this text with you has been very important and a relief for me. Thank you also for insisting on including more personal stories.

I want to thank Robert Schipper, Laurence de Fontenay, Carlos Murillo, Rufus Pollock, and Andrew Bovarnick for offering their precious comments. Thanks also to Matthieu Ricard, Tarek Toubale, Jo Confino, Gautier Machelon, Fabien Monteils, Julien Maury, Jean-Paul Meunier, Claudine Revol, Giovanni Beluche, Pierre Marchand, Mindahi Bastida, Jyoti Prevatt, and Arthur Dahl for their support.

Foreword

THOMAS LEGRAND'S *POLITICS of Being* is a profound, insightful, extensively researched, sensitive, and much-needed essay, which provides a precious roadmap for traveling together toward a better world; a world based on simpler, more essential values—solidarity and inner peace, benevolence and cooperation—a wise altruism combined with a sustainable and harmonious relationship with nature and with the eight million other species with whom we share this planet. Addressing the fields of spirituality, experimental psychology, governance, and organizations, *Politics of Being* provides a wealth of knowledge and hopeful solutions.

One of the main purposes of spirituality, which takes a central place in Thomas Legrand's book, is to actualize the potential of goodness and wisdom that is present within us—Buddhists speak of the Buddha nature being present in all sentient beings—but lies dormant unless one cultivates wisdom and compassion and removes the veils that mask such potential. Compassion without wisdom is blind, and wisdom without compassion is sterile: we need both, just as a bird needs two wings to fly. Spirituality is also about setting on a path of transformation, from delusion to wisdom, from self-centeredness to altruism, from entanglement with suffering to inner freedom.

One may wonder how to move from individual transformation to the transformation of our institutions and society at large. Individuals can change through training their mind, and societies change through the evolution of cultures (see the remarkable work of Richerson and Boyd, summarized in *Not by Gene Alone*, 2004), which follows the Darwinian process of natural selection but is much faster than genes and allows major changes of attitude within a couple of generations. Individuals and cultures mutually shape each other like two blades of a knife.

Just as a flower bed will look beautiful if every flower is fresh and beautiful, to transform the world we first need to transform ourselves. Besides two thousand years of contemplative practices meant to go from delusion to wisdom and from suffering to the removal of the causes of suffering, collaborations between contemplatives, neuroscientists, experimental psychologists, geneticists, and others have shown more recently that by training one's mind, one can induce functional and structural changes in the brain, through neuroplasticity, and even induce changes in the expression of our genes (epigenetics). It follows that much-needed altruism, compassion, inner freedom, resilience, discernment, and ultimately, wisdom can be trained as skills, just as one learns to read and write, play chess, or a musical instrument. Without practice, these skills will remain at their inherited baseline.

Throughout history, many philosophical and spiritual traditions, from the ancient Greeks to Buddhist philosophers and meditators, have given a central place to the pursuit of wisdom in their quest to bridge the gap between appearances and reality and dispel confusion while imbuing such wisdom with a resolute motivation to benefit others.

For this, education needs to play a major role by not only filling the students' minds with information and teaching them how to solve problems, but by inspiring them to become good human beings for the twofold benefit of themselves and others.

This indeed applies to politics alike, to quote, as Legrand does, Elinor Ostrom's Nobel Lecture: "A core goal of public policy should be to facilitate the development of institutions that bring out the best in humans." It is not the role of the state to embark on "making" people happy, altruistic, and wise, but it should provide the most appropriate conditions for people to bring the best of themselves to the surface and allow altruistic and wise people to thrive without being hijacked by selfish, reckless free-riders.

"Our old model is broken," Thomas Legrand keeps on emphasizing, quoting Ban Ki-moon. Indeed it is. Let's remember that the average North American citizen emits two hundred times more CO_2 than a Zambian, and a Qatari two thousand times more than an Afghan. How could this be right and sustainable? The concept of sustainable development is broken because, in too many people's minds, "development" evokes quantitative growth. What we need to establish as the norm is a "sustainable harmony," harmony now by remedying poverty in the midst of plenty, and harmony over time by remaining in equilibrium with nature instead of sucking Gaia's blood till the last drop.

We can live a perfectly good life with much less. One of the main crises of our times is the crisis of the superfluous, making us desire and buy what we don't need, either to live decently or to find fulfillment in life. As Buddhist Master Thich Nhat Hanh said, "To save our planet, we need to have a new view of happiness."

Let's hope that Thomas Legrand's most welcome book will inspire many to embark on this path.

—Matthieu Ricard
Author of *Altruism: How Compassion Can Change
Ourselves and the World.*

Introduction

"The way out is in."

—Zen Master Thich Nhat Hanh

OW IS THE time to tap into our highest wisdom to chart a new development path. The aim of this book is to propose a wisdom-based approach to politics, its definition, philosophical foundations, and concrete policies that can advance it through a robust science-informed reflection. Humankind is undergoing an intense and rapid process of transformation, whose inner and outer dimensions cannot be separated. If we are to survive and thrive, our whole civilizations have to change. In order to do so, we cannot avoid a profound cultural change, a change of mindsets, worldviews, and values, or, at a more fundamental level, a shift in consciousness.

As the interrelated crises we are facing are deepening, their true nature is becoming increasingly clear. Greed, hatred, fear, rage, ignorance, selfishness, lies, bigotry, and fanaticism seem to be spreading everywhere in the world, impregnating political leadership and obstructing the changes our society urgently needs. On the other hand, they are helping us touch what is wrong in our collective consciousness,[1] and, by doing so, they point the way out. They are the symptoms of a spiritual disease that we need to recognize, transform, and heal if humankind is to flourish in the future.

Darkness is said to be stronger just before dawn. Indeed, our awareness of this spiritual disease can allow us to develop the appropriate medicine. As we will see in this book, the required change needs to be so profound and all-encompassing, touching upon the very meaning of our lives and priorities, connecting us to our true nature, resonating with spiritual teachings, and constituting a deeply qualitative progress, that I can find no other way to define it than "spiritual." This also simply means growing up collectively so that, more and more, we act as mature, responsible, and reasonable human beings—no more than that. Each of us already has such people in his or her neighborhood and daily life.

There is no one definition for "spiritual," except that it is linked to the spirit or the soul, which you might have guessed anyway! Unfortunately, because of how it has been historically framed in the West, many definitions are based on an artificial opposition between spirit and matter, which translates into an understanding of spirituality as exclusively transcendent and not immanent (permanently pervading and sustaining the universe). Still, the spiritual is often associated with certain key concepts and feelings: essence, meaning and purpose, sacredness, connectedness, awe and wonder.

To me, everything is, in essence, spiritual, and spiritual development can be understood as the process by which we come closer to our true nature. From that connection, we naturally tend to manifest the highest qualities: wisdom, love, joy, peace, etc., or simply the best or most authentic version of ourselves currently available! If your own experience has not led you to believe that these qualities naturally emanate from a somewhat divine nature within us, then spiritual development is basically becoming who you are while cultivating these qualities and developing your own intimate relation to the above-mentioned concepts and feelings associated with spirituality. This is something we can find, for example, in secular humanism, a wisdom tradition that is as admirable as any other. Spiritual development can be defined as the way to human fulfillment, which is to say: being.

Spirituality is the science, art, and practice of this inner connection, transformation, and fulfillment. It is psychological science in action. It is not religion but its essence; the lived experience, the incorruptible spark that lies or should lie at religion's core. Religions are social institutions that are supposed to organize, facilitate, and support the spiritual lives of their followers. They are historical and cultural constructs that exert influence and power over their communities. As such they tend to reflect all human weaknesses and have contributed to countless wars and persecutions. Their attempts to encapsulate spirituality into narrow creeds, forms, rituals, rigid moral codes, and social systems have too often proved a hindrance to human evolution.

Religion can be considered useful only to the extent that it serves genuine spirituality. There is no reason to leave spirituality to theistic (whose spirituality involves a god or a supreme being) or nontheistic religious people. Spirituality belongs equally to atheists (who don't believe in God) and agnostics (who suspend their judgments on the existence or nonexistence of god/s), philosophers, poets, artists, or anybody else.

The inner dimension of development

To understand the need for spiritual evolution, all we need to do is to look at the roots of the many problems the world is facing and see that they fundamentally result from an imbalance between humankind's material and technological power and the relative underdevelopment of the wisdom, ethics, and consciousness we need to manage this power and the increasing complexity it has brought to our world.

Humankind has seen its power multiply, to the point that many scientists classify it as the main geological force on Earth. Now that we have entered the "Anthropocene,"[2] we could easily destroy ourselves and our planet, for instance, in a nuclear war. But our development path has not allowed the kind of human growth necessary to build a wiser society that makes good use of its power. On the contrary, this imbalance between outer and inner development and its repercussions is rapidly increasing, particularly with the development of artificial intelligence, biological engineering, and our capacity, in the near future, to drastically transform human beings.

Our technology, if used wisely, could solve most of our problems. However, its current misuse may provoke the collapse of our civilization. In the closing sentence of his best-selling book *Sapiens*, historian Yuval Noah Harari poses this frightening question: "Is there anything more dangerous than dissatisfied and irresponsible gods who don't know what they want?"[3]

This leads Harari to suggest we should invest the same amount of effort and money into advancing human consciousness as we do into improving artificial intelligence.[4]

In the twentieth century, humanity was torn between liberty and equality. If we want to retain and cultivate our individual liberties while addressing the many challenges we collectively face, we need more responsible individuals. Twenty years ago, in 2000, through a long, engaged, cross-cultural dialogue, global civil society already recognized that what we need is "a change of mind and heart." So says the Earth Charter, "a declaration of fundamental ethical principles for building a just, sustainable, and peaceful global society in the 21st century,"[5] initiated by the United Nations.[6] Behind this proposal, there is a very simple truth—so simple that we may have collectively forgotten it along the way—that our technological progress and ethical crises have made even more relevant nowadays: all the problems we face come from our minds and hearts. There also lie the solutions. As our problems grow more complex and develop unpredictably, we more than ever need to come back to this simple truth.

The greatest spiritual leaders all seem to be reminding us of what Plato already said long ago: "This City is what it is because our citizens are what they are." The fourteenth Dalai Lama believes that "the fundamental problem [...] is that at every level we are giving too much attention to the external, material aspects of life, while neglecting moral ethics and inner values."[7] "So long as people give priority to material values, then injustice, corruption, inequity, intolerance, and greed—all the outward manifestation of neglect of inner values—will persist."[8] The Indian spiritual and humanitarian leader Amma[9] also agreed:

> In short, today we search externally for the causes and solutions to all the problems of the world. In our haste, we forget the greatest truth of all that the source of all problems is to be found within the human mind. We forget that the world will become good only if the mind of the individual becomes good. So, along with an understanding of the outer world, it is essential that we also come to know the inner world.[10]

Pope Francis has expressed this in his encyclical letter on care for our common home, *Laudato Si*: "The external deserts in the world are growing, because the internal deserts have become so vast."[11]

While often loosely articulated, this need for a "shift in consciousness" or some kind of inner spiritual change has gained momentum and is now recognized by a growing community of anonymous individuals and thought leaders, from spiritual teachers to scientists or philosophers, as the key to the many interrelated challenges humankind is now facing. Regardless of wording, there is a growing emphasis on the need for a deep cultural change as recognized in the 2020 Human Development Report—a major reference in development thinking published annually by the United Nations Development Programme (UNDP): "Nothing short of a wholesale shift in mindsets, translated into reality by policy, is needed to navigate the brave new world of the Anthropocene, to ensure that all people flourish while easing planetary pressures."[12]

I believe this cultural change needs to be so profound that it necessarily implies an evolution of the spiritual and philosophical foundations on which our societies are built. Many of these foundations were contemporarily established in China, India, Persia, and the Greco-Roman world between the eighth and the third century BCE, a period German philosopher Karl Jaspers (1883–1969) has called the axial age.[13] We have now entered a new axial age.

An ongoing transformation

We can see several signs that this transformation is not only possible, but ongoing. Scientific development has considerably extended our knowledge and power not only over nature but also over our very human condition: breaking through the structure of the atom, looking beyond the boundaries of our galaxy, harnessing quanta as computational tools ... It is now challenging modern ideologies while inviting us to revisit spiritual wisdom and traditions, as we will see in this book. Together with science, globalization, and the development of information and communication technologies, especially the internet (also known as "humanity's brain"), are evolutionary forces in themselves, which have deepened our sense of interconnectedness. Humankind is experiencing an unprecedented process of information exchange and synthesis through which it can either get lost or get to know itself, reflect on its history, and consciously choose what direction to evolve in. These are important conditions for a collective spiritual transformation.

According to Ronald Inglehart, the most recognized political scientist studying the evolution of values on a global level,[14] in "developed countries," the unprecedented prosperity and security of the post-war era has already brought about a great cultural change. With most of the new generations taking survival for granted, these societies have seen a shift from materialist to post-materialist values—which was part of an even broader shift from survival to self-expression values.[15] Consequently, "spiritual concerns, broadly defined, are becoming more widespread in post-industrial societies,"[16] while religiosity declines. Indeed, this deep cultural shift moves from prioritizing economic and physical safety, as well as conformity to group norms, toward increasing emphasis on individual freedom and autonomy, openness to new ideas, tolerance and empathy for outgroups (including LGBTQ+ and foreigners), gender equality, participation in decision-making, environmental protection, secularization ...

According to Inglehart, values change mainly through intergenerational population replacements as one's basic values largely reflect the conditions that prevailed during one's preadult years. This cultural change is considered the main driver of long-term institutional changes, which tend to occur quickly only when the cultural change has reached a critical mass and is then diffused in society through media and education. That is why while our underlying values have been changing for fifty years, societal changes are relatively recent. However, a recent decline in economic and existential security, associated with rising inequalities and immigration, is causing a cultural backlash and the return of survival values—heavy emphasis on group solidarity, rejection of outsiders, rigid adherence to cultural norms, and obedience to strong leaders—among those who hold traditional cultural values and fear losing the world as they know it. This has invigorated xenophobic, populist, and authoritarian political movements and is, according to Inglehart, the main cause of the rise of far-right populism.

In addition to this widely positive cultural change and its recent backsliding, recent studies also reveal a longer trend of significant decline in interpersonal trust in all high-income Western countries,[17] with the consequent erosion of social ties. We see that, indeed, the best and the worst are on the rise.[18] While self-expression values as identified by Inglehart are tinged with a strong focus on individuality and do not necessarily correspond to the cultivation of our higher selves, I believe they represent one step in that direction, as part of an even broader trend toward the actualization of our true selves.

The spiritual dimension of the ongoing cultural change has been highlighted in particular by US sociologist Paul Ray and US psychologist Sherry Ruth Anderson. Studying the evolution of social values, they have named the growing sociological group at the forefront of current progressive cultural change "the cultural creatives." They have distinguished among them a core group of more educated, socially committed, and influential people who share a strong focus on spirituality. This has led to conversation about an "emerging planetary wisdom culture."[19]

If we are serious about addressing the current challenges, we need to recognize that our politics should turn inward and address this question of a cultural shift, and more precisely, of a shift in consciousness. This should not be opposed to the many other policy reforms we urgently need, which are in some cases well-known but often not implemented. In many cases, it should rather be seen as complementary, two sides of the same coin, with the inner change enabling the outer change and the outer change embodying and facilitating this shift in consciousness.

The politics of being

This book intends to share in a simple, clear, and robust way the rationale, vision, and potential policies for making the fulfillment of all beings the main compass for politics, what I call the "politics of being." I hope to bring to the policy level and convey as accessibly as possible the urgent need for a planetary change of consciousness in response to the current global civilization crisis we are facing. This vision has inspired brilliant books and great works. However, it has been virtually absent until recently from the media and academic and political debates.

Cultural change is sometimes identified as a potential key lever to fight, for example, climate change. However, this option often remains theoretical and is not really discussed, as if this is something out of our reach, that we cannot deliberately pursue. It is the "elephant in the room" no one dares to speak about, much less acknowledge its spiritual nature. The inner pathway to change is so foreign to our cultural software that its potential is left untapped. Like someone looking for a lost object in a dark street where the light is, rather than where the object fell, we keep searching for solutions through the traditional options we are comfortable with (technology, financial incentives, etc.), even though they cannot, by themselves, address the great challenges we are facing.

Still, as we will see in this book, this change of consciousness is slowly happening through many forms. While this vision is entering our lives fumblingly—crisis after crisis, not least the COVID-19 pandemic—this book invites us to consciously make this collective change in a generation's time. What we are missing today is a simple, well-defined, and logically articulated reflection, rooted in science and the conversation around politics and sustainable development, that speaks not only to the heart of people but can convince decision-makers and thought leaders. This vision remains often perceived as too embryonic, vague, and limited to inspirational discourse, and as such can be easily dismissed.

Moreover, we need an integral vision and framework that unifies a diverse array of relevant claims and initiatives. Most of the proposals that are being put forward tend to focus on specific perspectives (for example of a particular spiritual tradition) or dimensions of the ongoing cultural and spiritual transformation, such as compassion, happiness, or systemic thinking. This is impeding people from connecting all the dots and allowing this movement to become more aware of itself, get organized, and finally gain social and political traction. That is why in this book I attempt to compile and synthesize most of the many great ideas I have found in the existing relevant literature, often quoting texts to show that they all can fit into the general framework offered by the politics of being.

Finally, what we need is a policy agenda with actionable sectoral recommendations that can harness the power of politics and institutional change to bring this transformation to another scale in due time. In fact, the emphasis is often on the need for individual evolution and works at the grassroots level, leaving aside the question of institutional and policy changes. When this question is discussed, proposals are too often incantatory and not going beyond strategic visions, with no details on what concrete policies to implement. Having studied and worked in this field for the past two decades, in this book I intend to contribute to this effort.

I propose throughout this book a marriage of wisdom and science. Scientific knowledge per se cannot determine what we should strive for, the values we should hold, and the desirable direction of our societies' evolution. Hence we have lost our ways in the blind pursuit of economic and technological development as ends in themselves. We need wisdom to guide our nations, and the role of knowledge is to validate or reject (as erroneous applications or interpretations), specify, and operationalize wisdom's general orientations. This wisdom is to be found in the traditions that cultivated it over centuries and millennia—allowing it to impregnate our cultures, an essential condition for its legitimate and effective use nowadays—and updated to our current realities through the scientific lens.

The vision I outline is largely inspired by the many wisdom traditions that have flourished everywhere on this Earth throughout history. Beyond what are often called spiritual and religious traditions, there are also philosophical traditions, especially those which have remained faithful to their etymology, the "love of wisdom," and are thus, according to the definition I propose, "spiritual traditions," a term I will often use in this book. Unfortunately, due to the course Western philosophy has taken, this is often no longer the case in the West, which is deeply connected to the current spiritual crisis.

In ancient Greece, philosophy was born as an art of living, a way of being, an effort of inner transformation that relied on spiritual exercises.[20] Philosophical discourse was only a part of it. Anyone on the path of self-improvement or self-realization was a philosopher. All ancient philosophical schools warned against the natural tendency to get caught up in philosophical discourse, thus forgoing philosophy as a way of life. Greco-Roman philosophy was eventually absorbed by Christianity and shaped the Christian spiritual life, providing concrete exercises, models, and vocabulary. Christianity took over the spiritual role of philosophy and let what was then called "philosophy" become a mere theoretical, intellectual exercise, providing a conceptual basis for theology.

After the Middle Ages, "philosophy" progressively regained its autonomy over religion, inheriting many of the medieval features of abstract theology. Nowadays, philosophy is generally considered an art of thinking, concerned more with concepts and words than with discovering the essential laws and truth of our lives, and taught by university professors— the only ones with a claim to the title of "philosopher." Moreover, contrary to the Middle Ages, philosophy's lack of a spiritual dimension is often no longer balanced by religion nowadays. Spirituality has been confused with religion and somehow rejected by Western philosophy and modernity, something that has had important consequences on the evolution of society.

While religions have sometimes been used to divide humanity, true spirituality brings people together. I have come to the conclusion that all spiritual traditions share a common wisdom, whose different colors and forms ultimately enrich our common humanity. My own limited experience has drawn me closer to some of them, particularly that of my own teacher, Zen Master Thich Nhat Hanh, which to a greater extent enlightens this book. This Earth wisdom, that can emerge from the discussion between different spiritual traditions, provides the basis, through a continuous dialogue with science and history, for the development of the politics of being.

Spiritual traditions are humankind's most valuable common heritage, able to offer a profound understanding of human nature, as well as practical knowledge and tools for inner, and ultimately social, development. In fact, spiritual wisdom is not only relevant to our inner lives but can be applied to all areas of life, in everything we do, as spiritual teachers often embody. As societies reflect the psychological, emotional, and spiritual patterns and challenges of the individuals they are composed of, they, like individuals, can benefit from spiritual understanding and guidance. No individual can truly thrive without looking inward. The same is true for societies.

This reflection is also informed by science. Throughout this book, I will also cover recent developments in many fields of human science, in particular political science, economics, sociology, anthropology, psychology, biology, and development studies, with endnotes and references for readers who want to go deeper. I refer to a wide range of countries as examples, with some emphasis on France, my own country, and the United States, on which a wealth of data is available to document our views. The US is probably the country that has fallen farthest into the old materialistic and individualistic paradigm—what can be called the "story of separation" (see chapter 2) and the emphasis on economic development. Hence, the US exemplifies the troubles associated with this approach and the need to transition to the new paradigm of being.

I first thought about writing this book as a pure, objective, and science-based proposal like the ones I write for UN agencies or governments, and this book can provide the basis for that. However, I realized something fundamental would be missing. I reclaim it by interweaving science and spirituality, inspiration and hard facts, theory and practice, including those from my personal experience. We cannot divide ourselves, mind and heart, when addressing the subject of human evolution. Wisdom, deep understanding, and intelligence do not arise from our thinking mind alone. Still, it needs to relate to our existing body of scientific knowledge, which provides a common ground for any relevant discussion beyond narrow spiritual circles.

I hope those who generally share the vision I outline in this book will find the concepts, arguments, and references they need to fulfill their role in this great Earth transformation. I invite my dear skeptic readers who naturally resist arguments containing spiritual rhetoric and subjectivity to make full use of their scientific skills to judge the pertinence and solidity of this proposal based on the sources and evidence it cites. Thank you for your openness.

In the first part of this book, we will see why collective awakening is the way out of the civilization crisis we are facing, the key to sustainability, and how a politics of "being," as opposed to "having," can be conceived to support it. In the second part, we will go over how new ideas and practices in politics and science are preparing the ground on which spiritual values—understanding, life, happiness, love, peace, mindfulness, etc.— can serve as foundations of truly sustainable development. In the third part of this book, we will look at what kinds of policies and measures in different sectors could constitute a politics of being, before analyzing in part 4 how to develop and implement it nationally and internationally. I see this book as a meditation through which we look deeply from different perspectives into the most fundamental issues for our collective evolution and familiarize ourselves with the emerging paradigm of being.

My personal journey

As this shift of consciousness has to ultimately come from each individual and can only be truly understood through personal experience, I will begin by sharing about my personal journey. I hope this can help some of you better understand the ideas that are developed in this book. I will come back to a more traditional format for such an essay in the next chapter.

When I was starting to open to the world, as a late teenager in Paris in the nineties, I began to feel the same violence and awkwardness, the same life-denying disease in my mind and heart and in the people around me, as well as in the economic and social systems I was studying. I grew aware that there should be some links between the inward mess and the outward mess. For the most part, people pretended all was fine. I was not fine. Despite my privileged social condition, a good bunch of friends, and momentary glimpses of life's vast potentiality, I was in the grip of great suffering, fear, insecurities, and loneliness that manifested themselves in the still lulls between the exciting discoveries and joyful experiences of teenagerhood. I struggled to find meaning in life.

It took me some time to notice how most of the people around me were not in better shape. Then I realized they were not necessarily all lying and pretending, as I often did myself. Most were often simply unaware of how they felt inside. In specific circumstances, I could sense these blind spots in people's minds. It was frightening to feel these abysses of grief, grasping their depth in people's very incapacity to just be aware of them. I soon understood that all this pain, insecurity, and alienation were not only nourished by our economic system but were its very engines and perpetrators. I was not merely watching TV, but TV was watching over me, feeding me (and the rest of the cabled world) these fallacious myths that happiness is found (often in the future) through consumption, professional achievement, social status, power, ego ...

TV was policing my thoughts, constantly reminding me of this social paradigm that one can only deviate from at great cost. To exist or simply survive socially, we were taught that we needed to partake in this system. We needed to pretend not to see the fear or the absurdity or the violence that were inhabiting us. Our parents had not wanted to see these things in themselves, so they had not taught us to recognize them. Moving forward that way, humankind was somehow surprised about the tragedies punctuating its path. It seemed so unconscious. A famous historian, Francis Fukuyama, even promised the end of history with the general advent of democracy and market-based economies. We could keep on sleeping quietly.

I earned my bachelor's degree in management in Paris. Although I did not find it uninteresting, I also didn't find my vocation in it. I was curious about many things but found it difficult to conceive of a livelihood and a way of life in the system that would inspire and fulfill me. And I was already aware that my heart was desperately looking for inspiration and meaning, something that could make me dream. I did not know where to find this; my plan was to go traveling the world as soon as I could.

My chance was a six-month university exchange in Mexico City in 2002, following my admission for a master's degree in the Paris Institute of Political Studies, where much of the French political elite has studied. While it was fantastic to take a break from my own culture with lots of free time, parties, and rich cultural experiences, what changed my life was my encounter with native spirituality.

I once found myself in the red dust of a remote village of the Sierra Madre Oriental, where one of the most preserved indigenous people in

Mexico subsist: the Huichols. A deep canyon in front of me went plunging into the earth's entrails. It was all rocky, dry, and silent. Only a slight breeze was moving from time to time, wildflowers scattered among the high yellow herbs. It was really a harsh environment, and I could see no human trace in the vast panorama I was contemplating. At some point, I felt drawn to a conifer forest on the other side of the canyon, some two or three hundred meters away. As I focused on it, a vast space suddenly opened within me. For a moment I felt as if I was on the other side: I could feel the sensation of that forest within me, as if I was there. I staggered. I was part of the forest, and the forest was part of me.

Several profound experiences in which I reconnected to myself and Mother Earth followed. One night, I found myself in a small adobe house in an indigenous village hidden in the midst of southern Mexico's mountains. I was contemplating the beauty of the flower offerings placed at the center of a ceremonial circle. The unsteady lights of beeswax candles placed directly on the ground illuminated them, while projecting dancing shadows on the walls. The flowers reminded me of the deeply caring and respectful relationships the people here had established with their environment, which was palpable in the shaman's ritual that night. Everybody around me was already asleep, wrapped in blankets on the cold cement floor. I felt deeply at peace, filled with gratitude about what I had found in this country, and decided to return after finishing my last semester of study in Paris.

In the morning, a door opened. Rude daylight knocked us out of a deep sleep. A group of people from Mexico City had arrived, and I ended up spending the day with them. We went to the top of the mountain, where they asked the "Chicon Nindo," the spirit of that place, for permission to carry out their ceremony. When we returned to the village that evening (which involved a series of sprints along the mountain's slopes), I went to the shaman who led this group. I asked him if there was a possibility I could join them that night for their ceremony, though I was not sure that was what I wanted to do, as this was also my last night with the Mexican girlfriend I was traveling with. The shaman replied, "Sure, brother, you are welcome."

I cannot describe his voice at that moment. He touched me so deeply that my decision was instantly taken. I had observed him during the day and was impressed by his presence. He emanated a mysterious power that permeated everything he did, his movements, words, and gaze often concealed behind his hat. I asked him many questions that night during the ceremony. I first saw in his teachings a clear spiritual path, and I knew right away this was what I had always looked for, without having been able to put a name to it until then. I knew then why I would come back to Mexico: to learn shamanism with this man and his group.

I had found a worthwhile struggle, the fortune of the spiritual warrior, which is what the Toltec tradition calls someone on the path. I once and for all established my spiritual path as the priority in my life. I wanted to explore my full potential as a human being. The potentialities that I had a glimpse of were, for me, the motivation to get in touch with my willpower and do what I needed to do to manifest the best version of myself. When I started, with great effort, to actively take care of myself, heal myself, and cultivate my energy, I realized that until then I had been half living. I already had understood that life was somehow a struggle, whose worth I had questioned, and I decided to choose a struggle that was really worth it. "The trick is in what one emphasizes. We either make ourselves miserable, or we make ourselves strong. The amount of work is the same,"[21] said a Toltec shaman.

I felt deeply relieved and free as I suddenly let go of many ideas that my education, family, and culture had put on me about what life was about or ought to be, about what I could expect from it, or about how the universe worked ... Something in me had already known for a long while that I would not be able to fully believe in these things, respond to these expectations, and thrive among them. A space emerged for me to open to the vastness of life, to connect to what I really wanted, to follow my most profound and cherished aspirations and restructure my life, to walk a path with heart.

"All paths are the same: they lead nowhere ... Does this path have a heart? If it does, the path is good; if it doesn't, it is of no use [...] One makes for a joyful journey; as long as you follow it, you are one with it. The other will make you curse your life. One makes you strong; the other weakens you," is a Toltec teaching I related to.[22] I plunged into that mystery to see what was there for me, and found much more than I could have ever imagined!

My intentional spiritual journey started there, though I now can see that it has always been part of my life. When I was in the doldrums at nineteen, one morning, while I was painfully leaving home to go to college, I woke up for a second and stopped. I perfectly remember where I was: in front of the elevator on the first floor. Something in me at that moment understood that what I sincerely wanted to bring to the world was something good. To do so, I had to take care of myself, and I could legitimately claim support from the universe, which I knew would uphold me. For some reason, it seemed to make perfect sense at that moment, but life went on, and I forgot about this insight, which remained elusive for some time.

After my first stay in Mexico, I started to consciously entrust myself to the great spirit, asking for its support and for it to use me as an instrument of service, of its will, something I feel has been increasingly occurring.

The shaman I met that night in Mexico was also a modern doctor. I could see a unity between his personal and professional life. I wondered how to develop that myself. The deep reconnection to Mother Earth I had begun experiencing in Mexico made me more aware of how we are abusing it, so I decided to put environmental conservation at the center of my professional life. It seemed to me this was the most important contribution I could offer at this time in history. Contemporaneously, through experiences with street children in Mexico and impoverished indigenous communities, I came in touch with social injustice and the human suffering it brought. It was clear for me that my nascent spiritual path should also be a path of service. My profession should be aligned with this vision—I should have a "right livelihood," as the Buddhists say—and transform myself to be a better instrument for social change. For the first time in Mexico, I heard of a Mayan prophecy about a change in consciousness for which 2012 would mark a turning point. I thought, indeed, it could take a decade for the current system to stretch its limits and potentially collapse.

Back in France, I took some extra courses to conclude my master's and ultimately got a degree in international development instead of international trade. I wanted to work for the Earth, but I thought I did not really have the skills for that. So, I momentarily opted for microfinance, in which I could combine what I had learned in business administration and international development. I found a two-month internship with UNESCO in Paris. The first day, my supervisor told me she could offer me an additional one-month consulting assignment in Mexico!

Six months after leaving Mexico, I was back with a job at a microfinance institution in Chiapas, where I was sent to evaluate a UNESCO-funded literacy program. I spent almost three years in Mexico, continuing to learn as much as I could from shamans while working on microfinance with different organizations as a manager and consultant. While I liked the non-paternalistic approach of microfinance emphasizing trust, responsibility, and empowerment, I discovered the best and worst of it. A beautiful idea conceived for the greater good could easily be transformed into an instrument of exploitation by corrupt minds and systems.

After three years I came back to France, quite exhausted due to some personal issues. I had many wounds to heal, habit energies to transform, and my then-girlfriend was suffering anxiety attacks. I was still feeling a strong call to do something for the Earth without seeing the expertise I could bring, so I started to work in management consulting. I wanted to experience a different professional environment (and I was curious about the one I was geared toward before my experience in Mexico) and play a different social role—a practice Toltec shamans call "not doing"—knowing that it would always be helpful if I later chose to continue working on microfinance or simply as a consultant of some sort.

A year later, I started a PhD in (ecological) economics, in parallel to my work, which I finally left two years later, after a long assignment in Madagascar on financial sector reform, where I also got in touch with local traditions and medicine men. I studied the Costa Rican national program of economic incentives for forest conservation ("payments for environmental services"). This PhD thesis taught me three main things. First, by looking through a new lens, that of ecological and institutional economics, rather than more orthodox environmental economics, I was discovering a very different story than the one generally told. It was more about symbolically rewarding the efforts of people who were intrinsically motivated to fulfill their own responsibility to take care of the nature they and their neighbors enjoy, rather than making conservation financially attractive to some "homo economicus" only interested in their own financial gains.

Secondly, the question was then not so much how to influence selfish individuals to act for the common good. In addition to better regulation, it seemed to me the key to addressing these environmental challenges was to change this transactional mindset. This echoed the conclusion of a major scientific voice in the field of natural resources management, arguably the most influential voice in institutional analysis. American political economist Elinor Ostrom, in her Nobel Prize in Economics lecture in 2009, summarized the most important lesson she drew from fifty years of research:

> Designing institutions to force (or nudge) entirely self-interested individuals to achieve better outcomes has been the major goal posited by policy analysts for governments to accomplish for much of the past half century. Extensive empirical research leads me to argue that instead, a core goal of public policy should be to facilitate the development of institutions that bring out the best in humans.[23]

Finally, I understood that for sustainability to succeed, it needs to be built not only on the livelihoods of people but on their very identity as a nation, as Costa Rica has done. For instance, the country set a goal to achieve carbon neutrality by 2021 to celebrate the two-hundred-year anniversary of its independence. Being a green country, together with not having an army, is Costa Rican's main source of pride—some of my interviewees even told me that a Costa Rican who does not like nature was a bad Costa Rican.

In fact, my most important PhD result was my Costa Rican now-wife. Three months before this first mission, I had been through a personal crisis and wanted to put an end to everything I was doing—my PhD, my professional work, and the NGO dedicated to environmental consulting we had just launched with some friends—to dedicate myself to an energetic healing technique I had just discovered. Overcome with tiredness and the separation from my girlfriend of five years, I momentarily lost faith in the kind of change that could be achieved through this work. My PhD supervisor told me I was already committed to this first trip to Costa Rica, and I had to honor that commitment. The girlfriend I was breaking up with told me: "There is always a reason for things to happen ... who knows? You might have someone to meet there."

I arrived in Costa Rica in August 2009, staying in a cheap hotel that was renting rooms by the hour—usually not a very good sign—feeling lonelier than ever in this unknown place. The day I met Emelina, I decided to rent a room from her for two months. Before making the decision, I thought, She is practicing Zen meditation and works in environmental conservation, so in principle, we should be able to get by. We became best friends so quickly that at the end of my stay, I invited her on a trip to Mexico. Two years later, during which we gradually came to realize we were soul mates, we became partners. I was amazed a conscious universe had sent me directly from France to Emelina's very house in Costa Rica so that we could find each other. Retrospectively, I feel a bit like I was a pizza delivered on time.

Following my first encounters with shamans in Mexico, I did not, of course, change overnight in living my daily life up to my ideals. I'm still working on those. But I set my intention, and these personal agreements—which I always need to come back to nurture and meditate on—started to shape the main orientations of my personal and professional life. Little by little, my life—partner, friends, work, home location, etc.—started to unify itself around my spiritual path, and many wonderful gifts manifested themselves. Throughout the years I've had the chance to study and practice different spiritual paths, including meditation and the practice of energetic arts, and it became clear to me they were all fundamentally referring to the same kind of experience and understanding. I developed a great trust in the wisdom of all spiritual traditions and teachers, as I could see how they were transforming my life for good. I was always particularly interested in their views on our current collective reality and challenges.

In 2010, through a professional assignment in India, I discovered the teachings of Sri Aurobindo—a Hindu spiritual teacher whose work on humankind spiritual evolution, we will see later, has been very influential—that felt so close to me. This vision of humankind as undergoing a process of spiritual evolution has progressively grown in me and seems more and more the right lens through which I can understand the happenings of the world. It feels so incredible to me that it is still almost completely absent from our public debate. Nevertheless, during the 2008 financial crisis, we started to clearly see the obsolescence of our economic system and to open up to a whole range of new possibilities. From one day to the other, ideas that used to be considered completely inappropriate started being discussed, and that was promising. This is happening again with the COVID-19 crisis.

While obtaining my PhD, I started working as an independent consultant on environmental conservation and sustainable development in Latin America, Africa, and Asia, for international organizations, such as UN agencies, companies, and NGOs. This is what I have been doing for the last ten years. As an environmentalist, I have always felt we are working against the flow, as general economic dynamics so intrinsically oppose the logic of environmental sustainability. I have come to the conclusion that there is no hope for achieving sustainability without a real paradigmatic change, a profound reorientation of our economic systems, our societies, and lives.

Though I have led strategic work, such as national green development strategies, I have never really had a chance to approach my work from the perspective of this book and put forward this vision that has been growing in me. There is never the space to go back to the really deep roots of our problems. That is why I felt I should take the time to write this book that I have patiently nurtured and meditated upon since 2012. As I am finishing the manuscript in early 2021, I am working for the United Nations Development Programme (UNDP) on the early development of the Conscious Food Systems Alliance. The initiative aims at leveraging the power of inner transformation through proven approaches such as mindfulness, to support systemic change toward sustainability in the food and agricultural systems. It seeks to establish conscious sustainability as a field of practice through a dedicated lab and a global community of practitioners and institutional partners, as well as a portfolio of initiatives.

It is great to see the growing legitimacy of such an approach, as I have noticed that this has been an important artificial barrier set between us until now. This work has been an opportunity for me to share this perspective with people in many different organizations, who often feel isolated and tend to avoid expressing their deeper wisdom. However, when spaces open up to discuss these ideas, which has increasingly become the case with the COVID-19 pandemic, one realizes there are so many people supporting the integration of the inner dimension to our works, including at the highest hierarchical levels.

The first day I met my wife in Costa Rica, when she heard I was French, she told me, "There is a place I would like to know in France. It is called Plum Village." She was talking about the Buddhist monastery and mindfulness practice center of Zen Master Thich Nhat Hanh, often considered one of the most influential Buddhist and spiritual teachers of our times and the "father of mindfulness." Born in Vietnam in 1926, his lifelong peace activism began during the Vietnam war. In 1967, Dr. Martin Luther King Jr. nominated Thich Nhat Hanh for the Nobel Peace Prize, saying he did "not personally know of anyone more worthy of [it]."[24]

In 2014, a couple of weeks before going to Plum Village, I wrote in my diary that I could feel something important was there for me. It took my wife and I six months after this first visit to settle down nearby, in the southwest of France, which was soon followed by the arrival of two beautiful daughters. We have lived there since then and enjoy practicing mindfulness, community life, and engaged or applied spirituality.

I

SUSTAINABILITY AS COLLECTIVE AWAKENING

"There is nothing more powerful than an idea whose time has come."

—Victor Hugo, poet

1

An Obsolete
Development Path

"The old model is broken. We need to create a new one."[1]

—Ban Ki-moon,
former UN Secretary-General

An ambivalent development, no longer sustainable

DURING THE LAST two centuries, a model of development, originated in the West, has been widely promoted; first during colonization, and later on through globalization, and hence adopted by other cultures. It relies basically on modern science and its technical applications as a means to master nature and bring material prosperity, from which happiness supposedly stems. Indeed, this model has provided humankind with unprecedented power over nature and material development. The World Gross Domestic Product (GDP) has been multiplied by more than seventy during the last one hundred and fifty years. The global GDP per capita rose almost twelvefold from US$ 1,263 in 1870 to US$ 14,574 in 2016, while the global population was multiplied by six from 1.3 billion to 7.7 billion.[2]

Over the same time, the humanist ideals born during the Enlightenment have brought about significant improvements in human rights and freedoms in numerous countries. The number of democracies has increased tremendously during the twentieth century, exceeding the number of autocracies since 2002.[3] Discriminatory attitudes and behaviors are generally decreasing, with women's and minorities' rights progressing, though not linearly. While the last century was marked by two World Wars and the start of the nuclear age, since the second half of the twentieth century we have probably enjoyed one of the most peaceful times in human history.

However, development has also brought about enormous challenges, potentially jeopardizing humankind's own future on Earth. The possibility of a widespread collapse of society is now widely admitted and actively discussed. This model of development, founded on the pursuit of economic growth, has largely destroyed social and environmental capital to produce economic capital. Our planet is feverish and calling for help. It is now obvious that this system based on infinite material accumulation is not sustainable in a finite world. We are already consuming as many ecological resources as if we lived on 1.75 planets, and we would need the equivalent of five planets if all of humankind adopted the average US citizen's lifestyle.[4] The Earth is headed toward the sixth mass extinction of her long history, with a 60 percent decrease in wildlife populations since 1970,[5] while 25 percent of all plant and animal species are threatened with extinction.[6]

Global temperatures are currently on track for a three to five degree Celsius rise by 2100,[7] way above the estimated threshold of 1.5 to 2 degrees we need to avoid a climate catastrophe. Moreover, traditional livelihoods and community-based solidarities that used to provide for people's basic needs have been undermined, and societies disarticulated, bringing people into poverty[8] and marginalization. Inequalities have boomed between the poorest and richest nations and especially among most countries. According to Oxfam, the twenty-six richest people on Earth hold more wealth than the poorest half of humankind.[9] As we will see in chapter 8 and in the observations of Inglehart, rising inequalities have a deeply negative social impact, leading to more polarized and less open societies.

In the words of French philosopher Edgar Morin, "Development is complex, that is to say ambivalent, negative and positive at the same time."[10] But development has now reached its limits: its negative impact is now undermining the benefits it brought us, threatening the very future of humanity.

The decorrelation between happiness and material accumulation

As it increasingly appears that material development is not the main avenue for societal happiness, this model is also losing its legitimacy, in particular for high-income countries. If economic development can strongly increase subjective well-being in its early stages—an indicator based on interviewees' own assessments of their level of happiness and life satisfaction—once a certain level of material prosperity is reached, its correlation to well-being plateaus (see figure 1 below). That is why, for example, some Latin American countries seem happier than many so-called "developed countries" with a higher GDP, a very deficient metric even when it comes to measuring material wealth.

We can also observe the diminishing returns of economic development in other key social indicators, such as life expectancy (which had started to diminish in the US before the COVID-19 pandemic), whose curve in relation to GDP is very similar.

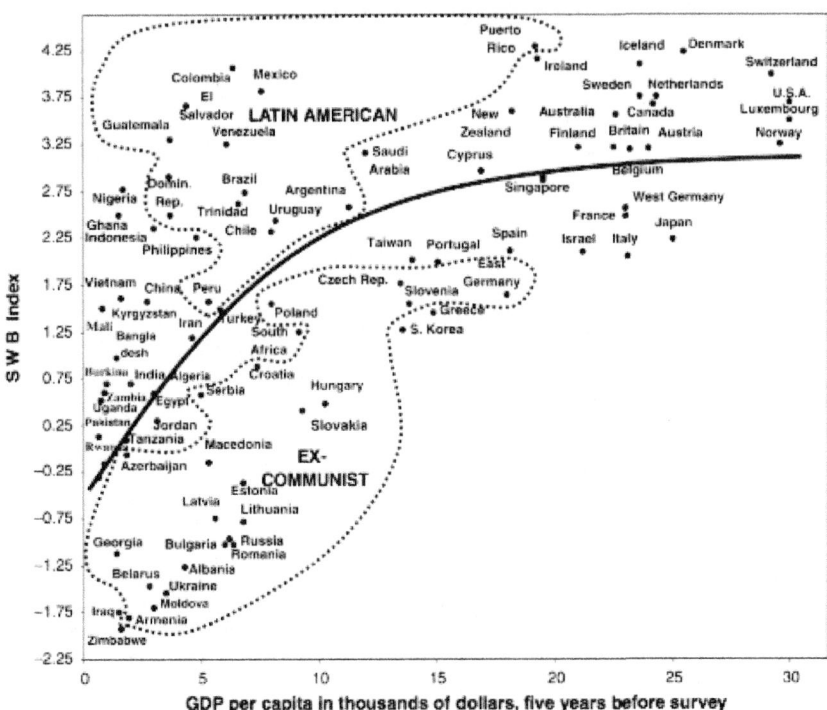

Figure 1. Subjective well-being and GDP.[11]

Moreover, the science of happiness emphasizes the quality of our relationships and social capital[12]—which our growth-based model has destroyed over the last decades—as a more important determinant of society's happiness than material wealth[13] (see chapter 6). Inglehart has also shown that the rise of global happiness in the last thirty years is less due to economic growth than greater social tolerance on the one hand and democratization on the other hand, which are currently threatened by the rise of inequality.[14] Furthermore, as we will see in chapter 3, it has been demonstrated that materialism is unhealthy and not conducive to well-being. Our self-esteem and sense of purpose are being endangered by consumerism and its pervasive advertisements.

Finally, the modern human condition is plagued by an emotional burden characterized by profound dissatisfaction, stress, and loneliness.

Many countries seem to be facing mental health crises. According to the World Health Organization, it is estimated that 15 to 20 percent of the world population has one or more mental or substance abuse disorders,[15] while depression has become the main cause of invalidity.[16] Though difficult to analyze because of data availability and national specificities, high-income countries are particularly hard-hit. In Europe, every year, 25 percent of the population suffers from depression or anxiety,[17] while in the US an estimated 18 percent of the population faces a mental health or substance abuse problem.[18]

Global suicide rates have increased by 60 percent in the second half of the twentieth century.[19] In the US, they have risen nearly 30 percent between 1999 and 2016.[20] All these rates are now soaring due to the COVID-19 pandemic. In August 2020, one in four young people (eighteen to twenty-four years old) in the US reported having seriously considered suicide in the last thirty days.[21] The erosion of social ties is at the heart of this mental health epidemic, which makes us feel (sing, Police!) "so lonely, so lonely, so lonely, so lonely!" Among its main causes are the collapse of communities' traditional social frameworks and, eventually, of industrial societies organized in classes in which work supported socialization, as well as the rise in inequalities, and a deepening process of individualization. Interpersonal capacities are decreasing. More and more young people socialize through social media and have a hard time building relationships and conversations in real life. While competition tends to dominate social relations, a general mistrust toward others is increasing in all high-income countries in different proportions and is at the basis of votes for far-right populist movements, as we will see in chapter 7.

Objectively, in many parts of the world where a certain level of economic development has been achieved, the focus on material accumulation is an obsolete and destructive compass. It aims at sustaining a failing economic system, rather than improving our collective well-being. Don't get me wrong: economic development is a good thing, per se. It is only when placed above all the rest and considered people's main end goal, rather than a means to pursue a collective vision of the good life, that it naturally becomes destructive and imposes its own logic. Our economic system not only destroys social ties and the environment but feeds on these destructions that create new market opportunities. It seeks to adapt humans to its own requirements rather than adapting itself to human needs. Based on fundamental misconceptions, this system can only perpetuate itself through ever more propaganda that feeds our disconnection from ourselves, our true needs, and ultimately, our apathy.

An inner underdevelopment[22]

Our model of development has not only caused psychological and relational failures but is also associated with an intellectual one. Our reductionist knowledge is making us increasingly ignorant, unable to understand the complex world we live in and answer the systemic, multifaceted crisis we are facing (see chapter 4).

Most importantly, we are also facing an ethical crisis, from which most of the world's problems arise. The rise of individualism, the weakening of traditional solidarities and religious moral frameworks, as well as the mechanization and dehumanization of our lives associated with the scientific and technical mentality,[23] have undermined our sense of responsibility. They have allowed the spread of the neoliberal economic idea that our own material interest is the natural basis for decision-making. Greed, competition, and egoistic behaviors are increasingly legitimized. This is particularly apparent in the US. In 1952, half of all Americans thought people led "as good lives—moral and honest—as they used to." In 1998, three in four Americans believed people are less moral than they used to be.[24]

Shortly after the subprime financial crisis in 2008, Jeffrey Sachs, a famous American economist, wrote a book, *The Price of Civilization*,[25] in which he shows that the "aggressive pursuit of higher income in the United States came at the cost of declining social capital, mental well-being, and ethical behavior."[26] On this last and most fundamental point, Sachs wrote:

> At the root of America's economic crisis lies a moral crisis: the decline of civic virtue among America's political and economic elite. A society of markets, laws, and elections is not enough if

the rich and powerful fail to behave with respect, honesty, and compassion toward the rest of society and toward the World [...] Without restoring an ethos of social responsibility, there can be no meaningful and sustained economic recovery [...] Too many of America's elites—among the super-rich, the CEOs, and many of my colleagues in academia—have abandoned a commitment to social responsibility. They chase wealth and power, the rest of society be damned. We need to reconceive the idea of good society in the early twenty-first century and find a creative way toward it.[27]

In general, we now have solutions to solve most of our problems, but they persist due to our indifference, our moral bankruptcy. When people hold more compassionate values, they tend to act for the common good and are more civically engaged than those with more selfish values (such as money, success, and personal image)[28] that our economic system tends to promote.[29] As Sachs put it, "Poverty is caused by a failure of ethics, not economy."[30]

All these failures expose our inner underdevelopment as the root of the current crisis in our model of development.

While Western civilization initially thought the development of knowledge would unavoidably bring happiness and human fulfillment through material prosperity and education, it is now clear that this optimistic vision is erroneous. Economic development has brought real progress, but in the last decades, its destruction of social and environmental capital has produced enormous problems and now threatens our very future on this Earth. We also have to admit that access to education does not necessarily translate into moral progress. Science has been used to develop weapons that could easily destroy humankind; the terrorists that crashed their planes into the Twin Towers on September 11, 2001, were among the most educated members of their societies. Humankind's belief in unavoidable progress, widely shared until recently, has now turned into a fundamental doubt. We don't know where we are headed. We are looking forward with anxiety and fear, as our model of development has now entered a systemic crisis.

2

An Evolutive Crisis

"We are on the threshold of both heaven and hell."[1]

—Yuval Noah Harari, historian

A civilization crisis

THE WORLD IS facing a multiplicity of crises. This became evident after the 2008 financial crash, the biggest economic crisis since 1929. It became apparent that not only our economic system was dysfunctional but all aspects of society. In 2020, the COVID-19 crisis is currently shedding new light on these dysfunctions. Our crises are not only economic or sanitary; they are also environmental, social, political, food-related, energetic, demographic, ethical, cognitive, etc. Together, these issues point to an overall obsolescence of our current model of development. Edgar Morin called this multifaceted systemic crisis (or metacrisis) a "civilization crisis" that highlights the dark side of Western civilization. Indeed, this model is rooted in a cultural program: our modern paradigm and its set of values—materialism, reductionism, individualism, humanism, scientism, etc. It has been adopted globally and pushed to its limits and contradictions. Within the historical context in which it emerged, it brought considerable progress, bringing solutions to the problems societies once faced in the past.

But this model is reaching the end of what it can do for us, as the solutions of the past have created new problems that can no longer be left unattended. The materialism that historically improved our living conditions has now turned into widespread greed. The individualism that allowed individuals to free themselves from harmful social conventions is morphing into egocentrism, destroying social capital and isolating individuals. It is corrupting humanism, whose anthropocentrism already obstructs our sense of belonging to the natural world. Reductionism prevents us from understanding reality as an interconnected whole, and the different crises we are currently facing as a systemic crisis. Scientism keeps us trapped in the naive expectation that technology will solve our problems.

The current crisis is an opportunity to look deeper into the causes of our problems and realize that only a different model, based on a different cultural program, can generate different outcomes and solve these challenges. As symptoms of an obsolete development model, these problems are bound to reappear with greater and greater force until we really change this model. This "civilization crisis" is an evolutive crisis that invites us into a profound cultural evolution, which many of us believe is, in essence, spiritual.

Toward a new story

Charles Eisenstein has provided one of the best analyses of the kind of cultural change we need to undergo. These analyses are presented in some of his books, including *The More Beautiful World Our Heart Knows is Possible.* According to him, "At the bottom of our civilization lies a story, a mythology [...] a matrix of narratives, agreements and symbolic systems that comprises the answers our culture offers to life's most basic questions."[2] We are currently mainly driven by the "old story," the one Eisenstein calls the "story of separation," which articulates our cultural answers to these basic questions, as shown in table 1 below. It is a simplification of our actual cultural answers, which form its core but have never dominated completely, even when the old story reached its zenith in the last century. Some of these answers are scientifically obsolete but continue to frame our understanding of what is "real, possible and practical."[3]

Table 1: The story of separation[4]

Basic questions	Main answers
Who am I?	"A separate individual among other separate individuals in a universe that is separate from you as well."
Why do things happen?	Because of the impersonal forces of physics that shape a "blind and dead" universe.
What is the purpose of life?	"There is no purpose, only cause," no meaning except to live and maximize rational self-interest.
What is human nature?	As ruthless maximizers of self-interest, we are fundamentally evil. "To protect ourselves against this hostile universe of competing individuals and impersonal forces, we must exercise as much control as possible."
What is sacred?	"Science and religion have agreed: the sacred is not of this world." We need to overcome our biological programming and pursue "higher things."
Who are we as a people?	We are the only species to have a soul or a rational mind. We can use the latter to model the world according to our desires and become better off thanks to science and technology.
Where did we come from, and where are we going?	While we once lived miserable lives, science and technology have allowed us to conquer the world and be much better. "Our destiny is to complete that conquest: to free ourselves from labor, from disease, from death itself, to ascend to the stars and leave nature behind altogether."

We see that this story of separation has been forged by the history of the West, including Christian loathing of flesh and pagan beliefs of a living nature; Descartes's view of nature as a soulless machine and of humans as other than nature; the economic understanding of humans as rational maximizers of self-interest (egoistic); Darwinism and the survival of the fittest; the modern pursuit of happiness through material progress that is based on science and technology; the separation of the realms of science and religion as a solution to their conflict ... Throughout this book we will explore how these views—which once served as solid foundations for our sense of reality—are evolving, particularly through new scientific findings that are beginning to shape a completely different story, one that brings, together with new answers to these questions, the promise of a whole new civilization.[5]

Like Eisenstein, I believe we are moving out of this old story toward the story of "interbeing." Interbeing is a term coined by Zen Master Thich Nhat Hanh, which goes beyond interconnectedness to touch on the very nature of our being. It expresses the nature of reality based on the Buddhist teachings of interdependent co-arising ("that is because this is"), non-self, and impermanence (see box 1). A flower, for example, like everything else, has no independent self: it is made of non-flower elements such as the sun, the rain, the earth, the air ... It is co-arising in an interdependent manner with these non-flower elements, which is also why it is not permanent, always in transformation. We are also made of our parents, cultures, education, the friends and partners we have had, all our life experiences ... We inter-are with all of this, and ultimately with the whole universe. As Thich Nhat Hanh said, "We are here to awaken from our illusion of separateness." This is the essence of any spiritual path, as we will see in the next chapter.

Box 1—Interbeing by Thich Nhat Hanh[6]

If you are a poet, you will see clearly that there is a cloud floating in this sheet of paper. Without a cloud, there will be no rain; without rain, the trees cannot grow; and without trees, we cannot make paper. The cloud is essential for the paper to exist. If the cloud is not here, the sheet of paper cannot be here either. So we can say that the cloud and the paper inter-are. "Interbeing" is a word that is not in the dictionary yet, but if we combine the pre-fix "inter" with the verb "to be," we have a new verb, inter-be.

If we look into this sheet of paper even more deeply, we can see the sunshine in it. If the sunshine is not there, the forest cannot grow. In fact, nothing can grow. Even we cannot grow without sunshine. And so, we know that the sunshine is also in this sheet of paper. The paper and the sunshine inter-are. And if we continue to look, we can see the logger who cut the tree and brought it to the mill to be transformed into paper. And we see the wheat. We know the logger cannot exist without his daily bread, and therefore the wheat that became his bread is also in this sheet of paper. And the logger's father and mother are in it too. When we look in this way, we see that without all of these things, this sheet of paper cannot exist.

Looking even more deeply, we can see we are in it too. This is not difficult to see, because when we look at a sheet of paper, the sheet of paper is part of our perception. Your mind is here and mind is also. So we can say that everything is in here with this sheet of paper. You cannot point out one thing that is not here— time, space, the earth, the rain, the minerals in the soil, the sunshine, the cloud, the river, the heat. Everything coexists with this sheet of paper. That is why I think the word inter-be should be in the dictionary. "To be" is to be inter-be. You cannot just be by yourself alone. You have to inter-be. You cannot just be by yourself alone. You have to inter-be with every other thing. This sheet of paper, is because everything else is.

> *Suppose we try to return one of the elements to its source. Suppose we return the sunshine to the sun. Do you think that this sheet of paper will be possible? No, without sunshine nothing can be. And if we return the logger to his mother, then we have no sheet of paper either. The fact is that this sheet of paper is made up only of "non-paper elements." And if we return these non-paper elements to their sources, then there can be no paper at all. Without "non-paper elements" like mind, logger, sunshine, and so on, there will be no paper. As thin as this sheet of paper is, it contains everything in the universe in it.*

Here are some principles of this new "story" Eisenstein has set out:

- That my being partakes of your being and that of all beings. This goes beyond interdependency— our very existence is relational.

- That, therefore, what we do to another, we do to ourselves.

- That each of us has a unique and necessary gift to give to the world.

- That the purpose of life is to express our gifts.

- That every act is significant and has an effect on the cosmos.

- That we are fundamentally unseparate from each other, from all beings and from the universe.

- That every person we encounter and every experience we have mirrors something in ourselves.

- That humanity is meant to join fully the tribe of all life on Earth, offering our uniquely human gifts toward the well-being and development of the whole.

- That purpose, consciousness, and intelligence are innate properties of matter and the universe.[7]

While the story of separation has turned into a spiritual disease, the story of interbeing can be the medicine for our societies. It emphasizes cooperation over competition and can reconcile individual freedom and thriving with the common good. This change of story has received different names, including moving from an ego-system focused entirely on oneself to an ecosystem awareness that emphasizes the well-being of the whole, as we will see with the work of Otto Scharmer in chapter 4.[8] At the core of this change is the view we hold of human nature, whether we emphasize its potential for goodness or for evil, and the consequent need to build our social systems on trust and intrinsic motivation or, on the contrary, control and extrinsic motivation (see chapters 7 and 13). We can now understand the complex nature of the current historical phase in which, increasingly, the worst and the best in human beings and societies are competing.

Humankind's spiritual evolution: An idea whose time has come

As mentioned in the introduction, Eisenstein's work echoes a growing recognition of the spiritual nature of the cultural change that the current state of the world demands. This relates to a more general belief in humankind's capacity to evolve spiritually, which has been most prominently emphasized by spiritual teachers across different traditions, as we will quickly review. While some readers might think that these spiritual teachings can take us away from a rational, grounded, and practical political thought that this book intends to develop, I offer them as deeper perspectives, in which this reflection can—but does not necessarily need to—be embedded.

The belief in humankind's spiritual evolution is inherent to many spiritual traditions, for example those with cyclic cosmologies or others believing in reincarnation and the existence of the divine within living beings, that we can, life after life, learn to manifest more fully. These include many traditional cultures and religions, such as Buddhism, Jainism, and Hinduism. Many interpretations of the latter seem to agree that we are moving out of the "kali yuga," the "age of quarrel and strife." The faith in the upcoming unification and progress of humanity is also present in numerous indigenous prophecies. The indigenous people's track at the 2018 Parliament of the World's Religions was titled: "The Spiritual Evolution of Humanity & Healing Our Mother Earth."

Most religions also have an eschatological dimension: they are concerned with the destiny of humanity, which, after many crises, is said to be ultimately radiant. For instance, this is illustrated in Christian concepts such as the "kingdom of God"—which is generally considered to be the central theme of Jesus's teaching, and, according to some interpretations, means the earthly fulfillment of God's will—or the "new Earth." In the last two centuries, three spiritual teachers from different traditions have been particularly prominent in proclaiming not only humankind's destiny toward spiritual fulfillment, but its upcoming realization.

The first is Baha'u'llah—"the glory of God" in Arabic—who was born in 1817 in Persia. He was the founder of the Bahá'í faith, which is estimated nowadays to have between five and eight million adherents[9] spread throughout the world. He was a follower of Siyyid Mírzá `Alí-Muḥammad, a young man who, in 1844, claimed to be the promised redeemer of Islam, the long-awaited Imam Mahdi in Shia Islam, and called himself the Báb ("the gate"). The Báb took that name as he announced the imminent coming of "he whom God will make manifest." Together with thousands of followers, he was severely repressed and finally killed in 1850.

As one of the Báb's followers, Baha'u'llah was imprisoned in an underground dungeon of Tehran in 1853, where he had a vision of a maiden from God, who announced his mission as a messenger of God, the one whose coming the Báb had prophesied. Baha'u'llah was soon released from jail but continued to live his life in exile in the Middle East, most often under surveillance or jailed again by the Ottoman authorities. Before his death in 1892 near Acre—now part of Israel—he left an abundant body of works, which established a solid foundation for a new religion.

After Abraham, Krishna, Zoroaster, Moses, Buddha, Jesus, Muhammad, and others, Baha'u'llah stated that he was the last Manifestation of God for this age, whose mission was to unite the human race so that a thriving planetary civilization could be established, a new world order whose institutions would embody Bahá'is' ideals of unity and justice for all. Baha'u'llah considered justice the main condition for the unity of humankind, without which its "well-being [...], peace and security, are unattainable."[10] "It is not for him to pride himself who loveth his own country, but rather for him who loveth the whole world. The Earth is but one country, and mankind its citizens,"[11] he proclaimed. He taught that religious truth is progressively revealed by God through a series of divine messengers, whose teachings are tailored to suit the needs of the time and place of their appearance, for the progress and advancement of human morals and civilization.

In fact, Bahá'i scriptures consider religion to have "been the basis of all civilization and progress in the history of mankind."[12] This view of a "progressive revelation" and oneness of all religions is summarized by Shogi Effendi, who was the head of the Bahá'i faith from 1921 to 1957:

> The fundamental principle enunciated by Baha'u'llah, the followers of His Faith firmly believe, is that religious truth is not absolute but relative, that Divine Revelation is a continuous and progressive process, that all the great religions of the world are divine in origin, that their basic principles are in complete harmony, that their aims and purposes are one and the same, that their teachings are but facets of one truth, that their functions are complementary, that they differ only in the nonessential aspects of their doctrines, and that their missions represent successive stages in the spiritual evolution of human society.[13]

These different stages of evolution are considered to be analogous to those of an individual's life, our current stage being adolescence, which precedes full maturity. As Shogi Effendi put it:

> The long ages of infancy and childhood, through which the human race had to pass, have receded into the background. Humanity is now experiencing the commotions invariably associated with the most turbulent stage of its evolution, the stage of adolescence, when the impetuosity of youth and its vehemence reach their climax, and must gradually be superseded by the calmness, the wisdom, and the maturity that characterizes the stage of manhood. Then will the human race reach that stature of ripeness which will enable it

to acquire all the powers and capacities upon which its ultimate development must depend.[14]

In their book on the Bahá'i faith, Hatcher and Martin explain:

Baha'u'llah envisioned the establishment of a World Order as occurring in three successive stages. The first stage is a period of social breakdown and widespread suffering, suffering greater in scope and intensity than any previously known. Bahá'is believe that this first stage is already well advanced and that the turmoil presently afflicting the world will, in time, test every human life and all existing social institutions [...] According to Bahá'i belief, the present period of suffering and difficulties will culminate in a worldwide spiritual, physical and social convulsion.[15]

This crisis will lead to the establishment of the "Lesser Peace," in which some of the institutions of this new world order will be established to guarantee political peace. It will be the prelude to the third stage of establishment of the new world order, the "Most Great Peace," that will come about far more gradually to establish "the Kingdom of God on earth," the "coming of age of the entire human race"[16] based on the conscious recognition and application of the teachings of Baha'u'llah.

In fact, the works of Baha'u'llah include many teachings related to this new world order that is based on spiritual principles, in particular the oneness of humanity. It will necessitate and allow a major restructuring of political, social, and economic institutions based on an intense dialogue between science and religion, the two systems of knowledge available to humankind. Among his priorities, Baha'u'llah emphasized science and religion, the equality of men and women, universal education, economic justice, cultural diversity, and an auxiliary international language, as well as institutions of international governance: a world government, parliament, code of law, tribunal, police, etc.

The second spiritual teacher to announce the spiritual evolution of humankind was the Indian political leader, poet, and evolutionary philosopher Sri Aurobindo. Born in Calcutta, India, in 1872, he moved to England at the age of seven and lived there fourteen years. He studied at Cambridge, where he gained extensive knowledge of European history and cultures. He was briefly one of the top Indian nationalist political leaders, ending up in jail and close to execution before he dedicated himself to his spiritual work and writings. Based on the Indian spiritual tradition, Aurobindo built a synthesis of different spiritual paths ("yogas") he called "integral yoga." This yoga does not aim at spiritual realization as a divine escape from human life and material experience—something Aurobindo critiqued in other practices. Rather, it seeks to constantly ascend to the divine and bring this down to transform one's human condition—mind, life, and body—thus setting the basis for a collective transformation on Earth.

Indeed, Sri Aurobindo believed that humankind, whose distinctive type of consciousness is mental, is not the last rung in the evolutionary scale and is bound to spiritually evolve to a higher state of existence that he called the "supramental." He said:

> There is therefore no reason to put a limit to evolutionary possibility by taking our present organization or status of existence as final. The animal is a laboratory in which Nature has worked out man; man may very well be a laboratory in which she wills to work out superman, to disclose the soul as a divine being, to evolve a divine nature.[17]

Politics and spirituality, Western thinking (especially evolutionary theories), and Eastern spirituality converge in Aurobindo's vision of human progress. In one of his books,[18] he applied the traditional yogic view of inner development and self-realization as the main driver and ultimate goal of man's experience on Earth through the reincarnation cycle to understand societies' evolution and development. According to him, societies are not only composed of human beings, but are beings in themselves ("national souls") in search of their realization, whose development obeys the same spiritual laws.

Sri Aurobindo refers to the traditional Indian conception of humans, also found in other civilizations, such as ancient Greece, as composed of and governed by different levels of being—physical, "vital" (life force made of emotions, passions, desires, likes and dislikes, etc. that other systems would call the emotional being), mental, and psychic (or soul).[19] Each of these forces is associated with specific questions, attitudes, and patterns of conduct. They coexist within each human and society. Inner development or the process of civilization is one in which humans and societies learn to govern their lives from higher levels of consciousness, putting at their center either the spirit or the highest cultural ideals of truth, beauty, and good cultivated through science, art, and ethics. To endure, the process of civilization needs to embrace the majority of people, otherwise it is "always in danger of submergence by the ignorant night from below."[20]

The satisfaction of physical, vital, and even mental needs carries "man no more than a certain distance; afterwards he flags and tires for want of a real self-finding, a satisfying aim for his action and progress. These three things do not make the sum of a complete manhood; they are means to an ulterior end and cannot be made forever an aim in themselves."[21] This pursuit leads ultimately to either deception, loss of vitality, or disaster. Only the spirit can be a safe guiding light and its realization a satisfying aim. The mental consciousness that characterizes human beings does not have the capacity to transform our lower animal nature of the physical and vital consciousness. When it does not subject itself to them, it can only try to subdue them. Societies then lose their vitality and decline.

Sri Aurobindo explained some of the great civilizations' achievements and failures by the economy, development, and interplay of these inner forces, which spiritual seekers learn to know, organize, and progressively harness on their paths towards self-realization. Ancient Athens, for example, initially concentrated on the "beauty and the delight of living"[22] and later on emphasized philosophy, but lacked the self-discipline and character—both signs of ethical development—to successfully translate these into practice and sustain the city's flourishing. The ethical impulse behind Republican Rome led it to an exceptional development of self-mastery, which allowed it to conquer and rule a vast territory. But this unnatural repression of life forces ultimately led to revolt, and the "early

Roman type collapsed into the egoistic and often orgiastic licence of later republican and imperial Rome."[23]

Other cultures, dominated by ascetic religions and the denial of humanity's material and vital nature, ultimately discourage the life force they channel, thus stagnating and degenerating. That was the case in India when illusionism (or mâyâvâdâ) prevailed—a doctrine first taught by Shankarâchârya (788–820 AD) that teaches that the universe is an illusion and the only reality is the unmanifested divine, Brahman. Reason, whose divine essence is to search truth for itself, can also submit itself to our lower nature and become an instrument to serve its needs. Sri Aurobindo considered modern societies to be ruled by a new:

[K]ind of barbarism—for it can be called by no other name— that of the industrial, the commercial, the economic age which is now progressing to its culmination and its close. This economic barbarism is essentially that of the vital man who mistakes the vital being for the self and accepts its satisfaction as the first aim of life. [...] the vitalistic or economic barbarian makes the satisfaction of wants and desires and the accumulation of possessions his standard and aim. His ideal man is not the cultured or noble or thoughtful or moral or religious, but the successful man. To arrive, to succeed, to produce, to accumulate, to possess is his existence.[24]

Sri Aurobindo thought that societies, like the human beings they are composed of, are bound to move from an infrarational age, where they are mostly governed by passions, to a rational age, and finally to a spiritual age; he considered this the unavoidable destiny of humankind on Earth (see box 2). This evolution does not need to be linear. Human societies have to go back and forth through the human development cycle until they are able to complete it.

**Box 2—Societies' Development Cycle
According to Sri Aurobindo**

To describe this cycle, Aurobindo uses German historian Karl Lamprecht's psychological theory of history and its categories of the psychological stages through which human societies progress (symbolic, typal, conventional, individualist, and subjective). In the first stage of this cycle—the symbolic stage, corresponding, for instance, to that of Vedantic Indian, Ancient Greek, or Egyptian civilizations—the divine is seen as permeating all reality, and social institutions express a religious and spiritual symbolism. Then comes the typal stage, in which great social ideals emerge from the spiritual visions of the symbolic stage. Moral principles become more important than the spiritual truth from which they derive and start to shape the social organization. Codes of honor and knighthood are good examples of this. But at some point, these moral qualities lose their living roots, their natural expressions, and become conventional.

In the conventional stage, moral principles are turned into rigid rules, which have to be followed closely. They tend to fix the social order and ensure its reproduction. "The form prevails and the spirit recedes and diminishes,"[25] explains Sri Aurobindo. Medieval Europe is a good example of the conventional stage. When any effort to revive the core truths behind conventions is in vain, conformism starts to be considered a hindrance to humankind's expression and progress. Sooner or later, the conventional stage is supplanted by an individualist age governed by reason, such as during the Enlightenment, which in the religious sphere sometimes manifests as atheism. "Often we find atheism both in individual and society a necessary passage to deeper religious and spiritual truth: one has sometimes to deny God in order to find him; the finding is inevitable at the end of all earnest scepticism and denial."[26]

As the question of individuality grows in importance, and the limits of reason are increasingly recognized, in particular to account for personal life experiences, the subjective age arrives. It initiates the inward turn toward the essential truth of the self and of things. Societies can then easily get lost, such as in relativism or vitalism (Germany in the nineteenth and early twentieth centuries), but Sri Aurobindo believes that this search will eventually lead to a spiritual age in which societies start governing themselves in accordance with spiritual laws.

Aurobindo saw widespread disorders as the manifestation of an evolutive crisis:

Often the decisive turn is preceded by an apparent emphasizing and raising to their extreme of things which seem the very denial, the most uncompromising opposite of the new principle and the new creation. [They] need be no index of a practical impossibility of the new birth, but on the contrary may be the sign of its approach or at the lowest a strong attempt at achievement.[27]

Sri Aurobindo spent the last twenty-five years of his life in seclusion, dedicated to anchoring the supramental consciousness in terrestrial matter. He died in 1950, three years after the Indian independence he had long fought for, which occurred on his birthday.

The third famous spiritual teacher who perceived humankind's ongoing spiritual evolution came from the Western world. Pierre Teilhard de Chardin (1881–1955) was a French scientist, philosopher, and Jesuit priest. His study and work as a paleontologist and geologist led him to reflect on the evolutionary process of the universe, from primordial particles to the development of life and human beings, from the geosphere to the biosphere, and finally what he called the "noosphere," "the sphere of human thought." Inspired by French philosopher Henri Bergson's view on "creative evolution,"[28] Teilhard de Chardin perceived in the evolutionary process a clear direction toward an ever-increasing level of material complexity and consciousness: "Evolution is an ascent [of matter] toward consciousness." [29]

Teilhard de Chardin thought evolution was bound to achieve a supreme consciousness, which he called the "omega point," which was "pulling" all creation toward it. This would be achieved by the future of humankind, that would realize its psychic unity, a process he termed "unanimization." Teilhard de Chardin wrote that he first had the vision of the "noosphere," which he considered "Earth's own soul," during World War I, in the trench warfare from Yser to Verdun, where he spent months serving as a stretcher bearer. In this extreme physical, psychic, and energetic density, where a million men were fighting each other, he started to perceive an evolutionary process, not at all distinct but rather of the same kind of physical matter's evolution he had studied. He proclaimed:

> A new Faith, in which the ascensional Faith that rises up towards a transcendent, and the propulsive Faith that drives towards an Immanent, for a single compound – a new Charity in which all the Earth's dynamic passions combine as they are divinized: it is this, I now see with a vision that will never leave me, that the World is desperately in need of at this very moment, if it is not to collapse.[30]

Teilhard de Chardin's work, which has had a profound impact among scientific and spiritual communities, was first condemned by the Catholic Church[31] before being finally rehabilitated with great recognition by leading figures such as Pope Benedict XVI and Pope Francis.[32]

Sri Aurobindo, Teilhard de Chardin, and many others have shaped a spiritual vision of evolution that honors the current scientific knowledge while transcending its materialistic paradigm. According to this vision, it is the spirit in nature that springs higher orders of complexity, consciousness, and freedom. While evolution has unfolded unconsciously during billions of years, we can now start to understand the nature, direction, and patterns of evolution. "We are evolution becoming self-aware,"[33] said Barbara Hubbard, another great futurist and evolutionary thought leader. In her book *Conscious Evolution, Awakening The Power Of Our Social Potential*, she explains that for the first time in history, we can choose to evolve by choice, not by chance. We can align ourselves with this universal intelligence at work and tap into our great scientific, spiritual, and social knowledge to cocreate the next stages of our evolution. She also sees in our current crisis a natural process inherent to evolution patterns: that of the difficult birth of the universal humanity that we can help to deliver smoothly.

Many of the most respected spiritual teachers of recent times have considered the need and possibility for humankind to undergo in the coming decades a great spiritual evolution that will transform societies worldwide. This vision, very present nowadays in spiritual circles, increasingly manifests in the fields of philosophy and social science, for example. Two current examples are integral thinkers such as Ken Wilber and Israeli historian Yuval Noah Harari, who, from respective fields and perspectives, with their own languages, are articulating similar views and reaching similar conclusions.

Ken Wilber is an American philosopher who has created his own "integral theory," in which every form of knowledge and experience can fit together coherently. We will review this theory in more detail in chapter 4. An important aspect of integral theory is its perspective on cultural evolution. For this, Wilber draws on spiral dynamics, which is based on the works of American professor of psychology Clare Graves (1914–1986), and other similar researchers in the field of developmental psychology. They have empirically identified different stages of human consciousness—also called levels of human existence, core ways of thinking, worldviews, value systems, "MEMEs" in spiral dynamics, etc.— that shape and color all our thinking and actions. These stages unfold progressively during a human life and, perhaps surprisingly, also within societies and organizations, to respond to changing life conditions over time, in the dialectical (moving alternatively to a primary focus on individuals or the collective) form of an ascending spiral.

Each level of development includes the previous ones (recognizing their value) and also transcends them (recognizing their limits, circumscribing their areas of validity), representing "a more complex way of dealing with the world."[34] A brief description of these "MEMEs" or levels of development, which are usually named (for convenience) after a color, is presented in table 2. They are not "good" or "bad" per se, but can express healthy (for-better) or unhealthy (for-worse) qualities, depending on their adaptation to life conditions and their capacity to allow the expressions of other levels along the spiral.

Table 2—The different MEMEs or levels of development[35]

Color	Self and consciousness	Culture	Social system	Basic concerns	Estimated percentage of global population (in 2001)[36]	Estimated percentage of power (in 2001)[37]
Turquoise	Holistic (2nd tier)	Holonic (postmodern)	Holistic meshworks	Life and harmony	0.1%	1%
Yellow	Integrative (2nd tier)	Integral (postmodern)	Integral commons	Flexibility and natural flows, big-picture views	1%	5%
Green	Communitarian (1st tier)	Pluralistic (postmodern)	Value communities	Equality and community	10%	15%
Orange	Achievist (1st tier)	Scientific-rational (modern)	Corporate states	Autonomy, self-interest, success	30%	50%
Blue	Purposeful (1st tier)	Mythic order (premodern)	Early nations	Meaning and order	40%	30%
Red	Impulsive (1st tier)	Power gods (premodern)	Feudal empires	Dominance and power	20%	5%

Color	Self and consciousness	Culture	Social system	Basic concerns	Estimated percentage of global population (in 2001)[36]	Estimated percentage of power (in 2001)[37]
Purple	Magical (1st tier)	Animistic-magical (premodern)	Ethnic tribes	Harmony and safety within tribes and with the spirit world	10%	1%
Beige	Survivalistic (1st tier)	Archaic (premodern)	Survival clans	Survival	0.1%	0%

A key feature of integral and spiral dynamic theory is the belief in a fundamental change, a jump to "second-tier consciousnesses" or "being levels" between yellow and green. The first six levels, including the green one, are called "first-tier consciousnesses" or "subsistence levels." They are unable to fully appreciate the value of other levels and are more resistant to the unfolding of higher levels. Starting with the yellow level, the awareness and capacity to think in terms of the overall spiral of existence and make the best use of each level in an integrated manner develops, together with a more important focus on the self. A wide space for new possibilities opens.

Integral theory, spiral dynamics and other developments stage theories have been particularly influential in the Western world in thinking about the current need for a change of mindset or consciousness. While I use them in different parts of this book as an important resource that can provide illuminating insights on specific issues, I tend to disagree with some key aspects of their views on cultural evolution inasmuch as I understand them.

First, I don't believe that every culture necessarily follows the same path of development drawn by the Western world, which these theories seems to suggest.[38] I consider this low cultural sensitivity a general weak point. The use of these typologies and categories, which are often constructed by westerners can make us blind to other cultural and social potentials. Secondly, I would not equate spiritual development with the way one thinks or operates in the world and moving up along the spiral as affirmed by spiral dynamics (but not integral theory), something Christopher Cowan, the cofounder of spiral dynamics, also disagrees with.[39]

While I do not oppose the view that some individuals and nations may be more spiritually evolved than others—though I do believe we have inherently equal value as people—I think the spiral does not adequately account for that. In reality, some traditional indigenous cultures, generally considered purple, let's say, for example, the Kogis in Colombia, seem to me much wiser and more spiritually evolved than many "developed" Western societies, whose center of gravity is usually dominated by orange. This second point relates to a third weakness of spiral dynamics (and not integral theory): it does not adequately distinguish social and cultural development from personal development, while people from all development stages can be found in each society and culture. For these three reasons, I consider development stage theories unfit as a common cross-cultural conceptual framework for the kind of politics this book is calling for.

Israeli historian Yuval Noah Harari has recently become famous for different best-selling books, including *Sapiens* and *Homo Deus*. These have been praised and received by some of the world's most important leaders. According to him, the superhuman that Sri Aurobindo prophesized a century ago is not a remote destiny for humankind but is likely to become reality in the very near future. It will be biologically engineered and could well emerge in this century, as these technological capacities fully develop. According to Harari, "the real potential of future technologies is to change Homo Sapiens itself,"[40] and this human enhancement will not only have the capacity to improve our bodies and health, but also our intellectual, emotional, and ethical capacities. It may well change our very consciousness and identity.

From this recognition, Harari derives a fundamental question: "If the curtain is indeed about to drop on Sapiens history, we members of one of its final generations should devote some time to answering one last question: what do we want to become?"[41]

3

Being as the New Paradigm

"When basic needs have been met, human development is primarily about being more, not having more."

—The Earth Charter (2000)

The need for a new development paradigm

THE CIVILIZATION CRISIS we face calls for a new development paradigm. This is widely recognized and was at the center of the UN's debate on the post-2015 global development agenda when then-UN Secretary-General Ban Ki-moon said, "The old model is broken. We need to create a new one."[1] He specified "a new model for economic growth" and called for "sustainable development goals that will lay the foundation for dynamic economic growth, respect for the planet and social equity." These sustainable development goals (SDGs) were adopted in 2014 as the general framework for international development for the 2015–2030 period.[2] Designed through a very participative process, for the first time they include all countries, including "developed" nations. The SDGs propose an ambitious global transformation and take on a high moral standpoint on human dignity by promising that "no one will be left behind." In this regard, they constitute a very important achievement, maybe the best that we could have hoped for given the international political situation.

Unfortunately, while culture has been referred to as the fourth pillar of sustainable development[3]—at the Rio+20 conference, indigenous people even claimed that culture should be considered sustainable development's most fundamental dimension[4]—the UN 2030 agenda for sustainable development does not say what is wrong in our cultural software and how it might be transformed. To my knowledge, it does not offer a convincing general theory of change but rather provides specific answers in separate sectors, focusing mostly on the symptoms rather than the root causes of our spiritual disease. The emphasis on "economic growth" (see SDG 8[5]) is suspicious as it perpetuates our old model; growth should be a means rather than an end in itself.

This is directly linked to how we conceptualize sustainable development. While its objective of meeting "the needs of the present without compromising the ability of future generations to meet their own needs"[6] is valid, the often-proclaimed need to find a balance between economic growth, social equity, and environmental protection to achieve sustainability can be misleading. With its relatively short-term perspective, economic growth for its own sake often trumps social equity and environmental concerns, which it tends to see as limitations. Finding a balance between these three competing objectives is inherently difficult, and that is why sustainable development, which is a compromise, is often a very ambiguous concept (which can explain its political success). It lacks the inner strength to become an inspiring force for transformation. We will see that, on the contrary, happiness and inner development can go hand in hand with sustainability.

Sustainability is a tired word that has suffered many abuses. I use it throughout this book—to refer to overcoming our environmental and social challenges—only to make my general messages clear in the current mainstream conversation. But what do we want to sustain? The Earth and our societies or "development" as we know it? Isn't it rather the time for a deep human, social, and environmental regeneration? I think we should aim toward the flourishing of the whole Earth community, and let go our idea of sustainability as a fixed outer destination to accept the fact that it is a never-ending adaptive journey to changing circumstances, grounded in the evolution of our mindsets, values, and human capacities.

As we grow aware of the systemic nature of our problems, everybody talks about the need to shift our paradigm. In books or reports dealing with our current global issues, you will often find this quote from Albert Einstein: "You can't solve a problem with the ways of thinking that created it." In my professional field of environment and climate change, I have come across this quote time and time again. Ironically, the different solutions or "new paradigms" most often proposed only represent a minor deviation from our current development paradigm and, as such, are doomed to fail, just like Einstein said! The Green Climate Fund, the main UN financial facility for addressing climate change, seeks to promote a "paradigm shift to low-emission and climate-resilient development." But, how is this challenging our cultural operating system based on the idea of separation? Theoretically, it could go on in a low-carbon world. It often seems as if the proposed solutions could prevent us from making the fundamental paradigmatic shift we need: "Everything needs to change, so everything can stay the same."[7] Why don't we get to the bottom of things and recognize that the new paradigm needs to be essentially spiritual, with all other paradigmatic changes as mere reflections of it? This book wishes to recognize the fundamental direction of this change, set the horizon, and discuss how we can move forward with all relevant ideas and solutions.

This relative confusion around paradigms also has to do with the plurality of definitions associated with this notion. Among these are (i) an example or archetype, (ii) a philosophical or theoretical framework that defines what is scientifically valid, and (iii) a cultural framework that shapes our perceptions.[8] In line with the latter, I find this definition useful:

A constellation of concepts and assumptions that structure how we see the world. It is not the same as our perceptions of the world; it is the framework that shapes our perceptions. Paradigms are also a structure for our future. By extrapolating from our present paradigm, we develop expectations about the future, and within the paradigm we formulate policies to achieve the future we want. Thus, a paradigm defines and limits the future that we can imagine.[9]

In that sense, as a cultural "framework that shapes our perception" and guides our actions, a paradigm resembles what Charles Eisenstein (2013) calls "story" and what we have called a cultural program or software.

From having to (inter)being

As we have mentioned, the old story of separation that is at the core of our cultural program until now has shaped our development model's priority: that of "having," measured in countries' GDP, which still prevails as the metric for assessing countries' relative levels of development. This focus has created an imbalance, a relative inner underdevelopment, an ethical crisis that threatens our future. We need a more integral development, which is not merely focused on the external material dimension but a truly human development with the inner dimension at its center. It should represent a second stage of investment in human development, emphasizing not only physical and mental development through health and education, but also emotional, psychological, ethical, and aesthetic—which is to say spiritual—development. We need to move from having to being, which many believe means interbeing.

This need for a more integral development is generally emphasized, among others, by religious organizations. The interreligious statement at the Rio + 20 Conference claims that "to make development truly sustainable, our economic, scientific, and technological accomplishments should assist the processes of individual and collective, psychological, and spiritual development. We must reorient our economic bottom line to support this full human development if we wish to live in a flourishing Earth community."[10]

In the same document, they use a statement from the Earth Charter: "When basic needs have been met, human development is primarily about being more, not having more."[11] This is congruent with Inglehart's observations, according to which, in "developed countries" over the last decades, there has been a transition from materialist to postmaterialist values, and more generally from survival to self-expression values. It is also consistent with the work of American psychologist Albert Maslow, who distinguished "being" (or "growth") needs and "deficiency" needs.[12]

The latter include physiological, safety, belongingness, and love, as well as esteem needs; the motivation to meet them decreases with their fulfillment. The former, which stands at the top of its pyramid of needs, relates to self-actualization (achieving one's full potential), and the motivation to fulfill these needs increases as they are met.

Finally, as we will see in chapter 6, happiness science confirms the primacy of "being" needs once basic needs are met. Being is not only the way for societies to balance their power and ensure social harmony but also for individuals to thrive. Going beyond the view of an integral development, in which there is a balance between our material needs and our inner needs, this statement seems to put emphasis on "being" over "having" "when basic needs have been met." In fact, inner growth is also the key to meeting "basic needs" as conveyed by the Indian spiritual and humanitarian leader Amma:[13]

> In today's world, people experience two types of poverty: the poverty caused by lack of food, clothing and shelter, and the poverty caused by lack of love and compassion. Of these two, the second type needs to be considered first—because, if we have love and compassion in our hearts, then we will wholeheartedly serve those who suffer from lack of food, clothing and shelter.

In fact, "being" precedes "having." We are spiritual beings having a human experience with material needs. Having is a material condition to being. It is a means, not an end. That is why, together with the current imbalance between "being" and "having," I propose that we emphasize "being" as the new paradigm. This applies to any country, independent of its economic development level. Even though part of the underlying rationale (e.g., Inglehart and Maslow's analyses) makes it particularly relevant to countries with higher income levels, investing in personal development at scale can also have an important positive impact on the development of poor countries, as shown by the example of Nordic European countries in the nineteenth century (see box 7). The politics of being needs to be adapted to the prevailing cultural and socioeconomic conditions but, for the sake of clarity, I will not address this in detail in this book.

"Being" poses the question of our true nature. First, as we will see, every major spiritual tradition teaches us that we are connected at the level of our being. I often use the term "interbeing," a Buddhist way of understanding this nature, but it can also be called "relational," something that is more and more recognized in human science. We are made of relationships. From birth, we develop our identities and potential through relationships, and we live our lives and flourish within relationships.

Secondly, the question is about the good or meanness of human nature. On the one hand, as we will see, our spiritual nature makes us fundamentally good. On the other hand, as human beings living in the historical reality, we have the potential for goodness and meanness. Our culture and social institutions play an important role in helping us manifest one or the other.

A basic theory of change

Before exploring what this change from having to being could entail, it is worth mentioning that science increasingly underlines the human capacity for change. While for some time, human behaviors and psychology have been assumed to be significantly determined by our genes—whose natural evolution is a matter of tens of thousands of years[14]—culture is now recognized as another factor of great importance.[15] In fact, by shaping our environment and life experiences through many social institutions, culture even has an important effect on the expression of our genes, as shown by the recent development of epigenetics. Moreover, neuroscience has long believed that, once formed and structured, our brain could no longer change and could only decline with age.

In the last decades, we have discovered and further researched the brain's neuroplasticity. It turns out all our experiences are continuously reshaping our brains, constantly creating new neurons, strengthening or reducing neuronal activities, or even changing the functions of specific areas of the brain. Scientists were surprised to realize the extent to which the brain can change. Neuroscientific research has in particular documented the effects of meditation from this perspective, and its potential for human and social flourishing, as we will see in chapter 9.

So, how would this change of emphasis from "having" to "being" materialize in terms of individual behaviors and their social outcomes, in particular from the perspective of sustainable development? As we will see in the next chapters, science shows that happiness and pro-social (including pro-environmental) behaviors tend to go hand in hand. Both naturally develop with self-actualization and the development of our capacities and virtues, which can be cultivated, including through educational programs and spiritual practices such as meditation. On the other hand, self-disconnection, unhappiness, selfishness, and antisocial behaviors also go together. These two different paths fundamentally reflect differences in values.[16] Changes in values are possible and tend to precede institutional changes[17] that can also in turn support them. Inner development and the cultivation of the best of human values, both at the individual and institutional levels, have the potential to bring about wiser, happier, and more sustainable societies.

Let's now look at this in greater detail. As we have seen, the current model of development, focused on economic growth, fosters and feeds on egocentrism and individual disconnection. It not only fuels excessive materialism, which has been shown to be associated with ill-being;[18] more generally, it impels people to prioritize what self-determination theory[19] calls extrinsic goals (money, fame, image, conformity, etc.), on which our model of development relies for its continuation, over intrinsic goals (autonomy, social relationships, personal growth, mental health, physical fitness, etc.). The former are those through which we are searching for a positive evaluation of others, while the latter "are inherently satisfying to pursue because they are likely to satisfy innate psychological needs."[20] The prioritization of extrinsic goals not only reflects a sense of insecurity about oneself,[21] but leads to a lower level of subjective well-being and to suffering "disproportionately from a host of maladies including anxiety, depression, physical symptoms, unpleasant emotions, drug abuse, alcohol abuse, behavioral disorders, lower levels of self-actualization, less vitality, less life satisfaction and fewer pleasant emotion."[22] The scientific literature also shows that those who pursue extrinsic goals tend to have attitudes and behaviors toward others and the environment that are more harmful.[23] Our economic system is based on this disconnection, which fuels consumerism, greed, and the focus on having, workaholism, and the primacy of doing over being.

When thinking of such an individual, I can't help remembering an encounter I had a couple of years ago. I was having breakfast in a nice hotel in Accra, Ghana, when a white man in his fifties, John, sat down in the empty seat in front of me. The conversation started, and he soon asked me what I was doing here. I explained I was supporting the country in protecting its endangered forest. He paused, stared at me, and said distinctly: "I am wondering when the last tree of this country will be cut." At eight o' clock in the morning, that was a real wake-up bell, and I immediately knew that I needed to be careful in how I handled this, that something special was happening.

John started to tell me about his life: he was an English entrepreneur based in Singapore, who dealt with oil palm plantation investments in neighboring countries Indonesia and Malaysia, and as such was actively involved in deforestation. He recognized this was a tragedy, telling me about the painful feeling he had a couple of months ago when traveling to Indonesia. He saw the last remnant of tropical forest ready to be cut, with some chimpanzees completely lost there, amid vast areas of oil palms. But as an entrepreneur and the head of a family, he had no choice but to make these investments. "If I don't do it myself, another one would do it anyway; that is how business works," he said.

He went on explaining how he was smuggling palm oils in Ghana, avoiding taxes with no financial risk for him: "If the authorities catch me, my company in Singapore goes bankrupt, and I am only losing a couple of thousand dollars that I need to have in equity in it." He was speaking a lot; his story felt almost like a confession, and I could feel he was testing me, eager to hear the reaction of the environmentalist he had in front of him.

I did not speak much. I was observing him: he really looked very anxious, restless, unhealthy, a strange mix of pride and shame. Despite the financial situation he was somehow proud of, I could really see there was no happiness, no peace in him. The world he was living in was like hell, full of fear and competition, doomed to tragic absurdities. He was not a bad guy; I could see he loved and wanted to take care of his family, and he was not insensitive to the destruction he was part of. He was just completely disconnected, torn into different pieces.

At some point I asked John how he could possibly divide himself between the entrepreneur who was destroying the forest and the human being who was lamenting this catastrophe. He did not seem quite sure what to answer. I had tried to express that in the most compassionate way, as I was really, above all, feeling sorry for him and wanted to reflect my acceptance to him, but I felt my nonnative English might have made that sound a bit accusative. When he finally left the table, I wished him good luck, thanked him for the conversation, and told him to take care. When asked why people were not responding to the threat of climate change, Zen Master Thich Nhat Hanh answered that because people are often not able to save themselves from their own suffering, we cannot expect them to worry about the plight of Mother Earth.[24]

On the contrary, what would the development of truly mature human beings result in at the social level? The many scientifically demonstrated effects of meditation inform us of the changes in attitudes and behaviors inner development can help promote (see chapter 9). We may also consider the testimonies of the most spiritually advanced people that have walked this earth to clearly understand the direction that spiritual development entails. In fact, according to Wayne Teasdale (1945–2004), an American Catholic monk, the great mystics of all spiritual traditions have basically shared a common divine experience: that of unity or oneness with all that is.[25]

"Only by admitting and realising our unity with others can we entirely fulfil our true self-being,"[26] said Sri Aurobindo. This can be conceptualized differently, such as through the Buddhist conception of "interbeing," but these traditions all express a dissolution of the distinction between self and others (in other words, "ego"), which naturally leads to the highest purpose: that of service. While only exceptional individuals are able to undergo this full transformation, it can certainly inform us about our nature. As we come closer in touch with our true selves, we tend to express our nature of interbeing or, more simply, our relational nature: we also get closer to and take more care of other human and nonhuman beings. We naturally develop pro-social behaviors and a sense of service (chapter 6).[27]

This path of inner development leads us to nourish three essential connections: to ourselves, to other human beings, and to nonhuman beings. As they reflect our true nature, these connections tend to develop together, each one leading to the others. As more mature human beings, we are becoming more aware of our true needs, which are, to a large extent, relational.[28] This tends to lead us to take more care of our partners, family, and friends, and maybe even reconcile ourselves with a brother or cousin we have not seen for a while. We grow aware of the many benefits and wisdoms that nature offers us freely,[29] and become more sensitized to the need to protect it. We learn to take care of ourselves; we become happier and feel better,[30] often while consuming less and finding more time for what really counts. We may decide to change our job for one that is more meaningful to us and which is in line with our values, to make our own little contribution to a better world.

As we grow wiser, we develop the ability to see things as they are, to make better and more conscious decisions that can help translate our care for one another and the Earth into effective actions. We also become more creative and open to change, more resilient. Of course, on our path, we tend to be more in touch with our own suffering and that of others, but we realize these knots and tensions have always been there, and we can learn and develop the confidence to transform them.

This human transformation, this change of story we are calling for, is something I get to hear and see every day here in the Plum Village Mindfulness Practice Center through many individual examples. People come here and often quickly relate to what is written on the main bell tower in four languages: "I have arrived; I am home." They connect to themselves, to their true home, seeing in the community the possibility of a very different way to relate to each other and to the Earth. Some of them, often unexpectedly, choose to stay weeks, months, years here.

When we first came here, it took my wife and me two days to realize that something really special was happening, something we wanted to be part of. It is not that people become enlightened and transform themselves in a day, but getting in touch with our true nature, our real needs, and following a spiritual path and practice, or simply letting our own deep wisdom guide us, is something that can make a tremendous difference in our lives and the world. As our teacher Thich Nhat Hanh said:

> We need a collective awakening. [...] Awakening about what? When we breathe and bring our mind back to our body; when we are truly there, body and mind united, there is already awakening. We know that we are alive, we are present and life is there for us to live. That is already a kind of awakening. So awakening is not something very far away. [...] Being in the present moment, we recognize that there are so many wonders of life that are in us and around us. And if we know how to get in touch with these wonders of life, we can get the nourishment and the healing right away, and peace and happiness can be possible right away. With mindfulness, you can realize that you already have more than enough conditions to be happy. [...] You don't have to struggle anymore, you don't have to run into the future anymore, you don't have to look for happiness elsewhere and in the future because happiness is possible in the present moment. That is the teaching of the Buddha [...], living happily right in the present moment. And that is a practice that can help many of us to release our craving, our anger, our fear. [...] With a collective awakening, we can stop the course of destruction of our societies and of the Earth. With awakening, we don't think anymore that more power is needed for us to be happy, more wealth, more sex, more fame is needed.[31]

I am sure you have around you some examples of this kind of personal transformation. Look deeply into them; go beyond the surface—they probably still look the same outwardly—and make your own judgment. They probably have not developed all the qualities that I have mentioned above, but at least some of these are already making a difference. Thanks to our current crisis, it has become very clear and simple; there are now but two paths for humankind: the path of suffering, destruction, and separation, or the path of interbeing in which we could all thrive together as one Earth family. Only by flourishing can a tree sustain itself, the birds, the bees, and the whole ecosystem it is part of. Being is the key to the harmonious coexistence within societies and the whole Earth community.

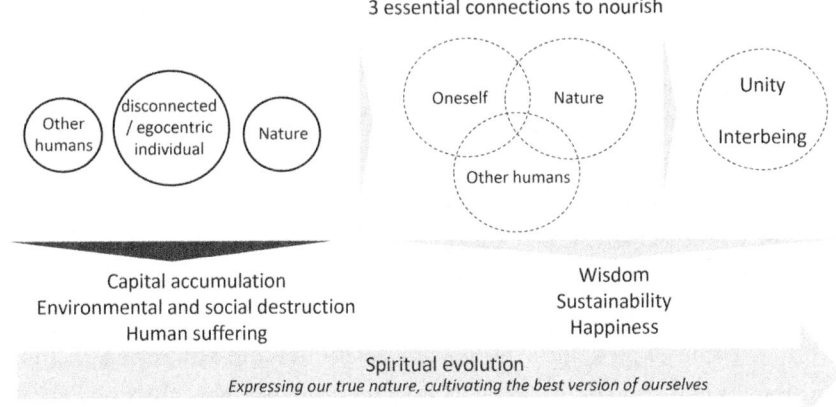

Figure 2. The inner path to sustainability: a theory of change.

The politics of being

How would a more spiritually advanced civilization be governed? I personally believe it would be based on the simple insight that all our problems come from within us, from our minds and hearts, and can be solved by us. That is why such a civilization would partner with evolution and put at the center of its efforts the inner development of its members in a continuous process. A wiser civilization would know that by organizing itself in a way that honors the highest values and waters the best seeds in everyone—truth, freedom, justice, respect for life, happiness, love, peace— it could best support its flourishing and that of societies' members.

Social sciences are increasingly pointing toward this truth. Elinor Ostrom, who is probably the most respected scholar in the field of institutional analysis, summarized the most important lesson she has learned through her work by arguing that "a core goal of public policy should be to facilitate the development of institutions that bring out the best in humans."[32] I call this wisdom-based approach to politics, which places being as its main objective and means, "the politics of being." Here, "being" means the fulfillment of all beings and, for humans, the realization of our full potential, that is to say of our highest and truest being. Our highest being refers to the development of inner values, virtues, or qualities, while our truest being relates to the process of becoming who we really are. They both converge in the manifestation of our true interbeing nature.

The emphases on highest and truest being complete, balance, and ultimately meet each other. Focusing only on our highest being is neither healthy nor sustainable. Self-improvement comes with many pitfalls (e.g., ego strengthening, disconnection from oneself, masking deeper problems, etc.). At the social level, the exclusive focus on righteousness can foster a hypocritical morality when it fails to recognize that it is natural and fine to make errors, which are necessary parts of any evolutive process. People at all developmental stages should feel respected and supported in their journey. This focus could also slip into legitimizing new forms of social control. The social credit system in China offers us a glimpse of such risk. It assesses the trustworthiness of individuals, companies, and government entities, and, based on their scores, offers rewards and punishments. Reciprocally, when the subjective quest to become who we are does not lead us to objectively develop the best in ourselves, as is often the case in individualistic societies, it is a vain attempt and comes with many social ills.

This definition of "being" makes it similar to other terms that I also use at times. They include spiritual or inner development, self-actualization, human flourishing, or eudaimonia (see chapter 6). All the dimensions of being, as well as our relational nature, need to be considered. Thus, being is about "realizing one's unique potential through physical, emotional, mental, and spiritual development [...] in relation to self, others and the environment."[33] The politics of being recognizes that life is a spiritual journey and aims at aligning our institutions with our true reason for being here on Earth: becoming who we are, the best and most complete version of ourselves. Societies can help us "be" by offering the means to fulfill our deepest healthy aspirations, through institutions grounded in the (inter)being paradigm.

Spiritual teachings tell us that we cannot separate the means from the end. "There is no way to happiness; happiness is the way," the Buddha once supposedly said. "There is no way to peace; peace is the way," said both Gandhi and Christian American pacifist A. J. Muste. Well, then ... there is no way to being; being is the way! Being is a path, an endless process of unfolding. Many socialist regimes during the twentieth century hoped to produce a "new man" but failed. Our societies can't make us mechanically more conscious, more mature human beings just by getting institutions right. Bad minds and hearts can corrupt the most perfect institutions on paper. Nonetheless, our institutions should embody and facilitate this inner change, which remains, at the end, every person's choice.

Institutions are often defined as "rules of the game" and include laws, policies, organizations, social practices, etc. They should be designed in a way that favors the daily experience, practice, and nourishment of the greatest qualities in each individual—our capacity for cooperation, love, awareness, harmony, respect, and creativity rather than for greed, competition and selfishness. Virtues are developed through practice, as sages from Buddha to Aristotle have long taught. These in turn can help to refine, adapt, and wisely implement our institutions. When our current institutions try to fill our needs and address the challenges we face through solutions based on competition, greed, and selfishness, that is to say, through more separation, they only strengthen the root causes of the very problems they want to solve. Our institutions should provide solutions that are based on cooperation, intrinsic motivation, and positive emulation, our sense of solidarity and interbeing, our need for connectedness and creativity.

Our social engineering is based on minimal expectations of human nature, as if these "conservative" assumptions provided a more solid basis for our institutions. The technical mentality believed that by developing our social rules and practices with the assumption we are all selfish, we would be shielded from any bad surprises. It turned out that our institutions tend to produce realities that reflect their assumptions about human nature and actually make us more selfish and separate from one another (see chapter 7). We can no longer afford not to cultivate and tap into our human potential. The solutions to our problems could build on this potential, rather than relying more and more on technologies, machines, and standardized processes only.

Vlady Stevanovitch (1925–2005), who founded the "inner path school" where I first learned tai-chi-chuan, once wrote about acupuncture, which he practiced himself. He had read that researchers had discovered (who knows how?) that the best acupuncturists are the ones most in touch with their inner center, called Tang Tien or Hara, which is both an energetic and physical (gravity center) located inside our body, a bit lower than the belly button. From their own paradigm, the researchers came to the logical conclusion that there should be a way to decrease this human variability, and we should focus our efforts on finding how to do that.

Well, from our own paradigm of "being," we would rather, together with Vlady, establish the conditions to better train acupuncturists so that they can develop this capacity, a treasure that has been patiently cultivated by great masters for thousands of years and passed on to us. I believe that in doing so, they would not only become better acupuncturists, but probably also healthier, happier people, deeply connected to themselves, life, and others, who can better contribute to society, including by sprucing vibrations up here and there! The human dimension is not something we need to eclipse as the technical mentality suggests; it is the real potential for societies to develop and tap into.

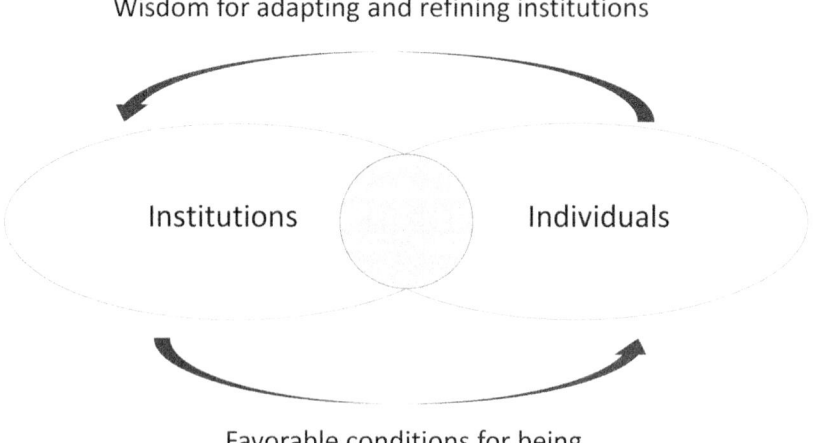

Figure 3. Institutions and individuals in the politics of being.

This idea of making inner development the center and goal of societies and politics has already been expressed in different ways. From a spiritual point of view, Bahá'is consider development an organic process in which "the spiritual is expressed and carried out in the material,"[34] and Baha'u'llah taught that societies should create a milieu favorable to the healthy growth of all their members, to the development of their spiritual qualities and virtues. Likewise, Confucius's essential teaching is for nations to support the cultivation of their members' virtues that are necessary both for social order and for each of them to become more fully human.

Sri Aurobindo wrote that "the radical defect of all our systems is their deficient development of just that which society has most neglected, the spiritual element, the soul in man which is his true being."[35] He considered that human societies never really approached their development from an authentically spiritual perspective. "If we look at the old religions in their social as apart from their individual aspect, we see that the use society made of them was only of their most unspiritual or at any rate of their less spiritual parts."[36] He also believed that the largely failed endeavors to socialize spirituality and apply it to societies underline religions' incapacity for regenerating humankind. He believed, "A society which was even initially spiritualized, would make the revealing and finding of the divine Self in man the supreme, even the guiding aim of all its activities, its education, its knowledge, its science, its ethics, its art, its economical and political structure."

Aurobindo warned against the error of "thinking that this change can be effected by machinery and outward institutions; they will know and never forget that it has to be lived out by each man inwardly or it can never be made a reality for the kind."[37] Thus, "a large liberty will be the law of a spiritual society and the increase of freedom a sign of the growth of human society towards the possibility of true spiritualization."[38] Aurobindo believed a spiritualized society would not use its institutions to force the transformation of its members but rather to present them with spiritual truths and invite them to grow as human beings. It would not compel science and philosophy "to square their conclusions with any statement of dogmatic religious or even of assured spiritual truth,"[39] knowing that if "left free in their action, they will find the unity of Truth with Good and Beauty and God and give these a greater meaning than any dogmatic religion or any formal ethics or any narrower aesthetic idea can give us."[40]

This idea has also been very present in Western philosophy. For example, Aristotle considered the purpose of the good state to be forging the virtues of its citizens,[41] providing them the means for self-fulfillment.[42] More recently, French sociologist and philosopher Edgar Morin, ninety-nine years old as I write, has developed a similar viewpoint. Having earned honorary doctorates in different social sciences from twenty-seven universities, Morin has developed an influential transdisciplinary theory on complex thinking that we will review in the next chapter. He is particularly renowned in the French-speaking world, Europe, and Latin America, and less well known in the anglophone world due to the limited availability of English translations of his over sixty books.

According to Morin, "The gigantic planetary crisis is the crisis of mankind that does not manage to access humanity," [43] as revealed by its inner underdevelopment. "There is above all the immaturity of nation-states, of minds, of consciousnesses, that is to say, fundamentally, mankind's immaturity to accomplish itself."[44] As a humanist, Morin believes in a process of "hominization" by which human beings could become more evolved and truly human. One of his books opens with a quote from German philosopher Friedrich Schlegel: "To attain humanity, there is a need of a sense of beyond humanity."[45]

In 1965, in *Introduction to a Politics of Human*, Morin adopted a rather anthropological perspective to call for "a politics of the whole human being."[46] He called this "anthropolitics" or "politics of human," whose advent he considered natural, engraved in the very new (quoted by US president Truman in 1949) notion of "development" in politics. Morin predicted that "more and more, the nuclear center of politics would be the human to become in the world"[47] and that this anthropolitics should allow us to "unify in one multidimensional politics all the fragments of politics."[48] He recognized that since the French Revolution and during the last two centuries, politics has progressively extended its field of action from its initial focus on social order. It has included, on the one hand, all the aspects of social life (economics, health, education, demography, culture ...) and, on the other hand, philosophical problems related to the meaning of life (Marx's conception of politics as a way to fulfill philosophy, the French Revolution's recognition of happiness as the ultimate goal of politics, our contemporary search to fulfill human aspirations ...).

This led Morin to conclude that "all the avenues of the living (from the 'surviving' to the 'is this how men live?') and all the avenues of politics are starting to cross themselves and announce an onto-politics, concerning in an increasing intimately and globally the being of human."[49] Morin believes the current political crisis rests on the inability of politics to assume this endeavor. According to him, "An ideal of consumption, supermarkets, gains, productivity, GDP, cannot satisfy the deepest aspirations of a human being, which are to realize themselves as a person in a solidary community."[50] Thus, "the development of human beings, of their mutual relations, of the societal being, is the purpose of the politics of human in the world, which calls for the pursuit of hominization." "It is about going on with the millenary search for consciousness, love, science, going on with these streams by making them converging."[51]

Within governments, this idea is also making its way. The UK Government Office for Science conducted a study on "Mental Capital and Wellbeing: Making the Most of Ourselves in the 21st Century" that was released in 2008.[52] This document drew upon "the advice of over 400 leading experts and stakeholders from across the world, and from diverse disciplines such as: economics; modelling and systems analysis; social sciences and ethics; neuroscience, genetics and mental development; psychology and psychiatry; and sciences relating to education, work and wellbeing." It is rooted in recognizing the importance, in the twenty-first century, of mental capital—defined as encompassing "a person's cognitive and emotional resources"—and mental well-being—considered as equivalent to "mental health" or "mental flourishing"—which combines positive feelings, attitudes, and functioning in life.

The study took note of the future social and economic challenges associated with an aging, more diverse population with new values and expectations, and an economy driven by international competition with constant technological changes that will change how we work. It mentions that "the scientific evidence reviewed in the Project clearly shows that a high level of wellbeing is associated with positive functioning, which includes creative thinking, productivity, good interpersonal relationships and resilience in the face of adversity, as well as good physical health and life expectancy." The study emphasizes that "an individual's mental capital and mental wellbeing crucially affect their path through life. Moreover, they are vitally important for the healthy functioning of families, communities and society. Together, they fundamentally affect behaviour, social cohesion, social inclusion, and our prosperity."

The study proposes a range of interventions to strengthen mental capital and well-being through a lifelong perspective, from early childhood to old age. The study clearly recognizes, based on the most up-to-date scientific findings, that the development of cognitive, emotional, and psychosocial resources will be the key to allowing people and nations to thrive in the twenty-first century. As such, it constitutes an interesting first step in the direction of a politics of being, one that, unfortunately, no British government took. However, it is still framed very much in the language of the old paradigm, with its consideration of human inner resources as capital to develop and of holistic human development as a new competitiveness strategy. The focus on mental capital and well-being is somehow to the politics of being what personal development is to spirituality: a bit more superficial, a bit less transformative, still quite self-focused and ego-driven, but that nonetheless prepares the ground for the transformation to come.

II

SPIRITUAL VALUES AS THE FOUNDATION OF THE POLITICS OF BEING

"For the spirit of man must strain towards the heights; when it loses its tension of endeavour, the race must become immobile and stagnant or even sink towards darkness and the dust. [...] To follow after the highest in us may seem to be to live dangerously, [...], but by that danger comes victory and security. To rest in or follow after an inferior potentiality may seem safe, rational, comfortable, easy, but it ends badly, in some futility or in a mere circling, down the abyss or in a stagnant morass. Our right and natural road is towards the summits."

—Sri Aurobindo,[1] Hindu spiritual teacher

To STRIVE, NATIONS need to cherish high ideals. They are usually engraved at the heart of our nations as in the French official motto—"liberty, equality, fraternity," —or in the 1776 American Declaration of Independence recognizing "life, liberty, and the pursuit of happiness" as unalienable rights, which governments are created to protect.

Given our definition of spirituality, we believe that societies progress and advance as they increasingly honor the highest values, helping their members to cultivate and express the best in themselves while actualizing their truest being. In this part, we will reflect on the importance of spiritual values—in particular understanding, life, happiness, love, peace, mindfulness, and light—for social progress. These values, which are at the heart of virtually all wisdom traditions, embodying spiritual realization, as well as the divine or God, are increasingly at the core of new scientific research fields. These growing bodies of research highlight their importance for sustainability, while framing new narratives, new understandings of our human and social potentials, as well as the possible policies and institutions that could help realize these potentials. As we will see, these universal values are also quickly entering the political field, shaping new political debates and agendas, concrete policies and initiatives, overcoming long-standing divides and traditional alternatives. Together, these spiritual values are the foundation of the politics of being.

4

Understanding

Interconnectedness, Wisdom, Systemic Thinking, Integral Thinking, Complex Thinking

"Wisdom is the recognition of interdependence of things.
True wisdom is to understand the nature of reality without prejudice
or attachments, seeing things as they are. When attained,
this understanding blends with compassion, and helping others
becomes an endless personal mission."[1]

—Sulak Sivaraksa, social activist and philosopher

WE SELDOM SEE how deeply our problems are rooted in our way of thinking and that the paradigmatic shift we need requires an evolution of nothing less than the fundamental instrument through which we understand the world: our very concept of science.

The paradigm of simplification

Descartes formulated our modern scientific paradigm, which Edgar Morin calls the "paradigm of simplification," by "disjoining the thinking subject (ego cogitans) and the thing being thought of (res extensa)"—in other words, philosophy and science—and by positing "clear and distinct ideas" as principles of reality; in other words, disjunctive thinking itself.[2] Modern science has developed ever since according to this paradigm. Physics, biology, and human sciences have been isolated from each other. The understanding of ever-smaller parts has been prioritized over that of the totality or system to which they belong, while all realities that do not match modern scientific methods and instruments (experiments, quantitative modeling ...) have been excluded from the field of inquiry.

This simple thinking, in science and its applications, in society and politics, has produced great advances in knowledge, technology, and many material benefits over the last few centuries. It has tried to control and shape the world, optimizing all the areas of our lives, extending its reach continuously to the point where it is now facing its own limits as its ultimate harmful consequences are unfolding. In fact, it has currently become the philosophical root of our most serious challenges— "mutilating thought necessarily leads to mutilating actions,"[3] said Morin—and of our inability to understand and address them effectively. Ever-more-specialized scientific knowledge—that is to say parceled, fragmented, and compartmentalized—has also produced the regression of our understanding and capacity to think of reality as an interconnected whole.

On the contrary, as we have seen, spiritual traditions emphasize the interconnected nature of all things. The Buddhist noble eightfold path, for example, starts with "right view" or the capacity to see reality in its true interbeing nature. Spiritual traditions have profound teachings to offer on the problem of knowledge, which, as we will see, resonate deeply with the alternatives that are being developed to this simple thinking. More generally, wisdom is fundamentally related to our capacity to see the bigger picture and put things into perspective.

Systems thinking

What Morin refers to as "simple thought" or "simple thinking" is often simplistically (sic) termed "reductionism." This is the tendency to understand a phenomenon in terms of its simple or fundamental constituents and consider this sufficient, as if the whole would equal the sum of its parts. Reductionism has proved particularly limiting in the field of ecology, from which the systems theory has been progressively developed in the second half of the twentieth century. Systems theory leads us to consider any reality as a system—embedded in larger systems as everything is connected, and often composed of subsystems—that is more than the sum of its parts, as it is also made of interconnections between the different elements that compose it and has its own function or purpose.[4]

Nowadays, systems thinking is widely recognized as a critical tool for addressing many of our current environmental, social, economic, political challenges, their interconnection, and the possibility of addressing them in an integrated manner through systemic changes. In many instances, it is particularly helpful in moving beyond disciplinary silos and direct causality to reach root causes through a transdisciplinary analysis. We are often used to assuming direct linear causality and come with solutions that are constrained by the particular disciplinary lens through which we analyze reality. We naturally assume that economic—or social, political, psychological, etc.—problems should be addressed by an economic—or social, political, psychological, etc.—solution that can be identified by a specialist of this field. However, these disciplines are human constructs, and in the real world, the social, political, economic, psychological ... are all mixed up together, and the root causes and solutions to any problem are often surprising. For example, we naturally tend to think that the main avenue to public health issues is to enhance access to health care, but it is now widely accepted among public health specialists that major determinants of health ("the causes of the causes") are social and economic, rather than access to health care or individual characteristics or behaviors.[5]

Changing a system's goals and the paradigm[6] (or mindset) from which it arises are considered among the most powerful leverage points for systemic change,[7] though also the most difficult to activate (on the right side of figure 4). As we have seen, this lies at the heart of the politics of being.

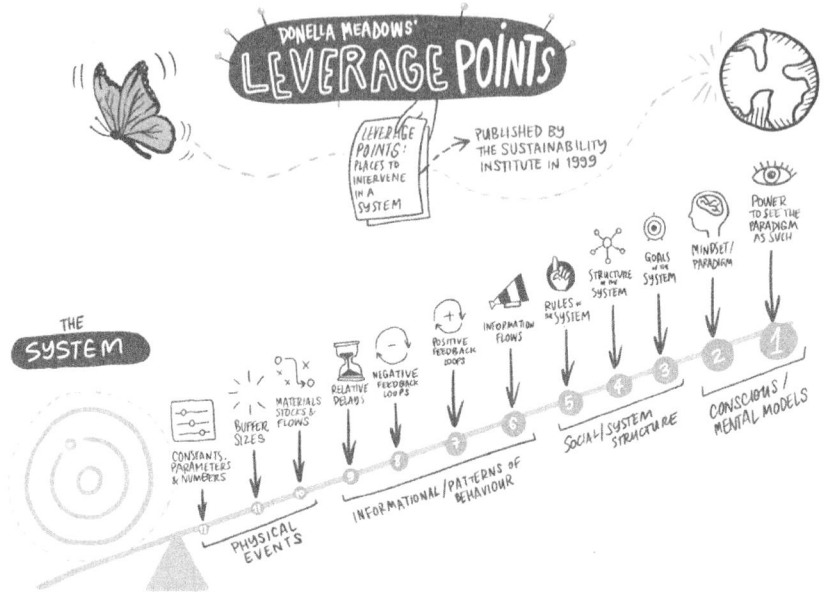

Figure 4. Donella Meadows's leverage points: places
to intervene in a system.[8]

The importance of mindset or consciousness is increasingly
emphasized in systems thinking. The theory U of German MIT professor
Otto Scharmer has recently found a large audience. It argues that the key
to systems change and to many of the most pressing challenges lies in the
field structure of our attention: "I and We attend this way, therefore the
social field emerges that way"[9] or "form follows consciousness."[10] Scharmer
identifies four types of attention structures or states of operating:

- Habitual awareness, in which we simply enact patterns from the
  past: nothing new can get in;

- Ego-system awareness, in which new information can get in
  (open mind) and prompt adaptation but only from one's own
  perspective;

- Stakeholder awareness, in which we can truly listen to others (open heart) from their own perspectives: the system becomes self-reflective, being able to see itself through the eyes of other stakeholders.

- Ecosystem awareness, in which we are able to let go of our old identities and intentions (open will) to connect and operate from "the source of the highest future possibility that is seeking to emerge."[11] This awareness allows the system to sense and see itself and adjust accordingly.

Scharmer calls the process that occurs when human systems start to operate from this ecosystem awareness "presencing." "Presencing" is a blending of the words "presence" and "sensing." It means to sense, tune in, and act from one's highest future potential—the future that depends on us to bring it into being.[12] "The root of the word presencing is *es, which means 'to be,'"[13] he explains. In fact, the gateway to presencing is "the connecting to our authentic or higher-self,"[14] which he considers the most important leadership tool, expressing itself through linking the intelligence of the head, heart, and hands. Scharmer believes that "the number-one leadership challenge in the world of business, government, and civil society is the same. It is to enable stakeholder groups that need each other to change the system to move from me to we—that is, from ego-system awareness to eco-system awareness."[15] According to him, the shift to such a state of operating is "the central phenomenon of our time"[16] he sees emerging in the way we think, converse, organize, and govern ourselves.

The theory U process is a method to help groups shift their attentions and access a state of presencing to increase collaboration and achieve positive systemic changes. It helps people realize they are part of the system they want to transform and take responsibility for the way they attend it. Former head of UN climate negotiations Christiana Figueres describes this very well in her book *The Future We Choose* (coauthored with her colleague Tom Rivett-Carnac):

As we learned during our stewardship of the Paris Agreement, if you do not control the complex landscape of a challenge (and you rarely do), the most powerful thing you can do is change how you behave in that landscape, using yourself as a catalyst for overall change. All too often in the face of a task, we move quickly to "doing" without first reflecting on "being"—what we personally bring to the task, as well as what others might. And the most important thing we can bring is our state of mind.[17]

Through its recognition of the interconnected nature of reality, systems theory reconnects knowledge to wisdom, as mentioned by Donella Meadows (1941–2001), one of the most recognized experts in systems theory: "It is often possible (...) to make a direct translation from system jargon to traditional wisdom."[18] However, systems thinking has sometimes been used as a very partial and fragile answer to some of the problems of knowledge, in particular the current imbalance in our thinking, "reductionism." We cannot address it by thrusting ourselves to the other extreme of "holism," at the risk of producing general and vague "holistic" principles that lack the capacity to be fully operational. We need to develop methods and knowledge that articulate the whole and its parts.

Integral thinking

Developed to a great extent around Ken Wilber's work during the last decades, and embedded in both science and spirituality, integral theory considers reality as made up of "holons," wholes that are simultaneously parts of other wholes, or "whole/parts." It intends to move beyond the fragmentation of our knowledge and develop a comprehensive view of our reality—in all its physical, biological, social, psychological, and spiritual dimensions—by bringing together a diversity of theories into one single framework. It proposes to consider each problem in its different dimensions, including psychological and cultural ones. It considers that any holon or system should be understood as a whole through its division in four "quadrants," corresponding to the interior and the exterior of the individual and the collective, as presented in figure 5.

INTERIOR   EXTERIOR

	INTERIOR	EXTERIOR
INDIVIDUAL	« I » Subjective (self and consciousness)	« IT » Objective (brain and organism)
COLLECTIVE	« WE » Intersubjective (culture and worldview)	« ITS » Interobjective (social system and environment)

Figure 5. Four quadrants in humans according to integral theory.[19]

The cause and cure (or management) of any particular illness, for example, should be looked at from the perspective of the four quadrants:

- Objective: that is the traditional focus of modern medicine on the body of the patient.

- Subjective: it has now been demonstrated that the subjectivity (emotions, psychological attitude, intentions ...) of the patient play an important role in both the cause and cure of the illness.

- Intersubjective: the cultural representation and acceptance of the illness (e.g., AIDS) will impact the patient, in particular through the very medical definition of the disease and the communication the patient has with the doctor, families, and friends, as well as his or her own internalization of cultural representations.

- Interobjective: this includes health insurance, health-care services, environmental pollution, economic and social context, etc.

Moreover, integral theory complements this view of the four quadrants by considering the stages of developments or worldviews associated with each quadrant, that of individuals (in their physical, emotional, mental, and spiritual dimensions), cultures, and social systems. For this, Wilber draws on spiral dynamics, as presented in chapter 2. This consideration allows a finer understanding of how individuals, culture, and social systems operate, to better understand the potential causes of any problems and adapt solutions. For example, it is common among ethnic tribes (purple) to link a specific physical or mental illness to a cosmic disorder within the patient's family, tribe, or environment (including the realm of spirits). Traditional treatments, which may also include rituals for the patient and his or her family, tribe, or environment, in this (inter)subjective context may be the most effective cure.

On the contrary, scientific-rational culture (orange) tends to favor modern medicine and may impose, as occurred recently in France, mandatory vaccinations, which may irritate postmoderns, who value the recognition of a plurality of approaches (green), while integralists (yellow), aware of the ideological backgrounds of the discussion, may try to accommodate the different perspectives in some kind of compromise.

While integral theory is based on "All Quadrants All Levels" (AQAL), it also identifies additional dimensions to combine with the AQAL and expand it towards a more integral perspective. These include, for example, lines of development (one can be cognitively orange, emotionally purple, morally blue, etc.) and types of consciousness (personality types, gender types, etc.). It is beyond the ambition of this book to present integral theory in detail and the spiral dynamics theory it builds on, of which I am not a specialist. Both can be quite complex, for their core concepts can be nuanced and combined in multiple ways. Making the best use of these theories requires the capacity to think (or flow?) in a multidimensional way and is thus a practice, an art, a "wizardry" as spiral dynamics founder Don Edward Beck puts it.

Integral thinking is a crucial necessity in an increasingly more complex and diverse world. Its perspective on cultural evolution provides many interesting keys for change and conflict transformation, in particular to address the cultural wars between different worldviews we are now facing. Integral theory is increasingly used and influential in academia, organizations, governments, and social discussion, helping to develop more effective approaches in a wide range of sectors, from health to education, business, ecology, security, geopolitics, and spirituality. I personally consider integral theory an impressive body of work that has the capacity to link many realities together, especially inner and outer ones. It is a wonderful toolbox, full of enlightening insights that one can tap into and assemble to understand and address a specific question. However, I use integral thinking more as a practice than a general framework, because of the fundamental theoretical disagreements I have outlined in chapter 2.

Nonattachment to views

Finally, in the attempt to build a theory of everything, I think there is a point that may be recognized by integralists but is not given enough space, and this is the complexity of our world and how this fundamentally affects how we can understand it. I feel that, as a system that intends to fit the whole reality into many typologies, integral theory relies on too many simplifications and partial truths, and by doing so, ironically, can perpetuate the "paradigm of simplification" initiated by Descartes. As we have seen in general with modern science, reflections based on this paradigm, when pushed to their limits, can be very harmful. In its noble attempt to push the limits of knowledge, integral theory sometimes gives the impression it forgets the old Socratic wisdom: "I know that I know nothing." In its pursuit of systematization, integral theory seems at times too much a mental endeavor, where everything could make sense and could automatically produce all the answers to our problems. Like any lens through which we view reality, it can be useful but need not be confused with reality.

As a Plum Village practitioner, I have committed to practice, among other Buddhist principles, "nonattachment to views."[20] This means that we should be mindful not to be stuck in our own views or any theory, and always remain open to others' insights and experiences and remember that truth is found in life and not in any system of thought. Ultimately, we should aim at not being caught in any view, at being free of views in order to be able to experience nirvana. Not being caught in our views is very difficult; psychologists have shown that people tend toward reducing cognitive dissonance because it is uncomfortable. We tend to avoid information that challenges our views, look for information that confirms them, and go to great lengths to justify and retain our current perspectives.

The difficulty also comes from the fact that our perspectives frame our perception of reality and our behavior, which in turn shape our reality and corroborate our views. We read the newspaper that tells us what we want and are prepared to read. The internet selects materials based on what we've already seen, liked, and known. We may distrust someone who may perceive our resistance and act in a way that confirms it. I have even come to consider that our lives are, to a great extent, the unfolding of our inner realities as some spiritual teachings affirm. They are woven into our thoughts, beliefs, dreams, or fears; they are the material expressions of our journey as spiritual beings. So be careful with your thoughts, fears, and expectations: they may well materialize!

The more we grow in our understanding (not in the Socratic sense), the greater the temptation to think we know and close ourselves to new knowledge. That is why in the shamanic Toltec tradition, it is said that clarity is one of the four main enemies—together with fear, old age, and death—on the path of spiritual warriors: it can easily blind them and keep them stuck in their evolution. We should always ask ourselves, "Are you sure?", particularly in such a fast-changing and disruptive world, in which new possibilities constantly emerge. Its spiritual and evolutionary nature makes "being" not a fixed paradigm but one that constantly aims at transcending itself. Meadows considers the capacity to transcend paradigms, to not be caught in any of them in particular, as the ultimate leverage point for systemic change.[21]

Complex thinking

As semantically suggested, complexity is the missing part, the shadow of modern science founded on the "paradigm of simplification" and its almost messianic ambition to make the whole of reality intelligible. While there has always been the tendency to use systems thinking as part of a mechanistic approach to social engineering, systems change usually requires dealing with complexity. The world we live in and the challenges we face are increasingly complex, and our ways of thinking and acting have to adapt to this new reality.

Climate change, for instance, combines environmental and social hyper-complexity, which makes it so difficult to address. We cannot fully understand how climate will evolve because of factors such as threshold effects and feedback loops that are generally not reflected in our climate models. For example, climatic conditions can suddenly turn the Amazon rainforest into a savannah, releasing greenhouse gases in the atmosphere and fueling further climate change.

Nor can we really predict climate change's impacts on our lives: while our existences have been seriously disturbed by the COVID-19 pandemic, the melting of permafrost can liberate a multitude of viral pathogens. Climate change costs cannot be fully anticipated as they are too complex, uncertain, and result from too many interactions. Their evaluations generally focus on the simplest and most certain impacts and those whose values can be estimated, thus often underestimating their true costs and values. The monetary approach is also not well-suited as it assigns the same value to US$ 1 of essential products (e.g., food, water, etc.), whose production is often most affected by climate change, as to US$1 of unessential products (e.g., video games). An approach in terms of well-being may be better suited. Climate destruction may also spur an increase in economic production to prevent its effects and repair its damages. Still, the negative impacts of climate change will be huge and call for a drastic increase in international cooperation and across all kinds of stakeholders, as well as a redesign of our economic system.

As with systems theory, ecology has been particularly instrumental in the development of complex thinking. Such complexity is well exemplified by the effects of wolves' reintroduction in Yellowstone National Park since 1995, which caused a trophic cascade of ecological change that the authorities say "will take decades to understand."[22] The absence of wolves since the 1930s took a huge amount of predatory pressure off the elk, which multiplied and browsed too many willows, which affected the beaver population. The reintroduced wolves killed more elks, which benefited ravens, eagles, magpies, coyotes, and bears. It also alleviated the pressure on the vegetation: aspens, cottonwoods, and willows. The growth of the latter helped the songbirds and beavers to multiply.

Beaver dams have multiple effects on stream hydrology and helped provide habitats for a wide variety of species: moose, otters, mink, wading birds, waterfowl, fish, amphibians, and more. Fewer elks also meant more berries available for grizzly bears. The wolves also drove down the population of coyotes, which also had to shift territories, allowing the number of foxes to rise. More foxes meant that coyotes could focus on them, instead of other prey such as hares, young deer, small rodents, and ground-nesting birds. "These changes affect how often certain roots, buds, seeds and insects get eaten, which can alter the balance of local plant communities, and so on down the food chain all the way to fungi and microbes,"[23] concluded a journalist.

Beyond ecology and the many challenges we are facing, science is now facing complexities everywhere, which are challenging its general epistemological framework. The complexities are not only quantitative phenomena linked to the extreme quantity of interactions and interferences between nearly countless units (counted at least in the billions for any auto-organizing (living) systems such as cells or organisms). They also relate to disorder and uncertainty, to ambiguity and logical contradictions as shown, for example, in physics (e.g., quantum physics, the general theory of relativity at the macro level, etc.), which traditionally provided the model for science.

The paradigm change that we are calling for requires and entails not only new ways of thinking or some new scientific content, theories, methods, or instruments, but a real alternative to the domination in science of the "paradigm of simplification"—one that can deal with this complexity science is now facing. This is the ambition of complex thinking (or complex thought) proposed by Morin that can be the basis for what he calls "a modification, a transformation, an enrichment of the current concept of science."[24] In fact, as Jacob Bronovski, a British mathematician and historian (1908–1974), said, this concept is "neither absolute, nor eternal,"[25] and Morin reminds that "any pretension to define the borders of science in an assured way, any pretension to the monopoly of science is by the same logic not scientific."[26]

Complexity theory grew out of systems theory in the 1960s and 1970s as an interdisciplinary theory drawing from research in natural sciences that examines uncertainty and nonlinearity. Founded in 1984, the Santa Fe Institute was the first research institute dedicated to the study of complex systems, and it is estimated that there are now some fifty research centers or institutes focusing on this subject.[27] Complexity theory is now influential in a wide range of scientific fields—from physics and biology to human science, finance, and management—and in redesigning educational systems.

Among other researchers, Edgar Morin has been particularly instrumental in developing the basis of complex thinking that "connects theory to methodology, to epistemology, and even to ontology."[28] We will focus on his approach to this subject. While it is beside the point of this book to present its approach to complex thinking and try to convince the readers of its depth, coherency, and robustness, we will present below some of its very general features.

At a theoretical level, complex thinking, as conceived by Morin, can be based upon "a theory of self-eco-organization,"[29] which is still in the making. It originates from a paradox: according to the second law of thermodynamics, our physical reality is subject to entropy, that is to say, an increasing disorder or disorganization, while biological evolution shows a contrasting trend towards increasing organization. Living systems are auto-organized systems in which the information necessary to such organization is encoded in DNA. Since the apparition of life and the encounter between DNA and amino acids, living systems are open systems whose evolution always occurs in relation to their environment (the "eco"). This evolution has led to an increasing complexity that culminates with human beings and their organizations in social systems. Their study should consider both the natural dimension of human beings and phenomena, as well as their hyper-complexity.

According to Morin, this "theory of self-eco-organization that is open towards a general theory of physics" can be the basis for the unification of science, in which physics, biology, and anthropology "cease to be closed entities, but do not lose their identity."[30] In fact, the study of complex, autocatalytic, self-organizing, nonlinear, and adaptative systems is increasingly recognized by scientists as the core of the emerging scientific agenda for the twenty-first century.[31]

While complex thinking humbly recognizes the impossibility of full and perfect intelligibility of reality, and thus the ambition to control and dominate it, it seeks to "treat with reality, dialogue with it, negotiate with it."[32] Morin has developed his method over six books,[33] so clearly this chapter can only provide a superficial overview. A general principle "with incalculable consequences" is that "the object must not only be appropriate to science, but science must be appropriate to its object."[34] Complex thinking entails "a methodology that is at the same time open (that integrates the preceding) and specific (description of complex units)."[35]

Three principles can help us understand these complex units. First, they follow the holographic principle that "the whole is in the part that is in the whole," as we can see with societies (the whole) and humans (the part). Second, if we consider this in a time perspective, we can see it as a "recursive process [...] where the products and the effects are at the same time causes and producers of what produce them,"[36] a view that opposes the reductionist, linear opposition between cause and effect, product and producer. Third, understanding complex units requires also a "dialogic principle," which "associates two terms that are simultaneously complementary and antagonistic,"[37] allowing the maintenance of the "duality at the heart of unity,"[38] such as order and disorder, for example, which, as we have seen, collaborate to produce organization and complexity.

Transcending dualistic thinking

The need to transcend dualistic thinking—the instrument of separation, which functions in terms of "either-or"—has been emphasized by many spiritual traditions as the key to truly understanding reality. In fact, any idea is by definition different from reality, and dualistic thinking is somehow inherent to the way thinking and language are built: around opposite notions. The notion of subject makes sense because of our notion of object, the same for right and left, birth and death ... That is why spiritual teachers often ask their students to meditate on paradoxical statements that challenge dualistic thinking, such as koans in the Zen traditions: "What did your face look like before you were born? What is the sound of one hand clapping?" are good examples of this. Feel free to stop reading and meditate on these for as long as you need!

The Buddhist path starts with "right view," that of interbeing, which transcends all dualistic concepts, including that of self and non-self, being and nonbeing, of birth and death, of sameness and otherness ... "Right view" is so fundamental that the Buddhist path's goal, "nirvana," literally means "the extinction of all concepts." This has also been an object of profound meditation in ancient Chinese Taoist philosophy through its yin-yang concept. According to it, opposite or contrary forces may actually be complementary, interconnected, and interdependent polarities that may give rise to each other as they interrelate to one another.[39] In a natural system like a body or a forest, life necessarily produces death (that of cells or trees, for example), which in turn is necessary to allow life to regenerate itself. They are two faces of the same coin, indissociable: they cannot exist separately. In fact, we should not talk about the yin and yang concept but the yin-yang concept.

This dialogic principle also leads Morin to challenge many traditional ontological distinctions, including Descartes's fundamental disjunction between subject and object, that set philosophy and science apart. According to Morin, all living systems are self-organized; that is to say, each of them "creates its own determinations and its own finalities,"[40] and biological evolution is not a product of hazard but of "the meeting of hazard with an organizing potentiality."[41] Thus it appears that each living system has some degree of autonomy, as well as some other features— individuality, complexity, uncertainty, ambiguity—that were generally considered inherent to the subject.

Reciprocally, biological and social constraints need to be reintegrated in the notion of subject, including through the emphasis on its relationship to its environment. "To be subject is to be autonomous while remaining dependent,"[42] which means subjects are also objects. Thus, involved in a complex relationship, the notions of subject and object are indissociable. The metaphysical subject or positivist object are concepts that are both per se insufficient and incomplete. While this distinction has long been fruitful, these concepts should not have been petrified, and the recognition of their limits can now certainly open the way to a better understanding of reality, and most importantly, to the reconnection of philosophy and science.

Seeking to articulate the understanding of the whole and its parts, complex thinking moves beyond both general holistic principles—that we can find in systems thinking and wisdom traditions—and reductionist knowledge, to provide the basis for an evolved concept of science that would not only be more scientific but also wiser. By reconnecting philosophy with reality as understood by modern science, it can give it back its power to transform our lives and societies. It reminds us that intelligence can never be chained to any dogma, whether scientific or spiritual. It is rather the true spiritual quality, whose path is endless. Complex thinking naturally calls for an epistemology that is open and self-reflective. This epistemology needs to control for the biological and social conditioning and constraints to the production of knowledge and integrate different forms of knowledge. These include marginalized actors' (e.g., patients and doctors in medicine, peasants in agronomy, indigenous people in ecology, etc.) and practitioners' knowledge, the latter often having a better sense of the complexity of the problems than academic scholars.

For example, as we have seen, environmental processes are very complex, and their study very costly and thus often limited. They do not easily fit in the simple and so-called "evidence-based" reasonings that modern decision makers appreciate and thus tend to be overlooked. It is, for instance, simple to ask people about their lifestyles—are they smoking, drinking, eating healthy, exercising, etc.—and correlate these data with whether or not these people have developed cancer. It is much more complex to establish measurable links between cancers and specific environmental factors. This is due to the difficulty of tracking people's exposure to pollutants and establishing correlations with cancer rates, especially when the effects of pollution can only be perceived in the long term, or because the impact of one source of pollution can vary greatly because of interactions with other sources of pollution (the so-called "cocktail effect").

In some cases, the omnipresence of a source of pollution makes it also impossible for researchers to find a control sample. As a result, only those resulting from unhealthy lifestyles tend to be called "preventable cancers," as if those resulting from environmental pollution were not. Public efforts toward cancer prevention tend also to focus on lifestyles (though they only account for 40 percent of cancers in France) rather than environmental factors, as in the case of the 2021 French government's plan against cancer.[43] Addressing environmental pollutants would not only challenge our modern epistemology and its focus on what is simple and measurable (even when this only allows us to cover a minor portion of the problem), but also powerful economic interests and the paradigm of economic growth.

Moreover, as any system relies on some assumptions that cannot be proven,[44] epistemology should always be open to dialogue and recognize the capacity to go beyond itself, rather than claiming a monopoly on the truth. "Epistemology [...] is the place of both uncertainty and dialogics. In fact, all the uncertainties we have raised must confront and correct each another; there must be a dialogue, without, however, hoping to stop the ultimate crack with an ideological Band-Aid."[45]

A cure for our times

I believe Morin's complex thinking can be a cure for many pathologies of our modern thinking. As he said:

> The modern pathology of mind is in the hyper-simplification that makes us blind to the complexity of reality. The pathology of ideas takes the form of idealism, where the idea obscures the reality it is supposed to translate, and takes itself alone as real. The pathology of theory is in doctrinarism and dogmatism, which turn the theory in on itself and petrify it. The pathology of reason is rationalization, which encloses reality in a system of ideas that are coherent but partial and unilateral, and do not know that a part of reality is

unrationalizable, and that rationality's mission is to dialogue with the unrationalizable. We are blind to the problem of complexity. [...] This blindness is part of our barbarism. It makes us realize that in the world of ideas, we are still in an age of barbarism. We are still in the prehistory of the human mind. Only complex thought will allow us to civilize our knowledge.[46]

In fact, complex thinking naturally develops crucial personal qualities such as openness, humility, and a sense of solidarity—"If you have the sense of complexity, you have the sense of responsibility," said Morin[47]— emanating from the recognition of the interconnection of all things. Most importantly, it goes along with the capacity to let go of an artificial sense of control ("Relax: nothing is under control" says a board in Plum Village) and approach complex problems and situations from the perspective of "being" rather than traditional problem-solving mindsets as we have seen with theory U.

This leadership based on being, rather than only doing, calls for a whole-person intelligence, integrating mind, heart, body, and spirit, and the ability to pay attention to our attentions, intentions, feelings, sensations, intuitions, and subtle perceptions. It is a collaborative leadership, which recognizes the value of all stakeholders' viewpoints to activate our collective intelligence—as no individual has the cognitive capacity to process alone the complexity of the issues we are facing—and hear the voice of the system.

We participate in the system we want to change and the paradigm from which it operates. Changing how we engage in it can have a powerful impact, even in mysterious ways. "Life is a mystery to be lived, not a problem to be solved," said Gandhi. We can accept living amid mystery, that of the world, of our lives and our selves in the making, which knowledge will never exhaust. And that capacity to step into life, into its mystery, into the unknown, into what has not yet been tried, into what is to be invented—that openness to change is probably what we most need collectively.

Complex thinking fundamentally relates to personal inner development. Indeed, developmental psychology tends to consider mental complexity the main measure of a person's developmental stage. Each stage (such as the ones mentioned for integral theory and spiral dynamics in chapter 2) represents an extra layer in our consciousness that allows us to be aware, make sense, and function at a higher level of mental complexity. What defines us at one stage (e.g., the social norms that we have internalized) can become an object of a broader sense of self at a later stage (e.g., when we become able to think by ourselves and self-author our lives).

As we grow as individuals, our identities also expand, and we tend to feel part of ever-larger circles of belonging and solidarity. We feel not only responsible for our families, friends, and local communities but progressively also for more abstract ("imagined") communities such as nations, humanity, or even future generations and the whole earth community with all living beings. These larger circles of belonging translate into more complex identities and moral reasoning capacities. We see that it is our own inner complexity that allows us to make sense of and navigate the world as it is nowadays (or not to make sense of it, as the case may be).

The fundamental mismatch between our collective inner and outer complexity lies in our inability to deal with most of our problems. The rise of populism (and the simple solutions it proposes) and conspiracy theories are in large parts failed attempts for people to make sense of a world that has become too complex. I am often surprised to see so clearly in some people how this capacity or incapacity to think complexly connects to their self-awareness, their narrow or inclusive sense of identity, as well as their worldviews and political preferences.

Our own self-consciousness may indeed be the most important basis for the human, so human, adventure of knowledge: "Know thyself, and thou shalt know the universe and God" was written on the temple of Apollo at Delphi. Knowledge is a spiritual exercise and quest. As I write, there are one hundred and eighty-nine cognitive biases listed on the dedicated Wikipedia page.[48] We should better know how our mind works so as not to get caught in them. We should also be aware of our way of thinking ("metacognitive awareness") and functioning, our conditioning, our psychological and emotional disbalances that inevitably shape the way we perceive reality, in order to always try to overcome them. Many spiritual traditions tell that we need to purify our ego—which includes healing our psycho-emotional traumas and overcoming our conditioning—so that the biases and distortions that tarnish our perception of reality can dissipate.[49]

Our mind can then become clearer, so we can get closer to a certain objectivity or capacity to see things as they are. This would also allow us to understand other's viewpoints at their roots and be more tolerant and compassionate. If this insight were to grow in our collective consciousness, the public debate would grow much healthier and constructive. The associated development of our capacity for perspective-taking, which is also called "de-centering," would also strengthen our capacity to consider others' points of views and collaborate, our collective intelligence and wisdom.

It is striking to observe how little objectivity is valued in intellectual debates and the field of politics and how this strengthens polarization. My country, France, has a long tradition of engaged intellectuals and a passion for politics, which tends to make debates very ideological. I am always surprised to see that if I say that one political leader has made a smart move or that one fact he or she mentions is true, it seems automatically as if I am generally supportive of his or her views and agree with his or her interpretations of facts. Objectivity or the capacity to be simply true does not necessarily seem to be the main quality praised in an intellectual or a philosopher—individuals who are often considered the wise men or women of our so-called rational societies.

Our minds and systems of recognition tend to be more seduced by sophisticated theories, enclosing a wealth of culture, expressed with a brilliant writing style. I am often puzzled to see the extent to which our public intellectuals' own psychological wounds, neuroses, conditionings, and limitations—that one can relatively easily relate to their personal trajectories—seem to influence their views so deeply, framing the public debate. An old, disenchanted communist will spend his time explaining to us how there is no more hope for the world, and each should cultivate his or her garden, something easier to say when you are seventy than twenty. A materialist philosopher with deep anticlerical feelings and rationalist views, shaped in the adversity of a Christian orphanage, reduces religions to their negative aspects, fueling hot debates in the media. A pious conservative politician defends the very reactionary values that repress his natural tendencies, to the point that he has developed sexual practices his morals condemn ... etc., etc. It seems to never end.

Am I the only one seeing this? I often wonder, as the media never seem to acknowledge it. "We do not see things as they are; we see them as we are."[50] We should always look inside and ask ourselves whether our ideas and decisions are related to any of our own psychological imbalances or conditionings. They almost always are, so let's at least be aware of them, transform them, and step by step, enter reality.

The interconnected, dynamic, and infinite nature of reality makes it impossible for reason to fully comprehend it. "The integral truth of things is truth not of the reason but of the spirit,"[51] proclaimed Sri Aurobindo. Reason, when purified, can lead us to this recognition. It can voluntarily renounce its sovereign power and become an instrument of the spirit, formulating in words and reasoning what the spirit knows intuitively from its secret oneness with all things and beings.[52]

5

Life

Ecosophy, Biophilia, Deep and Integral Ecology, Mother Earth, Regeneration, Living Systems, Harmony, Simplicity, Health

"We are as much alive as we keep the Earth alive."

—Chief Dan George (1899–1981) of the Tsleil-Waututh
Nation in current Canada

"LIFE, OH LIFE, oh life, oh life doo, doot doot dooo ..."[1] Oops ... sorry :).
Following a long Judeo-Christian tradition of body depreciation, modernity has led us to consider ourselves primarily as thinking minds—"I think therefore I am"—fundamentally different from nature. As a definitive victory over millenniums of paganism, nature could finally be considered a great mechanism composed of separate parts, devoid of consciousness or life, lacking any intrinsic relationship to each other. Some scientists are now looking for ways to scan and upload the human mind, including long-term memory and "self," into a technological device (computer, robot, etc.) so we can live eternally, free from this body, which is doomed to decay.[2] Descartes's insight has finally led us to this fear-based denial of and technology-driven escape from what we fundamentally are: living beings of the nature to die.

We are alive. We are ALIVE. WE ARE ALIVE. Can we fully realize this, in all the cells of our body, including those cells that have just died and those that have just been born as we read this sentence? What does this mean in terms of how we should live our lives? When we understand what it really means to be alive, we may no longer fear death. "A cloud never dies," says Thich Nhat Hanh. We may find counsel in death. Imagine yourself on your deathbed; with this awareness, how should you live now? We can cherish each moment and no longer let our fear build artificial cocoons that isolate us from life itself. Rather, we can let our old systems die and welcome what wants to be born.

While, according to French anthropologist Philippe Descola, the ontological separation between humans and nonhumans and the opposition between nature and culture historically only developed in the Western world,[3] it has recently spread like a disease over the rest of the planet. The environmental crisis is a cultural crisis: it is striking to realize that cultural diversity and biological diversity tend to go hand in hand.[4] Indigenous people remind us nowadays that humankind traditionally considered itself as part of nature, a sacred community to which we belong, together with all living beings who are our brothers and sisters, our friends and relatives, as many Native Americans say. Nature is sacred because everything is filled with life, spirit, a vital force: not only the animals and plants but also stones, mountains, rivers, the sun, the moon, the wind, the fire, and of course, our Mother Earth.

At barely two and a half years of age, one of my daughters once asked me, "Dad, what is e-ner-gy?" I was surprised! I took a pause, probably smiled, and breathed before answering her, "That is what makes all things alive." Traditionally, it is believed that this energy or spirit unites all that is, as part of a cosmic order, named, for example, Tao in China, Maat in Egypt, R'ta or Dharma in India, and Logos in Greece. We can contemplate this divine order, its beauty, harmony, and wisdom in the course, ways, and laws of nature, the original and permanent source of revelation.[5] "If your heart were pure, then all of nature would be to you a book of divine wisdom," said Saint Francis of Assisi.[6]

This cosmic order, embodied in nature, often also means and is translated as the "path." Spiritual practices and duties aim primarily at harmonizing ourselves with this path, not only individually but also collectively, as the social community and order are a part, an expression, of a wider sacred community and order. Nature's life-supporting laws and principles—e.g., self-organization, balance, mutuality, reciprocity, zero waste, localism, unity in diversity, etc.—and its wisdom have long inspired our social systems. This is attested to by many indigenous people,[7] whose collective organizations have allowed them to live long in relative harmony with Mother Earth and with a sense of community, belonging, respect, awe, and sacredness.

It is traditionally believed that violating these natural laws and principles inevitably causes a cosmic imbalance that can manifest itself through many different social problems. Preventing these problems through maintaining cosmic harmony is the main inspiration and principle for human "justice," a concept also sometimes used to translate this natural order. Whether we like it or not, all the systems we are part of or that we are trying to transform are living systems, which are subject to nature's laws and should align with them.

A living nature

As the Earth's desacralization and our separation from it become increasingly recognized as the philosophical root causes of our environmental crisis, science is slowly helping us to recognize the sentient, conscious, and intelligent nature of plants, trees, and animals. From CIA interrogation specialist Cleve Backster's[8] experiments with a polygraph instrument in the 1960s to the recent extraordinary success of Peter Wohlleben's *The Hidden Life of Trees*, the ancient idea that nature is alive and conscious is slowly finding its way back into our cultures in a way that is more acceptable to our rational modern minds. Science is now telling us that trees can communicate among themselves, including to alert their neighbors of a coming danger, and can modify their metabolisms to adapt to variations in the environment that they can detect. Cypresses, for example, can release an airborne substance, which, kept inside, would make them more vulnerable to fire.[9] Trees display unusual electric activity up to three or four days before an earthquake, according to a Japanese study.[10] Though they don't have a brain or neurons, plants display information, memory, decision-making, and problem-solving activities.

Scientific findings, such as the work of ethologist and primatologist Frans de Waal, are also showing us that animals use tools and concepts, develop cultures, and display emotions, strategies, and empathy. A chimpanzee, Ayumu, has even shown greater memory than any human.[11] The long-held view within the Western world according to which humans distinguish themselves from nonhumans through particular cognitive and moral abilities is now falling apart. According to Frans de Waal, "It is time to stop running after a human specificity. In my life, I have probably seen some twenty-five proposals on human particularity. They have all been rejected"[12]; "it is a difference of degree not of nature."[13] de Waal calls the deniers, who remain many in science, "neo-creationists," as they recognize that we humans have evolved from primates but act as if this does not relate to our brain or mind.

The Gaia hypothesis developed by British chemist James Lovelock posits that the organic and inorganic components of the earth have evolved together as a single living, self-regulating, complex system that helps to maintain and perpetuate the conditions for life on the planet. One example Lovelock uses is that even though the luminosity of the sun—the Earth's heat source—has increased by about 30 percent since life began almost four billion years ago, the living system has reacted as a whole to maintain temperatures at levels suitable for life. As such, Earth's system is similar to an individual organism that regulates body temperature, blood salinity, etc. Initial scientific opposition to the Gaia theory has now largely waned, and the concepts associated with a living planet are now widely accepted in mainstream science, according to American science writer Ferris Jabr who, in 2019, defended the definition of Earth as a living being in a *New York Times* column:

> Like many living creatures, Earth has a highly organized structure, a membrane and daily rhythms; it consumes, stores and transforms energy; and if asteroid-hitching microbes or space-faring humans colonize other worlds, who is to say that planets are not capable of procreation?[14]

While Lovelock's theory does not rely on the presumption that Earth's consciousness is coordinating this process as its reference to the Greek earth goddess could indicate, the theory shows that the ancestral vision of a living earth, which is found in virtually all indigenous cultures, is, in theory at least, compatible with scientific understanding. In practice, this can offer a wise framework to guide our relationships with the Earth.

Interbeing with Mother Earth

One of the main surprises when I first attended the Parliament of the World's Religions in 2015 was how this "Mother Earth" vision is increasingly shared and promoted by major religious and spiritual traditions, who recognize the profound wisdom of our indigenous brothers and sisters. It has now even been adopted by the UN. Proposed by the Plurinational State of Bolivia, international Mother Earth Day was established by the UN in 2009 and is now celebrated every April 22.[15] The UN resolution recognizes that "Mother Earth is a common expression for the planet Earth in a number of countries and regions, which reflects the interdependence that exists among human beings, other living species and the planet we all inhabit."

Indigenous people have a deep-rooted understanding of their interdependence with the natural world, of which we are part, something Amerindian cultures have captured in their "web of life" concept, as put forward by Chief Seattle (1786–1866) in 1854: "Humankind has not woven the web of life. We are but one thread within it. Whatever we do to the web, we do to ourselves. All things are bound together. All things connect."[16] We have largely lost track of this evidence in our complex modern societies in which water comes to us through tubes, food is found in supermarkets, and fish nuggets seem the most common aquatic species quoted by children.

The environmental crisis is now pushing us to relearn this profound truth. The biodiversity crisis and how it affects us as humanity is sometimes difficult to comprehend, more than climate change, for example. I remember a French environmental minister at a UN convention on biological diversity, who was summarizing the difficulties in reaching an ambitious agreement. She said something like, "People are not seeing the great apes' extinction as a threat for humanity." We are all part of the web of life, and our well-being inherently depends on the well-being of other species. This is something we increasingly understand. Science tells us that 75 percent of our food crops and nearly 90 percent of wild flowering plants depend at least to some extent on wild pollinators such as bees.[17] It also emphasizes that deforestation was a major cause of both the last large Ebola outbreak in West Africa in 2014 and the return to Madagascar of the black plague the same year; it forced the bats and rats that carried the diseases into closer contact with humans.

But, beyond these very direct and linear cause and effect relationships, we need to move to a more systemic wisdom, recognizing that the Earth is an extremely complex system—as we have seen, for example, with the reintroduction of wolves in Yellowstone National Park—in a constant search for equilibrium. Environmental degradation can have unexpected consequences through a long chain of causes and effects. All species are interconnected, and each of them plays a role in the ecosystem. So it is not only about bees or rats or trees or a specific beautiful endangered species but about preserving the whole living system. We inter-are with all that exists: the food that we eat, the air that we breathe, the water that we drink ... Even our body hosts more microorganisms—bacteria, archaea, fungi, protists, and viruses—than human cells. They represent some 99 percent of the total number of genes in our body and are mostly located in our intestines. These microorganisms help us with digestion and immunity; impact babies' motor skills and language development; influence our choice of sexual partners; affect our food, health, and weight; and even have a bearing on our emotional state, our very personality, and social behaviors.[18]

Nature's benefits

Whether we like it or not, we are part of life, and we need to build harmonious relationships with life inside and outside of us. A great way to nourish life in us is to spend time in nature—"a pure source to which we can drink without any fear of being poisoned,"[19] according to French poet Guillaume Apollinaire—as confirmed by a growing body of recent scientific works. Table 3 below presents the many mental and physical health and well-being benefits of spending time in nature identified a couple of years ago by a review of scientific studies. These can help us understand why some talk about nature-deficit disorder.[20] I remember that when observing people at the university, I noticed those who had grown closest to nature seemed healthier and fresher to me. Their energy was different; there was more life in them.

Most of us have not waited for science to confirm what we know intuitively through experience: how a nice walk in the forest can nourish, calm us, and make us feel well. Dr. Qing Li, a researcher at the University of Tokyo, has recently been instrumental in scientifically restoring the legitimacy of an ancient Japanese therapeutic practice: Shinrin Yoku, or "forest bathing." With his best-seller, *Shinrin-Yoku: The Art and Science of Forest Bathing*, Li is part of a growing movement worldwide shedding light on the many health and well-being benefits that a walk in the forest can offer. This includes strengthening our immune system, lowering our blood pressure and stress levels, boosting our concentration and creativity, and stimulating and awakening all our senses. This recognition is leading to the quick development all over the world of commercial offers by certified "forest bathing" professionals, in which a walk in the forest can be accompanied by some guided meditations and exercises.

By supporting our reconnection to nature, these practices can also yield important environmental benefits. A scientific study was able to establish a correlation between our connection to nature, which tends to grow as we spend time in it, and our environmental attitudes and behaviors.[21] The individual benefits from exposure to nature can occur in a wide range of settings, including our homes or working spaces. I remember when I brought my first plant into my small flat in Paris. A few days later, I entered my home and felt the energy was completely changed, full of life. The contrast was so stark. How could I have previously lived in such a desolate place without noticing it? I was, with some difficulty, coming out of one of the toughest periods of my life, and it seemed as if my place was reflecting my inner void. A couple of years later, I felt sad and preoccupied when a close relative of mine, who has never been attracted to nature, told me she wanted to give away the last plant in her large flat. It seemed to me she was removing life from her existence, something that echoed her other unhealthy attitudes and behaviors.

Table 3—Typology of the benefits of interacting with nature

Benefit	Description	Examples
Psychological well-being	Positive effect on mental processes	Increased self-esteem
		Improved mood
		Reduced anger/frustration
		Psychological well-being
		Reduced anxiety
		Improved behavior
Cognitive	Positive effect on cognitive ability or function	Attentional restoration
		Reduced mental fatigue
		Improved academic performance
		Education/learning opportunities
		Improved ability to perform tasks
		Improved cognitive function in children
		Improved productivity
Physiological	Positive effect on physical function and/or physical health	Stress reduction
		Reduced blood pressure
		Reduced cortisol levels
		Reduced headaches
		Reduced mortality rates from circulatory disease
		Faster healing
		Addiction recovery
		Perceived health/well-being
		Reduced cardiovascular, respiratory disease, and long-term illness
		Reduced occurrence of illness

Source: Keniger et al. (2013)

The benefits of urban nature are also increasingly documented by science and do not only materialize at the individual level but seem to be significant drivers of social health. Beyond many other well-known benefits, "urban greening" also helps cities build social capital—as parks, gardens, and open spaces promote social interactions[22]—significantly reduce crime rates (though the impact pathways remain a bit mysterious),[23] improve safety on the streets,[24] etc.,[25] findings that are now being applied by many cities.

The current environmental crisis is so rooted in our minds and the very structures of our social and economic systems, and so intertwined with all the other crises we are facing, that addressing it will entail a different form of civilization. In a way similar to the industrialization process, which transformed societies in all their dimensions, we now need an integral ecology that seeks to transform all our institutions, our economic, political, social, cultural systems, and align them with ecological principles.

China's ecological civilization

The above is something China recognized in 2012, when it included the goal of achieving an ecological civilization in its constitution. We may see that as mere political rhetoric, but still, China is making considerable investments to green its development pathway and, maybe more importantly for the long-term future, the country has great cultural, philosophical, and spiritual resources to mobilize in support of this goal. Xi Jinping, China's current leader, called for an "ecological civilization." He mentioned it should ensure "harmony between human and nature" and noted "we, as human beings, must respect nature, follow its ways, and protect it." His administration will "encourage simple, moderate, green, and low-carbon ways of life, and oppose extravagance and excessive consumption."[26]

Paying attention to the semantics, it is easy to recognize how this concept resonates deeply in Chinese culture. The "Tao" concept is central in East Asian philosophy and religions, including Confucianism, Taoism, and Chinese Buddhism. Though the Tao is "eternally nameless,"[27] it is often translated as the "way" and considered as the primary cosmic principle, the flow of the universe, the natural order that permeates and governs all things and keeps the universe in balance. It is often closely associated with the chi—"breath" or "energy"—of which all things are made, and which makes all of them—humans, animals, plants—fundamentally equal.[28]

According to these traditions, spiritual practice aims at becoming one with the Tao or at harmonizing oneself with nature and following its way to achieve "effortless action" ("wu wei"). Importantly, this view has not been confined to individual spiritual practices but has long been instrumental in Asian political philosophy to reflect on good governance. The Tao can be contemplated in nature, the main source of wisdom, guidance, and nourishment. Thus, the sage will naturally tend to choose a simple, humble, frugal life, close to nature. "One that has penetrated life's meaning does not struggle anymore for what does not contribute to life,"[29] said Tchouang Tseu, the famous Taoist philosopher from the fourth century BC, nowadays echoed by the voluntary simplicity movement.

More generally, according to traditional Chinese philosophy, for everyone and every nation, the good life is the life lived in harmony with the way, which can lead to different interpretations and priorities. Indeed, this natural order is not only present in nature but can also be found in relationships, family, arts, and traditions, for example. But it would be vain to search for it in material goods, power, or fame.[30] In attempting to build an "ecological civilization," China—this five-thousand-year-old culture—will simply return to its longtime quest for the good life, honoring the great wisdom of its ancestors, and potentially offer a new model to the world in its search for sustainability.

"Vivir bien" and "buen vivir"

Taoism has lots in common with indigenous philosophies. Across South America, the latter has been the basis for developing an instrumental political reflection on development goals and how to align our societies with life's needs and wisdom. The Andean concepts of Suma Qamaña (in Aymara) and Sumaq Kawsay (in Quechua) are imperfectly translated in Spanish as "vivir bien" ("living well") and "buen vivir" ("good living").[31]

Rooted in indigenous cosmovisions and nourished by modern reflections, particularly on post-development, these concepts emphasize living in harmony with nature and one another[32] (or "harmonious coexistence"[33]).

Decolonization, respect of traditional cultures and cultural identities, the importance of community, equilibrium among the various elements that make up the whole (including the material and the spiritual), are other key features of these plural concepts, which are being developed on an ongoing basis between indigenous communities, social movements, and academia. They have gained attention in the late twentieth and early twenty-first century as an alternative to neoliberalism, extractivism (a development model based on mining and natural resource exploitation), consumerism, and even development, perceived as a Western idea fundamentally alien to indigenous cultures.

The two concepts, which are echoed by different indigenous cultures across Latin America,[34] have become central within the governments of Rafael Correa in Ecuador and Evo Morales in Bolivia and were introduced into the constitutions of both countries respectively in 2008 and 2009. "Buen vivir" is recognized as a right in the Ecuadorian constitution, while "vivir bien," together with other similar indigenous concepts,[35] is recognized in the Bolivian constitution as a fundamental principle and value of the State of Bolivia, which is now recognized as "plurinational." In both countries, these concepts have been recognized as the main political goal, and the countries' development plans bear their names.[36]

With its 2008 constitution, Ecuador became the first country in the world to codify the Rights of Nature. Article 71 states:

> Nature, or Pacha Mama, where life is reproduced and occurs, has the right to integral respect for its existence and for the maintenance and regeneration of its life cycles, structure, functions and evolutionary processes. All persons, communities, peoples and nations can call upon public authorities to enforce the rights of nature.

In Bolivia, nature rights were recognized in 2010 through the Law on the Rights of Mother Earth, which, in practice, has been poorly effective.[37] With their institutionalization and state cooptation, "buen vivir" and "vivir bien" have lost much of their spirit. A developmentalist, productivist vision has remained dominant. The extractivist models have thrived as a means to accumulate resources in order to then be able to transcend it, according to the National Plan for Buen Vivir in Ecuador,[38] often with significant environmental costs, in particular in Bolivia. Complemented by social measures, this has allowed these countries to improve many traditional development indicators without getting closer to the good life as envisioned originally in these concepts.

These governments, in particular in Bolivia, have become more authoritarian, undermining the capacities of communities and societies to self-organize, a fundamental means of building buen vivir or vivir bien from the bottom up. Nevertheless, the Bolivian and Ecuadorian governments have actively promoted these concepts, philosophies, and policies (i.e., rights of nature) at the global level. Their efforts included the development of a draft Universal Declaration on the Rights of Mother Earth (see chapter 16) and the adoption by the UN of international Mother Earth Day, as well as different UN resolutions on "harmony with nature."[39]

Biomimetics

Analyzing the philosophical roots of the concepts of "buen vivir" and "ecological civilization" reminds us today that our ancestors have long been busy looking deeply into nature and life, as the original sacred book, to understand how it works, our place and role in it, and how we can align and harmonize our societies' functioning with it. Nowadays, nature's intelligence, its 3.8 billion years of research and development, and proven innovative, efficient, sustainable, and resilient solutions are again attracting enormous interest. Biomimetics is the imitation of the models, systems, and elements of nature for the purpose of solving complex human problems.[40] Though it has ever existed, it is a growing and very promising field of research and application, which has recently allowed the development of many innovative, often green and sustainable, technologies. For example, Velcro was developed through observing how certain plants propagate their seeds by hooking them to passing animals' coats, while architecture has studied termite mounds to design passive climate control systems as in the Eastgate Centre in Harare, Zimbabwe.[41] Studying shark skin has allowed the development of high-performance swimsuits, as well as varnish for airplane fuselage,[42] and Japanese high-speed trains have copied the kingfisher's beak to reduce noise when entering tight tunnels while also saving 15 percent of energy through improved aerodynamics.[43]

The economic potential of biomimetism via the development of innovative technologies in a wide range of industries—including health care, agriculture, energy, construction, transport, chemistry, textiles, etc.—is huge, furthering the economic case for arresting the current loss of biodiversity. Perhaps more importantly, we can return to valuing nature as a source of wisdom and inspiration that can help us develop sustainable, resilient, and effective systems in the domains of economic, social, and natural resource management. In fact, circular economies,[44] industrial ecologies,[45] and permacultures[46] are all based on imitating nature and system thinking, which, as we have seen, comes from the field of ecology, in itself the only new political ideology of the twenty-first century.[47]

Natural wisdom is currently spreading into many fields, such as governance,[48] organizational theory, or urbanism. Fréderic Laloux, in his best-seller *Reinventing Organizations,* which we will discuss in detail later, states that organizations embodying the highest development stage to date often consider themselves as "living organisms" or "living systems."[49] The new city of Lavasa, India, is designed to play the role of a humid forest that once occupied the same space, delivering the same ecosystem services, which are key with regards to land dryness and monsoon-related floods.[50] All these innovations outline the emergence of new cultures of life. These regenerative cultures recognize that, as part of nature, nature is our way, and we can only thrive with it and not against it.

According to Thich Nhat Hanh, "What we most need to do is to hear within us the sound of the earth crying."[51] There is no "human nature" separate from nature itself, as we have seen with Frans de Waal. If we can truly be in touch with our own nature, we can connect with the Earth and automatically feel the need for rising up in defense of all life. We are part of Mother Earth; we are her immune system. It is now time to come back to her, recognizing her as the material basis of our lives, as well as an inexhaustible source of nourishment and wisdom. As ex-prisoners rehabilitating themselves by working the land, in collectively shifting our lives to take care of Mother Earth, we may well heal ourselves.

6

Happiness

Well-Being, Eudaimonia, Flourishing, Positive, Quality of Life

"To save our planet, we need to have a new view of happiness."
—Zen Master Thich Nhat Hanh[1]

ONE THING THAT unites us all is our common search for happiness and well-being. In recent history, our societies have focused on the production of goods and services as a way to achieve this and have tended to confuse what was supposed to be a means with the end goal. As it is now becoming clear that economic growth does not necessarily translate into real happiness, especially once a certain level of economic development has been achieved, it has become more important to reaffirm happiness as a legitimate orientation and measure of social progress and see what kind of development can move us in that direction.

Bhutan's Gross National Happiness

In 2008, the government of Bhutan instituted Gross National Happiness (GNH) as its main development goal in the country's constitution, enacted thirty-six years after then-king of Bhutan, Jigme Singye Wangchuck, proclaimed, "Gross National Happiness is more important than Gross National Product." GNH is currently defined in Bhutan as a "multidimensional development approach seeking to achieve a harmonious balance between material well-being and the spiritual, emotional, and cultural needs of society,"[2] relying on four pillars: good governance, sustainable socioeconomic development, preservation and promotion of culture, and environmental conservation. An institutional framework has been put in place, including the GNH Commission, in charge of the design and implementation of development plans and policies; a GNH index relying on objective and subjective indicators;[3] and GNH screening tools for policies and projects.

The GNH has provided the overall rationale for an original development path. Its main features include cultural preservation, with low exposure to Western influence in particular through the strict limitation of tourism, as well as a TV and jeans ban;[4] protection of the local economy through limited integration with the international trade system, such as when Bhutan decided not to join the World Trade Organization;[5] and environmental conservation, with forests representing some 81 percent of the national territory (constitutionally, this rate is legally required to remain above 60 percent at all times).[6]

It has to be noted that Bhutan is not the ideal country, as sometimes portrayed as a result of effective marketing at the international level. Bhutan has been strongly criticized for ethnic cleansing and human rights abuses. In the early nineties, with the intention of preserving its culture, the country forced more than a hundred thousand ethnic Nepalese (one-sixth of the country's population) to leave. A gradual transition to a constitutional democracy was initiated in the early eighties and continued up until the nation's first democratic elections in 2008.

Happiness as a new development paradigm

On July 19, 2011, by consensus, the UN General Assembly adopted resolution 65/309, "Happiness: towards a holistic approach to development." Cosponsored by sixty-eight countries, the resolution's goal is to support, share information, and discuss the relevance of happiness and well-being in the global development agenda, recognizing happiness "as a fundamental human goal." A high-level meeting on well-being and happiness was then organized at the United Nations headquarters in New York in April 2012. Attended by more than eight hundred delegates, it requested the Kingdom of Bhutan to convene an expert working group to frame a new development paradigm based on the Bhutanese GNH approach.

The result of this work was a seventy-five-page document, "Happiness: Towards a New Development Paradigm," through which the Kingdom of Bhutan proposed putting happiness and well-being at the core of the new sustainable development paradigm for the post-2015 global development agenda.[7] In this proposal, happiness is described as "arising from a sense of connectedness with nature, communities, and the world, and as stemming from service to others."[8] Following Bhutan's GNH approach, the document proposes to assess well-being according to nine domains or needs: ecological diversity and resilience, living standards, health, education, cultural diversity and resilience, community vitality, time balance, good governance, and psychological well-being. For these outer conditions of well-being to translate into the experience of human and societal happiness, they have to be accompanied by the "transformation of our own mind-sets and behaviours." The development of "happiness skills," such as "mindfulness [...], loving-kindness, compassion-meditation, and the conscious practice of gratitude, empathy, and patience,"[9] is emphasized.

Back in 2013, it was a real source of hope and inspiration for me that such an amazingly mature proposal would be on the table of the United Nations to shape their post-2015 agenda. Unfortunately, it has not been really taken into account in the SDGs. The world was not ready yet. Had it been, we probably would have advanced by a generation in terms of global development thinking.

Many countries, such as the United Arab Emirates, the UK, and Canada, for example, along with regions such as Tasmania[10] in Australia, and cities, have started to use the happiness lens.[11] They are rethinking their development path and public policies (we will see some examples in part 3)[12] and developing social progress indicators[13] as part of the worldwide trend of searching for an alternative to GDP. In 2019, under the leadership of Prime Minister Jacinda Ardern, New Zealand adopted its first "well-being budget." It prioritizes relevant investments to tackle issues identified for the population's happiness, in particular inequality, homelessness, mental health, as well as domestic violence.[14] Five investment priorities have been defined in that perspective, beyond which there seems to be little scope for approval of new investments. These priorities are supporting mental health (with a focus on youth), reducing child poverty, lifting the incomes and opportunities of indigenous Maori and Pacific Islanders, moving to a low-emission and sustainable economy, and supporting a thriving nation in a digital age.[15]

More and more companies are also taking their employees' well-being seriously, especially as it has been shown to make them more productive, creative, healthy, engaged, loyal, and cooperative.[16] They implement dedicated programs and redefine their values, organization, and management practices, including greater autonomy for their employees or the use of remote working. Well-being at work has even become a key investment criterion, as in the case of the Happy@Work investment fund launched in 2015 by Sycomore. It has also become a matter of public policy, with some countries mandating companies manage and report on psychosocial risks.

Nongovernmental initiatives, such as the "action for happiness,"[17] are also spreading. Launched in 2010 by the Dalai Lama, this is a movement of people committed to building a happier and more caring society. It first requires its members to make a simple pledge: to try to create more happiness in the world around them. Then it offers them a happiness training based on modern positive psychology and traditional wisdom from both the West and East, providing ideas and resources to enable people to take action at home, at work, or in their community. Members are also encouraged to form local groups to take action together. By the end of 2018, more than one hundred and twenty-three thousand people from one hundred and seventy-five countries had registered as members.

The science of happiness

The development of the scientific study of happiness has accompanied its emergence in the field of politics. While happiness and well-being have long been discussed by moral philosophy, the development of scientific studies represents a real breakthrough in starting to provide evidence-based answers to age-old debates. Developed in the nineties, positive psychology has been a major foundation of this new science. It is defined as the "scientific study of optimal human functioning [that] aims to discover and promote the factors that allow individuals and communities to thrive,"[18] contrasting with the traditional dominant focus of psychology on psychological pathologies. In 2009, the founder of this new field, professor Martin Seligman, called for this discipline to expand its boundaries and transform into "positive social science" that would unite psychologists, sociologists, economist, policy-makers, educators, health and business researchers and practitioners, as well as philosophers and thinkers in the field of religion and spirituality.[19] The new happiness science has been characterized by important debates on the definition, determinants (especially regarding its relationship to income level) and measurements, as well as public policies, measures, and tools[20] for happiness and well-being, which reflects the significance of what this new approach has at stake and the extent to which it could potentially redirect our development path.

International happiness rankings have tendentially been dominated by Northern European countries such as Denmark, Norway, Iceland, Finland, and Sweden, as well as other European countries such as Switzerland and the Netherlands, followed by countries such as Canada, Australia, or New Zealand.[21] These rankings tend to rely on country-level statistics on subjective well-being (SWB), which is measured through self-reported appreciation of (i) life satisfaction or happiness (cognitive measure) and/or (ii) positive or negative affects (affective measure). It is important to keep in mind that any specific approach we take to analyze happiness may influence the conclusions we draw. For example, the frequent domination of cognitive over affective measures is not free from bias and may overestimate the role of life circumstances, in particular socioeconomic factors, favoring rich countries in international rankings on happiness.[22]

According to Gallup's 2019 global emotions reports, Paraguay, a middle-income country, was the country where people reported the most positive experience on a given day.[23] This is in line with popular wisdom: the joy and positive emotions expressed by poor people in "developing countries" are often striking for many westerners, while Northern European countries, which consider themselves very satisfied with their lives, are not necessarily known for enjoying such strong and positive emotions. The symbolic domination of materialistic values associated with the social comparison tendency may create a cognitive bias, leading people in richer countries to estimate themselves more satisfied with life while the people from the so-called "underdeveloped countries" could logically consider themselves less satisfied with their lives.

Subjective well-being analyses have allowed us to identify the main social conditions that are favorable to happiness. They highlight in particular the social and cultural foundations of happiness. Social capital, defined as "the extent of trust, social support networks, and pro-sociality in a society,"[24] has been stressed as the prominent determinant of subjective well-being,[25] well above wealth.[26] One of the surveys of reference, which is published almost every two years in the World Happiness Report, provides a cross-national comparison of levels of self-evaluated life satisfaction.[27] It uses six variables[28] to try to understand the respective influences on happiness levels, which together account for three-quarters of the variation of the national levels of happiness between 2005 and 2018.

Researchers found the following contributions to national happiness: social support (34 percent), GDP per capita (26 percent), healthy life expectancy (21 percent), freedom (11 percent), generosity (5 percent), and corruption (3 percent).[29] The four variables associated with the quality of the social context (social support, freedom, generosity, and corruption) represent more than half of the contributing factors. This is certainly an underestimate, for the measure of the quality of social contexts' contribution to happiness is limited by the availability of data for other variables that may express it, and the quality of the social fabric is itself a key determinant of wealth and health. Material prosperity does matter, but its effect diminishes once a certain threshold is reached, after which it becomes less significant.[30]

Happiness is negatively associated with social inequality—in particular well-being inequality—which has recently increased at the national and international levels. Raising the well-being of the lowest segment of the population through the improvement of the social fabric can be beneficial to the whole spectrum of society.[31] Finally, social capital can drastically affect societies' resilience, an important result considering our future's uncertainties and risks, including that of major collapses. Following a crisis, subjective well-being can plummet if the social fabric crumbles further when "the crisis triggers blame and strife rather than cooperation and repair" (e.g., Greece in the decade following the 2008 economic crisis), or, conversely, well-being can rise if responding to the crisis is taken as an opportunity to strengthen social capital (e.g., Iceland and Ireland during the same period).[32]

Cultural determinants of happiness, in particular attitudes of power and gender equality, have also been emphasized, along with strong in-group feelings and a humane orientation (societies valuing people for "being fair, altruistic, generous, caring, and kind to others"[33]). Researchers have found that cultural factors could account for more than 90 percent of country levels of subjective well-being, with more traditional indicators linked to income, education, human rights, and urbanization accounting for less than 10 percent.[34]

From another perspective, Inglehart, a leading American political scientist, has identified freedom of choice as the main condition of happiness. According to him, global happiness had been rising sharply since the eighties, before declining or stagnating since the 2008 financial crisis. This exceptional upward trend was mainly due to "a remarkable conjunction of favorable circumstances."[35] The most important factor was rising social tolerance (on gender roles, homosexuality, ethnic backgrounds, etc.), followed by democratization and, to a lesser extent, economic growth. All of these factors enhanced people's freedom of choice in how to live their lives.

The relative importance of these factors depends on the level of development of the countries; rising social tolerance has been particularly important for rich countries to increase their happiness, while democratization has played a key role for middle-income countries, and economic growth has proved more critical for less prosperous countries. This trend also reflects the general evolution from survival values to self-expression values that are more conducive to happiness, and the current cultural backlash and return to survival values that are now threatening this promising evolution.

Beyond pointing out the conditions of good societies, happiness science also highlights the elements of a good life at the individual level, which may also depend on national contexts: income, for example, is more important for happiness in low-income countries than in upper-income countries. The quality of relationships, in particular with a partner and family, is generally recognized as the most important factor,[36] confirming humans' relational nature. "Good relationships keep us happier and healthier"[37] is the key conclusion of the famous eighty-year-long Harvard Study of Adult Development.[38] That is why people who adopt a relational view of existence are in general much happier than those stuck in an individualistic and materialistic vision, something evidenced by many studies.[39] Physical health is also generally recognized as an important condition, one that actually benefits from good relationships, with clear belief systems, religion,[40] income, and work fulfillment coming much after.[41]

Happiness as a way of being

More fundamentally, premodern philosophical and spiritual traditions all over the world have emphasized for centuries that happiness fundamentally depends on us, rather than our life conditions. The concept of eudaimonia (see box 3), which goes back to Aristotle, has been central for reflecting and discussing the scientific literature about happiness. Sometimes translated as fulfillment, psychology professor Veronika Huta defines eudiamonia "roughly speaking" as including "states and/or pursuits associated with using and developing the best in oneself, in accordance with one's true self and one's deeper principles."[42]

Box 3—Eudaimonia[43]

According to Huta, "Aristotle defined eudaimonia as active behavior that exhibits excellence and virtue in accordance with reason and contemplation—those faculties which differentiate from other species—and is performed for its own sake. His conception includes moral virtues like justice, kindness, courage and honesty, as well as intellectual activity and high performance at any activity, such as one's profession."[44]

Huta identified the following themes as being associated with eudaimonia: excellence, authenticity, development ("personal evolution and realization of one's potential"[45]), full functioning, broad scope of concern (service ...), engagement, autotelism ("seeing the means or process as an end in itself"[46]), contemplation, acceptance, meaning, elevation, awe, connection, aliveness, fulfillment, and competence.

As the practice of virtues and a long-term endeavor, eudaimonia has often been opposed to the search for pleasure, enjoyment, and comfort, known as hedonia. Research shows that, though both orientations can lead to happiness, eudaimonia seems a better and more sustainable way than hedonia. But most importantly, it is the combination of these pursuits—"the full life"—that leads to greater life satisfaction than any single pursuit.[47] This has led researchers in the field of positive psychology to develop the concept of human "flourishing." While it is also sometimes used as a translation of eudaimonia, researchers have defined flourishing as a state of mental health associated with positive emotions and positive psychological and social functioning through which one can self-actualize, and researchers have placed it at the center of their agenda.[48] They have identified the main psychological features associated with flourishing, highlighted by decades of research in psychology, and found they correspond to a large extent with the opposite symptoms of depression.[49]

On that basis, scientists have argued that mental health should be positively defined as flourishing, rather than negatively as "the mere absence of mental illness."[50] They have studied how to best develop the characteristics associated with flourishing, which are presented in box 4. While part of our subjective well-being is related to our genetic heritage,[51] these are capacities that we can all develop to lead a psychologically healthy and happy life.

Scientists have also tried to assess the proportion of the population that is flourishing among different societies. While many of us declare ourselves happy or satisfied with our lives, it turns out that only 18 percent of US adults[52] or 12.2 percent of Europeans are flourishing, with enormous differences between Northern Europe (Denmark, 33 percent) and Eastern Europe (Russia, 6 percent), with countries such as the UK (18 percent), Germany (12 percent), and France (10 percent) in between.

Measuring flourishing, rather than just subjective well-being, seems to me a much more complete and appropriate approach. Someone experiencing a manic episode would report subjective well-being. People can easily feel satisfied with their lives for erroneous reasons, like a vision of success that has been imposed on them. Mental health gives a more objective account of well-being.

This vision of happiness as flourishing has the potential to radically transform our model of development and make it more sustainable. Simple living does not hinder, but often rather enables flourishing. In 2007, as part of a twelve-year-long program, neuroscientists[53] found in Matthieu Ricard, a French Buddhist monk close to the Dalai Lama, physiological measures[54] associated with happiness never reported before in the scientific literature.[55] This promptly led the media to call Ricard "the happiest man in the world," which he said is an overstatement.

It was surprising for some that a chaste man, without money, dressed in the same clothes every day, living in a monastery in Nepal in very basic material conditions, with little use of technology, and probably not even believing in God, could be that man. In fact, Ricard, who was born in 1946 to an artist mother and a famous philosopher, grew up among the French intellectual and artistic elites of his time and completed a PhD in molecular genetics under the supervision of a Nobel Prize winner. He decided when he was twenty-six to quit this promising life to become a monk in the Himalayas.

Box 4—The Recipe for Personal Happiness

The Action for Happiness initiative has tried to summarize positive psychology's findings into "ten keys to happier living:"[56]

- "Giving" or doing good to others;

- "Relating" or connecting with people, which includes enjoying a sense of support and belonging to a community;

- "Exercising" or taking care of our body, which includes a healthy diet and good sleep;

- "Awareness" or living life mindfully;

- "Trying out" or continuing to learn new things;

- "Direction" or having purpose or goals to look forward to;

- "Resilience" or finding ways to bounce back including through an appropriate attitude towards adversity, for which a sense of purpose can be very helpful;

- "Emotions" or cultivating positive emotions and attitudes, as well as savoring happy moments;

- "Acceptance" or accepting ourselves and others as we are;

- "Meaning" or being part of something bigger.

In addition to these, psychological science stresses the importance of:[57]

- Autonomy or the capacity to follow one's own direction, to act in harmony with oneself and resist unsavory social pressures;

- Competence or the capacity to master our need for satisfaction;

- Commitment to personal growth;

- Self-knowledge;

- Optimism;

- Gratitude and contentment;

- Forgiveness;

- Etc.

Scientists have already established the extraordinary potential of meditation—even practiced in very moderate dose such as twenty minutes a day for three weeks—to develop our capacity for happiness, and meditators from all backgrounds, in this study, fell outside the standard curve in a very tight, clearly defined cluster. Ricard then shared his happiness secrets in one of his first best-sellers.[58] Basically, he invites us to focus on inner conditions that are more under our direct control and more fundamental to generating true, enduring happiness that is different from momentary pleasures. According to him, "Achieving durable happiness as a way of being is a skill. It requires sustained effort in training the mind and developing a set of human qualities, such as inner peace, mindfulness, and altruistic love."[59]

Through meditation we can transform our mind and cultivate our true nature, purging mental toxins such as hatred, anger, pride, or craving, and generating naturally positive emotions and ways of being that are less self-centered and more compassionate. As this will ultimately determine the quality of each instant of our life, we should dedicate time to training our mind for happiness—"life's most important skill"—through meditation in a similar manner to how we dedicate time to education or to keeping ourselves physically fit.[60]

We see that wisdom, personal development and transformation, and spiritual practices have a great deal to bring to our well-being. Bhutan's happiness paradigm is culturally rooted in Buddhist teachings, which put the search for happiness (or the end of suffering) at the core of the spiritual path. Moreover, many mystics have reported great feelings of joy and happiness associated with their realizations. In Hinduism, "Ananda" or bliss is considered one of the three key features of the ultimate reality (together with "sat"—existence—and "chit"—consciousness), an experience to which many Hindu sages have attested. Thirteenth-century Sufi poet and mystic Rumi advises us, "If you are seeking, seek us with joy. For we live in the kingdom of joy."

But what about religions? Do they help us to be happier? Well, there is evidence for a "religious engagement paradox."[61] If we compare countries, we see that those with less religious engagement are happier (and sometimes abide more by virtues endorsed by religions, such as not smoking or obeying the law). But, if we turn to individuals, studies show that religious engagement is generally correlated with a higher level of happiness.[62] This is particularly true for highly spiritually committed people, who also display more compassionate attitudes and behaviors (work, volunteering, charitable giving, etc.).[63] While nominally religious people, for whom religion is, above all, a question of social and cultural identity, tend to be more prejudiced against others than nonmembers, those more committed to their religious and spiritual lives are less prejudiced.[64] Researchers have highlighted healthy lifestyles, social support, self-control, meaning and purpose, civic involvement, and charitable giving as some of the pathways through which individual religious engagement translates into more happiness.

Because I am happy ...

High-quality relationships, pro-social behaviors, health, and work performance are not only determinants of happiness; they are also benefits derived from happiness.[65] Science corroborates what French philosopher Voltaire (1694–1778) once said: "I have decided to be happy because it is good for my health." In fact, positive emotions have been found to improve the immune system, along with cardiovascular and endocrine functioning, and ultimately, longevity. Subjective well-being has also been proven to be a causal factor of work performance. Most importantly, individuals with higher well-being are reported to have longer-term time preferences; to spend less and save more; to donate more time, money, and blood to others; to engage more in social activities and networks; and to have more pro-environmental behaviors.[66]

Interestingly, analyses have shown that social and environmental benefits from happiness stem from a eudaimonic and not a hedonic orientation to happiness.[67] All of this has important consequences: happiness can be associated with virtuous circles at the individual and social levels. As some researchers put it:

> Happiness has the potential to generate positive snowball effects in
> society. Research has shown that people who are happier are likely

to bring happiness to those around them [in family, workplace, community, etc.], resulting in networks of happier individuals. It was found that happiness extends up to three degrees of separation, and longitudinal models show that individuals who are surrounded by happy people are likely to become happier in the future.[68]

Unlike other development paradigms, such as capitalism or socialism, which originated in the West, the happiness paradigm has been largely promoted through the experience of Bhutan, a small Asian country whose traditional culture has been relatively preserved and which became the first country to put the happiness paradigm at the center of its development path.[69] This has made it particularly appealing to other countries in Asia,[70] an important strength as world political leadership is slowly transitioning to the East.

In any case, countries' reorientation toward well-being and happiness may take time but seems unavoidable, which should give us hope for the future. Happiness science tends to indicate that by shifting our priorities from economic growth to happiness, we can be both happier and take more care of our communities and environment. Unlike economic growth, happiness may be able to go hand in hand with sustainability. Self-actualization and the development of the best in each person, including our capacity for enjoyment and positive emotions, have the capacity to move us forward on that path.

"It might seem crazy what I'm 'bout to say ..." The year Bhutan released its happiness proposal to the United Nations, the planet, surprisingly, got caught in an unprecedented international happy movement. "Because I'm happy ... Clap along if you think that happiness is the truth ... Because I'm happy ... Clap along if you know what happiness is to you ... Because I'm happy ... Clap along if you feel like that's what you wanna do," sings Pharrell Williams in his famous feel-good "happy" song released in November 2013, which spread virally and reached the top of the charts to become the best-selling song of 2014.

Groups of people from around the world started to dance in their homes or in the streets. They shared their videos on the web, including on a platform created for this purpose,[71] where you can find more than fifteen hundred such recordings. By expressing their happiness, they were also representing their cities and countries, spreading the winds of freedom—such as in post-Arab Spring countries like Tunisia, where I was a fortunate witness—and eventually, protests against political oppression, as in Iran, for example, where the dancers were arrested. The Iranian police chief said the song represented vulgarity and hurt public chastity.

The arrests went public, and Williams reacted in a tweet, stating, "It's beyond sad these kids were arrested for trying to spread happiness." Iran's president, Hassan Rouhani, criticized the arrest in a highly political tweet: "Happiness is our people's right. We shouldn't be too hard on behaviors caused by joy," and the dancers were finally released.[72] For the 2015 international day of happiness, "Pharrell Williams and the United Nations Foundation invited everyone to join a global HAPPY PARTY, spread happiness, and demand climate action," resulting in thousands of happy people from all over the world dancing and posting their own videos online.[73]

Who says that God does not have a sense of humor? I believe sometimes the universe bursts out laughing.

7

Love

Altruism, Empathy, Compassion, Goodness, Care, Brotherhood / Sisterhood, Solidarity, Cooperation, Trust

"If you want others to be happy, practice compassion.
If you want to be happy, practice compassion."
—His Holiness the 14th Dalai Lama[1]

HAPPINESS'S BEST FRIEND is love. Love is the most positive emotion: it is the state of mind that most activates areas in the brain associated with positive emotions, contributing greatly to our well-being, health, and development.[2] Indeed, love tends to encompass many other emotions and feelings, such as gratitude, joy, awe, and a sense of connectedness. Scientific studies show that parental love is the key source of all human development: physiological, emotional, psychological, cognitive, and behavioral.[3] It is the foundation for secure attachment, the basis of our empathic and relational capacities that are indispensable for our happiness and our social functioning.[4] "All you need is love. Love, love, love is all you need," sing the Beatles.

God is love

All spiritual and religious traditions place love at the core of their teachings and experience. It is often seen as the most divine attribute—"God is love," reads the Bible![5]—and the source of goodness in each of us that dissipates the artificial frontiers between us and others, allowing us experiences of elevation beyond the limits of our small egos. "Love is the bridge between you and everything," said thirteenth-century Persian Sufi poet Rumi.

This is exactly what I experienced in 2013, near Paris, after receiving a hug or "darshan" from Indian spiritual leader Amma (Mata Amritanandamayi). I felt my heart so open, my energy field so vast that I was experiencing others' presence within me, as if the boundaries that separate us had vanished for a split second. Amma, who has hugged more than thirty-four million people all over the world, often says that her religion is love.[6] When asked where she finds the energy to help so many people, she answers: "Where there is true love, anything is effortless." Amma demonstrates it all the time, not only through her constant spiritual transmissions that have changed the lives of so many people—she has sometimes given darshan for more than twenty-two hours without interruption—but also as a humanitarian leader.

Embracing the World (ETW), a global network of local and regional charitable organizations inspired by Amma, is currently active in more than forty countries.[7] It helps the world's poor to meet their basic needs—food, shelter, education, health care, livelihoods—provides relief from natural disasters, supports environmental conservation, and designs innovative solutions through its research programs. The selfless actions of this humble woman, who only speaks her native language—Malayalam—show us the social potential of compassion in action: no ETW administrators, nationally or internationally, receive any remuneration, and the vast majority of the ETW work is carried out by volunteers. This mirrors the organization of Amma's darshan ceremonies, which are open to everyone for free—the costs are covered by donations raised beforehand—and are carried out thanks to the support of hundreds of volunteers.

Attending these events was a revelation for me, not only in my inner journey; it also opened my eyes to the miracles that become possible on a collective level when love guides our actions and inevitably spreads. Contemplating all the work that is being carried out in Amma's name, that addresses the most important human needs—from schools to hospitals, companies, and even a university—I have come to realize that love could become the main operating principle for whole communities and even societies. The establishment of a "civilization of love," an expression first coined by Pope Paul VI and now established as the main goal of the Catholic Social Doctrine of the Church,[8] is truly possible.

Altruism

At the social level, in the way we interact with one another, love manifests through altruism,[9] which is enabled by empathy, our capacity to feel and resonate with others' joy and pain. Altruism has been ascribed many definitions. Matthieu Ricard, who reviewed these definitions in his book *Altruism: The Power of Compassion to Change Yourself and the World*,[10] emphasizes a couple of features: altruism is a lasting concern for the well-being of others that translates into acts. Altruistic actions must be primarily motivated by this concern. While they do not necessarily require a sacrifice or exclude personal benefits, these should not be the main motive.

Our capacity for altruism has been emphasized by all the major religions and ethical traditions, in particular through the golden rule, the principle of treating others as we would like to be treated. The golden rule forms an ethic of reciprocity that is the basis for social cooperation, which is itself generally considered the measure of a given society's functionality and health. The ancient Greeks also recognized that "philia," often translated as "brotherly love," "friendship," or "affection," was indispensable to their societies' cohesion and proper functioning.[11] According to American social theorist Jeremy Rifkin, "Civilization is detribalization of blood ties and the resocialization of distinct individuals based on associational ties. Empathic extension is the psychological mechanism that makes the conversion and the transition possible. When we say to civilize, we mean to empathize."[12] The great challenge of our times is not only to rebuild the empathic foundations of our local and national societies but to expand these associational ties to the whole of humanity.

The old story of egoism and competition

However, egoism and competition have until recently been central in our understanding of life, human nature, and evolution, as well as the basis for our societies' organization in the field of economics and politics, for example. Seventeen-century British philosopher Thomas Hobbes thought that "man is wolf to man"[13] and, from this natural condition, derives the State or "Leviathan," according to his doctrine of Social Contract, vastly influential in modern political philosophy. Western liberal democracies are based on the premise that democratic governance requires individuals and groups to compete for political power.[14]

In economics, since Adam Smith wrote the *Wealth of Nations*, it has been widely assumed that people only take their own (material) interests into account when making decisions, even though the same author advocated for the social importance of virtue in his *Theory of Moral Sentiments*. The theory of evolution developed by Darwin has long been summed up through expressions such as "survival of the fittest," a term originally coined by the philosopher Herbert Spencer and later adopted by Darwin; or the "selfish gene,"[15] which emphasizes competition over cooperation in natural selection. Our supposedly selfish nature has received more press than our natural capacity for goodness and altruism. In the field of psychology, Freud stated that "the child is absolutely egoistic,"[16] and it is only at the age of five and six that children learn to behave in a socially acceptable way.

Over the last decades, the transformation of our cultures and institutions along this selfish line has become more obvious and seems to lie at the center of many of our social problems. This is particularly true in the US. Studies comparing members of different generations (baby boomers, generation X, millennials) in the US over the last fifty years, particularly among teenagers and young adults, have shown a trend in recent generations toward greater individualism and self-focus. There has been a decrease in empathy, interpersonal trust, and connection. Younger generations put relatively more emphasis on extrinsic life goals (money, fame, image) over intrinsic goals (meaning, affiliation ...) and are less prone to moral reasoning and civic engagement.[17] Surprisingly, and no less worryingly—as this should be of particular concern to millennials—there has also been a significant decline in willingness to take actions for the environment,[18] something that may hopefully be starting to change.

The US is facing a "narcissism epidemic," according to some authors,[19] a trend nowadays fueled by social media. In 1951, 12 percent of US teenagers from fourteen to sixteen years would consider themselves "important," which rose to 80 percent by 1989.[20] It is estimated that in 2006, one US adolescent in four fit the criteria for being diagnosed as a narcissist.[21] One in ten suffer from narcissistic personality disorder,[22] a long-term pattern of abnormal behavior characterized by exaggerated feelings of self-importance, excessive need for admiration, and a lack of empathy.[23] Ninety percent of students think they are part of the 10 percent most gifted![24]

These inquiries reverberate with research that exposed the decline in US social capital over the same period,[25] such as that conducted by US political scientist Robert Putnam. Social bonds, trust, and interactions during the last decades have been significantly eroded due to urbanization, technology, work transformation, and inequalities.[26] Between 1950 and 1998, the percentage of people who a priori trusted a stranger fell from 60 percent to 30 percent[27] in North America and Europe. This is particularly worrying as our dispositions to support one another and cooperate fundamentally depend on this trust, this "invisible institution"[28] that stands at the heart of the "social contract."

We can have cooperation with little empathy. It can be fueled by self-interest, as in the case of our economic system. However, this kind of cooperation is limited and fragile; it is no longer sufficient in the world we live in. In addition, below a minimum level of empathy, the whole system tends to become dysfunctional. Studies[29] have shown that this decrease in interpersonal trust or social empathy is at the root of the rise of the far-right populism vote (and not at all of far-left populism, whose voters have much higher interpersonal trust but share a high level of anger and a lower level of life satisfaction with far-right populist voters). Daniel Cohen, a French economist who authored one of these studies, says,

"The electors of Marine Le Pen, Salvini, Trump, but also those who voted for Brexit, have a level of interpersonal trust extremely weak [...] These electors are wary of everything, of immigrants, of colleagues at work and of their neighbors."[30]

Retreating into nationalist ideas is a way of maintaining a sense of belonging to a community when interpersonal trust is deficient. In the US, Putnam believes that this decline has resulted in a wide range of negative impacts on happiness, educational performance, health, crimes, tax evasion, and inequality.[31] This trend has also had a huge cost at the individual level in terms of anxiety, mental health, and well-being.[32] The search for egoistic happiness is doomed to fail; by focusing too much on ourselves and denying our true nature as social, interdependent beings, we easily fall prey to our tormented egos.

The new story of goodness, altruism, and cooperation

Recently, science has started to tell us a very different story. While it recognizes our potential for both cooperation and competition, good and evil, altruism and egoism, it is increasingly emphasizing our higher nature as more authentic. In fact, even Darwin's initial views in *The Origin of the Species*[33] highlighted both competition and cooperation as mechanisms involved in natural selection. He later emphasized cooperation in *The Descent of Man and Selection in Relation to Sex,* in which he wrote, "Those communities, which included the greatest number of the most sympathetic members would flourish best, and rear the greatest number of offspring."[34]

The preponderance of cooperation over competition in natural selection is now being increasingly recognized on a scientific level. While competitive ethos/genes may be an evolutive advantage individually,[35] it is in the interest of people to cooperate, and cooperative societies are more prone to survive and develop, passing on their genes and cultures to the following generation.

The ability to cooperate is what characterizes our species, a message that is nowadays spreading quickly, such as in the best seller *Sapiens: a Brief History of Humankind*. It is what has founded our success, as highlighted in the title of biologist Edward Wilson's famous book,

The Social Conquest of Earth.[36] As social animals, our human nature may be better characterized by goodness than evil. Recent research, such as studies by Michael Tomasello and Felix Warneken of the Max-Planck Institute in Leipzig, has shed light on the natural altruistic tendency of children that is then tempered by social norms to become more selective by the age of five.[37] In contrast to Freud and Hobbes' views, new scientific works conclude that aggressiveness is neither inherent to humans nor animals but rather results from external conditions.[38]

On the contrary, humans are naturally repelled by killing.[39] A healthy person naturally does good, which feels good, as we are biologically wired for empathy and compassion,[40] reciprocity and mutuality.[41] A series of studies shows that people—adults as well as children—who have been offered money feel happier when they use it for others rather than when they use it for themselves.[42] The fact that one can enjoy doing good and receive psychological benefits has caused many who are trapped in the story of separation, in particular economists, to erroneously deny an authentic human capacity for altruism. However, there is plenty of evidence, in scientific labs[43] as well as real life (e.g., people risking their own lives for the sake of others), that supports the reality of true altruism.

The truth is that goodness is everywhere. We see it in NGO workers and blood donors, and everywhere we turn our heads, to the point that Ricard argues that we should instead talk about the "banality of good." Even the study of economics has been refining its basic assumptions on human psychology, recognizing the importance of personal and social norms, together with self-interest, in shaping economic behaviors.[44]

From delusion to reality

We as a society believe we are much less altruistic than is true.[45] A recent study from the Common Cause Foundation, based on interviews of a thousand people in the UK, showed that 77 percent of respondents underestimated the proportion of people whose values are more compassionate (also labeled by academics as "self-transcendence" values, showing greater concern for others) than selfish (also denoted as "self-enhancement" or "extrinsic" values").[46] In reality, 74 percent of individuals placed greater importance on compassionate values than selfish ones.[47] Why the misperception? As evidenced by this study, it is because our institutions (e.g., the media, politicians, schools and universities, businesses and economic institutions, etc.) are constantly telling us that people are out for themselves and tend to emphasize values of wealth, power, image, and ambition.

Moreover, as one social psychologist put it, "The image of humans as self-interested leads to the creation of social institutions (e.g., workplaces, schools, governments) in that image, which, in turn, transforms that image into reality."[48] In fact, studies have shown that the "self-interest norm" leads people to act and speak as though they care more about their material self-interest than they actually do.[49] The introduction of extrinsic rewards or incentives can crowd out intrinsic motivation for pro-social behaviors.[50] For example, in a daycare center in Israel, the introduction of fines for parents who pick their children up late actually led to a substantial increase in late parents and the need for teachers to stay longer.[51] Establishing performance incentives for schoolchildren collecting donations for a charitable organization led them to collect less money.[52] The same was true for volunteers in Switzerland, who worked less when they started being paid.[53] The power of social norms and altruistic motivations can decrease when self-interest is emphasized.

The perception that others are more selfish than they actually are has important consequences. According to the Common Cause Foundation study:

> People who hold this inaccurate belief about other people's values feel significantly less positive about getting involved—joining meetings, voting, volunteering. These people also report greater social alienation. They report feeling less responsible for their communities, and they are less likely to feel that they fit in with wider society—relative to citizens who hold more accurate perceptions of a typical British person's values.[54]

Our current cultural software is lying to us on the nature of human psychology, pitting us against each other, activating our lower nature to keep the system running, and preventing us from expressing the most authentic and best version of ourselves. This widespread erroneous view undermines the basis for cooperation and a paradigm change out of the story of separation. We all need to pay attention to the kinds of assumptions on human psychology we are relying upon when interacting with other people or designing social institutions.

Cultivating compassion

Contrary to the dominant values of egoism and competition that lie at the core of our current institutions and problems, the supreme moral values of altruism, empathy, compassion, care, brotherhood, solidarity, and cooperation are now receiving considerable attention again from scientists and policy makers to address the great challenges we are now facing. If we were more compassionate, would we let some seventy-five hundred children die every day because of malnutrition,[55] allow homeless people to suffer from the cold and exclusion, or permit our grandchildren to inherit a world about to plunge into climate chaos and civilization collapse? Would people keep running after money, power, and fame, crushing whatever stands in their way, if they felt sufficiently accepted, loved, and supported? Would climate change and other global challenges be so difficult to solve if every country treated others as they would like to be treated themselves? Probably not. "Compassion is no longer a luxury, but a necessity if our species is to survive," said the Dalai Lama.[56]

One of the major promises of our time is that compassion, empathy, kindness, and cooperation can be cultivated and spread. At the individual level, science has recently started to demonstrate the effectiveness of meditation-based and educational programs to develop these qualities.[57] For example, Compassion Cultivation Training (CCT)[58] has been developed by a team of clinical psychologists, neuroscientists, and contemplative scholars at Stanford University. Though it is influenced by Buddhist contemplative practices, it is a secular, nondenominational eight-week educational program designed to help cultivate compassion for oneself and others, as well as resilience and well-being. It integrates meditation techniques, lectures, and group discussions, as well as practical exercises to put learning into practice at home between sessions. Research has shown its positive impact in terms of self-compassion and compassion toward others, emotional regulation, interpersonal skills, well-being, and mindfulness.[59] This can be the basis for embedding compassionate values with family, at school, at work, in hospitals, etc. Furthermore, institutions can reward or hinder these capacities that are, to a large extent, contagious. Numerous studies on altruism show that it is enough for someone to see another person helping a stranger for the bystander to then be more likely to also help.[60]

This promise is the basis for the Charter for Compassion[61] that was launched in 2009 by Karen Armstrong, a famous religious scholar, after she received a TED prize. Supported by a group of leading inspirational thinkers from the three Abrahamic traditions—Judaism, Christianity, and Islam—it is a call to activate the golden rule and has been signed by some two million people, including many influential personalities. The Charter for Compassion organization is helping with the support of a network of partners to build compassionate communities. While it initially focused on cities, they soon recognized that other types of communities, both small and large, were eager to join the movement. As a result, the charter now also supports towns, townships, shires, hamlets, villages, neighborhoods, islands, states, provinces, counties, republics, and even countries, and is now forming an international network of communities committed to making compassion a living reality.

These communities are usually organized through a diverse and inclusive coalition of people and organizations representative of the diversity of the population and its challenges.[62] They define their own path and priorities based on their cultural appreciation of what suffering, in their context, is most important to relieve. This spans youth violence, drug use, teen suicide epidemics or environmental racism, to a lack of equitable health care, the hardships of immigrants, homeless individuals, LGBTQ groups, or the need for restorative justice. It can also focus on spreading a culture of compassion in neighborhoods, businesses, schools and colleges, health care, the arts, local government, peace groups, environmental advocacy groups, and faith congregations, through specific trainings and measures.

As of mid-2020, the Charter for Compassion is supporting hundreds of initiatives in almost fifty countries in the world. Over seventy cities globally, such as Belfast, Cape Town, Karachi, Bali, Denver, and Monterrey, have affirmed the Charter for Compassion through city and community councils or other government entities. They have identified issues on which they are working and are committed to a multiyear action plan. Countries such as Botswana or Australia, and states such as Nuevo León in Mexico, have already done the same.

In Botswana, it is called the Botho movement. As Mehring[63] puts it, "Botho incompletely translates from the national language Setswana into English as 'respect.'" The concept is commonly expressed in the phrase "Motho ke motho ka batho," meaning "I am because you are." Botho is a value shared across the South African region that promotes harmony and respect amongst people living together. The concept defies simple explanation, but a close friend of mine in Botswana distilled Botho as "Having a deep sense of another person's humanity—how to demonstrate being a human being to another human being." Botho is one of Botswana's five national principles (the others being democracy, development, self-reliance, and unity).

The Charter for Compassion is supporting compassionate communities through methodological and educational resources, events, and initiatives, as well as a large network of partners organized by sectors—business, education, health, environment, justice, science, art ... Coopetition is an effective way of social emulation for the good, and an interesting resource used by the Charter for Compassion is the compassion games organized by a partner,[64] through which communities compete in displaying compassionate actions. Through the power of play, these games, subtitled "survival of the kindest," help catalyze engagement at the local level, learning through the experience of other groups, and a sense of belonging to a global movement.

Since 2012, Compassion Games has mobilized more than one million volunteers in over forty countries, who have served over fifteen million people.[65] Teams have been created by community groups, faith congregations, schools, families, government agencies, businesses, and even among inmates in women's prisons.

According to the first woman to win a Nobel Prize in Economics, Elinor Ostrom, our institutions should be designed to "bring out the best in humans." It is time to name, without shame, what is the best in us, and collectively cultivate it. "We need to pronounce the word that has embarrassed us so much that never, politically, we have dared to use it,"[66] said Edgar Morin about love. And in fact, to confront the politics of fear, hate, and division, the time has come for *A Politics of Love*, the name of a book authored by Mariam Williamson, a US spiritual leader and political activist who ran for the 2020 Democratic presidential nomination. As she wrote:

> It was love that abolished slavery, it was love that gave women suffrage, it was love that established civil rights, and it is love that we need now ... [67]It's not naïve to suggest that we reorient our politics around love's purposes. What's naïve is to think that we can afford not to, and retain either our freedom or our survival as species. When fear has coalesced into a terrible sickness, the only medicine is love. A worldview centered on love is no less sophisticated or psychologically astute than any other—in fact, it is more sophisticated than any other. It is the only worldview that nurtures and sustains life.[68]

"Fear can stop your love; love can stop your fear," sings Morcheeba, an English band. A clear political and social commitment in that direction has the potential to produce the major cultural transformation that we need, in less time than we think. "Someday, after mastering the winds, the waves, the tides and gravity, we shall harness for God the energies of love, and then, for a second time in the history of the world, man will have discovered fire,"[69] said Teilhard de Chardin.

8

Peace

Nonviolence, Partnership, Gender, Justice, Deep Equity, Democracy, Human Rights

*"Since wars begin in the minds of men, it is in the minds of men
that the defenses of peace must be constructed."*
—Constitution of the UNESCO (1945)[1]

ALL ETHICAL AND spiritual traditions celebrate peace. As-salamu alaykum—"Peace be upon you"—is the Muslims' way of greeting one another, while Jews prefer to say "shalom," which in Hebrew means "peace."[2] Catholics do not end Mass before wishing each other Christ's peace.

A culture of peace

As a basic prerequisite for humanity's well-being and a key signal of our social health, peace has, of course, also been a central political concern for ages. However, in the last decades, it has started to be increasingly understood as not only the absence of overt violent conflicts—"negative peace"—but rather also as collaborative and supportive relationships—

"positive peace"[3]—between groups or nations. Following the trauma of two World Wars, positive peace has allowed a more proactive and preventive approach to conflicts, looking at their root causes rather than their manifestations. It has turned the lens from outward physical violence toward more inward structural violence, defined by Johan Galtung as the systematic ways in which a regime prevents individuals from achieving their full potential, such as through institutionalized racism or sexism.

Violence is not only physical but can also be psychological, social, or economic. At the same time, peace studies have started to be developed with the creation in 1959 of the first academic department of Peace Research by Galtung, the International Peace Research Institute in Oslo. The study, which is highly interdisciplinary, has gained recognition, and there are now hundreds of peace research centers in the world.

UNESCO has promoted the development of a culture of peace since the nineties, which led the UN General Assembly to adopt in 1999 the Declaration and Programme of Action on a Culture of Peace,[4] setting the ground for the International Year for the Culture of Peace (2000)[5] and the International Decade for a Culture of Peace and Non-Violence for the Children of the World (2001–2010).[6]

The culture of peace concept emphasizes ending all forms of oppression—political, social, economic, and cultural—and the peaceful settlement of conflicts. This means, in particular, rejecting all discrimination (based on gender, ethnicity, sexual orientations, etc.), recognizing and respecting the dignity of all individuals, promoting human rights and democratic participation, creating an economic system that works for all, and restoring our planet's balance. The Manifesto 2000 for a culture of peace and nonviolence was launched by a group of Nobel Peace Prize winners, who wanted to translate the UN resolutions into everyday language that all people could grasp.

The manifesto, which has been signed by more than seventy-five million people, was prepared by my friend Pierre Marchand, who initially titled it "Universal Ethical Charter of Human Duties for a Culture of Non-Violence for the Children of the World." Pierre knows that "what founds the dignity of human beings are not their 'rights' but their voluntarily accepted and applied 'duties.'"[7] Pierre was an early follower of Zen Master

Thich Nhat Han, and the manifesto draws to a large extent on the Five Mindfulness Trainings, an adaptation of the five precepts of the Buddha that members of the Plum Village community use to guide their lives.[8] According to Thich Nhat Hanh:

> The Five Mindfulness Trainings are one of the most concrete ways to practice mindfulness. They are nonsectarian, and their nature is universal. They are true practices of compassion and understanding. All spiritual traditions have their equivalent to the Five Mindfulness Trainings. The first training is to protect life, to decrease violence in oneself, in the family and in society. The second training is to practice social justice, generosity, not stealing and not exploiting other living beings. The third is the practice of responsible sexual behavior in order to protect individuals, couples, families and children. The fourth is the practice of deep listening and loving speech to restore communication and reconcile. The fifth is about mindful consumption, to help us not bring toxins and poisons into our body or mind.[9]

Since 2015, UN Sustainable Development Goal number sixteen has been emphasized, together with peace, justice, strong institutions, and the rule of law. As the politics of being proposes a cultural evolution, the culture of peace concept, with its long and successful history within the UN system, provides an opportunity for advancing such proposals at the intergovernmental level.

Domination or partnership

The culture of war that we want to transform is in essence a culture of domination. Riane Eisler and Douglas Fry, in their remarkable book *Nurturing our Humanity: How Domination and Partnership Shape Our Brains, Lives, and Future,*[10] show that the real cultural alternative is not between religion and secularism, modernity and traditionalism, east and west, north and south, capitalism and communism, but between a culture of domination and a culture of partnership. These opposite cultural configurations, which can be found in different degrees throughout history and geography, shape our brain—and thus the way we think, feel, and act—as well as our social, economic, and political systems, in two fundamentally different ways.

In cultures of domination, people consider inequality, control, and violence as inevitable, moral, and desirable. Hierarchies of domination underlie all social institutions, from gender roles to family and religion, from authoritarian education and punitive justice to top-down control of economic resources and politics. Maintained by control and fear, they go along with the cultural acceptance of psychological violence and physical abuse, such as child-and-wife beating, slavery, and warfare. Extreme examples of cultures of domination, which all share most of these features, include secular societies such as rightist-capitalist Nazi Germany in the West and current leftist-communist North Korea in the East, or religious societies like Europe during the Middle Ages, ISIS in the Middle East, and Boko Haram in Africa.[11]

On the contrary, partnership systems are democratic and egalitarian. They equally value women and men, and celebrate values such as caring, caregiving, and nonviolence in both women and men (these values are often denigrated as "feminine" in domination systems), as well as in social and economic policies. These cultures hold empathic, mutually beneficial, nonviolent relations as the norm and display a low degree of violence and a general respect for diversity and human rights. They often solve their conflicts without violence through mediation mechanisms. Cultures of partnership examples include modern Nordic countries (Finland, Sweden, Norway, Denmark, Iceland), as well as traditional societies such as the Minangkabau people, a four-million-people Muslim ethnic group in Indonesia, the Tiruray (or Teduray) in the Philippines, or the Moso in China. While these societies are sometimes called matriarchies, Eisler and Fry note that the term is in general inadequate, reflecting our incapacity to think outside of the domination lens, as in most of the societies mentioned, women and men are equal.

Historically, domination systems have been widespread for the last five thousand to ten thousand years, which has often led us to consider it the natural norm. However, according to Eisler and Fry, "Archeological and ethnographic evidence suggests that a durable legacy of cultural orientation to partnership lasted for at least two million years,"[12] being the general feature of nomadic forager cultures. It is only when settlement, agriculture, population expansion, and social complexity developed that domination systems appeared. Then war arose and became more common and destructive some four thousand to six thousand years ago. We see that war is not inextricably bound up with human nature but is a rather recent social invention. Furthermore, in Eisler and Fry's words, "Over the last several centuries, we have seen strong movement toward the partnership side of the continuum,"[13] which is still ongoing. "This struggle between those trying to move to a more peaceful, equitable, and sustainable future and those trying to push us back to more rigid patterns of domination is the real culture war,"[14] they conclude.

The decrease in violence

Together with the historical progress of democracy and human rights,[15] as well as the fall of some forms of structural violence such as the ones associated with discrimination, the marked decrease of physical violence testifies to the advancement of a partnership culture. Violence seems to be omnipresent in the world today, and most of us are not aware of this important fact. This is evidenced by recent scientific research confirming that physical violence in all its forms (homicides, rapes, child mistreatment, etc.) has been decreasing markedly during the last millennium, and in particular for the last sixty years. In Europe, the number of annual homicides per one hundred thousand people, which is estimated to have been forty-one in the fifteenth century, has continually decreased to reach 1.4 in the twentieth century.[16] In 2017, globally, annual intentional homicides were estimated at 6.1 for one hundred thousand people.[17]

This makes Steven Pinker, a famous Harvard professor and author of the best-seller *The Better Angels of Our Nature: The Decline of Violence in History and Its Causes (2011)*, think that we are probably experiencing "the most peaceful time in our species' existence."[18] He shows that over the last few centuries, wars have tended to be less frequent (except in Africa) and have provoked fewer deaths. The main causes, according to Pinker, include the consolidation of larger functional political entities with a monopoly on the legitimate use of force, commerce, reason, femininization, and cosmopolitanism (our capacity to understand and empathize with each other that has increased with literacy, mobility, and media). He also recognizes the importance of the rise of democracy, economic development, and global governance and notes the current "rights revolutions" since the late fifties to address discrimination against ethnic minorities, women, children, homosexuals, and animals.

So, we can note a clear long-term cultural evolution toward the rejection of violence; what was once common, accepted, and even enjoyed as entertainment, such as public torture, is now completely unbearable for us. Pinker identifies four "better angels" that "can orient [humans] away from violence and towards cooperation and altruism": empathy, self-control, moral sense, and reason.

Flourishing and partnership cultures

The advancement of partnership cultures has a unique potential to contribute to human flourishing. Indeed, Eisler and Fry show that domination systems produce high levels of stress, which affects the neurochemistry of the brain, tending to keep people at a less advanced level of overall human development, one that makes them less happy and healthy but that is compatible with these systems' functioning. As shown by numerous studies[19] (and quite logically, as culture shapes individuals), in cultures of domination, people are less empathic, more violent, less creative, and more prone to conform to authority and to prejudice against outlying groups. They display more mental rigidity, in particular a lack of tolerance toward ambiguity, a strong aversion to complexity, and difficulty in letting go of preconceived assumptions and dealing with change. As demonstrated by some experiments, this can entail selective perception and denial of reality, something we can observe in relation to climate change.

Frenkel-Brunswick, one of the pioneering scientists of this field, concluded that in highly stressful families, "Certain aspects of experience have to be kept out of awareness ... to reduce conflict and anxiety and to maintain stereotyped patterns."[20] In general, chronic stress limits not only perceptions but also behavioral options, as expressed by neuroscientist Debra Niehoff. She writes:

> As stress wears away at the nervous system, risk assessment grows less and less accurate. Minor insults are seen as major threats. [...] Surrounded on all sides by real and imagined threats, the individual resorts to the time-honored survival strategies: fight, flight, or freeze. [...] More constructive coping strategies are lost, and the brain fixates on an increasingly smaller portfolio of counterproductive reactions. With fewer and fewer alternatives, violence, depression and fear stop being options and become a way of life.[21]

Like plants, humans tend to grow and flourish less when they are under stress. Like flowers, we express a richer diversity of colors and nuances, as well as more complex patterns, as we flourish.

Partnership cultures' capacity to serve human flourishing is well reflected in European Nordic nations, which often call themselves "caring societies." As discussed earlier, these countries tend to dominate happiness indexes, human development indexes, and social health indexes (see below), while displaying high levels of economic equity (see below), gender equity,[22] democratic participation,[23] and commitment to nonviolence[24] and sustainability.[25] As Eisler and Fry emphasize, "These Nordic practices are not coincidental development. They stem from the fact that the Nordic world orients more to the partnership than the domination configuration."[26] Unlike what is sometimes argued, these examples show that progressive social policies—universal health care, government-supported childcare, paid parental leave, etc.—can be the cause and not the effect of greater prosperity.[27]

Cutting the roots of domination: children protection and gender equity

So how come domination systems are able to sustain themselves? They are supported by cultural narratives that frame our vision of what is normal, possible, and good. Children learn early on through authoritarian education, physical violence, and abuse that domination is natural, and the alternative is between dominating or being dominated. They come to understand quickly, often including through family example, that one half of humanity is dominating the other half, what is often termed "patriarchy." They learn to hold so-called "feminine values" of care, empathy, and nonviolence as inferior. The construction of masculinity is equated with domination and violence, and boys learn to dissociate themselves from their emotions, in particular ones considered "feminine," such as distress or compassion.[28] On the other hand, girls are taught that a whole range of emotions and behaviors are off-limits to them.

Though domination systems are maintained by all social institutions, ending violence against children and women has the potential to cut at the roots of their reproduction. Gender equity, in particular, holds a tremendous potential to establish a culture of peace not only by reasserting the equal inherent worth of men and women, but also because it is such a powerful driver of value change in society. "As the status of women rises, so also does the value a society gives to stereotypically 'feminine' traits and behaviors such as caring and caregiving—in women, men, and economic policy,"[29] explain Eisler and Fry.

It is a well-known fact that girls' education may be the most effective development policy, with a wide range of positive impacts for them (less abuse and discrimination, less death in childbirth, empowerment, etc.); their children (better health, nutrition, education, etc.); families (higher income, higher investment, etc.); and communities (fewer conflicts, more sustainability, less demographic growth, etc.).[30] Women generally hold significantly more compassionate, progressive, peaceful, and sustainable values than men.[31] When in positions of political and economic leadership, their votes and investment decisions are also much more inclined towards sustainability.[32] Hence, gender equity strategies, which can also significantly contribute to our happiness,[33] are necessarily central in a politics of being. They include better access to education, economic and political responsibilities, protection from abuse, and the recognition of the importance of their work as caregivers (through social security, pensions, and subsidies or tax credits).[34]

Per a former leader of the Baha'i faith:

The world of humanity is possessed of two wings: the male and the female. So long as these two wings are not equivalent in strength, the bird will not fly. Until womankind reaches the same degree as man, until she enjoys the same arena of activity, extraordinary attainment for humanity will not be realized; humanity cannot wing its way to heights of real attainment. When the two wings [...] become equivalent in strength, enjoying the same prerogatives, the flight of man will be exceedingly lofty and extraordinary.[35]

Gender equity is a major avenue to help both men and women express their full potential and humanity through less stereotyped gender roles. Eisler and Fry note that "men in more partnership-oriented cultures no longer find it such a threat to their status—to their 'masculinity'—to adopt more 'soft' feminine traits and behaviors."[36] Men can more freely express their sensibilities while women are no longer kept from expressing their strength and natural aspirations.

As exemplified by gender roles, domination systems are built not only on our disconnections from one another and reality, but they also sustain themselves on the disconnection from ourselves. In fact, instead of recognizing the suffering that domination systems unjustly inflict on them, people learn to recognize this violence as legitimate and deflect it on others. Thus, genital mutilation is in general performed by mothers on their daughters; racism is regularly passed down through a long hierarchy of domination; and people who were abused as children are often drawn to political leaders who advocate a punitive social agenda. As mentioned by Eisler and Fry:

Since children are helpless in the face of adults who ostensibly love them but treat them harshly, many children rely on denial and identify with the powerful and supposedly "good" adult rather than the weak, powerless, and allegedly "bad" child." As adults, children raised in such punitive contexts not only may fail to empathize with the pain caused by policies that harm people or neglect their basic needs but also identify with and support leaders who decree such policies.[37]

This "serves as a means of deflecting repressed pain and anger against those perceived as weak and evil—exactly how they were taught to perceive themselves as children when their parents punished them."[38]

Economic equity

While some forms of violence are decreasing, other forms of structural violence have recently developed, in particular through the rise of economic inequalities that are now threatening the social and political fabric of many countries. In their great book *The Spirit Level—Why Equality Is Better For Everyone*,[39] epidemiologists Richard Wilkinson and Kate Pickett show that, among rich countries, income equality is the best predictor for health and social woes with a "social gradient," meaning those that are most common at the bottom of the social ladder. These health and social indicators include, among others, level of trust, mental illness (including drug and alcohol addiction), life expectancy and infant mortality, obesity, children's educational performance, teenage births, bullying, homicide, imprisonment rates, social mobility, women's status ...

The higher the inequality level, the higher these problems are (see figure 6 below). Importantly, this is true at all levels of societies, which means almost everybody can benefit from a higher equality level. Of course, in a given society, the rich will generally be less affected by these problems, but they will be relatively more affected than people with the same income level who reside in a society with lower inequality levels. Income per capita is generally weakly correlated to these problems: even though some highly unequal countries, such as the US, have a per capita income that is almost twice that of other rich countries such as Greece, they still perform worse. Wilson and Pickett think their conclusions on the impact of inequalities are valid for any country, but they have focused on rich countries for methodological reasons.[40]

Large income differences are socially divisive and translate into bigger social distances and, more importantly, social stratification. They provide the material foundation for more distinction between people in terms of clothing, education, aesthetic taste, sense of self, and all other social and cultural markers. They negatively affect our capacity to identify with, empathize with, and trust each other, undermining social cohesion and cooperation, with a wide range of negative consequences. They also represent an important source of insecurity and stress for individuals. In fact, social status is widely perceived as an indicator of one's ability and value. Thus, social distinction increases "social evaluative threats"—the threats of being judged negatively by others—which, in experiments looking at cortisol levels, has been found to be the most powerful type of stressor. This is particularly important considering that the break-up of the settled communities of the past has led us to constantly interact with strangers today in a way that is inevitably shaped by quick assumptions or judgments on who we are. By increasing the importance of social status, inequality increases status competition and anxiety.

Figure 6. Health and social problems and their relationship to income inequality.[41]

This helps us to understand how the structural violence associated with inequality translates into physical violence, a relationship well established and accepted in the scientific literature. Levels of physical violence can have astonishing differences: murder rates in the US are four times higher than in the UK and twelve times higher than those in Japan. These rates are seven times higher in Louisiana than in New Hampshire. However, the age and sex distribution are very much constant: violence is a male phenomenon. Murder rates reach their peak in the late teens and early twenties for men, while rates for women are much lower at all ages.[42]

To understand this, Wilkinson and Pickett start by quoting James Gilligan, a famous American psychiatrist and scholar who has been the director of the Harvard Institute of Law and Psychiatry and has important experience working on mental health in prisons. In his book *Violence: Our Deadly Epidemics and its Causes*, Gilligan argues that acts of violence are "attempts to ward off or eliminate the feeling of shame and humiliation—a feeling that is painful and can even be intolerable and overwhelming—and replace it with its opposite, the feeling of pride." Gilligan goes so far as to say that he has "yet to see a serious act of violence that was not provoked by the experience of feeling shamed and humiliated ... and that did not represent the attempt to ... undo this 'loss of face.'"[43]

Men are particularly responsive to the triggers of disrespect and humiliation as their success in sexual competition depends primarily on their social status (for women what matters most is physical attractiveness), as shown by evolutionary psychologists Margo Wilson and Martin Daily.[44] If the societies men live in are highly stratified and males are already deprived of all the social markers of status, they will tend to struggle even more to defend the little status they have and react explosively when it is threatened.

Wilkinson and Pickett's index of health and social problems shows the great performance of highly equitable countries, such as Japan, Scandinavian countries, the Netherlands, and Switzerland, which—with the exception of Japan—are often measured as the happiest countries in the world. It also shows the poor performance of the US and the UK, where levels of inequality have reached levels unknown for several generations, as well as Portugal. The differences are huge among these countries, ranging from one to two for infant mortality, one to five for mental illness or imprisonment, one to six for obesity or social trust,[45] one to eleven for teenage births, and one to twelve for homicides.

The reason for these large differences is that inequality affects not only the poor but the vast majority of the population. This entails huge economic costs. At the beginning of the new millennium, some states in the US were spending as much public money on prisons as on higher education.[46] Inequality has increased among almost all rich countries in the last decades. While globalization and technology are often blamed, a deeper analysis and a look at history show that changes in political attitudes and ideology seem to have been the more central cause.

Published in 2009, just after the financial crisis, *Violence: Our Deadly Epidemics and its Causes* was very influential in the political debate in the UK. Full of graphs and very didactic, the book made clear that among developed market democracies, the quality of our social fabric, and the way we relate to each other is strongly determined by the inequality level. *The Economist*, famous for its (neo)liberal mindset, even recognized that "the evidence is hard to dispute."[47] Indeed, this insight meets the wisdom of traditional hunter-gatherer societies, whose economic and social lives were based on reciprocity and gift systems, as well as high levels of equality and "counter-dominance strategies" to keep peace and maintain social harmony.[48]

Equality as a fairness principle remains well-rooted in our modern minds, shaped by a long history of life—over 90 percent of our existence as human beings—in those highly egalitarian societies. An economic experiment, the "ultimate game," asks an individual who is given money—the "proposer"—to share part of it with another participant—the "receiver." The "receiver" needs to accept the proposed amount for the "proposer" to keep the rest. The experiment shows that the "proposers" tend to share the money relatively equally (43 to 48 percent of the sum in "developed societies").[49] Polls in highly unequal countries such as the US and the UK also show strong awareness (some three people in four) of inequality as an important problem.

However, while inequality appears as the main structural driver of so many social problems, this has not translated much into policies. "Every problem is seen as needing its own solution—unrelated to others. People are encouraged to take exercise, not to have unprotected sex, to say no to drugs, to try to relax, to sort out their work-life balance, and to give their children 'quality' time,"[50] explain Wilkinson and Pickett. "The unstated hope is that people—particularly the poor—can carry on in the same circumstances, but will somehow no longer succumb to mental illness, teenage pregnancy, educational failure, obesity or drugs."[51] But, in the face of our current challenges, we need to overcome this failed reductionist approach to our problems and address their root causes.

Reducing inequality is no longer an option, in particular to move toward sustainability. In fact, inequality levels in rich countries are also correlated negatively with innovation (number of patents granted per capita), waste recycling, spending in development aid, performance on the global peace index,[52] ecological footprint, waste production, and water consumption. Moreover, in our efforts toward sustainability, for the relevant policies to be implemented, burden sharing needs to be seen as fair, something well known by governments in times of war and recently highlighted, for example, by the yellow jackets movement in France.

Finally, by concentrating economic power, inequality seems to generally undermine the basis for democracy and the functioning of our social and political institutions, which are recognized as key pillars of a peaceful society. Indeed, studies strongly suggest that corruption in poor countries,[53] government distrust,[54] and lack of voter turnout[55] all increase with inequality. By enhancing social trust and cohesion, economic equality seems also to foster public-spiritedness and responsibility, including at the international level. "At the most fundamental level, what reducing inequality is about is shifting the balance from the divisive, self-interested consumerism driven by status competition, towards a more socially integrated and affiliative society,"[56] conclude Wilkinson and Pickett.

Nonviolence

Together with economic equity and democracy, the capacity to solve conflicts without violence is at the core of a culture of peace. Nonviolence is the natural way to advance the politics of being, for which the quality of our being is our main resource and means for action. Drawing significantly on spiritual traditions, including the concept of "ahimsa" in Jainism, Hinduism, and Buddhism, nonviolence is the political embodiment of all the highest values: truth, love, understanding, courage, strength, justice, and of course, peace! Nonviolence is an exercise, an educational path for a society to cultivate these higher qualities and establish a solid basis for peace and justice. Nonviolence is the only path to authentic and lasting progress: "Peace is the way." Nonviolent protests are twice as likely to succeed than armed conflicts, and nonviolent campaigns that engage more than 3.5 percent of the population have always succeeded.[57] The greatest political leaders of the twentieth century, including Mahatma Gandhi, Nelson Mandela, the Dalai Lama, and Dr. Martin Luther King Jr., all used nonviolence. The latter beautifully articulated what nonviolence means in his six principles of nonviolence (see box 5).

Box 5—Dr. Martin Luther King Jr's Six Principles of Nonviolence[58]

1. Nonviolence is a way of life for courageous people.

   - It is active nonviolent resistance to evil.

   - It is assertive spiritually, mentally, and emotionally.

   - It is always persuading the opponent of the justice of your cause.

2. Nonviolence seeks to win friendship and understanding.

   - The end result of nonviolence is redemption and reconciliation.

   - The purpose of nonviolence is the creation of the Beloved Community.

3. Nonviolence seeks to defeat injustice, not people.

   - Nonviolence holds that evildoers are also victims.

4. Nonviolence holds that voluntary suffering can educate and transform.

   - Nonviolence willingly accepts the consequences of its acts.

   - Nonviolence accepts suffering without retaliation.

   - Nonviolence accepts violence if necessary, but will never inflict it.

   - Unearned suffering is redemptive and has tremendous educational and transforming possibilities.

   - Suffering can have the power to convert the enemy when reason fails.

5. Nonviolence chooses love instead of hate.

   - Nonviolence resists violence of the spirit as well as of the body.

   - Nonviolent love gives willingly, knowing that the return might be hostility.

   - Nonviolent love is active, not passive.

   - Nonviolent love does not sink to the level of the hater.

   - Love for the enemy is how we demonstrate love for ourselves.

   - Love restores community and resists injustice.

   - Nonviolence recognizes the fact that all life is interrelated.

6. Nonviolence believes that the universe is on the side of justice.

   - The nonviolent resister has deep faith that justice will eventually win.

As recognized by Gandhi, in the face of oppression, violent actions may be better than apathy. But at this stage of our evolution, there is little violence can do for us. Only peace can bring forward the type of societies able to deal with current challenges. It is also instrumental for us to evolve our development paradigm, as many countries emphasize economic development in order to feel stronger and safer against the possibility of military conflicts.

Reconciliation

Violence only seems to end conflicts. But they are not resolved and remain alive in people's hearts, eager to reappear at the first opportunity, prompting polarization, paralysis, or wars. Many current conflicts have long historical roots that our minds often resist acknowledging. It is surprising to hear Russians treat Ukrainians as "fascists" today, seventy years after the end of World War II, or US president Trump threatening to strike fifty-two Iranian sites representing "the fifty-two American hostages taken by Iran many years ago"[59] (in 1979). Today's Islamic terrorism has partially grown out of the frustration and humiliation of nineteenth-century colonization. Colonization and a long history of abuses of all sorts are central in the general mistrust that currently plagues international cooperation. Proactive efforts of reconciliation are needed to prevent conflicts and provide us with the social cohesion we need to evolve collectively. Societies cannot move forward haunted by their past demons; simply forgetting is not an option. This was Spain's choice after Franco's dictatorship,[60] a choice that is still parasitizing the country's democracy, including in the Catalunya crisis (2019–2020).[61]

The recognition of truth and the reparation of injustices are important steps to heal past wounds and learn from our mistakes, understanding their causes so that we can transform and not repeat our errors. Many of us are able to see that problems in our lives tend to manifest again and again, more and more strongly until we are able to recognize and address their real causes. Problems are invitations for us to grow and heal, as often recognized by alternative therapists. As life increasingly invites each of us, calling us, forcing us to evolve and transform ancestral memories, I have come to see the current resurgence of some of these ancient political conflicts as a natural process of purification for humankind to be able to establish itself on higher grounds. War crimes, colonization, slavery and racism, and the abuse of women and children are among the major wounds we need to heal, as emerged in recent years with the campaign against sexual abuse in the Catholic Church, the MeToo movement, or the Black Lives Matter movement. "You have to dominate,"[62] President Trump—who is himself the product of an authoritarian education—told US governors dealing with the massive George Floyd protests.

Many national reconciliation efforts have been institutionalized through truth and reconciliation commissions following civil wars or the end of oppressive regimes, such as in post-apartheid South Africa in 1996, led by Bishop Desmond Tutu. Some older conflicts, like those in relation to the indigenous people of Canada or Australia, have also been recently addressed by such commissions. In Canada, Justin Trudeau has proclaimed reconciliation with indigenous people a national priority. As he rightly pointed out in a meeting of indigenous leaders and senior government officials in 2017, "Reconciliation, reconciliation, reconciliation, RECONCILIATION!! Reconciliation, rec ... on ... ci ... llliiiiiiiation ..."[63] No, he was not having a stroke as some attendees reported they believed; he just meant it sincerely, and for some of the participants, that was worth shedding tears.

Reconciliation does not happen once and for all through institutionalized initiatives. It is a long, iterative process, allowing healing to happen at a deeper level each time. The 2019 political crisis in Chile, for example, is a new attempt—after the National Commission for Truth and Reconciliation created in 1990, shortly after the country's return to democracy—to leave behind the Pinochet dictatorship's legacy. It prompted an agreement to replace the country's constitution, put into place by the Pinochet regime in 1980.

Deep listening and loving speech

To be able to solve conflicts, whether old or new, or even to have the profound constructive political conversations that are required, we need to be able to listen deeply to each other and communicate in a peaceful way. This is our practice in the Plum Village tradition, and it has been used in the context of lasting political conflicts. Israelis and Palestinians, for example, have been able to sit together and truly listen to one another, expressing their suffering, regrets, admirations, hopes. It often takes some time and practice for this to be possible, but just speaking respectfully and listening deeply can transform our relationships. That is why these grassroots initiatives are important for building peace from the bottom up, one heart at a time.

Political polarization has recently soared, affecting the political debate and threatening societies' cohesion. Violent and hate speech have spread, with political opponents increasingly demonizing each other. Discussions among people holding different political views are becoming more and more difficult. Internet and social media have fueled this trend, with people irresponsibly venting their anger and receiving only the kind of information that reinforces their particular views. Nonviolence practitioners cannot sink to the level of the haters. "When they go low, we go high," said Michelle Obama.

I was shocked recently to see so much hate and violence in Trump's opponents when watching a documentary on TV. People in the streets were shouting and insulting Trump's supporters, who were walking silently to a meeting. In these faces full of rage, I could almost see Trump himself. Hate, anger, and violence are the real enemies that lie in each of us, and they can only be transformed through nonviolence.

In 2018, at the parliament of religions in Toronto, I met William and Olivia, who decided at the last moment to come to learn more about other religious traditions. As white Christian conservatives from Canada, they told me they were astonished at feeling so denigrated by other participants, with some people even shouting at them. I told them I was sincerely sorry for what happened to them.

It was clear we had very different backgrounds and ideas. I was a progressive environmentalist, very at ease in an interspiritual context, and William worked for the oil industry. However, they could feel my empathy and openness, and after some pleasant personal discussions, we started to discuss several social issues, such as climate change. They were aware of the environmental and climate crisis but could not understand why people were so critical of Canada's climate policy, if Canada's forests were absorbing more GHG than all the country's emissions. I learned later that this lie had been heavily propagated by social media.[64] While recognizing I did not remember the exact numbers, I explained to them that this was very unlikely for different reasons.[65] I also helped them understand how the government of Canada's decision not to fulfill its commitment under the Kyoto protocol played a big part in undermining international cooperation on climate change.

The couple paid attention to what I said, as they could sense I was not trying to defeat them but rather wanted to have a respectful dialogue where they could have the space to express themselves. They even thanked me for sharing with them this information they had ignored, which helped them realize how erroneous some of their views were. We spent a nice moment together. Later on, we exchanged warm greetings when seeing each other, and William came back to me with some more questions about controversial political issues, such as what I thought of Fukushima. I saw he trusted he had finally found a reliable person who could provide him with information that differed from what he was usually exposed to.

I am grateful for this encounter as it helped me remember that when we are able to build respectful human relationships, communication can happen and bridge gaps of misunderstanding, distrust, and contempt.

Spiritual teachers, such as the Dalai Lama, remind us that "world peace starts with inner peace." All spiritual traditions emphasize peace of mind or equanimity, and peace of the soul as the ultimate life goal.[66] This inner peace that can free us is the fruit of spiritual practice. It starts within our body, in every breath, every step we take, in the way we think, communicate ourselves, and consume, in the smallest acts of our daily lives. We can be the peace that we want to see in the world.

9

Mindfulness

Awareness, Conscience, Presence, Slowness, Responsibility

"I have arrived, I am home, in the here and in the now."

—Zen Master Thich Nhat Hanh

W E HAVE MANY appointments, but we often miss the most important one: our appointment with life, in the here and now, says Zen Master Thich Nhat Hanh. In fact, neuroscience is now showing that our brain spends most of its time predicting reality rather than actually experiencing it. Ignoring the majority of information provided by our senses, except when reality deviates from prediction, is metabolically more efficient and allows an increased speed of reaction. If, for instance, you are eating an apple while reading this book, you may not really pay attention to the fruit's taste, because your brain already knows what an apple tastes like, and it will cause you to perceive the usual taste. But were this apple rotten, you might be surprised by its real taste and finally step into reality.[1] Experiencing reality, at least from time to time, may be a first wise step toward building a better world, don't you think?

The mindful revolution

On February 3, 2014, *Time* magazine published its cover on "The Mindful Revolution" with the following subtitle: "The Science of Finding Focus in a Stressed-Out, Multi-Tasking Culture."[2] In fact, we are facing a stress epidemic, and hundreds or rather thousands of messages compete every day for our attention through increasingly sophisticated means and technology. Our minds are full of thoughts, which are mostly repetitive and negative.[3] "If distraction is the pre-eminent condition of our age, then mindfulness, in the eyes of its enthusiasts, is the most logical response," wrote *Time* magazine, suggesting that mindfulness may be the key to surviving and succeeding in the twenty-first century.

Mindfulness is the energy of being aware and awake to the present moment, to what is happening in our mind, body, and external environment. Through this open, nonjudgmental presence, we can be truly alive and touch life deeply, at one with those around us and our actions. Mindfulness can help us cut through our habit energies, conditioning, and prejudices. It can bring us closer to seeing things as they are and help us manifest our true nature of compassion, peace, and joy. Mindfulness can be cultivated through meditation, in particular the attention to our breathing while sitting, walking, or doing our daily activities, without being caught in thoughts, feelings, or sensations.

Mindfulness, attention, or the ability to live in the here and now, have been viewed by many spiritual traditions as the key quality of being and the basis of any contemplative practice. How can we truly live or experience anything real if we are not in the here and now, our "true home," according to Thich Nhat Hanh, often presented as the father of mindfulness? As Meister Eckart, a German Christian mystic (1260–1328), put it, "There exists only the present instant ... a now which always and without end is itself new. There is no yesterday nor any tomorrow, but only Now, as it was a thousand years ago and as it will be a thousand years hence."[4] A famous answer to a king's question on what Zen means was "attention, attention, attention," and Greco-Roman philosophical schools emphasized "prosoche," or attention to the present moment, something passed on to many Christian and Islamic philosophers, mystics, and poets.

All the major wisdom traditions agree that the best way to live our lives is in the present moment, as expressed in this quote by Iranian Islamic philosopher Omar Khayyam, "Once yesterday has passed, it's best forgotten. Tomorrow's still to come; give it no thought. Do not be ruled by future or past; be happy now, and squander not your life."[5]

Nowadays, the practice of mindfulness is being used to revive many spiritual traditions, in particular the religions of the book—Christianity, Judaism, and Islam—to open the deepest meanings of their teachings through meditation.

Mindfulness science

As the *Time* magazine cover suggests, mindfulness has now become mainstream, with widespread media coverage, best-selling books, online resources, and more than five hundred peer-reviewed scientific papers published every year.[6] Rooted in Buddhism, mindfulness's success is largely due first to its transformation into an everyday secular fitness practice for the mind—in which attention is compared to a muscle to be trained—applicable to all that we do. Its promoters take great care in avoiding any talk about spirituality. Second, mindfulness's great usefulness has been validated by science, which has shown its capacity to reshape our brain:

- Reducing the gray matter in the brain's amygdala, a region correlated with stress;

- Thickening gray matter in the prefrontal cortex, an area responsible for things like planning, problem solving, and impulse control;

- Increasing gray matter concentration in the hippocampus, an area involved in memory and learning.[7]

Science has evidenced a wide range of potential benefits associated with the practice of mindfulness:

- Physical health: chronic pain reduction, aging reduction, immunity strengthening, heart disease reduction;

- Mental health and happiness: reduced stress, improved well-being, self-respect, confidence, resilience;

- Social skills: pro-social attitudes and behaviors; emotional and self-regulation; communication; empathy and compassion; anger reduction, the reduction of discriminatory behaviors; care for the environment; values clarification and alignment;

- Cognitive skills: attention; concentration; mental clarity; acceptance (non-attachment to views); meta-cognition awareness; cognitive flexibility and resilience; openness to change; resistance to cognitive bias; creativity; productivity; decision-making; memory, etc.[8]

Mindfulness exemplifies how a spiritual practice can support both individual and collective well-being. It has the potential to help us develop most of the qualities outlined so far as central for a politics of being (understanding, well-being, empathy, etc.), leading us to pause and connect with our values, which usually leads us to greater alignment on pro-social values.[9] It nourishes our capacity to care for one another and the Earth, and to collaborate, as well as the necessary wisdom for effective intentional action.[10]

Mainstreaming mindfulness

John Kabat-Zinn, a professor of medicine who graduated from the Massachusetts Institute of Technology (MIT), has been a pioneer and one of the most prominent figures of the mindfulness movement. After learning mindfulness from Buddhist teachers, in 1979 he founded the Stress Reduction Clinic at the University of Massachusetts Medical School, now called the Center for Mindfulness in Medicine, Health Care, and Society (CFM). He started to offer a mindfulness-based program, completely removed from its Buddhist framework and transposed into a scientific context, that would later evolve into the Mindfulness-Based Stress Reduction (MBSR) program that spread worldwide.

MBSR is an eight-week course combining mindfulness practices, yoga, body awareness, and reflection exploration of patterns of behavior, thinking, feeling, and action to help patients cope with stress, pain, and illness. The program has been completed by more than twenty-four thousand people in the CFM alone,[11] which has already certified over one thousand MBSR instructors,[12] replicated in more than two hundred hospitals and clinics within the US and abroad,[13] and adapted to fit other contexts. In the health-care industry, mindfulness has also been widely adopted by staff members, who are particularly prone to burnout and exhaustion, to reduce stress levels and enhance quality of care, including through improved empathy with patients.[14]

With its secular, standardized, and scientific approach, MBSR has become a laissez-passer for meditation to enter a wide range of organizations ranging from hospitals to schools, from companies to armies all over the world, like a medicine spreading in every organ of our sick social body. A growing number of public and private organizations, including companies such as Google, Unilever, Barclays, Capital One, Starcom MediaVest Group, and Goldman Sachs, have introduced mindfulness programs to improve their employees' mental health and performance. In the US, a study found that 22 percent of employers had mindfulness programs in place in 2016, with an additional 21 percent planning to implement one in 2017.[15] Many schools have included mindfulness practices for their students, teachers, and staff with the aim of improving their students' character, mental health, and results.

The mindfulness movement in education reaches beyond the classroom (see chapter 12). The book *Sitting Still Like a Frog* by Eline Snel, a Dutch therapist, proposes mindfulness practices for children to practice at home and has been sold by the millions—four hundred thousand copies in France alone—and translated into thirty-three languages.[16] Mindful parenting programs are also being developed, with proven benefits.[17] Mindfulness programs are also being used to help war veterans cope with post-traumatic stress disorder (PTSD), policemen and military personnel to deal with extreme recurrent stress, and offenders in prisons to heal and transform themselves.

Mindful Nation UK

The wide range of benefits and applications of mindfulness has led some to consider it a potential means for transforming a whole nation. In 2015, the British Mindfulness All-Party Parliamentary Group (MAPPG) published a report whose title conveys an ambitious vision: "Mindful Nation UK." The MAPPG was set up in 2014 "to review research evidence, current best practice, extent and success of implementation, and potential developments in the application of mindfulness within a range of policy areas, and to develop policy recommendations for government based on these findings."[18] Its creation followed the establishment of mindfulness classes in Westminster, attended in 2015 by one hundred and fifteen Parliamentarians and eighty of their staff. In this report, the MAPPG expressed confidence in the role of mindfulness to play a key role in tackling the UK "mental health crisis in which roughly one in three families include someone who is mentally ill"[19] and "up to 10% of the UK adult population will experience symptoms of depression in any given week."[20] The report found mindfulness "to lead to an expansion of choice and capacity in how to meet and respond to life's challenges, and therefore live with greater wellbeing, mental clarity and care for yourself and others."[21]

In the report's preface, the MAPPG's cochairs mentioned they:

[H]ave been impressed by the quality and range of evidence for the benefits of mindfulness and believe it has the potential to help many people to better health and flourishing. On a number of issues ranging from improving mental health and boosting productivity and creativity in the economy through to helping people with long-term conditions such as diabetes and obesity, mindfulness appears to have an impact.[22]

This political rationale builds on previous initiatives, in particular the 2008 study on "Mental Capital and Wellbeing" I mentioned in chapter 3. The Mindful Nation UK report includes recommendations to the government, national research institutions, and other bodies in four fields: health, education, the workplace, and the criminal justice system. Given the huge and constantly rising costs associated with poor mental health, the report emphasizes the enormous economic potential of mindfulness-based interventions for the country. The cost of depression in the UK is estimated to be at least some £20 billion a year in the next decade (£9.19 billion a year in lost earnings alone, with an additional £2.96 billion in annual service costs and £8 billion a year for the effect of poor mental health on physical illnesses).

Mental health is responsible for some 54 percent of sick leaves in the UK, and "the indirect costs to the UK of mental ill health in unemployment, absenteeism and presenteeism (and the resulting loss of productivity) are estimated at between £70 and £100 billion."[23] Moreover, considering the relatively low cost of learning and practicing mindfulness and its important benefits, a key argument is the cost-effectiveness of mindfulness interventions. For example, it is estimated that every pound invested in Mindfulness-Based Cognitive Therapy (MBCT), which has been found to reduce the risk of depression relapse by 43 percent in comparison to control groups,[24] generates at least £15 of savings. Transport for London, which has offered mindfulness combined with other interventions like cognitive behavioral therapy (CBT) to staff, has experienced a 71 percent reduction in days off for stress, anxiety, and depression, while absences for all conditions dropped by 50 percent according to internal assessments.[25]

The mindful society

A couple of years before the MAPPG report, in 2012, Tim Ryan, a then-US congressman, had already expressed a similar vision for the US in his book *A Mindful Nation*, showing how mindfulness could be an effective response to many of the current challenges his country was facing and might even help "recapture the American spirit" by strengthening values such as self-reliance, determination, and getting the job done.

The same year, Jeffrey Sachs published *The Price of Civilization*, in which he calls for a "mindful society,"[26] stating that "we will need [...] to achieve a new mindfulness regarding our needs as individuals and as a society, to find a more solid path to well-being."[27] Sachs identifies eight dimensions in our lives for which mindfulness is crucial:

- Mindfulness of self: personal moderation to escape mass consumerism
- Mindfulness of work: the balancing of work and leisure
- Mindfulness of knowledge: the cultivation of education
- Mindfulness of others: the exercise of compassion and cooperation
- Mindfulness of nature: the conservation of the world's ecosystems
- Mindfulness of the future: the responsibility to save for the future
- Mindfulness of politics: the cultivation of public deliberation and shared values for collective action through political institutions
- Mindfulness of the world: the acceptance of diversity as a path to peace.[28]

Indeed, mindfulness has the potential to build the inner foundations for sustainability. Being in the here and now is a key condition to being able to connect with ourselves, each other, and nature. Fostering our inner connection can help us have more clarity about our values, what truly matters for us, and allow us to align our lives accordingly. As we have seen, consumerism feeds on this disconnection. Through pervasive advertisements, it also takes advantage of our autopilot mode, the exact opposite of mindfulness. In fact, mindfulness has been associated with more sustainable behaviors and consumption patterns.[29]

As with yoga, meditation and mindfulness have become an industry, whose revenues reached US$1.1 billion in 2016 in the US,[30] a number that does not take into account the booming market for mindfulness applications (nearly one thousand available worldwide in 2016),[31] such as Headspace (more than thirty million users in one hundred and ninety countries in mid-2020).[32] Success often corrupts, and one could wonder whether mindfulness is losing its soul. Mindfulness is now widely used by the military to wage more efficient wars and by companies to help workers cope with toxic management systems and improve their performance to make more money in the end. Was that really the Buddha's intent?

There seems to be a real risk of diluting the essence of mindfulness, as the large number of mindfulness companies and consultants that are serving this market often do not always have the experience or qualifications necessary to access and transmit its transformative, perspective-shifting potential. And we need much more of these teachers if we want to help people at risk of depression. The MAPPG found that the existing capacity of mindfulness teachers in the UK could only attend to 4 percent of these people. Fortunately, true mindfulness is kept alive in many places.

A fundamental difference I have come to appreciate in Plum Village is that mindfulness is not a tool, something used to achieve a given purpose. It is a path of liberation, a way of being. It cannot be half-practiced; otherwise it is no longer mindfulness. If people practice true mindfulness, their initial objective cannot matter. By practicing, they will let go of their original ideas and positively transform. If they keep clinging to the ideas of money, power, or fame, they won't be practicing mindfulness and will not experience the joy, compassion, peace, and freedom it can provide. "We need not fear that mindfulness might become only a means and not an end because in mindfulness the means and the end are the same thing. There is no way to happiness; happiness is the way," said Thich Nhat Hanh to the *Guardian* journalist who asked him about this.[33]

10

Light

Mystery, Vibration, Energy, Subtle Realms, Powers

"The Tao that can be spoken is not the eternal Tao
The name that can be named is not the eternal name
The nameless is the origin of Heaven and Earth
The named is the mother of myriad things
Thus, constantly without desire, one observes its essence
Constantly with desire, one observes its manifestations
These two emerge together but differ in name
The unity is said to be the mystery
Mystery of mysteries, the door to all wonders."

—Lao Tzu,[1] Chinese Taoist philosopher
(ca. 6th century—4th century BC)

REALITY IS AND will probably always remain profoundly mysterious. Science has considerably deepened our understanding of reality, to the point that in the past some came to believe there would soon be no enigmas left to elucidate, and the world would be perfectly intelligible. It is now clear that this was a myth. "Not only is the universe stranger than we think; it is stranger than we can think," said Nobel laureate and pioneer of quantum mechanics Werner Heisenberg.

A mysterious reality

I believe our material reality will always remain mysterious because it is not separated from the ultimate (or "spiritual" or "other") reality; they coexist.[2] The spiritual reality that Lao Tzu refers to as "the eternal Tao," the "origin of Heaven and Earth," and which can also be called soul, spirit,[3] God, higher power, spiritual force, or divine "light," permeates the world. It is beyond our understanding; it transcends concepts and cannot be named. Hence when our scientific investigations deepen to bring us closer to where these two realities meet, we face the "mystery of mysteries, the door to all wonders." In fact, modern science is, more and more, telling us the story of an energetic, vibrant, and maybe even conscious reality, made of parallel universes, that resonates deeply with spiritual teachings.

Through Einstein's famous formula $E=mc^2$,[4] science has shown that all material reality is nothing more than energy. When the energy is sufficiently dense, it becomes what we call matter. Each subatomic particle (proton, electron, neutron, etc.) that constitutes matter has an energetic charge that creates an electromagnetic field and is in constant vibration at measurable frequencies. This is also true for macro-objects such as planets, stars, and even galaxies. As Einstein said, "Everything in life is vibration."

Light is a form of energy, being the visible part of the electromagnetic field created by a given source, a star like our sun, or a lamp. In the same solar electromagnetic field, there are other types of energy that we can feel with other senses, such as touch, in the case of heat, or that, we, as humans, do not have the physiological capacity to perceive, as with ultraviolet, infrared, or gamma rays. Our scientific understanding of light highlights the quantum-mechanical notion of "wave-particle duality." According to this view, every particle or quantum entity may be described as either a particle or a wave—both concepts being unable to fully describe the behavior of quantum-scale objects. As Albert Einstein explained:

It seems as though we must use sometimes the one theory and sometimes the other, while at times we may use either. We are faced with a new kind of difficulty. We have two contradictory pictures of reality; separately neither of them fully explains the phenomena of light, but together they do.[5]

Quantum physics has revealed many other puzzling observations, such as:

- "Quantum indeterminacy," according to which the state of a system does not determine a unique set of values for all its measurable properties;
- The "observer effect," in which the mere observation of a phenomenon inevitably changes that phenomenon;
- "Non-locality," the apparent ability of quantum objects to instantaneously know about each other's state and behave in a correlated fashion, even when separated by large distances.

These observations have aroused considerable interest from philosophers and spiritual seekers who want to see in them not only the echo but the scientific confirmation of ancient spiritual beliefs and knowledge. There is certainly a lot of misuse and abuse of quantum mechanics in the name of spirituality, and many of these claims, especially when they come from non-physicists, are denounced by scientists for lacking scientific rigor. At the same time, some of the best quantum physicists have found that their knowledge revives ancient spiritual notions. Some of them, including renowned David Bohm, have interpreted quantum mechanics in a way that brings back the philosophical notion of panpsychism: the understanding that mind or a mind-like aspect—let's say consciousness— is a fundamental and ubiquitous feature of reality.[6] According to their views, whose acceptance is growing, our world—from suns to quarks or electrons—is endowed with consciousness. From this perspective, evolution cannot be considered a merely biological phenomenon, which, at some point, led to the emergence of consciousness, but also as an evolution of consciousness itself.

String theory, currently one of the most popular attempts to reconcile quantum mechanics with the general theory of relativity, provides a unified framework for the four forces in the universe,[7] describing reality as a manifestation of the vibration of very small (10^{-35})[8] interconnected strings that resonate at specific frequencies. It includes a theory of parallel universes, the many-world theory, which is an interpretation of quantum mechanics. Interestingly, in his last paper, just before he died, physicist Stephen Hawking predicted there are not infinite parallel universes in the multiverse (something this theory assumed until now) but rather a limited number of them, which implies that this theory might be able to be tested.[9]

I am not a physicist—indeed, I was pretty bad at physics in high school. I am not trying to prove any spiritual teaching by using physical science. I am just acknowledging that, unlike a century ago, the reality described by science seems much more open to the mystery at the core of all spiritual traditions. Likewise, good scientists should be particularly cautious of not refuting spiritual teachings just because they lie outside their field of investigations. As Korean Buddhist master and Harvard graduate Hwansan Sunim wrote:

Science, by its own definition, is the investigation of one domain, namely, the observable material world. As a scientist, then, saying that you're only going to investigate one domain of phenomena does not logically mean that no other such domain exists. It's one thing to say I'm only going to explore the Atlantic Ocean. It's something else entirely to go on and say that no other oceans exist. And it's downright unscientific to say no other oceans can possibly exist and you're crazy if you think they do. In a word, it's bad science to say that no observations, except the kind of ones that I make, are possible. By definition, science has limited itself to one realm of exploration. This means, like it or not, there's no logical or "scientific" basis for it to make comments about other possible realms. All you can really say is: "I don't know. Based on what I've observed, it seems difficult to explain, but the truth is, I haven't investigated that." I haven't put in the same kind of effort with the same kind of resources and the same level of enthusiasm to investigate that. I personally just find it hard to accept.[10]

Hwansan Sunim's words lead us to three interrelated points. First, our current scientific instruments allow for observing only a tiny portion—5 percent—of the known universe, with dark energy and dark matter (the mysterious energy and matter that we can't directly observe except through their gravitational effects) representing some 68 percent and 27 percent of the universe respectively. This allows NASA to humbly conclude on its website that "more is unknown than is known" and that maybe the matter we are able to observe "shouldn't be called 'normal' matter at all since it is such a small fraction of the universe."[11]

Second, as we have seen with neuroscientific studies of meditators' minds, science and spirituality are not two separate realms and nonoverlapping magisteria. The inner experiences of meditators or shamans in trances[12] translate into the material structure of their brains and neurophysiological processes. Science and spirituality can enter a mutually fruitful dialogue, and science necessarily builds on philosophical concepts.

Third, the refinement of our instruments of scientific observation can shed light on experiences that were once only part of the realm of spirituality. We already have access to more subtle, and sometimes not "material" (in the conventional sense of the word) realities such as waves and energy, whose possibilities we have learned to harness. Our daily lives are impregnated by the waves, radiation, and electromagnetic fields used in many technologies, such as telecommunication, energy, medicine, or defense, that are invisible to the human eyes.

"But what is science if not a magic whose mysteries we have been able to partly explain? And what is magic if not the sketch of tomorrow's science?" asked French writer Edouard Brasey,[13] remembering how it was once common to talk about "the electricity fairy."

There is no doubt that the development of new instruments will continue to push the limits of scientific observations toward more and more subtle aspects of reality, including those which have long been associated with spirituality. Some scientists and alternative medicine practitioners claim they can use technological devices to observe, measure, and act, through vibrational means, on bioenergetic fields or subtle bodies traditionally known as "auras," and that they have correlated these measures with health states, allowing evidence to be gathered of causal relationships.[14]

I am not qualified to say if this is scientifically proven and understood. I have not tried either of these machines to develop my personal opinion on this matter. But as an energetic healing practitioner (Reiki[15] master) and a tai-chi-chuan teacher, "chi"—the Chinese word sometimes translated as breath or energy—for me, is a very concrete and practical experience, as it is for millions of other practitioners. It is also central to traditional Chinese medicine and Ayurveda, and present in one form or another in most spiritual traditions.

Experiencing the ultimate reality

Beyond what science can tell us, the "spiritual" dimension of reality— which is often associated with vibrations, energies, spirits, and a conscious universe—needs to be experienced in person. Otherwise it is just a description or a mere belief, devoid of authentic transformative power. In Toltec shamanism, seeing energy directly as it flows through the universe is a crucial experience and capacity on the path towards personal liberation.[16] Similar experiences are present in other spiritual traditions, as described, for instance, by Hindu master Ramakrishna (1836–1886).

In 2011, just before we became partners, my wife Emelina and I were enjoying our holidays in Mexico as best friends. We were in the small village of Amatlan, where the god Quetzalcoatl[17]—"serpent of precious feathers"—is supposed to have been born, next to the officially "magic village" of Tepoztlán.[18] With the mysterious eroded mountains that circle the valley, this landscape is recognized as sacred by its inhabitants and is famous for its allegedly special energetic properties, something I directly experienced.

In this small village, where locals still speak their native language

(Nahuatl) and have kept their cultural traditions alive, I spent an hour in the living room of a friend's house built on rocks, feeling exactly as if I were receiving an energetic healing treatment. My friend showed me a smaller room on a big rock, saying that it was impossible for her to sleep there. During a walk in the forest, Emelina and I stopped along a small river to practice some energetic techniques. We sat on rocks in front of each other, separated by the river and some five meters, and started to circulate energy between us. At some point, Emelina ceased to answer me and seemed to faint, her eyes almost closing. When I insisted on calling her, she had much difficulty answering me, and I had to call her attention several times before I decided to go to her.

"I saw all in lights ... you, the trees ... the leaves were sparkling ..." she told me after a moment, as I held her. She was really confused, struggling to keep her attention on this material plane, and I told her to jump in the water, just in front of her, which I knew was the best thing to do in that case. She finally told me that at some point, the whole of reality disappeared, and she saw everything as shimmering lights, including myself as a luminous oval field of energy. I now joke with her that she fell in love with me the first time she saw me naked—and I mean truly naked—as a soul! Many traditions emphasize that one should not get attached to such experiences, capacities, and powers, as even they can prove to be a hindrance on the path of freedom, but they definitely can help transform our consciousness by opening us up to a new perception of reality.

Science and heresies

As our societies grow spiritually, we will become more inclined to look deeply, at the collective level, into the many mysterious aspects of the reality that connects us to the spiritual dimensions of our lives—from new forms of energy to subtle bodies, spirits, or psychic powers. Many puzzling phenomena that could easily be scientifically verified or denied have not received enough attention from the scientific community, often because of a lack of interest or distrust. It is sometimes a deterrent for scientists not to be able to provide explanations for certain experiences, but ruling out the facts because of our incapacity to explain them is a fundamentally unscientific attitude.

The history of science is full of breakthroughs that were first denounced as heresies. I will provide two relatively famous contemporaneous examples of supposed phenomena with spiritual overtones. I abstain from making any personal claim on these contested matters. The point is just to illustrate the many mysteries we have yet to explore—a reality that, in my own experience, is obvious—and the public discussions around them.

Among the many mysterious abilities that mystics all over the world and throughout history have reportedly displayed is the ability to survive without food or water for inexplicably long periods of time.[19] Often called inedia or breatharianism, this is in some traditions associated with the alleged capacity to use sunlight as a source of vital force ("chi" or "prana") to sustain the physical organism. This is the subject of an Austrian documentary film, released in 2010, *In The Beginning There Was Light*. A key example the film highlights is that of Indian yogi Prahlad Jani (1929–2020), who claims to have lived for more than seventy years without eating and drinking. In 2003 and 2010, two scientific experiments confirmed he was able to spend ten and fifteen days respectively without eating and drinking, while maintaining good health indicators, something that is completely at odds with our current understanding of human biology.[20] The film asserts that inedia is not only a reality for exceptional mystics but also for numerous common people. Were inedia's reality to become more firmly established, it would be naïve to expect any solution to the issues of hunger or malnutrition from it, and its potential should be handled with great care as its pursuit has led some people to death.

Another example of easily verifiable work, challenging the current scientific understanding of reality, is that of Japanese author Masaru Emoto (1943–2014), who affirmed that human consciousness has an effect on the molecular structure of water. He backed this assertion with microscopic photographs of water crystals, obtained through freezing water after it had been exposed to different words, pictures, or music. When the expressed messages were positive, the water crystals were beautiful and harmonious, while when the expressed intention was negative, the frozen water droplets were clearly ugly.

These photos have had a powerful impact, and Emoto's book *The Hidden Messages in Water,* published in 2004, was a *New York Times* best seller. Emoto even claimed that prayer and visualization could help clean polluted water. As a human adult body is on average 60 percent water, Emoto's claims, if proven true, would have important consequences on how we approach our health, our thoughts and speech, and environmental regeneration.

These kinds of assertions, which are obviously contested but also sometimes supported by prominent scientists,[21] deserve to be examined with great care and more attention than what they have so far received from the scientific community. The more science refuses to seriously investigate these supposedly mysterious phenomena, the more possibilities there are for crooks to manipulate people in their name, and the less knowledge and human possibilities progress.

The subtle and vibrational nature of reality has already entered the field of political decisions, such as when we address the health impact of wave-based new technologies like 5G networks. As our knowledge develops, new possibilities will emerge in the future, which may not only take the form of high technology, but also of different practices in, for example, the fields of human health, landscape management, and agriculture. We may come to rediscover the wisdom of traditional knowledge and practices in that regard. As science is only scratching the surface of these possibilities, the agenda for action that I will present for the politics of being is very conservative in that regard, beyond the need for more scientific research. Still, as an example of new possibilities, it outlines a potential policy that finds roots not in science but in indigenous practices for managing sacred sites so as to balance and activate the Earth's energies.

"To me God is truth and love, God is ethics and morality, God is fearlessness. God is the source of Light and Life and yet he is above and beyond all those. God is conscience [...] He is the purest essence."

—Mahatma Gandhi, political and spiritual leader (1869–1948)

The spiritual values we have examined constitute the basic foundations of the politics of being, together with some other values such as truth, freedom, or abundance. While these are the basis of our current model of development, they have often lost their true meaning (and evolutionary potential) along the way.

The associated research we have reviewed outlines the obsolescence of the old narrative behind our model of development, what Eisenstein called the story of separation. On the contrary, it emphasizes our relational nature and the importance for our fulfillment (happiness) of our capacity to connect. The ability to connect starts with ourselves, and through our mindfulness, embrace other humans (love, peace), nature (life), the whole (understanding), and the absolute dimension (light). All these values tend to go together, as we already mentioned in our theory of change.

Complex systems thinking naturally develops the awareness of our interdependence and our sense of solidarity. It is critical to our understanding of how life works. Life comes from love, and the contemplation of natural order has been a fertile ground from which human wisdom has grown. Like love, peace, and mindfulness, spending time in nature is key to our well-being and health. And happy people tend to treat others and nature better. A culture of peace would embody all these qualities that the practice of mindfulness and, more generally, meditation, can help us develop. These different values inter-are because they all spring from the same spiritual source.

Each of these values has some paradigmatic pretension. There are many declarations, initiatives, and organizations that highlight one of them as the solution forward. The politics of being builds on all of them. This can help us express our full potential and find a deeper understanding of each of these values by not losing sight of the ultimate reality behind them. When we focus on, say, integral thinking or love, there is a chance for us to develop a relationship with the absolute, individually or collectively, that can be partial and imbalanced; in this case either too intellectual or too emotional. While it is true that each of these values can ultimately embody the supreme reality, it is safer to acknowledge all of them, in particular at a theoretical level.

Like individuals, nations naturally tend to emphasize a value above others, as is most culturally appropriate to them. Bhutan has emphasized happiness. Ecuador or Bolivia have emphasized relationships with all life forms, while the Charter for Compassion is rooted in the Abrahamic religions. This is fine, as the values they emphasize lead them to the others.

This list of spiritual values is not exhaustive. The ones we mention in these chapters' titles are interrelated with many others. We have already come across responsibility, openness, creativity, harmony, simplicity, gratitude, justice, and forgiveness, to name a few. We will look at abundance (chapter 18), as well as unity and diversity later (chapters 20 and 21). In this chapter, I would also like to briefly mention the more traditional but eternally relevant values of truth, goodness, beauty, and freedom.

Truth, goodness, and beauty are known as the transcendentals or the Platonic triad of higher forms.[22] Transcendentals, which have been discussed throughout Western philosophy, from Greek philosophers to Christian theologians, also sometimes include "unity" (or "one"). Essentially, they have been considered properties of being, and the catechism of the Catholic Church promulgated by Pope John Paul II in 1992 considered them to "reflect the infinite perfection of God,"[23] in whose image and likeness man was created. As such, the transcendentals are regarded as ontologically one, and thus always accompany each other. These ideals are said to correspond to three human fields of interest: science, religion, and arts. They embody the highest human aspirations.

When it is associated with religion, goodness is often considered as above science and arts, with justice or ethics completing the triad below. Ethics is, of course, a central aspect of our higher selves and a politics of being. In fact, Protestant Europe, which is well-known for its high level of ethics (the Reformation was, above all, an ethical reaction to the evolution of Catholicism), appears at the top of many relevant international rankings. But what a politics of being emphasizes is that our higher selves naturally emanate from our true selves, like the transcendentals emanate from our being or God.

American Zen master Philip Kapleau (1912-2004) argues that "a deeply enlightened person [...] does not imitate [Buddhist] precepts, but the other way around: the precepts imitate them."[24] Our societies should encourage their members to find the source of their morality and ethics within, instead of only imposing on them dogmatically rigid social norms and codes of conduct. This is a fundamental difference that is often used to distinguish ethics from morality, some considering ethics to be provided by external sources and morals to refer to one's own principles, while others think it is the other way around.

Many spiritual teachers consider the manifestation of truth as the central issue of our times. Some consider it the "apocalypse" foretold in the Bible, a term that is often poorly understood and which means "revelation" or "unveiling." The cultural transformation we are calling for is going along with a deepening of our understanding of truth, with the rediscovery of spiritual insights and laws. It is confronting obsolete worldviews and corrupt power structures—corporate control over the media, educational and scientific research systems, classified national security information, etc.—which generates resistance. In 2015, Richard Horton, the current editor-in-chief of the *Lancet* journal, confessed "much of the scientific literature, perhaps half, may simply be untrue."[25] Bad science, fake news propagated by social media, and blatant lies by politicians are among the last possible means to block the great Earth transition. They are part of a tremendous spiritual confrontation.

Jesus said, "Ye shall know the truth, and the truth shall make you free."[26] He was not talking about the kind of outer freedom that relates to our purchasing power or our political institutions and that has grown much in many places during the last centuries. He was referring to inner freedom, that of the soul or the spirit, without which outer freedom loses its significance, and at some point, cannot be sustained anymore. Liberalism has supported a great development of our freedom, which is a central aspect of progress—as recognized, for example, by Indian economist and Nobel Prize recipient Amartya Sen in his famous book *Development as Freedom*—and should stand at the core of a politics of being. But what is the point of theoretically having so much outer liberty, if in practice, because of our egos, our passions, our conditionings, all manipulated by powerful interests, we all adopt the same standardized patterns of behavior that lead us to the brink of chaos? What if the irresponsible use of our individual liberties imprisons us collectively?

Inner freedom needs to be cultivated and should be able to express itself in our ways of life. German philosopher Georg Wilhelm Friedrich Hegel (1770–1831) regards history as moving toward the realization of human freedom, which he considers the essential quality of mind or spirit ("geist"). While economic development and modernity have historically freed us from many limitations, our current growth-based model of development has now escaped our control, and hinders our freedom. It is in fact very rigid, and struggles to deal with the relatively minor costs of tackling, for instance, climate change, even though it makes perfect economic sense.[27] Our material prosperity is supposed to grow every year, but it seems we are never rich enough to invest in solving our problems. Instead, we are bound to reinvest our resources in sustaining the economic system on which we very much depend. It praises freedom, but in practice often works against it.

It is a well-known fact that free markets without regulation tend to destroy themselves, and in the last decades they have concentrated enormous power in the hands of a few corporations. They control markets, limiting competition and innovation, as well as consumers through marketing strategies and an increasing wealth of personal data. More importantly, they also control a great deal of scientific research and knowledge, as well as media and political spheres. Our individual and collective freedoms now depend on our capacity to regain control over these markets, and consequently of our economic system, so that the cultural evolution we envision can translate in practice into sustainable behaviors. Freedom is also increasingly threatened by the rise of authoritarian regimes,[28] the fight against terrorism and COVID-19, pervasive surveillance based on artificial intelligence, and the use of our personal data.

Finally, ugliness is one of the faces of our collective spiritual illness. We see it in the external world: in polluted rivers, garbage dumps, mutilated mountains and burnt forests, in orangutans wandering desperately around oil palm plantations, in the gems of cultural diversity that we let disappear, in our slums and soulless projects, in skeletal children. We can also see it in our minds and hearts, in religious bigotry and in the hatred that stirs terrorism, in the greed that kills, in our cold indifference, in widespread moral failures and mental illnesses. Deep inside, we are all longing for a more beautiful world.

Beauty can awaken our hearts, our creativity, inspiring us to hear and respond to this longing, to live poetically, reconnecting us to our true purpose. It has the power to bring out the best in ourselves, so we connect with each other and love and respect the environment we live in. We can see this in the colorful mural—the biggest one in Mexico—painted in 2015 on the two hundred and two houses of the Palmitas neighborhood in the city of Pachuca. The project, which engaged artists and local residents, including members of gangs, aimed at lowering delinquency and regenerating social ties. It first entailed convincing the four hundred and fifty-two families to get their houses repainted. This was done in white at the beginning, to symbolize a new departure and the fact that everybody is equal. Then the mural was painted. Contemporarily, the streets were cleaned, car carcasses removed, lighting improved, and security cameras installed. Three years after the project, which brought the community together around an artistic project and vision, violence had decreased 35 percent, and life quality had drastically improved.[29] We will flourish, walking in beauty.

One of the most effective ways to support personal development is to help people connect with their deepest aspirations and values to consciously align their lives and behaviors with them. When they do so, studies show people usually emphasize the highest values.[30] The same is true at the collective level: all these values are nations' guiding stars, and together constitute the lexical field of most national mottos. What better source of legitimacy for the politics of being?

These qualities are all one in the spirit, reflecting the same ultimate reality. As Gandhi said, "To me God is truth and love, God is ethics and morality, God is fearlessness. God is the source of Light and Life and yet he is above and beyond all those. God is conscience [...] He is the purest essence."[31] In their deepest sense, these qualities don't oppose each other. They do not belong to the left or right wing; they are universal and appeal to every reasonable and healthy person. Still, in practice, the last century has been shaped by the struggle between freedom and equality. To materialize in our societies, these spiritual qualities are apprehended by our thinking minds and often converted into one-sided ideologies that make them appear irreconcilable. By reconnecting with the authentic spiritual truth behind each of these values, the politics of being has the capacity to heal political polarization and unite us. Spiritual teachings can guide us in experiencing their harmonious balance within ourselves and help us develop the wisdom necessary to understand what this could mean for the outer world.

III

AN AGENDA FOR ACTION

"Designing institutions to force (or nudge) entirely self-interested individuals to achieve better outcomes has been the major goal posited by policy analysts for governments to accomplish for much of the past half century. Extensive empirical research leads me to argue that instead, a core goal of public policy should be to facilitate the development of institutions that bring out the best in humans."

—Elinor Ostrom, political economist
and Nobel laureate (1933–2012)[1]

THE POLITICS OF being supports our growth as human beings, including our autonomy and freedom, our vitality, our aesthetic sense, our capacity for love and empathy, joy, peace, mindfulness, and complex thinking. It is not an ethereal vision. These ideals are guiding stars that orient it. But concrete public policies that can support its practical implementation already exist. Many of them are mentioned in the scientific literature related to these values. Indeed, for most sectors like education, health, the economy, and so on, you can find strategic visions—and proposed policies to turn them into reality—labeled as "integral," "holistic," "regenerative," "life-affirming," "positive," "compassionate," "caring," "nonviolent," "partnership," or "mindful." Together, these policies form the natural substrate of the politics of being.

More generally, the literature reviewed in previous chapters has highlighted some general orientations for the politics of being. It has highlighted the need for "second-stage" investments in human development through education, mental health, and childhood well-being policies. It has also emphasized the need for our institutions to be based on more positive assumptions about human nature in order to encourage the expression of our higher selves and intrinsic motivation, rather than relying on traditional carrot-and-stick incentives used when assuming people are merely selfish and utilitarian. Other orientations include the need:

- For systemic and intersectoral approaches, in which goals pertaining to one sector (e.g., health) can be achieved by interventions in another sector (e.g., environment);

- To protect and nourish life outside and inside ourselves and harmonize us with natural principles and wisdom;

- To cultivate empathy and relationships, strengthening communities and social capital (in addition to individual autonomy) instead of sacrificing them for more goods and economic capital;

- To develop a culture of peace, a culture of partnership and nonviolence, fostering in particular gender and economic equity, a sense of material and psychological security, the respect of human rights, justice and democratic practices;

- To protect integrity and deepen our scientific knowledge and its transmission;
- To consider the subtle, "energetic" aspect of reality.

We should consider all this when defining strategic priorities and designing solutions for each sector. These institutions should not only deliver results in their own fields but also foster "the best in humans" to support genuine overall progress. If instead we base specific "solutions" on the same old paradigm that assumes and conjures selfishness, we will keep reinforcing our systemic crisis.

In fact, even in their own fields, strategic sectorial analyses demonstrate our approach's pertinence. They confirm that in many sectors, the actualization of our human potential, of our connection to one another and the natural world, lies at the center of many ongoing paradigmatic changes, of new strategic priorities and levers of action. While well-known and more traditional policies often remain relevant, they are no longer sufficient to address the mounting problems we face. They ought to be replaced or accompanied by policies embodying the (inter)being paradigm. In this part of the book, we present some of these as examples, without pretending to be exhaustive.

11

Childhood and Family

"What can you do to promote world peace?
Go home and love your family."

—Mother Teresa, Catholic nun (1919–1997)

Early childhood well-being

SCIENCE HAS CLEARLY established that childhood, especially in the first years of life, is decisive in building our capacity to flourish and contribute positively to our communities.[1] What our children need for their development is a safe, healthy, loving, caring, and stimulating environment. This is a major determinant of their well-being, health, work performance, empathy, and pro-sociality.[2] As mentioned by specialists:

> It is quite extraordinary that, given what we know about how early lives affect brain and even genetic expression, we have such limited resources dedicated to the desire for 'every child to grow up in a compassionate environment.' This failure to grasp the size and nature of the problems of 'how children around the world are raised in appalling conditions' is probably humanity's greatest compassion failure.[3]

It is also a huge social and economic failure, as one study found that every dollar invested in early childhood well-being in the US can potentially generate US$8 in returns for society.[4] Any wise politics should consider this a national priority, something done by Jacinda Arden, New Zealand's prime minister, when she proclaimed in 2018 her intention to make her country the "best place in the world to be a child."[5] Commitment is growing: the numbers of countries with national multisectoral early childhood development policies increased from seven in 2000 to sixty-eight in 2014, 45 percent of which were low- and middle-income countries.[6] SDG target 4.2 calls for universal access by 2030 to quality childhood development, care, and pre-primary education.

Governments' efforts to promote early childhood well-being should start during pregnancy or even before to ensure the best conditions for the child to come, addressing both its needs and the mother's. It should promote developmental screening and access to quality nutrition, education, health care, and social protection for all children, effective parenting, as well as financial support for populations at risk, such as poor or single-parent families. In fact, the material determinants of the childhood environment are important. In general, social inequalities are correlated with child well-being (as measured by UNICEF) in rich countries,[7] where child poverty is a function of the generosity of public policies towards families.[8]

Poverty has important consequences on children's development.[9] This is particularly important in low- and middle-income countries, where a staggering 43 percent of children under five years of age—an estimated two hundred and fifty million—are at risk of suboptimal development due to poverty and stunting.[10] It is estimated that the loss of average adult income for these children is likely to be 26 percent, trapping families in poverty.[11] At a societal level, the long-term costs of neglecting childhood, leading to stunting and developmental delays—that can be easily addressed through home visits, nutrition programs, and preschools—are several times more than what some countries currently spend on health or education respectively.[12]

A 2018 study by McKinsey & Company on the role of US states in improving young children's well-being emphasized the need to improve the transparency and coordination of youth welfare systems, which involve many agencies,[13] a challenge also found in other countries.[14] The development of information and tracking systems that are common to all agencies can enable coordinated support for children at risk, a solution already tested in some states. Another solution implemented by the state of Washington is the creation of a single agency to manage all programs related to early childhood, from parenting to education to health.

Parenting and secure attachment

Above all, a politics of being considers parenting to be of the utmost importance. It should ensure every child can count on the presence, love, and support of parents to be able to develop what psychologists call "secure attachment." This is the key basis for children's development, associated in particular with adults' capacities for well-being (self-esteem, mental health, autonomy, intrinsic motivation …) and social relationships (empathy, pro-social orientation …).[15] Deficiencies in early infant parental nurturance have also been scientifically correlated with the search for extrinsic rewards, such as money, power, or fame, as a way to compensate for a sense of insecurity.[16]

Extensive paid maternity, paternity, and parental leave policies, including mandatory ones for fathers,[17] can contribute to this objective, while benefiting the parents' well-being. Paid leave for parents to care for sick children can also be important. Hence it is no surprise that Nordic countries such as Sweden or Norway, which dominate internal rankings on happiness and social health, have among the most generous parental leave policies in the world, while the US lags behind.[18] In Sweden, parents of both sexes are entitled to four hundred and eighty days (sixteen months) of paid parental leave at about 80 percent of their salary (with a cap), to be shared between both parents, with each parent having an exclusive right to ninety of those days. The US, on the contrary, is the only high-income country with no federal paid-leave policy.[19]

In addition to ensuring parents' presence, it is important to help them build the capacity for parenting. Parenting programs can address all domains of nurturing care: health, nutrition, safety and security, responsive caregiving, and early learning. These programs can be particularly successful and are often directed at the family as a unit rather than the child alone.[20] Becoming a parent is not easy, in particular for women: worldwide, about 10 percent of pregnant women and 13 percent of women who have just given birth experience a mental disorder, primarily depression.[21] Parents' and families' health and well-being can have serious consequences for children and are essential to promote. Among the different dimensions of family background (social, economic, psychological, etc.), a mother's emotional health has been shown to be the most powerful factor of future adults' life satisfaction.[22]

In terms of education, evidence-based parenting programs, which often emphasize communication and interaction skills, demandingness and responsiveness, can be effective and benefit not only children but also parents' well-being.[23] They can reduce rates of child maltreatment, as well as net costs for the community. The study of a specific parenting program has shown that every dollar invested reduces the cost of children in the welfare system by US$9.[24] Another academic work demonstrated that adults engaged in eudaemonic pursuits (developing the best in oneself) are most likely to have had demanding and responsive parents.[25]

Evidence-based parenting programs should be promoted as part of a public health approach, that is to say at a large scale, avoiding the stigmatization that can be attached to such endeavors, and taking into account the most up-to-date research on parenting, such as those emphasizing compassion, mindfulness,[26] and civic concerns. Breastfeeding should also be promoted as a basis for protecting the mother's health and developing secure attachment,[27] health, and developmental potential of the children. According to the World Health Organization, "Adolescents and adults who were breastfed as babies are less likely to be overweight or obese. They are less likely to have type-II diabetes and perform better in intelligence tests."[28] Governments need to pass legislation ensuring basic accommodations for breastfeeding mothers at work, including time for women to express milk in private spaces that are not bathrooms.

Being a parent is also a unique opportunity to learn about ourselves, heal, grow, and ... practice! Thanks to the support of our parenting adviser Esther Montmany, my wife and I are trying to pay particular attention to the quality of our presence, in particular when carrying out all the basic activities of daily life—bathing, dressing, eating, etc.—which often constitute a significant part of the time parents spend with their children. Rather than trying to get these tasks done as quickly as possible while thinking of more important issues, we have realized the importance of the quality of our attention in these very moments, through which children can experience our love, as well as feel and learn the importance of taking care of themselves.

Another key insight has been how to deal with our children's emotions. As parents, we naturally feel uncomfortable with our children expressing "negative" emotions such as sadness, anger, or fear. We tend to prevent their expression, such as by distracting children's attention through other stimuli: "Oh look ... what a beautiful photo!" By doing so, we teach our children to disconnect from their own emotions, and we get in the way of physiological mechanisms such as crying, by which children can process and regulate their emotions. Those unprocessed emotions tend to accumulate within, distorting our children's characters and behaviors. As a result, to find a balance, they often rely on specific habits that are not necessarily well suited to real life and which limit their autonomy.

To fall asleep, our first daughter, Sonia, still needed her bottle at the age of two and a half. She also needed one of us to lie next to her for a long period of time. As our second child was about to be born, this became increasingly unsustainable. We asked for Esther's advice. She said that at the root of this habit was an unprocessed emotion that we could help Sonia release. It would be a tough exercise, she told us, and we needed to be ready to face whatever came out, she warned.

That night, Esther and my wife stayed with my daughter next to her bed. Sonia had a tantrum, screaming and shaking all over her bed, calling for her mom to lie next to her, and even trying to hit her out of rage at some point. Esther and my wife's work was to accompany Sonia's crisis through their compassionate and solid presence, while maintaining our daughter's body on the mattress to avoid her hurting herself. This lasted for more than an hour, until at last, a profound and particularly hideous scream came out of her. That was it: something had been released, and she soon fell asleep. After that night, Sonia never asked for a bottle again, and it became easier for her to fall asleep on her own ... Being able to accompany and support the emotional life of our children is a tough practice for parents, especially because of the emotional responses their tears and shouts trigger in us, in our own inner child, whose wounds call for healing.

With my wife, I have come to understand that our problems as parents are not our children's difficult behaviors. Ultimately, the real challenge lies in ourselves; it is our capacity to really be here for our children and respond skillfully, with attention, understanding, and love. Our daughter's cries have become our mindfulness bell. From an evolutionary perspective, our parental instinct has been the most important factor for mammals, in particular humans, to thrive. It now needs to be revived and re-nurtured.

Preventing, detecting, and healing children's traumas

Beyond and in relation to parenting, another priority should be to adopt a holistic approach to prevent, detect, and heal children's traumas. This includes home visits, care coordination with schools and other institutions, mental health care for parents and children, nutrition and medication, and a ban on corporal punishment.[29] Adverse childhood experiences (ACEs) are traumatic events that can profoundly affect a child's developing brain and body. They can be physical, emotional, or sexual abuse; physical or emotional neglect; growing up in a dysfunctional family with one of the parents struggling, for example, with mental illness or substance abuse; an incarcerated relative; a mother treated violently; or a divorce.

It is incredible to realize how common ACEs are. In the ACE study carried out from 1995 to 1997 on over seventeen thousand adults in California, 63.9 percent of participants reported having one or more ACEs, while 12.5 percent reported having four or more. Physical abuse (28.3 percent), substance abuse by a household member (26.9 percent), and parental separation or divorce (23.3 percent) were the most commonly reported ones. In 2020, one in ten people in France declared themselves incest victims.[30]

As former president of the American Academy of Pediatrics Dr. Robert

W. Block noted, "Children's exposure to Adverse Childhood Experiences is the greatest unaddressed public health threat facing our nation today."[31] In fact, compared to a person with none, studies have shown that a person with more than four ACEs is:

- 2 times as likely to be overweight or obese,
- 2.2 times as likely to have ischemic heart disease,
- 2.4 times as likely to have a stroke,
- 1.9 times as likely to have cancer,
- 1.6 times as likely to have diabetes,
- 12.2 times as likely to attempt suicide,
- 10.3 times as likely to use injection drugs,
- 7.4 times as likely to be an alcoholic,
- 32.6 times as likely to have learning or behavioral issues.[32]

A person with six ACEs has a life expectancy twenty years shorter than a person with no ACEs.[33] This essentially results from the impact of toxic stress associated with ACEs on the fundamental biological functioning of the body, and in many children, the healthy development of their brain architecture. The effects can be so profound that they can be seen through brain imaging. While ACEs make one more likely to engage in risky behaviors (smoking, drinking, etc.) that can explain part of the negative health effects, they themselves are consequences of the unhealthy brain and body development of a child.

Toxic stress is the "extreme, frequent or extended activation of the body's stress response without the buffering presence of a supportive adult."[34] This overactivation of the body's stress response system leads to its dysregulation, with many negative effects in children's brains and bodies, including on the nervous, hormonal, immune, and cardiovascular systems, even interfering in the way DNA is read and transcribed.[35] While cognitive capacities may become more prone to anxiety and fear, they may also be affected negatively in the areas of attention, memory, decision-making, and critical thinking.[36] Beyond the developmental, health, and educational impact of childhood traumas, ACEs are at the root of many social issues: from violence and crimes—for childhood violence is the best predictor of adult violence[37]—to their impact on the economy through decreased productivity.

We can prevent, screen for, and heal these children's toxic stress. So why are they mostly left unattended? In 2019, Nadine Burke, a pioneer in this field, became California's first surgeon general with a mandate to scale up work on ACEs across the state. In her great TED talk, she confessed, "At first, I thought we marginalized the issue because it doesn't apply to us. That's an issue for those kids in those neighborhoods."[38] But she realized the data does not bear that out. In fact, the vast majority of the participants in the ACE study mentioned above were white (74.8 percent) and had attained a college-level education or higher (75.2 percent). In the US, 74 percent of the parents in 1999 reported hitting their children,[39] while 47 percent reported hitting very young children in 2004![40]

Burke's experience with ACEs led her to ultimately understand things completely differently. She concluded, "I am beginning to believe that we marginalize the issue because it does apply to us. Maybe it's easier to see in other ZIP codes because we don't want to look at it. We'd rather be sick. Fortunately, scientific advances, and frankly, economic realities, make that option less viable every day." It is time to start facing up to our traumas, that are often passed from one generation to the other, and grow aware of the toll trauma takes on societies and many of us. It is time to heal, so that something really new can develop. This is a considerable part of the politics of being. We need to develop trauma-informed approaches to health care, education, social work, criminal justice, etc.

Healthy partnerships

Finally, if family needs to be recognized as the basic unit on which society builds, we need to emphasize the importance of a healthy partnership as the basis for a healthy family. As nineteenth-century French historian Jules Michelet put it, "To harmonized souls, it is already a society. It is already a world. The harmony found once is the same from here to the stars, the same for the Milky Way."[41] While each partner's self-actualization is a condition for a good relationship, the latter can be cultivated through specific support and training.

In the Plum Village tradition, we use the practice of "beginning anew" as a way to take care of our relationships through deep listening and loving speech. This is particularly important for maintaining healthy and authentic communication within couples, impeding the accumulation of misunderstandings and frustrations by way of weekly practices. We sit in front of each other, with flowers in between. The one who speaks has the flower vase, and the one who listens needs to remain silent and not provide any answer or feedback to what his or her partner says, just listen deeply. The practice has the following four steps:[42]

- Expressing appreciation of our partner's qualities with as much concrete detail as possible. Good seeds need to be watered to grow. This is effective in preparing the ground for our partner to open up and listen to us, including our difficulties, but should be done authentically, with no ulterior motive.

- Expressing regrets and apologizing for anything you have done that may have hurt your partner.

- Asking for more information to understand what is going on in our partner's mind and heart: Have I hurt you? Do I understand you enough?

- Expressing hurt or disagreement, emphasizing your own way of receiving your partner's actions or words and their psychological roots as the cause of your hurt, rather than these actions or words by themselves. You may invite your partner to explain why he or she did something, recognizing your limited perceptions of what happened, and ask for his or her support.

Eventually, one can also practice this informally in daily life, as well as between adolescents and parents, to reestablish communication, allowing love and suffering to express themselves, fueling a process of reconciliation.

12

Education

"*Spiritual education is not a distinct and separate discipline;
it is part and parcel of all types and levels of education; in fact,
it is the very foundation on which a lasting edifice can be built.*"

—Sathya Sai Baba, Indian guru (1926–2011)

E DUCATION IS A cornerstone of a nation's transformation. It played a key role in the processes of industrialization and democratization, and its purpose should now be redirected to the next stage of our evolution. It lies at the core of the politics of being, itself a strategy for inner development. The purpose of our education system should be to support the awakening and actualization of children's true being. It should help them to grow as authentic human beings—in all their dimensions: physical, emotional, aesthetic, moral, intellectual, and spiritual, which, as we will see, all seem to reinforce one another— and to develop the highest qualities, such as the ones we analyzed in part II. As our educational system should reflect the society we want to inhabit twenty or thirty years from now,[1] learning should help children develop more evolved worldviews.[2] It should prepare them to embody the paradigm shift from the story of separation to the story of interbeing. Nowadays, this often means unlearning!

Character and positive education

In 2014, the World Education Summit for Education (WISE)[3] asked six hundred and forty-five education experts, representative of its worldwide community, about their views on the future of education. Seventy-five percent of those surveyed believed that the most valuable assets for students in 2030 will be personal skills (e.g., the ability to interact with others, make sound decisions, or manage time effectively), way ahead of know-how and practical skills (59 percent) and academic knowledge (42 percent). Knowledge is now widely accessible online for free, and work is rapidly evolving, including with the development of artificial intelligence that redefines the kind of added-value humans can have. In the twenty-first century, lasting professional success will increasingly rely on personal skills, maybe the only ones that will accompany people all their lives. These skills will help us navigate complex and changing environments, work effectively in teams, contribute positively to our communities, and address the many life challenges we face.

Modern education has tended to emphasize the transmission of knowledge and certain cognitive capacities to prepare for professional success. The emotional sphere has mostly been left out. According to American-Portuguese neuroscientist Antonia Damasio, this is a major factor in the decline in moral behavior in modern society due to the scientifically evident role of emotions in sound moral behaviors. The concept of emotional intelligence only appeared in the early 1990s with the work of psychologists John Mayer and Peter Salovey on overcoming the reductionist view of intelligence, as expressed in the intelligence quotient. Mayer and Salovey defined emotional intelligence as "the ability to monitor one's own and others' feelings and emotions, to discriminate among them and to use this information to guide one's thinking and actions."[4] According to them, emotions are internal events that coordinate physiological responses, cognitions, and conscious awareness. The concept became very popular after the 1995 publication of *Emotional Intelligence—Why It Can Matter More than IQ* by Daniel Goleman, who was then a science journalist at the *New York Times*. Goleman stressed five ingredients of emotional intelligence: self-awareness, emotional control, self-motivation, empathy, and handling relationships.[5] The concept was soon incorporated into education through the Social and Emotional Learning (SEL) movement.

A quickly growing body of experiences and academic research now emphasizes the individual and social benefits of a large variety of educational approaches centered on the integral development of children, teenagers, and young adults. Sometimes rooted in long-established so-called alternative pedagogic systems (Montessori, Freinet, Steiner-Waldorf, etc.), they often build on new scientific understanding of learning and brain functioning. While it is traditionally feared that the focus on individual characters and personal skills could supplant the time needed to learn content, studies show that, on the contrary, these approaches can generate benefits in terms of well-being and character, while improving academic achievement. Improving children's personal capacities just helps them learn better.

One of the emblematic umbrella terms for this approach is "positive education," which aims to develop well-being, resilience, flourishing, and optimal functioning in children, teenagers, and students, along with traditional skills.[6] Beyond the scientific evidence of the many benefits happiness brings to individuals' development, interest in positive education has also been a response to the mental health crisis that has hit children and adolescents. Globally, 10 to 20 percent of them experience a mental disorder at some point,[7] such as depression, anxiety, or behavioral disorders; it's a rising trend in Western countries.[8] The 2018 State of Mental Health in America mentions that the rates of severe youth depression have increased from 5.9 percent to 8.2 percent in the last five years.[9]

Positive education interventions encompass a diversity of approaches and labels. Common examples are the Social and Emotional Aspects of Learning (SEAL) program implemented in many UK secondary schools, Kids Matter in Australia, the Penn Resiliency Program implemented in many countries, and the high school positive psychology program.[10] Such programs usually focus on the development of a wide range of skills and capacities, such as emotional competence; self-awareness and control; problem-solving and decision-making (especially through flexibility, judgment, and ethics); social awareness and empathy; relationship skills; self-efficacy and realistic optimism; positive emotions (joy, gratitude, interest, hope, etc.); perseverance; meaning ... [11] Many positive education programs have proven to be effective in reaching their goals, in particular through increases in connectedness, engagement, perseverance, motivation, and concentration.[12]

The mental health benefits can be very significant. For example, the Life Skills Training that has been deployed in the US for the last twenty years has achieved a 45 percent decrease in cannabis, alcohol, and tobacco consumption six years after its end.[13] The Bullying Prevention Program, initially developed in Norway before spreading to many other countries (Germany, UK, US, etc.), has managed to cut the number of aggressions by half.[14] Contrary to many past programs that focused on values and character building, these now can claim to be evidence-based.

Mindfulness is becoming a central resource in character development because of its demonstrated benefits in terms of attention and learning skills, well-being, resilience, as well as social and emotional skills.[15] Mindfulness programs for teachers, students, and schools are multiplying around the world. They include the mindful school program, that has trained more than fifty thousand teachers, reaching over three million pupils all over the US and in more than a hundred countries; the mindfulness in schools project[16] in the UK; MindUp;[17] or the Wake Up schools[18] movement rooted in Plum Village's approach to mindfulness. By calming their minds and bodies, students and teachers can pay more attention to what is happening within themselves and others, as well as to what is being taught, and make the most of each school day. There is evidence that mindfulness may contribute to establishing a level playing field among students. Children with more learning difficulties, who often come to school with significant emotional burdens, may benefit most from it.[19]

Values, cooperation, community, and service

Cooperative learning is sometimes part of positive education programs. It consists of students working together to jointly complete specific tasks and assignments that require collaboration to achieve learning goals.[20] Implemented since the nineteenth century, cooperative learning has been proven successful in terms of academic achievement, as well as in improving cooperation, empathy, relationships, well-being, moral sense, and reducing discrimination, bullying, drug addiction, delinquency, and violence in school.[21] The best educative effects have been observed amongst the most diverse groups in terms of skills, sex, culture, and motivation.[22] Rather than looking down upon children with more difficulties, the more advanced ones feel responsible for supporting their peers, allowing them to gain self-confidence and motivation.[23] They all become more engaged in learning. We see that mainstreaming cooperative learning is instrumental for moving out of a worldview based on competition and separation and the disastrous consequences it brings, especially to our social ties.

Beyond cooperation, to achieve an ethical evolution, the politics of being calls for a reflection and practice on values, starting with young children. Modern education has generally shied away from teaching values, although it is permeated by some, such as competition. Nowadays, many schools in the world have adopted values education as an effective strategy for promoting a healthy environment in which students learn and grow as human beings.[24] Universal values, such as respect, responsibility, trust, tolerance, openness, kindness, courage, humility, generosity, etc., can be promoted by schools through teaching and interactive discussions among children. Children should not be passive receivers of abstract teachings, but on the contrary, should be able to openly discuss day-to-day conflicts and problems from the perspective of these values. This can help them to develop their capacity for philosophical inquiry, to understand each other's perspectives, and find effective responses to moral problems.[25]

There should be a particular emphasis on the development of communication skills to help resolve conflicts and develop healthy relationships. Nonviolent communication techniques have been adapted to suit children and classroom needs in that perspective. This includes, for example, the "clear message" method developed by Quebec teacher Danielle Jasmin, which is now taught in many schools.[26] Jasmin has also established "cooperation councils" to discuss and make decisions on class life with pupils.[27] Inspired by Freinet pedagogy, these councils are helpful in practicing values such as cooperation, citizenship, and democracy. Students' involvement in decision-making in their classrooms and schools has been shown to contribute positively to character development and academic achievements.[28]

Community service and service learning (which integrates community service with the academic curriculum) help to connect theory with practice and can enrich a value-based education system. They have great academic and character benefits.[29] They should be promoted on a large scale, including through regulation and the establishment of mandatory national civil services that can play an important role in fostering social cohesion, to endorse a culture of awareness of social issues, compassion, and service. This is particularly important for the better-off students and those attending tertiary education. As inequality grows, their daily experience drifts further and further away from most other people's. They are too often unaware of harsh social realities and challenges that they, as future leaders, should be sensitized to.

Studies have shown that, at least in the US, upper-class individuals display less compassion than their lower-class counterparts do.[30] Community work can be an eye-opening experience for privileged individuals that can fundamentally alter their professional trajectories and the decisions they make in the future.

Arts and sports

Artistic practices are essential to our cultures' vitality and the integral development of children, in particular their creativity, imagination, and emotional and aesthetic intelligence. Such practices are essential for awakening children's capacity for awe and appreciation of the beauty, greatness, and depth of our existence and world. Long-term artistic experience has been shown to nurture resilient plasticity in the brain,[31] which is associated with our creativity and personal evolution. As mentioned in the UNESCO Road Map for Arts Education:

> 21st Century societies are increasingly demanding workforces that are creative, flexible, adaptable and innovative and education systems need to evolve with these shifting conditions. Arts Education equips learners with these skills, enabling them to express themselves, critically evaluate the world around them, and actively engage in the various aspects of human existence.[32]

We see the intrinsic importance of stressing education in and through the arts in curricula. Moreover, research has shown that artistic practices improve academic achievement, including by allowing students to metabolize information in their own way.[33] This is particularly effective for students with more difficulties.[34] Other individual and social benefits— mental health, self-confidence, better relationships, school attendance, and lower drop-out rates, etc.—are also in evidence.[35]

Physical activity is another building block of an integral education. It is indispensable to health, well-being, and cognitive development, and supports the development of relational and cooperative skills, in particular through team sports. The World Health Organization published in 2019 a study of 1.6 million adolescents (eleven to seventeen years old) in one hundred and forty-six countries that concluded that some 80 percent of them do not comply with the recommendation of getting at least an hour of physical exercise each day.[36] While modern values, especially in the West, have tended to disproportionately favor intellectual knowledge, our physical fitness is also very important for our mental capacities. Improving students' moods and brain functioning helps them concentrate, learn, memorize, and ultimately perform better.[37] The benefits are greater when sports are practiced outdoors. An education of being strengthens our connection to our bodies.

Communities of inquiry

Instead of filling pupils with knowledge, which is constantly evolving, educators should rather teach them how to search for and think critically about the mass of information they are surrounded with, and build their capacity to unmask the most widespread types of errors and illusions on the way to knowledge. These often stem from simplification—the common mental structure behind all fanaticism, which Edgar Morin calls the "spirit of war."[38] Children should learn to envision problems systemically, in all their dimensions and interrelations, and develop complex thinking. Teachers can also support the development of children's meta-learning capacities (their capacities to reflect on and adapt their learning), including metacognition (their awareness and understanding of their own thought processes).[39]

As American futurist Alvin Toffler (1928–2016) wrote, "The illiterate of the 21st century will not be those who cannot read and write, but those who cannot learn, unlearn and relearn." Broad education, in particular humanities, should always go along with expert knowledge in order to be able to put this knowledge in context and develop the capacity to navigate a complex world and constantly approach new learnings.

Moreover, the organization of academic curriculums around subjects (mathematics, history, biology, etc.), which does not correspond to students' natural ways of inquiry, can be complemented by an approach based on interdisciplinary topics. This is precisely what Finland has done since 2015.[40] In Costa Rica, the environment is recognized as an overarching theme in all primary and secondary education, together with human rights and peace. This emphasis involves direct contact with nature, for instance through visits to protected areas, or environmentally themed service projects.

Schools should become communities of inquiry, with a particular concern for the central social issues of sustainability and equity.[41] This materializes in service learning, community service, and through participation in the school's management. "In the end, practitioners and students come to see school itself as a project, aimed at the transformation of self, school, and society."[42]

By learning the story of the universe, the Earth, and humanity, and most importantly, their own societies and cultures, students can better understand the current challenges we are facing and put them into context and perspective. They can reflect on the human condition and develop an evolutionary perspective, as well as a sense of interconnectedness in our earthling community. They can understand the very special times we are experiencing, how we got here, and what unique contribution they can bring to this great Earth transition. Thus school becomes a resource to fulfill one's purpose in life. As I write this, all over the world, students are striking against climate change, reminding us that education without purpose is unsustainable.

Personalized approaches

In the WISE study mentioned above, an overwhelming 83 percent of experts surveyed believed educational curricula in 2030 will become more personalized to suit each student's needs, a trend that is already observable in many OECD countries. Alternative pedagogies such as Montessori or Freinet have long emphasized the need for content to adapt to students' interests and rhythms. This way, learning becomes easier, more natural and harmonious, while students develop autonomy and responsibility. An integral education is an organic growth process through which children's unique potential or spiritual being awakens and flourishes. On the other hand, an education that tries to fit each pupil in the same mold can cause irreversible harm by disconnecting them from their own selves.

Seventy-three percent of WISE experts believe that the role of teachers will shift toward guiding students along their autonomous learning paths. Teachers are to accompany what is asking to be manifested in the children. Teachers' skills and personal development are instrumental for most of the approaches presented above to be fully effective. Their benefits will remain theoretical if they are not properly implemented in a way that is adapted to their context. I know many parents who are into alternative education, whose ideological convictions prevent them from recognizing that a good conventional education is sometimes preferable to an imbalanced alternative one. Teachers not only need to commit to these practices but must know how to integrate them as a coherent and effective whole.

They need also to personify these values in order to infuse their classrooms and provide a role model for their students. That will require a change in teacher selection—with inner development becoming a central criterion—experience and age, education, lifelong training, and a review of their position and salary.

Beyond teachers, what we need are whole-school approaches, in which educational organizations commit to these values and embody this cultural change all around. Some successful examples of this approach are UK's Wellington College or Australia's Geelong Grammar School.[43] More and more, the aim of educational organizations will become like that of Tecmilenio, a fast-growing private university with twenty-nine campuses across Mexico. It has committed to being a "positive university," delivering "a learning community that cultivates the best self in each person, allowing them to flourish, discover their purpose in life, and benefit society."[44] Finally, parents, whose involvement in their children's education is a well-established factor of academic success,[45] should be involved in these educational projects through school-based parenting programs so that they can also be in line with these pedagogical approaches.

Based on the above, we can better understand the success of the Finnish educational system, which is a globally acknowledged example. Indeed, it incorporates many of the highlighted strategic orientations, as well as others also emphasized by research.

Box 6—The Finnish Educational System

The main objective of Finnish basic education (from age seven to sixteen) is to support students' personal growth as individuals and as members of society.[46] Students are given a lot of freedom in how they spend their time in school, with many practices inspired by alternative pedagogies (Montessori, Freinet, etc.) and, at the upper secondary level, in choosing what courses to follow.[47] Students with learning difficulties are identified and receive part-time or full-time special education. This is the case for some 30 percent (22 percent part time, 8 percent full time) of Finnish comprehensive school students (aged seven to sixteen), a much higher rate than in any other OECD countries.[48] The rich Finnish learning environment encompasses technological facilities, lessons outdoors, and excursions to museums, companies, etc.[49]

According to the Government of Finland, "Highly competent and motivated teachers are the cornerstone of the Finnish education system."[50] All comprehensive school teachers have a master's degree. They are well-paid and socially recognized: there are five times more candidates than people selected to become teachers.[51] Particularly well-trained in pedagogy and teaching in a way that is tailored to how different people learn, teachers have a large autonomy in choosing their teaching methods. This reflects a culture of trust and delegation of authority that characterize the Finnish education system, in which a core curriculum is applied nationwide,[52] though there is no sanction where this is not respected. The rest is designed by teachers in cooperation with the school—which is generally maintained by local authorities or joint municipal consortiums[53]—parents, and the community.

Teaching methods often include cooperative learning, a focus on interdisciplinary topics, and project-based learning that connect students to real-world issues from multiple perspectives. Finnish teachers do not emphasize grades in their assessment, which usually fosters competition and can have a negative impact on pupils' self-esteem. Grades become obligatory when children are around fourteen years old.[54] Qualitative insights and encouragement are favored through a dialogue with the children. Children spend less time in school than in other countries—usually from 9:00 or 9:45 a.m. to 2:00 or 2:45 p.m.—and have very little homework.[55]

Finnish children are very physically active; schools ensure that all pupils get at least one hour of exercise each day.[56] The Finnish school system has been built on the egalitarian principle of a good-quality universal education, where almost all institutions are free and public. Free healthy lunches are provided to all pupils.[57] The learning gap between the weakest and the strongest students in Finnish schools is one of the narrowest in the world.[58] Only 1 percent of each age group leave basic education without a certificate, and over half of students complete their education at a later stage.[59] Education is a national priority that the Finnish consider fundamental for their country's success.[60]

Ninety percent of the WISE experts believe that education will become a lifelong endeavor. This may be even more true for the education of being, which cannot wait long. To this end, an adult education system should be put in place or strengthened. Such popular education for inner personal development of young adults was developed at scale in Nordic countries between the mid-nineteenth and twentieth centuries and has probably played an instrumental role in the successful development of these countries until now (see box 7). In addition to helping people adapt their professional skills to an evolving job market, it should help them deepen all the dimensions that have been outlined in this chapter and in this book. Further education can facilitate the cultural change we need, allowing people to grow as individuals and professionals and to adapt and improve their contributions to societies. Being trained and counseled in how to grow as human beings should be recognized as a fundamental human right.

Box 7 - The Nordic Secret: "Popular Enlightenment" ("folk-bildung")[61]

What is the secret of Nordic countries, which, at the beginning of the nineteenth century, were among the poorest in Europe and now rank among the most prosperous, stable, happiest, and culturally evolved countries in the world? Andersen and Björkman believe it has to do with a deliberate effort between the mid-nineteenth and twentieth centuries to lift the majority of the population to a higher level of personal development. These countries' elites understood that to be successful, the transition from feudal agricultural monarchies to industrialized democratic nation-states needed to go along with an evolution of the consciousness of their people. Large-scale investments in character development were needed, in particular to create a sense of belonging and civic responsibility toward their national communities, and later on the ability to think for themselves so that students could make good use of their political power as citizens of young democracies.

The German philosophical concept of Bildung ("folk-bildung" when applied to the people at large) was central in this understanding. While Bildung is a complex concept that can be translated as education or enculturation, it refers fundamentally to the development of personal character toward more consciousness, depth, responsibility, and freedom. It originally developed as a religious concept, and later on acquired a secular meaning while retaining a spiritual connotation akin to spiritual development, enlightenment, awakening, or education of minds and hearts.

From civil society, and with public funding, educational programs or retreat centers—"folk high schools"—were developed, aiming at the cognitive, moral, and emotional development of young adults, in particular the peasant masses, through four- to six-month stays. By 1900, there were some three hundred and twenty-five of these centers in Denmark, Sweden, and Norway. Beyond teaching new productive technologies, these schools provided knowledge that empowers participants, helping them make sense of a changing world while providing them with practical tools for civic engagement. Participants who lived together developed a sense of community and trust, which helped develop meaningful group discussions, through which they could learn to think by themselves and develop their own judgments, moral sense, and purpose. Poetry and songs also provided inspiration and motivation for personal transformations. These schools helped participants elevate their aspirations while deepening the cultural roots and a sense of belonging to the national community.

A century ago, up to 10 percent of each generation attended a folk high school. The folk-bildung philosophy and the values of emancipation and self-organization of the people also permeated national political agendas in the first half of the twentieth century, as did the development of organizations such as cooperatives and sports associations. This leads the authors to estimate that folk-bildung efforts directly or indirectly affected the vast majority of the Nordic population, allowing for the extraordinarily successful development of these countries over two generations.

13

Work and Organization

"Choose a job you love, and you will never have to work
a day in your life."

—Perennial wisdom[1]

WE SPEND A good part of our lives working. This should be an opportunity to develop and express our talents, cultivate meaningful relationships, and contribute positively to the community. Unfortunately, this is seldom the case. Suffering at work is enormous. Every day we come up with new words for it such as boreouts,[2] brownouts,[3] or burnouts. The main reason has to do with our obsolete organizational models that cut across all sectors and types of organizations—public or private, for-profit or nonprofit.

A book is hardly enough to cover all the perspectives on work and organizations relevant to a politics of being. Being skills are becoming central at work, especially for leaders, and many companies support their employees' personal development, including through spiritual practices such as meditation. The most famous example is the Search Inside Yourself Leadership Institute (SIYLI) that originated as a program within Google in 2007. We see the same trend in business schools. It is increasingly recognized that "the need to shift mind-sets is the biggest block to successful transformations," as a 2019 McKinsey quarterly article affirms.[4] Values-driven organizations are also developing and seem to significantly outperform their peers.[5]

Toward "teal" organizations

In this chapter, we will first look into *Reinventing Organizations*, the best-seller by Belgian management author Frédéric Laloux, who spent ten years working in the McKinsey consulting firm. Laloux's work is embedded in integral theory (presented in chapters 2 and 4), which he applies to organizations. According to him, as humanity has gone through different stages of development, our ability to collaborate has been multiplied through new organizational models and breakthroughs. Table 4 below presents an overview of the specific organizational models associated with each development stage before the most recent one, which is the focus of his book.

Laloux selected twelve organizations, which operate in a way that embodies the characteristics of the next developmental stage that he calls "Evolutionary—Teal," which is also often referred to elsewhere as "integrative," "integral," or "yellow," as we have seen. He decided that these organizations could be for-profit and nonprofit, coming from all sectors and geographical areas. They should be sufficiently old—at least five years old—and large enough, employing a minimum of a hundred people. In fact, many of them have been running for decades and have thousands of employees. Laloux studied their characteristics and provided advice on how to start or transform an existing organization into a teal organization. He was wondering if he could find a template for more soulful organizations. According to him:

> The answer, clearly, is positive. These pioneer organizations didn't know about each other and experimented on their own; they work in radically different sectors and locations; some have hundreds, others tens of thousands, of employees. Despite all this, they have—after much trial and error—come up with strikingly similar structures and practices. [...] It means that a coherent organizational model seems to be emerging. [...] This is not a theoretical model, not a utopian idea, but a very concrete way to run organizations from a higher stage of consciousness. If we accept that there is a direction to human evolution, then we hold

here something rather extraordinary: the blueprint of the future of organizations, the blueprint of the future of work itself.[6]

I would be wary of calling this a blueprint that one can dogmatically impose on any organization in any context, but Laloux's model can help us consider what work and organizations would look like under the new paradigm of being: an opportunity for personal growth and flourishing, driven by purpose and intrinsic motivation. This certainly takes on a special relevance at the teal or integral development stage, but it can also inspire healthier functioning modes in organizations operating from a different development stage that can also move toward these objectives without resorting to teal systems.

Self-management

Laloux believes that the new teal organizational paradigm relies on three major breakthroughs, which are all relevant to us. The first breakthrough is self-management, which has also been popularized under the term "liberated company."[7] Power is no longer concentrated at the top but evenly distributed across the company. The organization is usually structured around small self-managed teams, with no boss, no middle management, and a bare minimum of staff teams, support functions (HR, communications, planning, etc.) being incorporated into each team. There is often no organization chart, no job description, nor title. People are not meant to fit predefined jobs but pick up various roles and responsibilities according to their personal interests, talents, and the needs of the organization. Each employee is able to take any decision (including on investments and, to some extent, one's own salary), provided that they previously seek advice from all affected parties and people with expertise on the matter.

Violating this condition can be a cause of dismissal. Usually the decision-maker is the person most affected by the issue or the one who noticed the issue or the opportunity. The process is not based on consensus but in some companies, non-objection is required. All information is available freely to everyone across the organization, in particular through the intranet. Meetings are reduced to the minimum and planned on an ad-hoc basis. Coordination and knowledge exchanges across teams happen organically. Laloux presents common processes and practices that these companies rely on to make self-management work, giving us a concrete sense of how companies operate. We cannot share them all here, and I invite interested readers to dive into Laloux's fascinating book.

An example: Buurtzorg

Buurtzorg ("neighborhood care" in Dutch) is a nonprofit which, in a couple of years, has become the largest neighborhood nursing organization, providing home care to the elderly and the sick in the Netherlands. It is structured around self-managed teams composed of ten to twelve nurses who self-organize to serve fifty patients in a small, well-defined neighborhood. They are collectively responsible for all aspects of their work—including planning, administration, recruitment, etc.—and take all decisions themselves. They receive extremely limited support from regional coaches—who each help forty to fifty teams in finding their own solutions and managing difficulties and conflicts—and headquarters (where thirty people support some seven thousand nurses).

Buurtzorg's organizational model has emerged in stark contrast to the prevailing achievement-orange paradigm dominating this sector until recently. Neighborhood nurses are historically an essential piece of the Dutch health-care system. In the 1990s, the Dutch health insurance system started to promote the grouping of self-employed nurses into organizations. These organizations started soon to merge themselves in pursuit of ever more scale. Tasks were specialized, and new departments appeared, in charge of planning, supervision, communication with patients ... Rather than being responsible for all the treatment of their patients, nurses focused on specific health treatments according to their expertise, for which time norms were established.

Each of these changes makes perfect sense in the Achievement-Orange pursuit of economies of scale and skill. But the overall outcome has proved distressing to patients and nurses alike. Patients have lost the personal relationship they used to have with their nurse. Every day (or several times a day if their situation calls for it) a new, unknown face enters their home. The patients—often elderly, sometimes confused—must gather the strength to re-tell their medical history to an unknown, hurried nurse who doesn't have any time allotted for listening. The nurse changes the bandage, gives the shot, and then is out of the door. The system has lost track of patients as human beings; patients have become subjects to which products are applied. The human connection is lost, and the medical quality is compromised too: there is no continuity in care; the subtle but important cues about how a patient's health is evolving are often overlooked when a different nurse comes along every day. Nurses find these working conditions degrading. Most of them chose their profession out of vocation to care for those in need—nursing is hardly a profession in which to get rich—and these practices make a mockery of their vocation.[8]

Buurtzorg results, from a medical or business point of view, have been exceptional. Buurtzorg patients stay in care only half as long and on average need 40 percent fewer hours of care than patients do in other organizations. Laloux notes that it is ironic as, unlike other organizations, Buurtzorg nurses take time for coffee and talk with the patients, their families, and neighbors. It is estimated that their work allows them to avoid roughly a third of emergency hospital admissions and, when their patients need to be hospitalized, the average stay is shorter.

Ernst & Young estimated that were Buurtzorgs's results achieved by all home-care organizations in the Netherlands, it would result in considerable savings for the Dutch social security system: close to €2 billion. Patients receive the emotional and relational support they need, and nurses have recovered their sense of vocation. Buurtzorg has often been recognized as the best employer in the Netherlands. Six years after its creation in 2006, it employs two-thirds of neighborhood nurses in the Netherlands.

Table 4—Overview of the specific organizational models associated with each development stage[9]

Type of organization	Main features	Current examples	Key breakthroughs	Guiding metaphor
Impulsive –Red	Constant exercise of power by chief to keep troops in line. Fear is the glue of the organization. Highly reactive, short-term focus. Thrives in chaotic environment.	Mafia Street gangs Tribal militias	• Division of labor • Common authority	• Wolf pack
Conformist – Amber	Highly formal roles within a hierarchical pyramid. Top-down command and control (what and how). Stability valued above all through rigorous processes. Future is repetition of the past.	Catholic church Military Most government agencies Public school systems	• Formal roles (stable and scalable hierarchies) • Processes (long-term perspectives)	• Army

Type of organization	Main features	Current examples	Key breakthroughs	Guiding metaphor
Achievement – Orange	Goal is to beat competition; achieve profit and growth. Innovation is the key to staying ahead. Management by objectives (command and control on what; freedom on the how).	Multinational companies Charter schools	• Innovation • Accountability • Meritocracy	• Machine
Pluralistic —Green	Within the classic pyramid structure, focus on culture and empowerment to achieve extraordinary employee motivation.	Culture-driven organizations (e.g., Southwest Airlines, Ben & Jerry's …)	• Empowerment • Values-driven culture • Stakeholder model	• Family

Enabling skills and authentic human development

For self-management to work in practice, Buurtzorg employees receive important training in communication, listening, meeting management, coaching, and other practical skills and techniques for healthy and effective group cooperation and decision-making. Conflict resolution skills are particularly important as teal organizations rely on colleagues to hold each other accountable. Specific trainings, for instance in nonviolent communication, and practices such as mediation are implemented to proactively bring to light and address conflicts. The freedom employees enjoy goes together with a high level of responsibility. Teal organizations tend to believe that all employees have the responsibility to act on any issue or opportunity they sense, even when it falls outside of the scope of their roles. In that case, this implies discussing an issue with a colleague who is part of the conflict. People don't have any bosses to solve their problems or protect them from the harsh realities the company may be facing, as all information on the company is shared openly.

Self-managed organizations treat their employees as adults, giving them all the power they need to perform their work and express their full and healthiest potential. Domination hierarchies—in which one's value is artificially equated with a position on the organizational chart—give space to actualization hierarchies based on skills, talents, character, and colleagues' appreciation. Power, ego games, and extrinsic motivations are replaced by peer recognition, emulation, and intrinsic motivation.

> In teal organizations, people don't compete for scarce promotions. You can broaden the space of your work and increase your pay if your colleagues are ready to entrust you with new roles. They will grant you important roles if you've developed your skills and have shown yourself to be trustworthy and helpful. [10]

Laloux notes that this is similar to the world of the internet, where influence stems from contribution and reputation rather than position. It makes him think that millennials, who many organizational leaders find so hard to manage, may have difficulties putting up with anything other than self-management.

A different perspective on human nature

Laloux points out that teal organizations talk about something more fundamental than their values or missions: their very assumptions about human nature. These often-implicit assumptions determine both the need for hierarchical organizations to control their employees or the teal organizations' foundations of mutual trust. Some of these organizations have felt the need to formalize these assumptions explicitly. Jean-François Zobrist, the CEO of FAVI company—a brass foundry in France with some five hundred employees, who transformed it into a "liberated company," wrote a book on FAVI's management practices, which was subtitled "The Company that Believes that Mankind is Good."[11] Laloux explains that one day, for training purposes, he wrote down the following set of assumptions:

- "The analysis of our organization chart in the 1980s [when FAVI was still run like any other factory] reveals without a doubt that men and women were considered to be:
    - Thieves because everything was locked up in storage rooms.
    - Lazy, as their working time was controlled and every late showing punished by somebody ... who didn't even care to inquire about the reasons for being late.
    - Not dependable because all their production was controlled by somebody else who must not have been very dependable either because random controls ... had been put in place.
    - Not intelligent, as a 'manufacturing engineer' department did the thinking for them.
- Zobrist and his colleagues defined three new assumptions that, over time, have become mantras inside the factory:
    - People are systematically considered to be good. (Reliable, self-motivated, trustworthy, intelligent)
    - There is no performance without happiness. (To be happy, we need to be motivated. To be motivated, we need to be responsible. To be responsible, we must understand why and for whom we work, and be free to decide how)

○   Value is created on the shop floor. (Shop floor operators craft the products; the CEO and staff at best serve to support them, at worst are costly distractions)."[12]

As Laloux indicates, the two sets of assumptions evoke respectively theory X and theory Y developed by Douglas McGregor in the 1960s, when he was a professor at MIT. The natural question that arises is, which of these theories is true? Science has shown that both are. When managers mistrust their employees, considering they only pursue their own self-interests (theory X), they subject them to controls, rules, rewards, and punishments. The employees' responses follow then the same logic: they try to maximize their self-interests, including by gaming the system if needed. When managers assume the employees are intrinsically motivated by their work, they meet them with practices based on trust, to which employees respond with responsible behaviors.

Expressed in terms of development psychology, if you create a strong Amber-Orange structure and culture, people will end up responding in Amber-Orange ways, create a strong enough Teal context and people are likely to behave accordingly.[13]

Collective intelligence and intrinsic motivation as the main drivers of performance

As we will see, these organizations tend to perform remarkably. What is it about self-management that explains these outstanding results? On the one hand, Laloux notes that even though central planning has been proved less efficient than free markets in running economies, it remains the dominant paradigm within organizations. In pyramidal structures, information is split into many departments and has to be consolidated upward so that decisions can be taken by a few individuals. On the contrary, teal organizations trust the collective intelligence of the system and let employees coordinate themselves and make decisions all the time in an organic manner. This trust allows companies to save many of the costs usually associated with supervision, control, reporting, meetings, career management, internal politics, and infighting and dramatically reduces the complexity and length of the decision-making process.

On the other hand, self-management allows companies to drastically improve employees' engagement, which is currently low in most organizations, where only a third of people are considered engaged in their work.[14] People who pursue a meaningful purpose and have the decision-making power and resources to do so are intrinsically motivated. This makes a huge difference in teal organizations. Their employees don't need pressure from above, but they still require feedback on their performance. These organizations focus on team performance and make available all this information, creating a healthy peer emulation. Poorer-performing teams are motivated to improve out of pride. They know this information will not be used against them and that their peers will help them progress. Because teal organizations value intrinsic motivators (freedom, responsibility, fulfillment ...) over extrinsic (status, power, money ...), they have mostly done away with incentives, whether individual or collective, preferring company-wide bonuses.

Wholeness

Laloux calls "wholeness" the second breakthrough teal organizations build on. He notes that "organizations are for the most part, in the true sense of the word, soulless places—places inhospitable to our deeper selfhood and to the secret longings of our soul."[15] We are used to wearing a professional mask at work, which is often "mental, rational, masculine, self-centered,"[16] protecting ourselves out of fear of judgment. In order to feel safe, we distance ourselves from others and from our own emotions, intuitions, longings, callings, souls. "Wholeness" means that teal organizations create a space in which people can fully express who they are and find support to grow into the truest and highest version of themselves. Self-management is already an important step in that direction as it drastically reduces the fear and internal politics that poisons life at work and invites people to invent their roles and bring their unique contributions to the organization. While our ego helps create an artificial sense of safety out of separation, the soul is shy like a wild animal, a place of deep intimacy and vulnerability that needs a safe and caring space to express itself.

Teal organizations have developed general practices to create this evolutionary space. They not only formalize and cultivate their values through collective discussions but turn them into detailed ground rules, providing a concrete vision of a healthy workplace, as well as recommended or unacceptable behaviors. People in these organizations spend a fair amount of time in group discussions, team supervision, and peer coaching to reflect on these values and rules and how best to apply them in concrete work situations. Meeting principles and practices are clearly defined, allowing everybody's voice to be heard and involving, for example, a minute of silence at the beginning to reconnect to oneself, as well as rounds of check-ins and check-outs to share how everyone feels.

Soulful office spaces—self-decorated and warm; open to nature, pets, and children; with no status markers—invite our humanity into the workplace. Reflective practices, such as meditation or walking in nature, help deepen the connections to oneself and others, while specific story-telling practices invite people to self-disclose and build community.

A particular emphasis is on reflecting this culture in human resources processes. The main question about recruitment becomes, "Are we meant to journey together?"[17] Zappos.com, an online shoe retailer, went as far as offering a US$3,000 check to new hires who choose to quit during the first month. Onboarding becomes a crucial process to make sure new employees are well integrated into a company's culture and teams. Significant training, often led by colleagues, is used to establish a common culture and support personal development. One teal organization[18] offers ten free counseling sessions per year to employees and/or their families, trusting that it is worthwhile even if it does not address a professional topic. Working time and commitment versus other commitments in life are discussed and agreed on openly and consciously. Appraisal becomes a joint inquiry into one's learning journey and calling, while caring support is provided to turn dismissal into a learning opportunity.

A conscious approach to wholeness has the power to transform workplaces. "At first we can feel vulnerable when we bring more of who we are into our own awareness and into the community of our colleagues,"[19] points out Laloux. "But once we do, it is as if life has switched from black and white to full color: it becomes rich, vibrant and meaningful. It makes business sense too. Workplaces where we feel we can show up with all of who we are unleash unprecedented energy and creativity."[20]

Listening to evolutionary purpose

Laloux calls the third breakthrough characterizing teal organizations: "listening to evolutionary purpose." Members of these organizations use a new metaphor to describe them. They see it as "a living system, an entity with its own energy, its own identity, its own creative potential and sense of direction."[21] A teal organization's purpose is not fixed or rigidly defined in a written statement but rather evolutionary, discussed orally, and continuously unfolding. Hence, "instead of trying to predict and control the future, members of the organization are invited to listen in and understand what the organization wants to become, what purpose it wants to serve."[22] This is particularly relevant for the complex interconnected world in which we live, where predictions look increasingly irrelevant.

Teal organizations do not waste much time and resources in developing formal corporate and marketing strategies, fixing targets, elaborating sophisticated budgets, and tracking their variance. Decisions happen organically at any time by everyone in the organization. Thanks to self-management, like a living organism, each of the "cells" of the organization constantly senses and responds to its environment. These organizations don't look to define perfect solutions from above; they just look for workable solutions that can be implemented quickly and then can be potentially revisited and improved based on new information. There is no need for change management, one of the most widely discussed aspects of management nowadays; change happens rather naturally and continuously. The important question for decision-making is: what feels right? What is meant to be? This not a purely rational process, but involves the capacity to listen to feelings, intuitions, or even aesthetic sensibility—that can sometimes best process and respond to the multitude of information and signs that the organization members sense.

"Many wisdom traditions affirm that when we act from deep integrity and align with what we feel called to do, the universe conspires to support us,"[23] writes Laloux, who, through concrete examples, shows that this also seems to apply to organizations. Patagonia—a US$1 billion outdoor apparel maker, started based upon owner Yvon Chouinard's passion for nature—is used to making decisions that could negatively affect its profit out of the deep environmental integrity that defines the company's purpose. Unexpectedly, many of these decisions, which involved an initial leap of faith, have turned out to be good for business.

In the mid-nineties, Patagonia decided to sell its thermal underwear without any packaging. While the company feared this would drive its sales down, it resulted in an increase as consumers could feel the material and its quality. As the underwear was displayed like regular clothes, it incentivized the company to make it look like clothing. This prompted consumers to use undershirts like regular shirts, fulfilling the company's goal to make multifunctional clothes.

Around the same time, the company decided to replace all conventionally grown cotton with organic cotton (which cost three times more) in less than two years. This was a crazy bet, but Patagonia felt there was no alternative when it became aware of the extraordinarily high environmental footprint of cotton production. Against all expectations, not only did they retain good consumers and profits, but the whole industry followed the company's example.

Patagonia is also famous for its ad campaign "don't buy this jacket" as part of its "Common Threads Partnership," aimed at making clothes that last longer and at supporting Patagonia clothes' repair, reuse, and recycling. In the short term, this certainly means fewer sales for the company, but more important is its purpose. Teal organizations do not even look at competition as a threat if it can help them achieve their purpose. On the contrary, Buurtzorg has documented and published its innovative ways of operating and invites the competition to adopt them. Its founder even directly advises a competitor on this transition.

Teal organizations choose like-minded providers and do not fear consumer scrutiny. With its "Footprint Chronicles," Patagonia has chosen radical transparency, making all information available, including videos of their factories, to show how clothes are made and what their environmental impact is. While the initiative faced inner reluctance at first, it received so much outside support on improving its practices that it became evident that this was the right thing to do.

In teal organizations, profits and growth are not ends in themselves but accrue from serving the organizations' purpose. They accrue naturally by doing what feels right and help these organizations achieve their purpose. The business and financial results of the twelve companies Laloux studied are extremely impressive. Still, he recognizes they are only anecdotal and not statistical evidence, which would methodologically be very hard to gather. Laloux explains this success is due to teal organizations' doing away with "the many ills of corporate life: politics, infighting, bureaucracy, silos, resistance to change, and so forth."[24] According to him, self-management, purpose, and wholeness liberate "tremendous energies,"[25] and "these energies get harnessed and directed with more clarity and wisdom towards productive ends."[26]

In self-managing teal organizations, the role of top leaders is rather unusual, as decision-making processes no longer converge to them, and they have to let go of the idea of their own importance. Their main role is to hold the space for teal operating principles to go on. These are highly countercultural and always likely to be challenged. Every time a problem occurs, it is tempting, especially for CEOs, to go back to tried-and-proven solutions based on control and create new rules and policies. This can happen insidiously, and teal leaders need to be mindful of these tendencies within themselves and their organizations to defend and reaffirm their unique ways of operating based on trust.

Teal leaders also have a unique responsibility in terms of role-modeling. More than any others, they need to embody their organizations' values, such as trust, authenticity, vulnerability, or courage, to allow other employees to live up to them too. They need the humility and discernment to listen, recognize, and serve their organizations' purpose and soul.

Beyond holding the frame, like any other employees, leaders have to find themselves roles where they can generate value for the organization in a way that is recognized by their colleagues. We see that in their specific roles, their value no longer rests on the quality of their doing but of their being. While they don't have any specific power to make or overturn decisions, their personal, visionary, and relational qualities often confer upon them an exceptional moral authority and a profound influence, which have the power to bring out the best in everyone.

Enabling legal frameworks

Teal organizational practices have a lot to inform how a politics of being can be designed and implemented. Public policies can be important in protecting workers, including their physical and mental health, making companies more accountable to their stakeholders, and ensuring better social and environmental performance, but they don't have much power in shaping how organizations are run. To support the development of teal organizations, the main public issue is having adequate legal frameworks. Indeed, Laloux believes that only two basic conditions are necessary for teal organizations to develop: both top leadership and the owners of organizations should have embraced the teal worldview.

The main problem is that teal organizations may lose their unique way of operating when top leadership or ownership changes. One way to prevent this is for the company to include such principles (e.g., self-management, wholeness, purpose ...) in its constitutional documents or in shareholder agreements. However, the very nature of the company and its fiduciary duty—that, in general, compels it to seek profit maximization—may still stand against these prescriptions. That is why it is important that the legal framework in which teal companies operate allows them to define their specific purpose. This does not need to be profit but could include, in addition to any social or environmental mission, the flourishing of employees.

Many countries and states are adopting legal texts to recognize these new types of corporations, which in some US states are called social purpose corporations (SPCs). These legal texts often also recognize what in the US are called benefit corporations: companies that pursue, together with financial profits, environmental and social benefits. Provided that the right institutional frameworks are put in place to ensure that these types of corporations generate public benefits, fiscal incentives could be designed to favor such companies so that they can progressively replace traditional companies focused on sole profits. Why should we collectively accept that socially destructive companies dominate our economies? From a historical perspective, it is naïve to think this system could hold for long.

Universal Basic Income (UBI)

Beyond organizational models, another policy option with interesting potential to positively transform work has recently emerged. Universal Basic Income (UBI), also known as "citizen's income," is "a periodic cash payment unconditionally delivered to all on an individual basis, without means-test or work requirement."[27] By definition,[28] it is:

- Periodic: paid at regular intervals, such as monthly;
- In cash: so that those who receive it have full freedom on how to use it;
- Individual: and not, for instance, household-based;
- Universal: paid to all, and not targeted to a specific population;
- Unconditional: there is no requirement to work or to demonstrate willingness to work.

In practice, basic income proposals and schemes can take a wide variety of forms—some distinct from the ones mentioned above—differing in terms of:

- Amount: if it is sufficient to meet a person's basic needs, allowing someone to live above the poverty line, it is often called "full UBI." Otherwise it is referred to as "partial UBI." In high-income countries, the generally proposed, sometimes tested amounts are around US$500 for partial UBI and US$1000 for full UBI. In some cases, the amount varies according to the beneficiaries' resources.
- Geographic scale: global, national, regional, or local;

- Targeting and conditionality: it is often geared toward poor people and adults, and in some cases requires availability to work;
- Source of funding;
- The nature and size of reductions in other social transfers that might accompany it.

This idea has a long history, dating back at least to the sixteenth century, and has been proposed under different forms by several prominent figures. Among them are English philosopher Sir Thomas More (1478–1535), American revolutionary Thomas Paine (1737–1809), French socialist philosopher Charles Fourier (1772–1837), British philosopher Bertrand Russell (1872–1970), as well as many famous contemporary economists such as neoliberal Milton Friedman,[29] or (neo)Keynesians James Tobin and John Kenneth Galbraith. We see that its defense cuts across traditional political divisions and includes conservatives, progressives, and libertarians, who support the same idea from different perspectives.

On the right side of the political spectrum, UBI is, above all, considered an effective means of overcoming the scattered, complex, and bureaucratic traditional social safety net systems, which are often costly to run and impede a large number of potential beneficiaries from accessing the support they are entitled to. Basic income is then often targeted to poor people, and its proposed amount is relatively low. Libertarians also see in UBI an opportunity to cut governments' bureaucracy through a partial UBI but insist on its necessary simplicity, supporting its unconditional and universal nature.

Left-wing proponents emphasize UBI not only as an instrument for reducing poverty and inequalities, but also of emancipation and real freedom, as UBI has the potential to enable people to engage in a wider range of self-fulfilling and socially useful activities, a vision aligned with that of the politics of being. Hence left-wing proponents support a higher UBI amount without work conditionality. More recently, many leaders of the tech industry, including Mark Zuckerberg, have supported the idea of a UBI to balance the social effects of the job losses associated with automation and the winner-takes-all business model of the digital economy.

There is no real UBI national scheme yet. However, many countries have social safety nets that aim at guaranteeing a minimum income for every adult, though they often depend on the beneficiary's means and willingness to work.[30] In the past, two countries—Iran and Mongolia—briefly implemented a national UBI.[31] Under Nixon's presidency, the US almost established a guaranteed minimum income. The proposal was "adopted in April 1970 by a large majority in the US House of Representatives, rejected by the relevant Commission of the US Senate in November 1970, and definitively rejected in 1972, despite several amendments meant to assuage the opposition, owing to a coalition between those who found it too timid and those who found it too bold," according to the Basic Income Earth Network (BIEN).[32]

Nowadays, many experiments with "purer" forms of UBI (or "quasi-UBI") are underway in numerous countries, often at the initiative of local, regional, or national governments. As a very simple and transparent concept through which a wide range of social issues and visions can be discussed, UBI increasingly stands at the center of political debates.

The COVID-19 pandemic has strengthened this trend, with massive cash transfers in response to the socioeconomic crisis in countries such as Spain or Togo, sometimes with the support of donors in low-income countries. The United Nations Development Programme has advocated for a temporary basic income to protect the world's poorest people from the effects of the pandemic.[33] In fact, UBI could also play a large role in the future of overseas development assistance. Cash transfer programs in low- and middle-income countries have been used extensively during the last two decades. Research shows they have important lasting positive impacts, outperforming many traditional development interventions. By helping beneficiaries invest in the development of their economic activities and supporting the local demand for goods and services (when the program is universal, benefitting every individual or adults of, let's say, a given village), these programs display very high rates of return after a few years.[34] Children are particularly likely to benefit in terms of health, schooling, and decreased child labor.[35]

A paradigmatic change in our relation to work

I consider UBI a good example of a policy option that can embody and facilitate the necessary change of paradigm in our working lives. Its opponents see it as economic heresy, one that would deter people from work, as if money were UBI's sole purpose. Though not based on pure UBI, past experiences of similar schemes show that this fear is at least exaggerated; the resulting decrease in work is extremely limited or nonexistent.[36] In the Canadian Manitoba Basic Annual Income Experiment in the 1970s, the reduction in work was estimated to be "about one per cent for men, three per cent for wives, and five per cent for unmarried women."[37] Those who worked less often engaged in socially useful activities instead; mothers spent this time with their infants, while working teenagers could more fully dedicate themselves to their studies.[38] A poll in Germany clearly reveals our cultural misrepresentation. When asked what will happen in the case of a UBI, people are much more prone to believe that other people will stop working than that they would do so themselves.[39]

We could also argue that UBI reduces what economists call "unemployment traps," a situation where social benefits that would disappear with employment (unlike for UBI) discourage the unemployed from working. But that just plays on and reinforces the old paradigm of extrinsic motivation. It would be wiser to recognize that in many cases, it is poor mental health that prevents people from working, something that UBI can improve. Finland's experiment in 2017–2018 showed that it can increase unemployed people's well-being and decrease their stress levels.[40]

As seen with Laloux and many others, a more evolved and positive worldview would acknowledge that healthy people are intrinsically motivated to work as a way of fulfilling themselves and serving their communities. Only a sick economic system or certain personal traumas can derail this desire to work. By reducing the economic constraint to work, UBI can help people choose activities that pay less or not at all, but are still deeply meaningful and gratifying, and probably more beneficial for society as a whole. Some may choose a simple communitarian life in the countryside, growing their food and reducing their consumption needs and environmental footprint to the minimum. Others will be able to dedicate themselves more fully to the unique contributions—artistic, social, environmental, scientific, etc.—they want to offer to the world.

UBI would also revalue household work, such as raising kids or caring for a close relative, which is often performed by women. They will gain the financial autonomy that can make so much of a difference in their life choices, such as by allowing them to leave an abusive partner. People would be in a position to demand better jobs and develop their own ventures while enjoying more freedom to build life projects that suit their callings and priorities.

As we reengage in meaningful activities, unnecessary consumption, which often serves as compensation for our frustrated lives, will drop, along with its environmental impact. Contrary to certain fears, the evidence from cash transfer programs in low- and middle-income countries indicates that UBI will certainly not increase, but in some cases will decrease the consumption of goods such as alcohol or tobacco.[41] As a source of economic security, UBI has the potential to help us actualize our truest and highest selves.

Opponents of UBI question the legitimacy for people to receive money without working. Many UBI supporters consider it a right deriving from the natural common property of the earth. Long ago, before the invention of agriculture, there were no property rights on the land and other natural resources. We were free to sustain our lives through hunting, fishing, and gathering plants, fruits, nuts, wood, and water. With the advent of agriculture, farmers started to generate an added value by cultivating the land, but this value came from something they did not create: the land itself, over which they had no natural rights. While there was enough land for everybody, this was not a problem as it did not result in an actual loss of access to resources. Otherwise the loss of access to these resources could very well justify compensation for the rest of the people, as a percentage of the value produced from that land.

Nowadays, as Earth citizens, don't we all have the same natural rights over our planet's resources, which are, in one way or another, incorporated into any goods or services produced?[42] The question becomes increasingly relevant as our economic model is jeopardizing the ecological conditions—and social conditions, as in the case of automation—for human life on Earth.

Some UBI proponents consider that this right also stems from the inherited technical progress from previous generations. Unlike the story on which intellectual property rights are based, what we call innovation is often the last link of a long chain of innovations. So why should the last innovators reap all the benefits resulting from this long chain of innovation? Does Mark Zuckerberg really deserve to own US$70 billion[43] just for having envisioned Facebook a couple of weeks or months before others? Can we seriously believe that?

Finally, UBI critics believe that societies cannot economically afford such huge costs. This is a valid question for any significant social transfer, but this all depends on the specific form a UBI takes: its amount, the savings on other social transfers or tax increase (for example on non-poor receiving a UBI as a way to neutralize these costs) that would accompany it, its eventual conditionalities ... The debate has to integrate all aspects of UBI, including its funding. UBI source of justification can point toward different potential sources of funding, including general state budget, money creation, or earmarked taxes on carbon, robots, artificial intelligence technology, or wealth. I believe that one important point of attention is that a UBI should support our transition out of the paradigm of economic growth, rather than strengthening it as a means to fund a UBI. This means that a full UBI may only be suitable if it goes along with a deep social transformation.

A full UBI is a powerful vision that helps us rethink our relation to work, our social solidarity, and economic systems. However, it may not be politically feasible in the short term. It may emerge as a part of a broader cultural transition, along which its amount would gradually increase, its conditions progressively lifted as institutions, mindsets, and behaviors adjust to the new paradigm of which UBI is part. As recognized by the Basic Income Earth Network (BIEN), "The fight for basic income is not an all-or-nothing affair. This is no game for purists and fetishists, but for tinkerers and opportunists."[44] There are many pathways to UBI, such as negative income tax, or basic incomes subject to conditions of revenues, work willingness, or considering households rather than individuals.

All these conditions can have negative effects (shame and social stigma, complexity, costs, disincentives, etc.) and do not necessarily provide the expected advantages.[45]

As explained, work unconditionality, in particular, is central to the potential benefits UBI can bring in terms of emphasizing our intrinsic motivation to work, increasing the bargaining power of workers and the incentives for the work supply to provide meaningful and fulfilling jobs. However, instead of a willingness-to-work condition, I believe a broader condition of social contribution, including self-employment, education, housework, or volunteering, may be an adequate temporary solution as we transition toward the paradigm of being. This was proposed by British economist Anthony Atkinson under the name of "participation income." A politics of being reclaims the sacred nature of work: we should all have the right to express our full potential for the benefit of all.

14

Health

"Health is a state of complete mental, social and physical well-being, not merely the absence of disease or infirmity."

—World Health Organization

LIFE EXPECTANCY HAS drastically increased with economic development in the last two hundred years. At a global level, life expectancy at birth has increased from an estimated thirty-one years in 1900 (in the richest countries it was still below fifty years) to 72.2 years in 2017.[1] This was initially driven by improvements in sanitation, housing, education, vaccines, and antibiotics, that caused a decline in early and midlife mortality mainly associated with infections, such as smallpox, cholera, measles, polio, typhoid, or viral hepatitis. As the risk of infections has decreased, long, slow, chronic diseases—such as cardiovascular and chronic respiratory diseases, cancer, or diabetes—have become more prevalent, representing some 75 percent of global health-care expenses.[2]

A decline in late-life mortality, which has been linked to how we can now prevent and treat these chronic diseases, has been the main cause of the increase in life expectancy in rich countries over the last decades. Chronic diseases are not passed from person to person but, beyond our genetic predispositions, are a result of our lifestyles (physical activity, food, sleep, drug, alcohol, tobacco consumption, stress and mental health, etc.), as well as social and environmental factors.

COVID-19 has been a wake-up call about the importance of universal access to quality medical care. The politics of being also calls for a new paradigm for health care, more in line with the WHO quote above. We need to move away from a health approach focused on sickness, whose increasing costs for an aging population seem unsustainable,[3] to one centered on prevention and well-being, in which individuals are more responsible for taking care of themselves. In health as in other sectors, human potential is enormous. Leveraging this potential should accompany the many technological breakthroughs that are about to deeply transform this sector. They include big data and artificial intelligence, genetic engineering, regenerative biology and medicine, tissue engineering, cancer genomics, and immunotherapy, precision medicine.[4]

Promoting healthy lifestyles

Because of the evolution of our diets, as well as an increase in physical inactivity related to sitting down all day at work, urbanization, and changing modes of transportation, worldwide obesity has almost tripled since 1975. In 2016, it was estimated that more than 1.9 billion adults (39 percent of the population) were overweight, of which six hundred and fifty million were obese (13 percent of the population).[5] This was a significant factor in the development of chronic diseases that can be reversed through the promotion of physical activity and healthy diets (see next chapter).

The World Health Organization recommends that each adult do at least two and a half hours, or ideally five hours, of moderate-intensity aerobic physical activity per week. Beyond the benefits in terms of well-being and fitness, exercising reduces general ("all-cause") mortality, the risk of chronic diseases (e.g. coronary heart disease, high blood pressure, stroke, type 2 diabetes, metabolic syndrome, colon and breast cancer, etc.), depression, and vertebral fractures.[6] Alcohol, tobacco, and drugs also take a terrible toll on consumers' health. They cause an estimated 9 percent of the years of healthy life lost globally,[7] with some ninety-one million people affected by alcohol and fifteen million by drug-use disorders in 2002.[8]

Beyond diet, physical exercise, and tobacco and alcohol consumption, which were the traditional focus in preventing chronic disease during the second half of the twentieth century, recent research has increasingly emphasized the negative effects of stress. Stress is a healthy and protective physiological response: it makes our bodies work harder to effectively respond to danger. But when stress becomes chronic, it exhausts us. The constant need to mobilize energy in the form of glucose can lead to obesity or diabetes. Blood vessels' chronic constriction and higher levels of blood-clotting factors tend to cause hypertension and heart disease. Our immune, digestive, and reproductive systems are negatively affected, while our cognitive functions decline. We develop memory and sleep problems, as well as an increased risk of depression.

According to Gallup's 2019 global emotions reports, over a third of people worldwide said they experienced "a lot of stress" the day before the polling was carried out. The US ranked seventh among the most stressed-out countries, with 55 percent of respondents reporting having experienced a lot of stress, compared to 46 percent in 2006.[9] We have already seen in chapter 9 the potential of meditation, in particular mindfulness, to contribute to stress reduction and mental and physical health. Meditation should be made accessible to the widest possible audience, as part of a public health strategy, including public funding of associated costs.

Mental health

The mind's capacity to influence our body has been traditionally recognized in virtually all cultures. It is central in some traditional medicines such as Indian Ayurveda—often described as an art of being—or traditional Chinese medicine, according to which diseases originate fundamentally in people's minds and hearts. These types of medicine consider how such conditions affect our lifestyles and the way we treat ourselves, others, and the world, leading to metabolic and energetic imbalances, toxin accumulation, symptoms, and eventually acute illness. Thus the foundations of health are healthy minds, hearts, and lifestyles, and the harmony between body and mind, person, society, and nature.

These traditional medicines associate certain emotional or psychological imbalances with specific organs, functions, or pathologies. They emphasize cultivating our health potential, the life in us, to prevent disease before symptoms appear and address the fundamental causes of illness. From that perspective, a medicine of the whole being is necessary—"Health is a state of complete harmony of the body, mind and spirit," said the famous yogi Iyengar (1918–2014). Diseases, as manifestations of inner imbalances, call for a reconnection to our bodies, hearts, minds, and spirits. They can be considered an opportunity for personal evolution, which our health-care system could facilitate. This is also true at the collective level. In fact, we can hope that the COVID-19 pandemic will help heal our societies.

Modern science has only recently developed the understanding of how stress, depression, or hostility—i.e., mental health—can affect our physical health, including heart disease, infections, and aging.[10] The World Health Organization (WHO) defined mental health as "a state of well-being in which every individual realizes his or her own potential, can cope with the normal stresses of life, can work productively and fruitfully, and is able to make a contribution to her or his community."[11] We have seen that it is closely associated to human flourishing[12] and lies at the center of the politics of being.

More than one of every three individuals in the world experiences a severe mental health problem in their lifetime,[13] such as depression and dysthymia—persistent depressive disorder—(four hundred and four million people in 2010 or 6.8 percent of the world's population), anxiety disorders (two hundred and seventy-two million people in 2010 or 4 percent of the world's population), schizophrenia, or bipolar disorder.[14] These numbers have shot up during the COVID-19 pandemic. Mental health accounts for some 32 percent of years lived with disability, and together with all cardiovascular and circulatory disorders, it is the leading cause of years of healthy life loss.[15]

People who are mentally ill are 50 percent more likely to die than other people of the same age,[16] and those who have been admitted to a hospital for mental health reasons have a life expectancy fifteen to twenty years shorter than those who have not.[17] Mental illness is the single most important cause of unhappiness (before physical illness, income, or unemployment)[18] and also has huge consequences on families and society. Economic costs of mental ill-health have been conservatively estimated at 3–4 percent of GDP in the European Union, with most of these costs occurring outside the health sector through reduced work and productivity, as well as disability benefits.[19]

Mental illness and chronic diseases are highly interdependent and tend to co-occur. Chronic disease significantly raises the likelihood of mental illness, which in turn affects an individual's ability to participate in treatment and recovery.[20] Reciprocally, mental disorders are important risk factors of chronic disease, both directly and indirectly, through health-risk behaviors such as tobacco use, alcohol or drug consumption, poor diet, or low level of physical activity.[21] In fact, mental disorders share so many common features with chronic diseases—underlying causes and overarching consequences, integrated approaches as the best response, etc.—that the World Health Organization has called for a transformation of health systems to provide a common integrated and multisectoral response to them both.[22] For example, they require a life-course approach, the promotion of healthy lifestyles, and people-centered holistic care in which patients are actively involved, as well as coordination and integration between different professionals involved in health care.

Despite the considerable importance of mental health, access to treatments and care remain incredibly low. In rich countries, less than a third of people who suffer from mental illness receive treatment and care.[23] In low- and middle-income countries, the situation is considerably worse. Average spending on mental health stands at 2.8 percent of total government health spending,[24] reaching 5 percent in rich countries.[25] From 2000 to 2014, only 0.4 percent of development assistance funding was directed toward mental health, which was not included in the Millennium Development Goals.[26]

However, effective and relatively inexpensive treatments exist and should be made universally accessible. Drugs and evidence-based psychological therapies, especially cognitive behavioral therapies (CBT), have been developed, with rigorous assessments of their effectiveness.

Studies have shown that for depression and anxiety disorders, these treatments led to recovery in over 50 percent of cases, with psychological therapies having much lower relapse rates than drugs.[27] Mindfulness-based interventions are also effective and can be combined with these approaches.[28] Importantly, the growing understanding of neurological manifestations of mental health issues and the fact that those can now be detected through neuroimaging is paving the way for the development of precision psychiatry. Beyond making mental health issues more tangible, it should help detect and prevent them at an early stage and improve treatments' effectiveness.[29]

It is even more difficult to understand the treatment gap when considering the very low costs of these therapies and comparing them to the high social costs associated with poor mental health. Beyond the important well-being benefits for patients, it is probable that funding mental health treatments may result in a net economic gain for society. So why are mental illnesses so discriminated against? Some argue that mental illnesses are still often perceived as an individual or family problem in rich countries, and mental health care is considered a luxury in low- and middle-income countries.[30] I believe that addressing mental health essentially implies a cultural evolution of both our health-care system— whose operating system has long focused on depersonalized bodies—and societies, which need to grow more aware of the importance of people's inner lives for human and social flourishing.

Healing trauma

Psychological trauma lies at the root of many mental health issues. A global study in both rich and poor countries found 70 percent of respondents had experienced at least one type of a traumatic event in their life.[31] In fact, to varying degrees, we all have our own traumas that prevent us from living our lives fully. Many spiritual teachers nowadays encourage us to heal trauma as the condition for new individual and collective ways of being to become possible. To grow as individuals, we first need to heal the wounds of our past, which so often control and limit us.[32]

Trauma affects the brain in ways that make people more vulnerable to negative emotions, in particular fear, and others such as shame or anger, which often leads individuals to adopt emotional avoidance strategies. Trauma distorts perceptions, constricting the inner space from which we can respond and not only react to specific events. It tends to reenact the very situations from which it originated. Trauma disconnects us from ourselves and each other and keeps us at a lower level of human development. These issues are often passed down from generation to generation, through culture, education, and, as recent studies indicate, through epigenetics too. In fact, new research suggests that people's experiences can change the way their DNA is expressed or read, and this change can be passed on from generation to generation (see box 8).

Box 8—Epigenetics and Intergenerational Trauma

While analyses on plants and animals have generated more robust evidence to date,[33] studies on human beings have found some evidence of intergenerational transmission of trauma effects, even though the biological mechanisms for that are not yet clear. Children of Holocaust survivors, for instance, have been shown to have inherited epigenetic changes in relation to a gene that regulates the entire stress hormone system. As a consequence, they display lower levels of cortisol—a hormone involved in the stress response—which makes them more prone to developing post-traumatic stress disorders (PTSD), depression, and anxiety disorders. Second-generation survivors have also experienced changes in metabolism, leading to increased risk for obesity, hypertension, and insulin resistance.

Evidence of traumatic effects passed on to following generations though epigenetic mechanisms have also been documented in the case of US confederate prisoners of wars[34] or Swedish people confronted by food shortages in the late nineteenth century.[35] The fact that these traumas' effects have only been passed on to male descendants indicate that the modifications would concern the Y chromosome.

Because we all live in cultures distorted by trauma, we are used to taking for granted trauma's features in our collective lives—disconnection and antisocial behaviors, fear and anger, apathy and denial, addictions of all sorts: to wealth and power, to consumerism and oil—and the intractable problems this creates. "Left unacknowledged and unresolved, the dark energy we carry hardens into the wicked problems of our time,"[36] warns Austrian spiritual teacher and collective trauma therapist Thomas Hübl. Healing trauma has now become a necessity for the cultural evolution we need: it is the gateway to being. As physician Gabor Maté affirms: "Every human being as a true genuine authentic self and the trauma is that disconnection from it and the healing is that reconnection with it."[37] This healing needs to happen both at the individual and collective level.

Access to treatments for trauma should be developed and should go beyond traditional cognitive-behavioral therapy to include new therapeutic approaches such as Eye Movement Desensitization and Reprocessing therapy (EMDR).[38] Making trauma healing a priority requires greater investments in research to improve current approaches and support therapeutic innovations based on recent scientific developments, such as neurofeedback.[39] Beyond meditation, spiritual traditions have many valuable practices and insights to offer to this end. They deserve scientific inquiry and validation, something that has already started with psychedelics, which are traditionally used to heal trauma in different cultures (see box 9).

Finally, we need to also move beyond an individual approach to trauma, as many traumas have common causes, such as sexual assault, or are ingrained in our history, such as with the injustice against indigenous people in many countries. These are social and cultural issues we need to look at collectively. Public hearings of testimonies, talking circles, ceremonies, and reconciliation efforts, including through symbolic or material reparations, can help us heal. What matters is our capacity to be fully present with the whole of ourselves in such healing processes to be able to really feel and acknowledge what has happened, what we have done, and how that still resonates within each of us and our cultures. Only then can we integrate, heal, and transcend our pasts to freely build our futures.

Box 9—Treating Post-Traumatic Stress Disorders through Ecstasy?

In 2017, the US Food and Drug Administration (FDA) officially designated MDMA—a psychoactive drug that is the basis of Ecstasy—a potential "breakthrough therapy" and fast-tracked a phase III clinical trial of it to treat post-traumatic stress disorders (PTSD). The Israeli government has also approved clinical trials of MDMA-assisted psychotherapy for PTSD.[40] According to Matthew Johnson, PhD, associate professor of psychiatry at Johns Hopkins University School of Medicine, and author of psychedelic research studies: "In previous research, the improvements were so dramatic that two-thirds of people will look like they no longer meet the clinical criteria for PTSD a year after treatment. Even if large-scale trials can only demonstrate an effectiveness rate of half that, it's much better than anything available currently."[41] It looks so promising that in 2020, a *Fortune* magazine article was published, titled: "Business Gets Ready to Trip: How Psychedelic Drugs May Revolutionize Mental Health Care."[42]

Building health-care workers' human capacities

Investments in building the human capacities of health-care workers are also a priority for a politics of being. Most experts agree that doctor-patient relationships are increasingly strained as a result of hyper-medicalization and hyper-specialization, lack of time and emphasis on financial profitability, and lack of confidence and ethical failures.[43] This relationship is generally framed as a technical transaction, whose human dimension is neglected, with bodies treated as if nobody lived in them. Patients are implicitly asked to entrust their health to doctors, fostering disconnection from their bodies instead of empowering people to take responsibility for their health. This is very unfortunate as doctors' capacity to empathize, listen, and communicate with their patients has always been known to be important for health outcomes, even before scientific studies confirmed it.[44] This capacity influences access to relevant information from patients, compliance with treatments, and is even therapeutic in itself.[45] It is crucial in activating the potential for self-healing in patients, which is often called the placebo effect.

"Natural forces within us are the true healers of disease," said Hippocrates. Deep listening can in fact be very healing: it allows people to express their suffering, externalize it, and reduce their stress levels. As an energetic therapist, I can often physically sense in my hands the effects of the conversations I have with my patients. An emotionally charged sentence can catalyze a sudden release of blocked energies. Placebo effects are also based on the attitudes and beliefs of patients in relation to a cure and, more generally, the caregivers' personal capacities. If many traditional doctors were once called "medicine men," it was because they themselves were known as the medicine and needed to cultivate their own healing potential to be effective.

Building health-care workers' capacities is important to help them cope with stress, risks of burnout, and compassion fatigue, to which they are particularly exposed. According to a recent report from the National Academy of Medicine, between 35 percent and 54 percent of nurses and doctors in the US have substantial symptoms of burnout, an all-time high.[46] The main causes include unmanageable workloads; inadequate technology (that hinders rather than supporting patients' care); moral distress associated with suboptimal clinical experience; norms and processes that conflict with personal and professional values; administrative burdens; and a lack of support. Organizational solutions—positive work environments, reduced administrative burdens, improved technologies, etc.—can be complemented with training (in particular mindfulness, as presented in chapter 9) and personal support and services to help people prevent, alleviate, and recover from burnouts.

A multisectoral health policy

Finally, changing our focus from sickness to prevention and health would result in a multisectoral health policy. Childhood and family environments, work conditions, food and sports, urban planning, housing, social support, and gender equity are all important aspects to consider in such a policy.[47] The list becomes even longer when considering the importance of the environment and the sectors affecting it.

Our health is not separated from that of the planet. Environmental degradation takes a huge health toll, whose consideration should be sufficient per se to prompt us to take action. The World Health Organization has estimated that environmental factors account for 22 percent of the years of healthy life lost globally.[48] This is particularly true for low- and middle-income countries. The French public administration has conservatively estimated the health costs—health-care costs, production loss, loss of years of life, loss of well-being, etc.—associated with environmental degradation at some 7.5 percent of GDP.[49] Natural habitat losses are spreading zoonotic diseases such as dengue fever, malaria, yellow fever, or Ebola.[50] Climate change accentuates this trend and could unleash unknown lethal viruses and bacteria that have been trapped in the permafrost—which is now melting at an alarming rate— for thousands of years. COVID-19 may prove to be only a gentle warning for what could come as a result of widespread environmental destruction.

Another major threat to public health that has recently emerged is the growing exposure to radiofrequency electromagnetic fields (RF-EMF), such as those due to mobile networks and Wi-Fi. Biological effects at very low levels of exposure to electromagnetic fields and radiofrequency radiations have been clearly established.[51] It seems they result in adverse health effects, as many peer-reviewed scientific studies have shown for humans, animals, and plants.[52] The International Agency for Research on Cancer (IARC), the cancer agency of the World Health Organization (WHO), concluded in 2011 that EMF frequencies between 30 KHz and 300 GHz are possibly carcinogenic to humans. More studies are needed to better understand these health impacts, including on the specific frequencies the 5G networks will use.[53] However, in view of important business opportunities and concerns of competitiveness— the global 5G market is expected to reach US$277 billion by 2025[54] and will allow the development of new digital services, for instance with the internet of things[55]—many governments are already rolling out 5G networks, in clear violation of the precautionary principle.[56] In

France, frequency licenses have already been scheduled before the public agency in charge of evaluating associated health risks is due to finalize its report.[57]

5G deployment would substantially increase such exposure (and the electricity consumption associated with it[58]), with dramatic potential public health effects. This is a good example of putting essential needs (health) at risk for the sake of economic growth, through the development of digital services whose effects on well-being are dubious. On the other hand, as of mid-2020, many local governments, in particular in Europe (in Switzerland, Brussels, Rome, etc.), have halted 5G deployment due to health concerns.[59] In addition to this moratorium, current efforts to limit the exposure to radiofrequency electromagnetic fields (RF-EMF) should be strengthened.[60] This can include:

- Drastically lowering "maximum total exposure standards" as many studies have reported bioeffects and adverse health effects with much lower exposure levels: in the case of cell-tower radiofrequencies, adverse effects have been shown with exposure levels one thousand to ten thousand times inferior to current standards;[61]

- Reviewing the composition of scientific panels in charge of defining these standards to ensure these have the appropriate skills and no conflicts of interest;[62]

- Public information campaigns on the risks of RF-EMFs and adequate behaviors to mitigate them;

- Promoting wired digital communication.

However, the single most important social determinant of health, at least in rich countries, is income inequality.[63] To some extent, it affects all of us, from the richest to the poorest, in particular through the loss of social capital and greater stress due to the competition over social status. In rich countries, average life expectancy is unrelated to health-care spending. Americans spend on average five times more on health care per capita than Estonians but still have shorter life expectancies.[64]

By focusing on prevention, well-being, a healthy environment, and lower income inequality, we could greatly improve our health. A major hindrance for implementing such an approach is that it challenges our development model based on economic growth (and its reductionist mindset), which is the basis of our current disease-centered health system. In this obsolete model, the pursuit of economic growth creates health problems (through pollution, inequalities, stress, etc.), for which it offers treatments, both accounting as economic production. A health model centered on prevention and well-being would spur new business opportunities, for example in personal health data management, but would also mean abandoning certain economic activities that do more harm than good to our societies.

The new paradigm of integrative medicine

The policy agenda that we have presented outlines integrative medicine as the new paradigm for health care, with its emphasis on prevention and well-being, patients' empowerment, and the consideration of the full range of physical, emotional, mental, social, spiritual, and environmental influences that affect a person's health.[65] Integrative medicine is also patient-centric (not disease-centric); it favors personalized treatments and views patients and practitioners as partners in the healing process. Informed by evidence, it makes appropriate use of both conventional and complementary methods (also called "alternative," such as traditional Chinese medicine, Ayurveda, naturopathy, chiropractic, etc., which in many cases can be more cost-effective than conventional treatments[66]), favoring whenever possible natural and less invasive interventions that can stimulate the body's innate healing responses. Integrative medicine promotion entails new research, education, and reimbursement strategies, as well as improved coordination of treatments and public policies, well beyond the traditional field of health care.

15

Food and Agriculture

"We are what we eat."

—Perennial wisdom

OOD SHAPES INDIVIDUALS—NOT only bodies, but genes,[1] brains,[2] emotional states,[3] mental health,[4] and cognitive capacities[5]— societies, and environments. Through food, we interact with ourselves, the Earth, and each other. Hence our relationship to food needs to be very conscious, guided by an ethical framework. Almost all religions have some rules about what to eat or not eat that highlight the sacredness of food and the need for gratitude, respect, and compassion toward the animals we eat, as well as hygiene and health concerns. While religions hark back to these high ideals, unfortunately, these are often no longer in tune with current contexts and challenges.

Mindful diet

Changing our diet by reducing or eliminating our meat consumption is, in general, the most powerful action individuals can take against climate change. Our global food system is associated with roughly a third of global emissions of greenhouse gases and 70 percent of global freshwater use.[6] Meat, in particular red meat, as well as dairy are major contributors to climate change, because of the lands deforested for cattle ranching or feeding, and methane emissions.

According to the Intergovernmental Panel on Climate Change (IPCC):[7] "[M]eat [...] was consistently identified as the single food with the greatest impact on the environment." In the US, beef represents 4 percent of the food sold by weight, but 36 percent of food-related greenhouse gas emissions.[8] Meat and dairy products only provide 18 percent of calories and 37 percent of proteins consumed worldwide, but take up an overwhelming 83 percent of agricultural lands.[9] Reducing meat consumption has tremendous potential: if the world were to go vegan and no longer consumed meat or dairy products, net greenhouse gas emissions from the global agricultural sector would be more than halved.[10] In the case of a vegetarian diet, this decrease would be 39 percent, and 35 percent for a flexitarian diet with limited meat (one portion per week) and dairy consumption.

At the same time, reducing meat consumption in high-income countries would translate into a major improvement in public health. A recent study, consistent with many others, showed that adopting healthier diets (which entails reducing red and processed meat intake) could reduce relative risk coronary heart disease, colorectal cancer, and type 2 diabetes by 20–45 percent, while reducing US health-care costs by US$77–93 billion per year.[11] In most parts of the world, healthier diets are not necessarily more expensive: on the contrary, they often cost less or the same as unhealthy food.[12]

Another important study has demonstrated that by 2050, we could feed the whole global population well while respecting the Earth's limits through the worldwide adoption of a "planetary health diet."[13] This diet could be symbolically represented as a plate filled half by fruits, vegetables, and nuts, while the other half would consist of primarily whole grains; plant proteins (beans, lentils, pulses); unsaturated plant oils; modest amounts of meat[14] and dairy; and some added sugars and starchy vegetables. Governments should actively promote this kind of diet, including through information campaigns (including standardized, color-coded nutrition labels); customized educational support to households; public cafeterias (with the additional benefit in places like France of potentially ending toxic debates on whether or not to offer special meals for religious reasons); and regulation and taxes (e.g., on junk food, meat, etc.).[15] A healthy diet goes beyond meat and dairy reduction and also means consuming more unprocessed, unpackaged products, which is also important for the environment.[16]

Diet is a key factor, not only for our physical but also mental health.[17] This has been especially well documented in children and adolescents' emotional, cognition, and behavioral disorders,[18] as well as for adults' depression,[19] violence,[20] and cognitive decline,[21] for example. Our food does affect our brain, which can be confirmed by MRI scans. A Western diet—characterized by lower intakes of nutrient-dense foods and higher intake of unhealthy processed foods—has been associated with a smaller hippocampus,[22] the brain structure involved in learning, memory, and mood regulation, which is specifically implicated in depression. Reciprocally, stress and poor mental health (as in the case of eating disorders) can affect our food behaviors,[23] and mindfulness-based interventions have been proven effective in promoting healthy eating and treating eating disorders.[24]

Besides environmental and health concerns, my personal commitment to eating no meat is above all ethical, based on a respect for life that is, in general, completely absent from the modern meat industry. While humanity has eaten meat since time immemorial, traditional animal husbandry has nothing to do with the industrial meat production system, in which animals' sensitivity, their very condition as living beings, is simply denied. That is the basis of the growing vegan movement and the more general concern for animal well-being, which calls for improved regulation, including the recognition of some rights to animals. Watching videos of a slaughterhouse is the surest way to quickly become vegan and we, in general, don't take the plunge simply because we don't want to face up to it and take responsibility. Each year, one hundred billion animals are killed to feed humans,[25] and many of these through a soulless industry.

The suffering of these animals is not separated from our suffering. It affects us, in particular slaughterhouse workers. There are many personal accounts that suggest these workers are particularly prone to developing mental health pathologies. Beyond self-disconnection or "doubling" and post-traumatic stress disorders (PTSD) in these workers, a spillover of violence from slaughterhouses to their surrounding communities has been seen in evidence. Indeed, a correlation has been found at the county level in the US between slaughterhouse employment and increased arrests for violent crimes, rape, and other sexual offenses.[26] Violence against animals can easily turn against humans. Lakota chief Luther Standing Bear (1868–1939) reminded us: "The elders were wise. They know that man's heart, away from nature, becomes hard; they knew that lack of respect for growing, living things soon led to a lack of respect for humans too."

Another ethical issue with important environmental and social consequences is the need to reduce food loss and waste, that amount to roughly a third of global production and is closely associated with our global agri-food system organization. Food is sacred. In many families, wasting it is not acceptable. Why do we, as societies, allow this to happen? Target 12.3 of the SDGs aims at halving these waste and losses by 2030. This could roughly contribute to a 5 percent decrease of total greenhouse gas emissions.[27]

Industrial agriculture: an obsolete model

The transformation of our agricultural systems is emblematic of the great transition that needs to take place. This sector, more than any other, embodies the patterns and dysfunctions of our current growth-based development path. Over the last few decades, industrial agriculture has imposed itself as the dominant model. An increasingly concentrated set of corporations have had the power to shape the organization and functioning of the global food system for their own profit. They capture a growing part of the sector's value, added through the commercialization of technology-based solutions. Their business flourishes as they provide temporary solutions to the problems their model creates. To soil depletion, they respond with more fertilizers; to pests and diseases with more pesticides; and even now, to climate change with GMOs that could tolerate drought and store more carbon.

Industrial agriculture's mode of operation is reductionist. It considers agricultural land a mere production factor and not an ecosystem integrated into a landscape. Production relies on monocultures of a limited number of crops and varieties and the application of standard technological packages and external inputs to a single end: maximizing profit.

Production and profits have considerably increased, but at great cost for the environment (biodiversity losses, water pollution, climate change, etc.), public health, and even long-term agricultural productivity[28] as lands degrade, agrobiodiversity vanishes (around 75 percent of the world's agricultural diversity was lost in the last century[29]), and antimicrobial resistance grows. Furthermore, over the past forty years, this industrial agricultural model has not allowed us to significantly reduce the number of people suffering from hunger—eight hundred and twenty-one million in 2018—who are mostly smallholders. It is also associated with new forms of malnourishment (nutrient deficiencies, overweight, obesity), which increasingly affect all countries.[30]

Because of soil degradation and the way it is processed, industrial food tends to provide low levels of micronutrients (vitamins and minerals) that are fundamental for our nervous system and thus our general human development. Micronutrient deficiencies alter our epigenetics and can even lead to physical degeneration (chronic diseases, changes in skeletons such as damaged facial bone structure, tooth decay, etc.).[31] Additionally, agriculture is probably the industry with the highest suicide rate,[32] especially as the current model of production pushes farmers to go into debt to buy the inputs and machinery sold by corporations. It is clear that this industrial agricultural system needs a fundamental transformation to address the new challenges of sustainability, resilience, and food security in a changing climate.

The new paradigm: agroecology

The ongoing change of paradigm in agricultural science is toward agroecology, which is increasingly seen as the main strategic orientation needed to address the current failures and challenges of our global food system. Though agroecology as a term was coined in the 1930s, traditional agricultural methods have always included some agroecological practices.[33]

While there is not a single definition, agroecology aims above all at "maximising the use of ecological processes in the functioning of agro-ecosystems, with a view to achieving sustainable food."[34]

As a discipline, agroecology stands at the "crossroads between agronomy, ecology and social sciences, with a preference for systemic approaches."[35] It is also often associated with social equity issues such as power distribution, farmers' technical and financial dependency, food security, consumer choice, etc. While powerful economic interests—closely linked to governments, media, and academic institutions they finance—pretend to respond to the current crisis through more technology, markets, and export-oriented agricultural models, an international scientific and grassroots food movement is now calling for a transformation of the global food system in support of small-scale agroecological farming systems.[36] Leading international research agencies, panels of international experts and UN agencies, and social, environmental, and consumer organizations are calling for a transformation of the agri-food system based on agroecology.[37]

The agroecological transition is an evolutionary process toward smarter, more complex models of agriculture, better suited to the heterogeneity of local circumstances, that embody some of the highest values presented in Part II to characterize the shift in consciousness we are calling for. The transition is pointing toward the ecologization of our agricultural systems that should work with nature instead of against it, and the adoption of more integrated, systemic perspectives on all the interrelated challenges that come with agriculture, recognizing the complexity inherent to both endeavors.

In practice, agroecology opposes the domination of a handful of international corporations by building farmers' autonomy from the global agri-food system. Indeed, it encourages farmers' control of seeds and agro-ecosystems whose productivity and resilience builds on biological diversity and the optimization of biological interactions[38] rather than external inputs. Cultivating soil health, synergies between different components of diverse production systems (crop covers, associations and rotation, organic fertilizers, integrated crop-livestock systems, agroforestry, etc.), and the biological control of pests and diseases are among the main strategies. Agroecology also challenges conventional scientific practices and hierarchies by recognizing the need for farmers and scientists to cocreate knowledge.

While regenerative agriculture is sometimes used as a synonym for agroecology and emphasizes soil regeneration, permaculture is a widely popular form of agroecology rooted in indigenous worldviews. It is based on a particular philosophy and ethics emphasizing care for the Earth, care for the people, and fair share, with design principles that can be applied beyond agriculture.[39] Organic farming shares some aspects with agroecology—the rejection of synthetic inputs such as fertilizers, pesticides, feed additives, hormones, and the use of biological solutions—but in other ways they differ. Organic farming practices are controlled through certification and do not exclude all practices associated with industrial agriculture, such as monoculture, integration into international value-chains, and a greater reliance on external inputs. Organic farming in 2017 accounted for some 69.8 million hectares (1.4 percent of global farmland) and 2.9 million farmers,[40] and this market is growing quickly.[41] Such data is not available for agroecology, as it lacks clear definition criteria and entails practices that can be implemented to different extents.

An increasing body of research shows that agroecology in some circumstances can compete with industrial agriculture's yields, while being much more ecologically and socially sustainable, as well as resilient.[42] A recent study has shown that a fully agro-ecological production system in Europe could meet balanced food requirements for five hundred and thirty million Europeans by 2050 while generating multiple benefits.[43] They include improved public health (thanks to improved diet and reduced pollution); environmental gains (including, through reduced pollution, a 45 percent decrease in net greenhouse gas emissions compared to 2010 and the development of agro-ecological infrastructures[44] favorable to biodiversity on 10 percent of cultivated land); and greater resilience (climate change adaptation of the sector and increased food sovereignty).

In order to support this agroecological transition, governments should:[45]

- Shift public support and procurement toward diversified agroecological production, taking into account the true social costs and benefits of different production systems (considering the environment, public health, and resilience);

- Develop new holistic strategic approaches and indicators for sustainable food systems;

- Support short supply chains and alternative retail infrastructures;

- Strengthen movements that unify diverse constituencies (farmers, researchers, consumers, ecologists ...) around agroecology to gain political power;

- Mainstream agroecology into education and research agendas, which are currently dominated by private interests that favor marketable technology-based solutions over nature-based solutions. Because the latter are less commercially profitable, public institutions have a greater role in developing and promoting them.

Food localism

As mentioned, agroecology often goes hand in hand with food localism. While relocating our food production may not, per se, decrease greenhouse gas emissions through reduced transportation[46] (except for products imported by air[47]), it is essential to ensure food security and our general resilience, as the COVID-19 pandemic reminded us. Local food networks, as well as urban agriculture initiatives—especially in the case of community growing—can strengthen social ties and communities' resilience.[48] The incredible edible movement, which started in the UK in 2008 before extending to more than seven hundred locations worldwide, has done this by transforming urban public spaces into vegetable gardens open to all. By allowing everyone to work and harvest vegetables and fruits, it has provided a renewed sense of trust, abundance, and conviviality. By the way, why aren't there any fruit trees in our cities?

Local food networks can also reconnect us to the landscape. Everybody, both in rural and urban areas, should have the opportunity to be involved in farming on a small scale, with proven well-being, physical, and mental health benefits.[49] This would greatly enhance our connection to the Earth and its wisdom, making us more aware of its laws and dynamics, its seasons and subtle balances, and more respectful of the magic of life.

16

Nature

"Mother Earth is a living being. Mother Earth is a unique, indivisible, self-regulating community of interrelated beings that sustains, contains and reproduces all beings."

—Universal Declaration on the Rights of Mother Earth (2010)

MANY OF THE necessary policies to address our mounting environmental challenges are well-known. As a professional in this field, it is sometimes depressing for me to see that legitimate platforms, such as the Intergovernmental Panel on Climate Change (IPCC), stress these policies again and again, report after report, while governments take few concrete actions. Most of these policies concern specific sectors, and we have already had a chance to discuss some of them (see the chapters on Education, Food, and Agriculture, and Economics for example). They fundamentally entail a paradigmatic change, which is why it seems so hard to implement them. In this chapter, I will focus instead on a couple of policies that best embody this paradigm shift in the way we consider and relate to our planet: as a sacred living entity, of which we are part.

The rights of nature

We need to recognize that the Earth, its ecosystems, and nonhuman living beings also have rights. We should be wise enough to acknowledge these rights and enforce them, in order to protect ourselves from our own insanity. This movement has already started. In a growing number of countries, court rulings and legislations have started to recognize the rights of Mother Earth,[1] rivers,[2] forests,[3] mountains,[4] animals[5]—including great apes[6] and dolphins[7]—etc., whose legal status has traditionally been that of "objects." We have already mentioned Ecuador and Bolivia as pioneers on this front.

In 2017, after granting legal personhood to a forest and before recognizing the rights of a mountain, the government of New Zealand granted legal personhood to the Whanganui River through the "Te Awa Tupua Act" (in reference to the river's indigenous name). It recognized the river as a legal person with all the rights, powers, duties, and liabilities therein.[8] This was an attempt to settle an old legal dispute with a Maori community over the interpretation of the Treaty of Waitangi, a treaty declaring British Sovereignty in 1840 and defining Maori land ownership, which is generally considered the founding document of New Zealand as a nation. The legal text recognized the Maori tribe's spiritual connection to the river, expressed in their saying "Ko au te awa, ko te awa ko au" ("I am the river and the river is me"), and gave the Maori the legal capacity to represent the river in court proceedings. Maori consider the river their ancestor, and they believe they have the responsibility and privilege, as family members, to care for it.

While customary indigenous laws worldwide have recognized the rights of nature for centuries, the idea to recognize them in modern legal systems was introduced in 1972 by professor Christopher Stone, from the University of Southern California, in his famous essay "Should Trees Have Standing? Toward Legal Rights for Natural Objects."[9] Stone's article and its defense of nature's rights was a response to the US Court of Appeals in California. The court had just denied the Sierra Club, an environmental NGO, the right to oppose the Walt Disney construction of a ski resort in Mineral King Valley (in the Sierra Nevada Mountains), on the grounds that the Sierra Club itself had not been injured by the project. Stone admitted that his proposal might appear "frightening or laughable,"[10] as had any previous attempts to confer rights onto other similar entities in the past.

Women, children, and slaves were once considered "legal things" with no right to stand in court, and people's court claims were dismissed before these rights were finally recognized. From that perspective, the extension of rights to nature is somehow the continuation of an historical process—that of the widening of our "circle of concern." Together with the deep ecology philosophy, which insists on the inherent worth of all living beings, the Earth jurisprudence concept, forged by American Catholic theologian Thomas Berry (1914–2009), has also significantly influenced the movement to enshrine nature's rights into law. It recognizes that humans are only one part of the Earth community, in which the welfare of each member is dependent on the welfare of the Earth as a whole. It considers the Earth as the primary source of law and affirms that human governance systems must be derived from and comply with the natural laws that govern life.[11]

Together with many indigenous people's philosophies and spiritualities, Berry's concept formed the basis for the Universal Declaration on the Rights of Mother Earth. This declaration was drafted in 2010 during the World's People's Conference on Climate Change and the Rights of Mother Earth held in Cochabamba, Bolivia, in which thirty-five thousand people and delegations from more than a hundred countries participated. The declaration affirms that: "We are all part of Mother Earth, an indivisible, living community of interrelated and interdependent beings with a common destiny." It states:

> The inherent rights of Mother Earth are inalienable in that they arise from the same source as existence. [...] Just as human beings have human rights, all other beings also have rights which are specific to their species or kind and appropriate for their role and function within the communities within which they exist. The rights of each being are limited by the rights of other beings and any conflict between their rights must be resolved in a way that maintains the integrity, balance and health of Mother Earth[12].

These rights include the "the right to life and to exist"; "to maintain its identity and integrity as a distinct, self-regulating and interrelated being"; to "integral health" and "well-being." While the text called on the General Assembly of the United Nations to adopt it, this has not yet been the case. The text was adopted as Law 71 of the Plurinational State of Bolivia.

Many questions and flaws remain on this "rights revolution" and how to implement it, including the definition of a rights bearer (i.e. nature, species, ecosystems, etc.), the bearers' rights, and how to find a balance between the rights of different beings, including humans.[13] Furthermore, some critics believe that recognizing nature's rights is unnecessary as "modern environmental law is moving towards a recognition of the intrinsic value of nature, puts breaks on property rights, offers remediation actions for pure ecological damage and also increasingly grants environmental NGOs wide access to courts."[14] These critics also stress that the results of these policies on nature conservation in Ecuador and, to a greater extent, in Bolivia, are not convincing. In fact, the enforcement of these rights has relied to a large extent on the willingness of these countries' governments, which have prioritized economic development through extractive development models.[15]

However, giving rights to nature seems an increasingly appealing ecocentric alternative to the current anthropocentric paradigm, one that has been endorsed by prominent players such as the International Union for the Conservation of Nature (IUCN)[16] or Pope Francis.[17] As stated in the Universal Declaration on the Rights of Mother Earth: "In an interdependent living community, it is not possible to recognize the rights of only human beings without causing an imbalance within Mother Earth." The hope is that the rights of nature may balance the rights people and corporations have, to allow a harmonious coexistence between all living beings.

Decisions enforcing this balance would certainly be controversial, but our legal systems are used to adjudicating conflicts between different rights, such as human rights to free expression and nondiscrimination.[18] Recognizing the rights of nature has the merit of questioning our unlimited rights to exploit the Earth, and their legitimacy. It invites our legal systems to probe: what do we really need as human beings to thrive? How can we fulfill our material needs in a way that minimizes the impact on our environment? Recognizing nature's rights is the way for human beings to become responsible members of the Earth community.

The acknowledgment of nature as a subject of rights could go along with the legal recognition of severe environmental destruction as a crime. Making economic and political leaders accountable for such crimes would be a powerful legal lever to deter them. Like crimes against humanity, those against nature are starting to be legally recognized through the notion of ecocide.[19] This is already the case in more than ten countries, including Russia, Ecuador, and Vietnam. However, it is not yet recognized as a crime by the International Court of Justice, despite several attempts to do so, most recently in 2019 by Vanuatu and the Maldives. The deep environmental crisis calls for adding ecocide to the International Court of Justice's criminal statute, together with genocide, crimes against humanity, war crimes, and aggression.

Subtle medicine for the Earth

Recognizing Mother Earth as a living being would also lead us to consider that its body—which is also our extended collective body—needs healing and nourishment. It needs our love and care. This body has not only a material dimension, but also a more subtle one, with energetic centers and channels (some are called "ley lines") similar to what Ayurvedic medicine calls chakras and nadis in the human body. This subtle dimension should be cared for as part of an integral Earth medicine, a knowledge that is deeply rooted in many indigenous cultures, whose sacred sites often correspond with these energetic centers.

Many traditional cultures give offerings or "payments"[20] to the Earth (food, flowers, rituals, etc.), as a way not only to express their gratitude but also to feed and energetically sustain the deities in charge of these sites, which the Romans named genii locorum (singular genius loci). They know that taking care of these sacred sites, which could be considered as analogous to acupuncture points for the Earth, is important to maintain the balance of their territories and of the planet itself. Traditional cultures know these places intimately and are aware of how they need to be managed physically and spiritually. The Kogi people from Colombia are particularly respected for having preserved such knowledge and practices. They call this Earth energetic network "shikwakala" and say it:

[I]s an invisible thread, created in the spiritual world, that completely encircles the Earth from East to West, forming a web of connections between the Earth, the sun and the rest of the universe. [...] That is what we call shikwakala. It is the sum of all these threads that, connected, help to sustain the universe, that, under the forms of paths, traverse the Earth.[21]

Kogi shamans now travel out of their territories to perform their rituals on other sites. They have even started to participate, together with modern scientists, to territorial diagnoses—for example in 2018 in the Drôme region (France)—where they can identify these important energetic points, their functions ("missions"), and how they ought to be managed.[22]

I was once hiking with a friend and two guides in Andohahela National Park in southeastern Madagascar, where these beliefs are part of the local culture. I arrived breathless with my twenty-kilo backpack at the top of the hill and saw a tree covered with bills. Tired and giddy from the climb, I did something inconsiderate. I burst out laughing at this tree that seemed to grow money and began ripping it off, between one cracked joke and another. My guide took the bills right out of my hands and put them back on the tree. He seemed serious, concerned, and started to recite a prayer, asking for the spirit of this place to forgive my offense. I understood my lack of respect and felt sorry.

We spent the whole afternoon going down several hills along riverbeds, under the protective shade of this beautiful forest, until we reached our campsite for the night. It was next to a river, with natural swimming pools and waterfalls. Our two guides left us there, after having shown us which way our destination was for the following day. One good thing about spending a night alone in the middle of the forest in Madagascar is that there are almost no dangerous wild animals. The biggest land predator is the fossa, something between a cat and a mongoose, while snakes, spiders, and scorpions are mildly venomous at worst. These were my thoughts as I fell asleep.

But I had bad dreams that awoke me that night. Someone was hitting my tent overhead. Alarmed, I understood this was probably the spirit of the bill tree I had bothered that day. My body was so tired that it needed to sleep, though I feared that, when I fell back into slumber, the spirit would return to torment me. So, I collected energy to prepare for a fight, if need be, and slipped into a lucid dream. I was sitting on a bus, defensively shuddering at other people around me. I went on to shake two of them, who looked at me as if I were crazy before getting off. As soon as I touched the ground, someone grabbed me by the shoulder. He told me not to be afraid. A bold and burly man with light olive skin, all dressed in red—the color of wizards in Madagascar—said, "I know a wise man, and I will try to put you in contact with him," and several other things I don't remember.

As my energy level decreased, I felt I was becoming smaller while he grew bigger, and I increasingly struggled to understand his words. At some point, his body went up in the air and did a loop before plunging into a point on a shelf before me—not unlike Aladdin's genie with his lamp! But instead of a lamp, when I looked closer, I saw a little plastic dinosaur toy and finally woke up.

The next morning, before leaving, I offered my prayers to the river. A month later, I shared a taxi in Antananarivo, the capital of Madagascar. After a few minutes sitting next to a tall, brawny man, I found out he was a Malagasy wizard and thought back to the forest "genie's" prediction. We went for coffee, and he shared the practice and wisdom of his tradition with me.

This experience, among many others, helped me respect sacred sites and their dwelling spirits, as well as the work of many autochthonous caretakers in the world that sustain the Earth through these sites. To make their work possible, we should make sure that the traditional guardians of these sacred sites are granted property and management rights, which many indigenous people demand. Where no indigenous people remain, some people have maintained this ancestral knowledge and could be granted these rights and responsibilities. They could even be trained and informed by indigenous people, such as the Kogis, who can help us rediscover the sacred nature of our landscapes.

It is also important for nature in these sites to be well protected and, if necessary, restored, something that I realized while working on a documentary film on the work of Don José Carmen Garcia Martinez. Don José Carmen is an old indigenous farmer from Central Mexico who, despite never having attended secondary school, is known for growing gigantic vegetables and increasing agricultural yields thanks to uncommon and clean farming techniques, which include the use of cosmo-telluric energies.[23] Beyond photos of extraordinary big vegetables— cabbages up to forty-five kilograms, maize plants five meters high, chard with two-meter leaves, etc.—that have circulated on the internet, the results have been confirmed by the Mexican Autonomous University of Chapingo.

My friend Yvo Perez Barreto has made two documentary films on Don José Carmen's work,[24] including one on his farming techniques,[25] that include a complementary book.[26] In 2015, I was involved in the making of a second documentary, *Maya Rain on Andalusia*,[27] conducting research and accessing unpublished documents. This documentary shows Don José Carmen coming to Andalusia, Spain, in 1995 to bring rain to this arid region, which was suffering from a five-year drought. The mission was successful: as predicted in a legal act drawn up by a solicitor,[28] important rain started the day after the last activity was carried out, with tremendous effects on the economy and the population.[29]

In fact, Don José Carmen developed the capacity to provoke rain "by induction" and regulate rain patterns through the study of ancient Mayan knowledge and writings (codex) that he managed to decipher. His capacity to make rain has been demonstrated several times, on large scales, in different countries, including in desert regions. In Mexico, the projects have been discussed with high-level national and local political authorities and have been successfully implemented in some states, such as San Luis Potosí or Zacatecas. The techniques are based on tree planting in specific locations, or when that is not possible, on the precise use of specific chemicals to artificially recreate, for a limited time, the effects of trees, as done in Andalusia.

Don José Carmen explains that the trees send information to the sea and clouds, "asking them" to bring rain to these areas. He also refers to the trees or the chemical reaction used as "ions generators," the ions facilitating, in association with nucleating agents, cloud formation. The specific locations where trees are planted are energetic centers, with specific electromagnetic conditions that are connected to each other in networks that end up on the seashore. This network allows for communication from forest to forest—that is to say from energetic center to energetic center—up to the sea.

Science increasingly understands the role of trees and forests in rainfall. Trees' transpiration effect is now well-known and may account for some 40 percent globally of all rain generation.[30] Trees take water from the soil and release it into the atmosphere in the form of vapor. Tree leaves also catch falling rain, which then evaporates. But recent research has also started to explain the role of trees in cloud formation, an important point to explain why rain may fall on forests and not elsewhere. A study published in 2016 in *Nature* presented evidence that terpenes—a class of organic compounds produced by trees—when combined with ozone, can form aerosols, around which vapor condenses to form clouds.[31] This new scientific knowledge can provide a first step toward understanding Don José Carmen's extraordinary results.

At a time when climate change greatly threatens ecosystems and our own survival on this planet, in particular by dysregulating rain patterns, the Mayan knowledge and experience of Don José Carmen are much needed. It is a stunning example of how relevant indigenous traditional ecological and spiritual knowledge are as we face climate change.[32] We need to pay attention to these practices, facilitating and scaling up their implementation. The experience of Don José Carmen reemphasizes the importance of managing sacred sites, which are energetic centers, in accordance with this traditional knowledge, which often implies ecological restoration. Among the documents I received from Don José Carmen and his team are indications of all the locations in Northern Mexico that should be reforested (in the right way) to restore adequate rain patterns. Some of them are on private lands, which complicates things.

These traditional techniques represent much-needed alternatives to technology-based geo-engineering ones (such as cloud seeding, which involves shooting chemicals into clouds—often from a small aircraft—to cause rainfall or snow[33]) that try to deal with climate change. Technology-based geoengineering generally works with a very limited and reductionist understanding of the biosphere and can induce profoundly destructive changes upon the environment as has happened before. Such technology is conceived to control the symptoms (in this case, getting rain) of a disease (rain patterns disrupted by climate change, which in turn is caused by our development model), rather than provide lasting solutions.

On the contrary, traditional knowledge operates with great respect and understanding of the cosmos and the Earth, whose harmony these techniques try to reestablish. Unlike chemicals used in cloud seeding, trees increase water vapor in the atmosphere and rebalance natural patterns. Trees also sequester carbon, often protect biodiversity, prevent soil erosion, regulate water flow ... How could geoengineering techniques be favored over such powerful, nature-based solutions?[34]

Biocultural conservation and the promotion of environmental awareness

The politics of being, and this particular paradigm shift in our relationship with nature, as expressed by the policy options presented above, point to a cultural transformation. We have seen that cultural and biological diversities often overlap. Thus their defense should be promoted in a synergetic manner, an approach called biocultural conservation. Traditional cultures have long embodied specific ways of being and living in harmony with nature and are the basis for the policy options presented here: the rights of nature, the adequate management of sacred sites, and the use of traditional ecological management techniques, including those based on natural energetic fields. Hence we should support the efforts of traditional communities to get their collective rights recognized, as well as to recover, preserve, and adapt their cultural institutions: language, organization and governance systems, knowledge, spiritualities, celebrations, etc.

At the other end of the spectrum, modern societies need to undergo a deep cultural transformation. We are all autochthonous to this Earth; we are all children of Mother Earth. Public policies can foster a sense of place, of community and identity, of intrinsic motivation and pride to be a part of this environmental regeneration movement. One good example of that is the "bandera azul" ("blue flag") program in Costa Rica, one of the leading countries in the world in terms of environmental awareness. Managed by a set of public and private organizations, this program incentivizes the organization of different sectors of civil society and their voluntary efforts toward natural resource conservation, climate change, sanitation, and hygiene, as well as public health, by symbolically recognizing their achievements according to a set of criteria. The program aims at promoting quality of life and environmental awareness through education and community organization.

The process is based on the formation of local committees, which impel actions and prepare reports for the program authority to review and deliver ecological blue flag awards for free. The program, which started in 1996 to protect beaches, has broadened its scope to fifteen award categories, including communities, municipalities, churches, health-care centers, households, real estate projects, farms, transport organizations, special events, micro watersheds, protected areas ... [35] Depending on their level of achievement, participants can receive an award with anywhere from one to six stars. There are also special stars related to particular issues—waste management, recycling, management of beach pollution sources, coastal security, etc.[36] The winners receive symbolic awards—a blue flag with the earned stars—during formal ceremonies. Between 1996 and 2018, twenty-one thousand three hundred and thirty-seven local committees received blue flag awards.[37]

The Costa Rican ecological blue flag program has been instrumental in fostering environmental awareness and civil society engagement on these issues. Through healthy competition, it has contributed to making environmental performance a source of pride and a common goal for different groups of people, strengthening a sense of belonging to their community and territory. Awarded communities attract both more touristic investments[38] and like-minded individuals who want to benefit and be part of these positive local dynamics. The program has been replicated in different countries, including Panama and Honduras.

17

Justice

"It is possible to reconcile justice and compassion, and to demonstrate that true justice must contain understanding and compassion."

—Zen Master Thich Nhat Hanh[1]

Retributive justice: an impasse

OUR CRIMINAL JUSTICE system, on which we are focusing in this chapter, is often described as mostly "retributive." It is based on the view that justice is achieved when whoever breaks the law receives a proportional punishment in return. It is believed this may also help prevent future crimes or rehabilitate the offender. This paradigm is at the root of the current criminal justice system's crisis in many countries, characterized by rising delays and costs, mass incarceration, recidivism, and the unfulfilled needs of victims and offenders.[2]

With 2.3 million people locked up (equivalent to 0.7 percent of the population) and a total of some seven million people under correctional control,[3] the US has the highest rate of incarceration[4] in the world. The number of people incarcerated in the US has gone up fivefold in the last forty years. A study showed that, between 1980 and 1996, only 12 percent of this surge was due to increases in crime, while the remaining 88 percent was due to the increased proportion of convicted criminals sent to prison and the extension of prison sentence lengths.[5] Experts worldwide seem to agree in general that prison is not very effective at deterring crimes,[6] in particular when imprisonment conditions are harsh,[7] making people more violent,[8] more prone to mental illnesses,[9] and less able to reintegrate themselves into society.[10] As summarized by British Conservative politician Douglas Hurd: "Prison is an expensive way of making bad people worse."

More than a solution, high imprisonment rates are a political answer to the public demand for safety, fostered by media, in cultures of domination. On the contrary, partnership cultures, which hold more compassionate values and display lower level of violence, tend to rely to a greater extent on mediation mechanisms to solve conflicts.[11] In that case, with the help of an impartial mediator, the people involved in a dispute resolve it, agreeing between themselves on the terms of a settlement.[12] Retributive justice's legitimacy is increasingly questioned not only from an efficiency point of view but from the perspective of its supposed fairness. In fact, more and more, research highlights the social determinants of crimes and the discriminatory nature of criminal justice, while advancements in neuroscience and related fields emphasize the biological, neurological, and environmental influence on behaviors.[13]

Childhood violence[14] and abuse,[15] fatherless homes,[16] poverty,[17] or ethnicity[18] are all powerful predictors of crimes or imprisonment, making it increasingly difficult to attribute full free will and responsibility to arrested individuals. Today's criminals are often the victims of decades of personal and structural violence that find a new expression in their crimes—it's an endless cycle. These people get beaten, fight back, and our justice system beats them back once more. How do we break the chains?

Restorative justice: an alternative paradigm

Restorative justice has recently received considerable interest as a potential alternative paradigm to retributive justice, one that is forward-looking and aimed primarily at addressing and repairing harm. It has been the basis of many traditional community-based justice systems that are being reactivated, and it is now developing quickly,[19] being already present to different degrees in more than one hundred countries in the world.[20] Many use restorative justice for juvenile offenders, for whom it can be particularly helpful in teaching values. In New Zealand, for example, the law established that the police or prosecutors must refer young offenders to mediation or to other diversion-type programs.

Restorative justice is based on a non-adversarial process in which all parties with a stake in a particular offense—the offender, the victim, and community members—actively participate together to resolve the issues arising from the offense. Through a facilitated dialogue, they agree together on the appropriate responses and programs, such as reparation, restitution, and community service, aimed at meeting the individual and collective needs and responsibilities of the parties and achieving the reintegration of the victim and the offender. Unlike retributive justice, "the restorative model regards crime as a violation of people and relationships."[21] It focuses on healing the wounds of the victims, offenders, and communities; helping the offenders take responsibilities for their acts; and strengthening the role of the community in preventing and responding to crimes, as well as restoring social harmony. It is a flexible approach that considers each case individually, respects the dignity and equality of each person, builds understanding, incorporates problem solving, and addresses the underlying causes of conflict. As such, it can inform and determine crime reduction strategies and actions.

Let us see a concrete example, "the case of a sixteen-year-old in an urban center found guilty of arson" as related by Bria Huculak.[22] A judge in Canada, Huculak was involved in peacemaking circles in the nineties, which are rooted in indigenous cultures and have a deep healing focus. The teenager:

> [H]ad set fire to the room at the youth facility, where he had been serving a disposition for numerous offenses. Youth institution has been his "home" since he was twelve. He had lost contact with much of his facility. Even now on the day of the Circle he does not seem to belong anywhere. On the day of the Circle fifteen people have come to participate: his mother, two sisters, an Elder, his counsel, social series, and correctional staff among them. Ironically, the staff had looser connection to the youth than did

his family. The judge and prosecutor are there. For the next three hours, they talk and listen and feel. There is much emotion and pain, and many tears. The youth discloses for a first time to his family and the other participants that as a small child he had been sexually abused by a relative. His older sister discloses that she too had been abused, and she now offers to attend counseling with him so that they both can get help to deal with this tragedy. At the end of the day, he had reconnected with his family and been linked with a support system. He has been held accountable for his criminal action, yet will not serve any more time in a youth facility. Instead, he will have a community disposition which includes community services, counseling, and contact with Elders. Thus, a community has been constructed for him, and for the first time he has hope. Help is offered and accepted. The Circle closes with a prayer, smiles, handshakes, and hugs. Justice is done.

Existing restorative justice programs vary considerably, for instance in how they relate to the criminal justice system or how they are operated (by public sector professionals or trained volunteers from the community) and who participates in the process. Beyond victims and offenders, restorative processes may include family and friends, community members, and government officials (police or correctional officers, judges, etc.). Restorative justice programs are often used in conjunction with conventional criminal justice processes and sanctions. They can be initiated at different stages of the criminal justice process: at the police level (before charges), prosecution level (usually before a trial), court level, or as part of corrections (as an alternative to incarceration, during incarceration, or upon release from prison).

Restorative approaches are suitable for dealing with many different kinds of cases, including very serious offenses. Basic conditions are that victims are identified; there is sufficient evidence to charge the offenders; offenders and victims are willing to participate (which is estimated to occur in some 50 percent of the cases[23]); and no power imbalances or cultural differences distort the process.

A more effective approach

Assessing restorative justice's effectiveness is complex and still not fully conclusive due to significant methodological challenges. Some of these challenges are common to the evaluations of traditional punishment, prevention, and treatment programs,[24] while others are specific to restorative approaches. These include a wide variety of approaches and program quality, selection biases (as participation in these programs is voluntary), and the need to define evaluation criteria aligned with the restorative justice approach.[25] Still, available research allows us to infer a couple of things.

First, consistent with the restorative paradigm and its focus on the victim, victims' satisfaction rates are very high: between 75–98 percent.[26] This contrasts with the results obtained by conventional judicial procedures.[27] A meta-analysis has found that:

> [B]enefits victims see in a restorative justice process are grounded mainly in the opportunity for communication: they want to express their feelings to the offender, hope to receive an explanation, and hope to have an impact on what should be done. Many victims also are motivated by a sense of public responsibility and think that the process may contribute to more understanding in the offender and less reoffending. Only a minority is especially interested in material reparation or compensation. [...] Victims also suffer less post-traumatic stress after a conference, feel less fear and anger, and more sympathy for the offender.[28]

Offenders' satisfaction rate also tends to be very high: a meta-analysis estimated it at 87.7 percent.[29] As seen in the concrete example presented above, this is not an easy process to go through, but it can be very beneficial to offenders, too, because they often engage emotionally in facing the harm they caused, take responsibility, and share about their own vulnerabilities and wounds. Another review of the literature concluded that "there is evidence from a number of European jurisdictions that restorative processes can significantly and positively impact the self-esteem of offenders and contribute to their acceptance of responsibility for their behaviour and the consequences of it."[30]

Offenders' and victims' satisfaction go along with a high degree of perceived procedural justice, higher than in the conventional criminal justice system.[31] This can explain the high rates of agreement and compliance with agreements by the offenders associated with restorative justice.[32] Restorative approaches also have the potential to reduce the costs of doing justice and increase the response to crime efficiency, as documented in some cases.[33]

Finally, while this is very difficult to estimate, it seems that restorative justice in general performs at least not worse and probably better than conventional approaches in terms of reoffending.[34] This is somewhat disappointing with regard to what happens during restorative processes. It seems to depend to a good extent on the quality of the follow-ups to the restorative meetings ("circles," "conferences," etc.), including access to relevant support or treatment,[35] something restorative approaches have the potential to help with.[36] All of these positive outcomes, that are often neglected in conventional criminal justice, highlight the great potential of restorative approaches.

As recognized by most experts in the field, ultimately restorative justice's effectiveness depends on the quality of these programs, which rely very much on human qualities. This leads us to a fundamental point from the perspective of the politics of being. Independent of their respective outcomes, it seems much more appropriate to invest collectively in developing our human capacities for understanding, compassion, respect, repentance, and forgiveness that support restorative justice rather than relying on our lower instinct for retaliation and refining the institutional machineries for punishment.

Restorative justice is a good example of how institutions can help us cultivate the best in ourselves and strengthen our communities. It relies on more positive assumptions about our human nature empowers stakeholders and provides an opportunity for healing and reconciliation. It is more an art than the mechanistic application of laws, and to be effective, it requires some human qualities, such as empathy, respect, courage, presence, responsibility, sensitivity, and skillfulness. These are the conditions to create a safe place for the expression of feelings and views of all participants about the harm done through which healing can happen.[37]

A safe and supportive climate is necessary for participants to reconnect deeply to themselves and to one another in order for forgiveness, and eventually, repentance (yes, usually in that order[38]) to happen. In a politics of being, all these qualities are ends in themselves.

As seen earlier, many cultures use the same concepts—for example Dharma for Hindus—to simultaneously describe cosmic order, spiritual law, justice, and a spiritual path, showing that they are by nature one. Justice is a sacred endeavor, and restorative justice is a spiritual path, with roots in many traditions,[39] worth pursuing for its own sake. The Interfaith Committee on Chaplaincy in the Correctional Service of Canada, in support of restorative justice, stated:

> Our goal is to seek, shalom, harmony and security for all, with reconciliation and healing, replacing revenge and pain. We believe that the search for true and satisfying justice is forever linked to the spiritual growth of all concerned. The path of over-incarceration, of a vengeful spirit and a punitive mentality, can only dry up the soul of our country.[40]

Grassroots movements have historically supported the development of restorative justice through local programs initiated by NGOs and community-based organizations. The declarations from the United Nations Congress on Crime Prevention and Criminal Justice have repeatedly called for a greater use of restorative justice, and in 2002, the United Nations Economic and Social Council adopted a resolution defining "basic principles on the use of restorative justice programmes in criminal matters."[41] These principles recommend that Member States "consider the formulation of national strategies and policies aimed at the development of restorative justice and at the promotion of a culture favourable to the use of restorative justice among law enforcement, judicial and social authorities, as well as local communities."[42]

While many restorative justice programs have been successfully developed without any new legislation, legal texts can encourage the use of restorative justice (lack of referrals has been the main weakness of many programs), set standards, and establish all of the necessary legal safeguards for participants.[43] It is important to up-scale restorative justice carefully and ensure programs' quality through specific training, as "restorative processes are never risk free, neither are they always without failings or difficulties."[44]

A restorative and more compassionate approach to justice includes how prisons are designed and run. *Breaking the Cycle* is a documentary available on online,[45] comparing a traditional US prison with a Norwegian one. In Norway, inmates enjoy very normal life conditions in what resembles a nice house: they cook, socialize with prison staff, receive psychological support, and develop working skills and their own personal projects, including recording music or developing a restaurant. In the US, prison conditions are harsh: the cells are tiny; the toilets are next to the bed and in sight of anyone walking in the hallway; the food is often insufficient and bad; the punishments are extremely severe; and prison staff often used to beat inmates before cameras were installed.

It is striking to see the two systems operate from radically different paradigms, in particular different assumptions about human nature and how to achieve positive social outcomes. The systems tend to enact the paradigm from which they operate. By treating inmates as criminals, the American punitive approach makes individuals more ill, angry, violent, and ultimately renders them unable to reintegrate themselves in society after living many years in such conditions. By treating those who have committed crimes as humans, the compassionate Norwegian approach allows inmates to heal, develop their humanness, and eventually become good neighbors when they are released.

Mindful justice

The proper integration of restorative justice into the criminal justice system depends on the correct appreciation of its virtues by judges and magistrates, policemen, prosecutors, correctional officials, and defense lawyers. This often implies a profound change of mindset and values toward more compassion and understanding. In some countries, the logic of violence, anger, fear, and reactivity is deeply ingrained in the criminal justice system. In the US, this is exemplified by dehumanizing prison conditions, with the widespread use of solitary confinement and physical violence by core correctional officers against inmates, the sentencing of children as young as thirteen or of nonviolent offenders to life terms, the killing of unarmed African-Americans, or the numerous legal restrictions on individuals with felony records, which undermine their chances of reintegration.[46]

This logic is so embedded in the system that it impregnates, consciously or unconsciously, the minds and hearts of every professional who participates in it. The Mindfulness in Justice initiative[47] stems from the recognition that, by helping develop empathic connections and by regulating emotional reactivity, mindfulness has the potential to build a more fair, compassionate, and humane criminal justice from the bottom up. Launched in 2014 in the US, it is a national effort to integrate mindfulness into criminal justice from front to back. A pilot mindful criminal justice system was developed in Santa Clara County, California, where more than a thousand professionals (sheriffs, correctional deputies, prosecutors, public defenders, judges, etc.) have already been trained in mindfulness.

Mindfulness can have also a positive impact on mental disorders, such as anxiety, post-traumatic stress, or depression, from which people involved in criminal justice (prisoners, police officers, correctional officers, criminal attorneys, etc.) tend to suffer disproportionately.[48] This is particularly true for prisoners. In the UK, according to the UK Mindfulness All-Party Parliamentary Group report: "Nearly half the prison population have depression or anxiety, 25% have both and suicide rates are considerably higher than in the general population."[49] Mindfulness is recognized for its potential to help treat these mental disorders, which studies have shown to be associated to higher risk of recidivism.[50] More generally, mindfulness has the potential to address other psychological issues, such as self-regulation, negative affectivity, and substance addiction, which are all relevant to recidivism.[51] The healing and transformative potential of meditation-based programs for prisoners is now used in a growing number of countries.

Cheri Maples (1952–2017) was an American police officer who became a teacher in the Plum Village tradition. I was fortunate to be able to meet her when she gave a talk, "Mindfulness and the Police"[52] (available online), in Plum Village in 2016. I just reread it before writing this tribute to her, and I could not hold back my tears. In her talk, she shared her story as a police officer whose work and life were transformed by the practice of mindfulness. She explained the physiological effects of a police officer's work that she experienced and was able to overcome thanks to her meditation practice:

> What happens with police officers, and you can probably relate to this, is that adrenaline starts to shoot up because of hypervigilance—being worried about your own safety and the safety of everybody else. We're always taught about what can go wrong—not so much about what can go right, which is the majority of the time. The adrenaline shoots out of the normal range and peaks, then takes twenty-four hours to come back to normal, but people go back to work before that twenty-four hours is up. So adrenaline starts going up and down, above and below the normal range. When the adrenaline kicks in, people are fast on their feet, able to make command decisions, and they have a sense of humor. And then when they are at home, the adrenaline drops way down and this looks like no energy, listlessness, depression. Prior to 2016, about four times as many police officers took their own lives as were killed in the line of duty in the US. This is a very real phenomenon. Emotionally, what begins to happen is the effects manifest as irritation and impatience and anger and depression. There's a very cynical sort of response that develops. Spiritually, the effects of doing the job manifest as an armoring and numbing of the heart. It's very hard to be compassionate when those things are going on.

Maples tells how her first retreat with Thich Nhat Hanh changed her life, and eventually her work:

> The changes were incremental, but I stopped doing my job in a mechanical way. What I started to see is what was right in front

of me, which I seemed to have missed with the other attitude: a suffering human being who needed my help and often didn't have any place else to turn. So I started taking my time on the calls I went on. I started trying to connect with people from a different space.

Once she had to deal with a father who had locked his daughter at home so that her mum could not pick her up:

I knocked on the door. I'm about five feet and three inches tall, and this six-foot-four-inch man who looked very angry opened the door. I could just see the suffering. It was so obvious to me. In a very calm voice, I said, 'May I come in? I'm just here to listen and to help.' I came in and saw his daughter, and I said, 'You know what, I see your little girl over here, and I know you love her, and I know how much you care about her, and I see that she's scared, and I know you don't want that to happen. So how about if we let her go out and be with her mother, and you and I talk. ' And he did. Rather than escalating this situation to the point where an arrest had to be made, it was just a matter of being compassionate and mindful. I violated every policy in the book, and with my gun belt and my bulletproof vest I sat down next to this guy on the couch, which you're never supposed to do. And he started crying in my arms. That was an incredible experience for me in terms of what a little kindness and compassion can do, and that there are alternative ways to respond to people. Of course when you're angry, irritated, and cynical yourself, it's really hard to see those possibilities. I ran into this man three days later. I was walking down the street that I lived on and he came up behind me—you know, it's not good to come up behind a police officer. [Laughter] He picked me up off the ground and he said, 'You! You! You saved my life that night.' It was a wonderful experience.

Later on, Maples started to share her practice, organizing mindfulness training and retreats for criminal justice officers,[53] getting very involved in the mindful justice movement. She became a Dharma teacher in 2008. For her ordination, she offered to Thich Nhat Hanh this "gatha" (Zen poem), which took the form of a guided meditation:

> Breathing in, I know that mindfulness is the path to peace.
>
> Breathing out, I know that peace is the path to mindfulness.
>
> Breathing in, I know that peace is the path to justice.
>
> Breathing out, I know that justice is the path to peace.
>
> Breathing in, I know my duty is to provide safety and protection to all beings.
>
> Breathing out, I am humbled and honored by my duty as a peace officer.
>
> Breathing in, I choose mindfulness as my armor and compassion as my weapon.
>
> Breathing out, I aspire to bring love and understanding to all I serve.

Three months after Maples gave this talk, she was injured in a bicycle crash. She died on July 27, 2017, aged sixty-four, from complications due to injuries.

Restorative justice and mindfulness-based programs are just two approaches that can help break the cycle of suffering, violence, hostility, and retaliation, which affects many criminal justice systems. Instead, they can foster compassion, understanding, healing, and ultimately true justice.

18

Economy

"The world has enough for everyone's needs,
but not everyone's greed."

—Mahatma Gandhi,
political and spiritual leader (1869–1948)

"A person who lacks empathy or conscience is a sociopath. Similarly,
an economic system that is essentially amoral—that does not factor
empathy or conscience into its determination of right action—is a
sociopathic economic system."[1]

—Marianne Williamson, spiritual leader and political activist

Economy lies at the heart of our current model of development,
with all the material benefits it has brought us and also the seemingly
intractable problems we are now facing. Hence redesigning our
economic system is central to the paradigmatic change we are calling for.
Only a very profound transformation that challenges the current failing
economic ideology will do. This may take a generation—twenty years—to
complete and will build on the institutional changes we have outlined in
previous chapters.

While our economy may seem to have little to do with spirituality, the
material aspects of our lives are instrumental to the fulfillment of all beings.
Since we have created this insatiable economic system through a number
of decisions and policies, we can very well replace it by an economy of

(well-) being. In fact, it is our only alternative. While I fully acknowledge the material progress our economic system has brought to many of us, I focus in this chapter on its downsides that we no longer have the luxury to leave unattended.

From scarcity to abundance

Our economic system operates under a principle of scarcity, a scarcity it creates itself. It destroys our individual and collective capacities to autonomously fulfill our material, personal, and social needs, forcing us to rely instead on paid work and goods and services to buy on the market. As a limited number of companies increasingly control production, they answer our real needs less and less but instead manipulate them for their own benefits. The primary objective of pharmaceutical or agricultural companies is not to improve our health or agricultural production but to sell their products. This may be achieved by fostering our dependence on them, for example by making seeds nonreproducible or by favoring lifelong symptomatic treatments over real cures and preventive solutions.

Beyond work specialization, with the destruction of our communities, cultures, and environment, we are losing our primary sources of sustenance, support, and fulfillment, which were once freely accessible. Our economic system has made our livelihoods, self-esteem, and mental health insecure. Money now has the power to define our social status and personal worth and to allow or impede access to an infinite range of products and experiences. We try to fulfill our needs through consumption but never have enough, not only because we are conditioned to need and desire more, but also because consumption cannot answer our real "being" needs for connection, self-actualization, and meaning.

We are doomed to live in scarcity; to produce and buy ever more to compensate for the degradation of our human, social, cultural, and environmental wealth; to compete against each other for psychological and material security. Scarcity is built into the system and fuels it. It has many names, from planned obsolescence to intellectual property rights, monopolies, and hoarding. Our fear of lacking controls our lives.

Stone-age hunter gatherers spent less time catering for their material needs.[2] We once thought technological progress would free us from material necessities and allow us to develop more meaningful and fulfilled lives in an age of leisure and abundance, which still hasn't happened. A friend of mine told me about a speech by a Cambodian minister of agriculture he listened to in the sixties. America had just provided Cambodia with new seeds that would double agricultural yields, and the minister concluded "logically" that the farmers could work half as much as a result. That has not been the case; work has been reallocated to other production in order to keep up with new economic opportunities, or rather to make ends meet in a disrupted social and cultural context. Despite many limitations, precapitalist populations lived in an affluent world, with awe and gratitude. That world was rich in relationships in tightly knit communities, embedded in thriving nature.

We are not condemned to serve our current economic system. We can redesign one that operates under the principle of abundance to serve the fulfillment of all beings. Abundance here is understood in terms of "being," but this goes hand in hand with all beings having their basic material needs met. By regaining control over the economic system, our needs, desires, and priorities, we can have more than enough, and be more fulfilled. We need to rediscover the spiritual values of moderation and contentment. We can get rid of product waste and most unnecessary consumption: disposable products; statutory goods; toxic goods (e.g. fossil fuels, junk food, mind-altering substances and alcohol, advertising, etc.); goods that offer "solutions" to the very problems we created (e.g. weapons,[3] security services, depollution, drugs for chronic illnesses, transportation for long commutes, etc.).

We can redirect these resources toward worthwhile activities, as Costa Rica did seventy years ago when it abolished its army and chose to invest in education and health instead, which nowadays allows it to rank number one in Latin America for social progress.[4] We can also better serve many of our needs through the nature-based and community-based solutions that have long remained outside the commercial sphere.

Reforming intellectual property rights

Technology already enables us to share and often access many things for free: education, tools, cars, houses, cultural content, software, etc. In the future, technological breakthroughs, automation, artificial intelligence, and digitalization could drastically drive costs down to facilitate universal access to many products and services.[5] For this progress to benefit the whole population, intellectual property rights systems (e.g., patents, copyright, trademarks[6]) need to be reformed, in particular to adjust to the new reality of the digital economy. Supported by costless copying and platform effects (networks' value depends on their size, so it makes sense for everyone to go where most people are—Facebook, Amazon, Uber, and Airbnb, for example), monopolies have made the digital economy extremely profitable, leading to an extraordinary concentration of power and wealth.

The production and management of information is the world's largest industry: seven of the eight largest companies in the world are info-tech-based,[7] while seven of the fifteen richest people are tech billionaires.[8] But unlike tangible goods, information is non-rival: when I watch a movie online, it does not impede anybody from also watching, and the extra cost for me to watch it is close to zero. This should make abundance the natural law of the digital economy. Instead intellectual property rights have created lucrative monopolies that are restraining access, innovation, and competition, creating artificial scarcity.

As my friend Rufus Pollock from the Plum Village community points out: "We need an open world. A world where all digital information is open, free for everyone to use, build on and share; and where innovators and creators are recognized and rewarded."[9] In his brilliant book *The Open Revolution,* Pollock shows that we can replace the current intellectual property rights systems to give free and universal access to all non-private digital information, from music to medicine and software to statistics. To support innovation and fairness, market-driven remuneration rights would keep rewarding inventors and creators, based on the actual use of their works, in addition to specific systems to fund new creations. Countries and international agreements could establish funding arrangements for this open revolution, such as small levies on internet advertising or cell phone data plans. In the case of music and movies, for example, the state would provide a universal legal protocol for their licensing, and platforms such as Spotify and Netflix would no longer act as legal distributors but could only compete as technical distributors.

The benefits of such a system can be huge. The total revenue for music in the Netherlands is estimated to be €150 million a year, with probably less than 60 percent going to creators, and open access could increase the welfare of the Dutch society by over €600 million a year.[10] This does not account for the elimination of the costs currently necessary to exclude those that don't pay for accessing such services. Pollock notes that the fact that a whole legal and technology industry worth hundreds of millions of dollars has developed "to prevent the very thing that the digital worlds does supremely well—costless copying—[...] to frustrate and infuriate the rest of us [...] is a superb example of mankind wasting its time."[11]

In addition to free and universal access, the open revolution would establish the right to reuse innovations and share new ones that incorporate them. It would replace the current patent system, which hinders competition and innovation by giving early innovators an absolute right to prohibit reuse of their works. Instead it would grant them the right to an equitable remuneration that is proportional to the actual added value generated by their innovations. These often build on long chains of innovation, stemming not only from companies but also from nature, societies, and public-funded programs, that tend not to be properly recognized in the current system.

The open revolution can put an end to the digital platform monopolies. For example, Facebook's protocols could be open and universally accessible (like the internet) with an equitable remuneration. That could allow an open social network controlled by its users to emerge, on which unlimited new functionalities and networks could be freely developed. Another way to break the monopolistic positions of large internet companies is for the law to mandate interoperability and data portability.

The open revolution is technically, financially, and legally feasible; it can be implemented incrementally through multiple pathways and support open-source production models (e.g., GNU/Linux, Android, Wikipedia, etc.). It can strengthen the positive values associated with the digital economy—collaboration, sharing, and creativity—and enact the paradigm of being in which effort and thus innovation is not primarily motivated by the prospect of financial gains but by intrinsic motivations to contribute positively to society.

By allowing all beings to receive everything they need, to offer all they can, to become all they are, we can prompt human, social, and environmental regeneration and set up a dynamic of authentic mutual enrichment.[12] With the objective of being, all the system changes from competition and scarcity to cooperation and abundance; from greed, violence, and destruction to care, peace, and flourishing.

A new value system and indicators

The first thing is to change the meaning and measure of success from having to being. As we have seen throughout this book, this simply means uncovering the lies at the core of our economic system. When we collectively recognize that money is not the key to our fulfillment and its insane accumulation is often pathological, people will naturally cease to treasure it. "Success isn't about how much money you make; it's about the difference you make in people's lives," said Michelle Obama. When we agree that a truly fulfilled and admirable person is in service of all, people will work again for the greater good.

The quest for money, as for any extrinsic reward, is often based on insecurity and the need for a positive evaluation from others, which in turn is nourished by advertising and the economic system. When we see this understanding in the eyes of our partners, our friends, our parents and children, our colleagues and neighbors, we will certainly change our ways and heal. As humanity grows into adulthood, it will become less necessary to treat people as children, using systems of rewards and punishments to foster right behaviors. At the social level, many destructive activities will simply no longer be tolerated—the change in values we are contemplating might someday make them unthinkable. Our value system focuses our collective attention and determines what is possible.

At the national level, this would translate into new indicators of success. Instead of having the highest GDP, countries would pride themselves on having the most fulfilled, happiest citizens, who care for each other and respect nature. GDP shortfalls are well-known and recognized, and alternative indicators have multiplied. They not only provide a better measurement of economic wealth and production, but also look beyond the economic to integrate human, social, and environmental dimensions, and occasionally, subjective assessments of life satisfaction and well-being.

Some measurement systems aggregate these different dimensions in one indicator, while others provide a set of indicators. Developed under the technical guidance of professors Michael Porter from Harvard Business School and Scott Stern from the Massachusetts Institute of Technology, and based on the work of Economics Nobel Prize recipients Amartya Sen, Joseph Stiglitz, and Douglass North, the Social Progress Index is one of these alternative indicators. It has been adopted among others by Paraguay, the European Union, and California. Instead of looking at economic means, it focuses on human, social, and environmental achievements. Its definition of social progress to some extent resonates with our views:

> [T]he capacity of a society to meet the basic human needs of its citizens, establish the building blocks that allow citizens and communities to enhance and sustain the quality of their lives, and create the conditions for all individuals to reach their full potential.[13]

As usual, Nordic countries occupy the top ranking while the US lags behind (ranked twenty-sixth in 2019). A change in the international distribution of power could support this redefinition of success. If China, for example, is able to reconnect to its soul, it could tap into its rich culture and ancestral wisdom to promote new indicators of progress and a healthy global leadership.

This new "being" bottom line does not only apply to the public sector. Companies can also redefine their purpose and assess their performance, such as in terms of happiness and well-being. To change our value system, we need a critical mass of committed leaders in all sectors at all levels: business men and women, bankers, journalists, researchers, presidents, ministers, governors, mayors, civil servants, etc. They all need to take responsibility, stand up, and come together. What we need is the willingness to act; strong individual, organizational, and political commitments that can bring about this transformation in a generation's time. I can't think of anything more exciting.

Many people who are now holding money and power fear this change, but the present economic system will sooner or later either profoundly evolve or collapse. Fear is a human reaction often triggered by trauma, but there is no escape. Increasingly people will have to face their own responsibility in the upcoming tragedies. If they are able to elude their own consciousnesses, their children and the world around them will hold them accountable. It is already happening; can you imagine 2040? On our deathbed, we will all have to ask ourselves: what have we done for the Earth and all its children?

A global green new deal[14]

In addition to fostering a new value system, our priority is to invest in the ecological transition. The current environmental crisis is the biggest threat humanity has ever faced. Our very survival as a species is at stake. The window of opportunity to avoid climate chaos and a global collapse is closing down, as the greenhouse gases we emit will affect the climate over long periods of time.[15] Global greenhouse gas emissions have risen at an annual rate of 1.5 percent in the last decade, reaching 55.3 GtCO2e in 2018. Countries' international commitments to reduce their emissions—if honored—would lead to a global emissions level of 56 Gt CO2e by 2030, on the path of a 3.2°C rise. However, to limit global temperature rise from preindustrial levels to 1.5°C, emissions must drop rapidly to 25 GtCO2e by 2030 (41 GtCO2e for a 2°C rise). That means a 7.6 percent reduction in emissions every year between 2020 and 2030.

This demands a massive coordinated investment effort, a global green new deal to overcome our deep environmental crisis. In the energy system alone, we need annual investments of some US$2.4 trillion—around 2.5 percent of the world's economy (they currently amount to 1 percent)[16]—to limit the temperature rise to below 1.5°C.[17] The establishment of decentralized and efficient clean energy systems is a key aspect of the decarbonization of our economies. All countries need and can achieve energetic independence. This is an important aspect of sovereignty, one that can drastically improve international relations and that would have avoided some of the recent conflicts and wars over energetic resources.

Beyond energy, a global green new deal will help transform all aspects of our economies: transportation systems; cities and buildings; industry; land-use management, including agriculture; forestry and nature conservation; water management ... At the same time, a huge amount of investment is needed to achieve the SDGs with a financing gap estimated at US$ 2.5–3 trillion per year in "developing countries."[18] It has also been estimated that a US$90 trillion investment in infrastructure (for the energy, transport, telecommunication, water and waste management, agriculture, and forestry sectors) is needed globally for the 2015–2030 period, which involves almost doubling current levels of investment.[19] This is more than our entire current global infrastructure's stock. A global green new deal would converge with this effort, as shifting to a low-carbon infrastructure would only cost 5 percent more up front, which could be fully offset during the lifetime of these infrastructures through reduced operating costs.[20] It could significantly reduce poverty and create more than a hundred and seventy million additional jobs by 2030.[21]

Following the 2008 financial crisis, calls were made, including by the UN, for green recovery investment packages. These went largely unheard, and the trillions invested to bring the economy "back on track" have not brought us much closer to sustainability. Recent political discussions in the US, Europe, and many other countries for a green new deal have met the COVID-19 crisis. As I am writing this, countries are discussing how to better integrate the ecological transition into their recovery investment packages. Presented in January 2020 by the European Commission, the European Green Deal is a set of policy initiatives by the European Commission aiming at making Europe climate neutral by 2050. It initially planned to mobilize at least €1 trillion (mostly public funds) over the next decade, but additional funding will also come from the post-COVID 19 recovery plan.

Public investments to rescue our financial and economic systems following the 2008 and 2020 crises have made clear that there is enough money available to fund such a global green new deal. Public subsidies, for example in the agricultural and energy sectors—annual fossil fuel subsidies have been estimated at US$447 billion, representing 70 percent of total energy sector subsidies[22]—could also be rechanneled towards green activities. While sending the right price signal to investors, high carbon taxes could also generate resources. Regulations could oblige financial institutions to fund the green transition. The trillions of dollars and euros invested in quantitative easing to deal with the effects of the 2008 financial crisis could be channeled toward green assets this time.

Leveraging monetary creation to fight against climate change could be also carried out at the international level, through the IMF Special Drawing Rights.[23] "The resources are there. What we are missing is the political will,"[24] said Richard Kozul-Wright, head of the UN trade, investment, and development agency's (UNCTAD) globalization and development strategies division when presenting the agency's 2019 report on financing a global green new deal.[25]

The current rate of ecosystem destruction, resource extraction, and pollution is unsustainable, and we need urgently to transition to an economic system that regenerates nature and operates under the principle of a circular or closed-loop economy with zero pollution, zero waste, and 100 percent recycling, just as nature does. Many initiatives are already heading in that direction, such as the efforts of San Francisco or Seattle to reduce their waste or the European Union's circular economy action plan. The main economic constraints will increasingly come from limited natural resources and possibly, for some time, energy.

Physical limits to our environmental impact need to be established and enforced (see figure 7). Beyond cultural change, public investments, and regulation, this implies in particular factoring full environmental costs and benefits into economic systems. Ultimately, in many cases, companies will not be allowed to buy their way out of environmental destruction, as physical measures will replace economic values to manage environmental impact. Companies will have to assume full responsibility for ensuring that everything is reused or recycled: only if the right systems are in place to do that will they be able to fund these systems and delegate their responsibility.

A focus on basic needs

An ecological economy is the only way to bring about a new form of prosperity. It necessarily breaks up the old paradigm of economic growth. Denying it just creates confusion: we are constantly wondering whether consumption levels are high enough to keep the economy going, while knowing that consumer culture is actually destroying our planet. To achieve sustainability and regeneration, we should let go of the (un) economic growth[26] logic of endless consumption and needs and stop clinging to useless and destructive economic activities just for the sake of fueling the economic system and out of fear of losing jobs. Instead we need to come back to the fundamentals of economy and seek the best allocation of limited resources, in particular natural, and to a lesser extent human resources, refocusing them toward the satisfaction of our real needs, in a spirit of sobriety.

The aforementioned Earth charter reads: "When basic needs have been met, human development is primarily about being more, not having more." On the one hand, an economy of being helps us access goods and services that support the expression of our full potential, including spiritual, artistic, or cultural content and experiences; social connections; access to nature; physical and well-being activities. This means growing a service economy, which can, to some extent, be based on sharing and free access, in particular through the internet, as well as on care work. Consistent with our approach, the latter refers to work in service of others, in particular vulnerable individuals such as young people, the sick, and the elderly, and is usually intrinsically motivated. Nursing, teaching, healing, cleaning, and cooking, for example, are considered care work and are classified under the category of personal and social services.

On the other hand, this means focusing on the satisfaction of our basic material needs, that everyone needs to fulfill. In fact, since the Universal Declaration of Human Rights in 1948, international laws and norms have attempted to recognize the rights of each individual to fulfill these basic needs. With the SDGs, humanity has committed to reach this goal by 2030. These basic material needs include food, water, sanitation, and housing, and access to education, health, energy, information, and communication technology. In *Doughnut Economics: Seven Ways to Think*

Like a 21st-century Economist, which was published in 2017, English economist Kate Raworth considers these basic material needs, together with other needs—such as income and work, peace and justice, political voice, social equity and gender equality—as the social foundation required "for all people to lead lives of dignity and opportunity."[27] Combined with an ecological ceiling based on the nine planetary boundaries identified by the Stockholm Resilience Centre, this social foundation defines a "safe and just space for humanity"[28] (see figure 7).

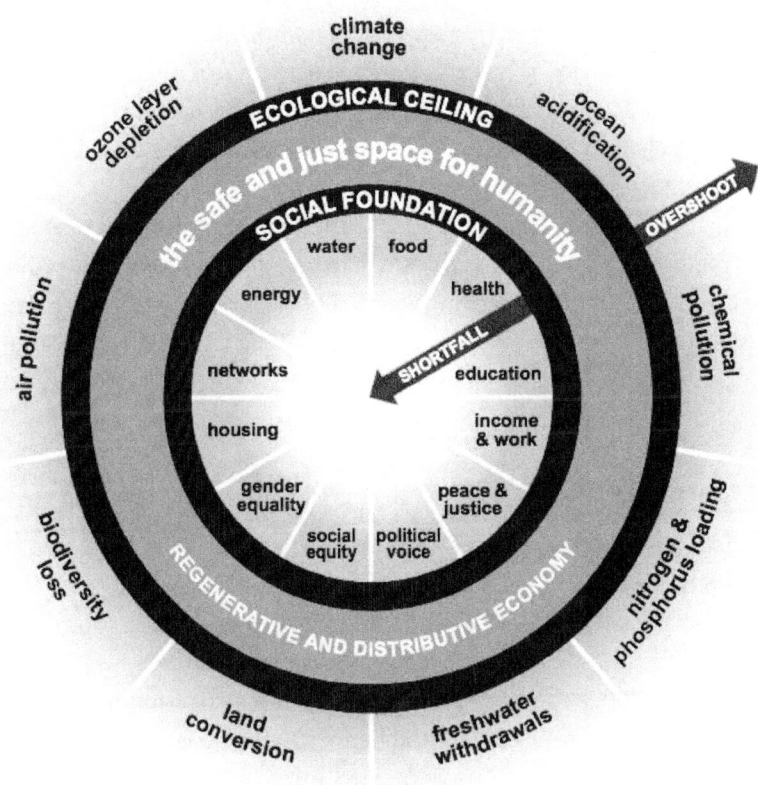

Figure 7. Doughnut economics.[29]

This focus on basic needs translates into different kinds of policies. Our tax systems, in particular value-added taxes, should favor products and services answering these needs, while luxury goods should be heavily taxed or simply prohibited. How is it possible that a purse gets 95 percent of its price from its logo? The business model of the luxury industry is basically based on making people look superior to others, even if they all have to buy the same purse for that! It does not create but instead destroys social value. I cannot see how this can fit in an economy of being.

Another possibility is to set a maximum price for a given product. Advertising, and the consumer culture it supports, is also clearly socially toxic, undermining our self-esteem, satisfaction, and well-being.[30] In many nonwestern countries, it has also provoked a sense of rejection of national and traditional cultures. To move away from the destructive economic system it fuels, we can severely restrain advertising as Bhutan did, and use it instead as a tool for promoting an economy of being.

I am not against economic growth per se. Activities that satisfy our basic material and being needs will have to grow within our ecological limits. But sacrificing everything to fuel economic growth that does not distinguish between destructive, unnecessary activities and those that can serve our fulfillment just makes no sense.

Reducing inequality

Our environmental challenges and the satisfaction of our basic needs and basic social health call for a drastic reduction of inequalities. The world's richest 10 percent produce half of all carbon emissions.[31] Some people emit more in a day than others in a year, or even a lifetime. Environmental taxation can reduce the negative impact, but it has to differentiate between average people's necessities and superfluous commodities. French economist Thomas Piketty proposes to introduce an individual carbon card, which would monitor the annual amount of greenhouse gases that each citizen is authorized to emit and apply substantial taxes beyond a certain threshold.[32]

Like energy in an ecosystem, money—that we use to maintain our human societies—needs to circulate, distribute itself, and not accumulate. The fact that there is so much debt in the world does not mean that we are collectively poor; it means the money is not where it should be: where it is needed and spent.[33] Indeed, debt has quickly grown during the last four decades as wealth concentration increased.

There are many possible ways to reduce inequality. The most obvious is to establish minimum and maximum income levels, as well as wealth taxes and high inheritance taxes. Before neoliberal ideas started to spread in the eighties, the US had a very high marginal rate of income tax: on average 81 percent between 1930 and 1980.[34] For the wealthiest, the inheritance tax rate was 74 percent. In 1944–1945, during World War II, the marginal rate of income tax reached 94 percent. During these fifty years, the US economy performed much better than it did during the last four decades, in which taxes on the wealthy have been drastically lowered.

In his best-selling book *Capital in the Twenty-first Century*, Piketty proposed a global wealth tax, topping out at around 2 percent. Wealth taxes, at a modest level, have been adopted by many countries, including the best-performing countries, such as Norway, Switzerland, and the Netherlands. As inequality grows, the attraction of a wealth tax increases. Running for the 2020 US Democratic primary, Elizabeth Warren and Bernie Sanders both built on Piketty's work and proposed such a wealth tax, topping out at respectively 6 and 8 percent of one's wealth every year.[35] They also included a high exit tax of 40–60 percent on the wealth of Americans that prefer to leave the country. Historically, wealth taxes have been successfully applied in dealing with public debt, the effects of wars, and the need for reconstruction: one-shot wealth taxes of 40–50 percent have been commonly applied in countries such as Japan, Germany, Italy, or France.[36] I believe today's situation and the threat of climate change is no less crucial and calls for higher income, wealth, and inheritance taxes on the wealthiest.

It could be possible to allow rich people who are using their money for the public good (though this should be strictly defined and well monitored) to deduct part or the totality[37] of these resources from the basis of this wealth tax. This would apply the principle of collective trusteeship defended by Gandhi or Bahá'u'lláh. As Gandhi wrote:

> Those who own money now are asked to behave like the trustees holding their riches on behalf of the poor. You may say that trusteeship is a legal fiction. But, if people meditate over it constantly and try to act up to it, then life on earth would be governed far more by love than it is at present. Absolute trusteeship is an abstraction like Euclid's definition of a point, and is equally unattainable. But if we strive for it, we shall be able to go further in realizing a state of equality on earth than by any other method.[38]

By incentivizing the rich to walk this path, they may discover how enjoyable it is and follow it naturally.

The money raised through these taxes could be used to promote public services and free access to health, education, urban transportation, water, culture ... A Universal Basic Income could be established and/ or a one-time individual capital endowment. In fact, Piketty proposes a system of "inheritance for all," in which each individual upon turning twenty-five receives a capital endowment equivalent to 60 percent of the average adult's net worth: in the US, this would mean US$231,000, in France €120,000.[39] Helping people establish their lives, buy a home, and invest, for example, in their own business, could greatly improve their autonomy and freedom to build their lives as they wish, following their calling.

Relocalizing the economy[40]

Against some of the above-proposed measures, some of you may have internally objected that they are not realistic as they would hurt national competitiveness, which needs to prevail in a globalized economy. In fact, economic globalization has created a race to the bottom in terms of regulation and environmental and social standards of production. With the deregulation of trade and finance at the global level, countries have started to compete to attract investments, including through tax breaks and subsidies. In the US, in addition to federal support, the *New York Times* found in 2012 that "state and local governments are giving out US\$80 billion a year in tax breaks and other subsidies in a foolhardy, shortsighted race to attract companies."[41] Capital is now able to establish itself where it is more profitable to produce, which has translated into a concentration of wealth, and the transferring of benefits into tax havens. According to UNCTAD, "Since the 1980s, in all regions and in almost every country, the share of national income accruing to labor has decreased,"[42] by an average of 7 percent in "developed countries" (from 61.5 percent to 54.5 percent) and of 2 percent in "developing countries" (from 52.5 percent to 50.5 percent).

Free movement of capital, in particular speculative and short-term funds, has drastically raised the risk of financial crises while expanding inequality levels as recognized by IMF economists.[43] Free trade has severely affected our economies' resilience, and the COVID-19 crisis has revealed the vulnerabilities of global supply chains and the risks of concentrating the production of essentials like medical products in very few places, such as India and China.[44]

Financial markets and large transnational corporations are increasingly dominating the global economic system. In 2016, among the world's top one hundred economic revenue collectors, only twenty-nine were states and seventy-one were corporations.[45] According to Paul Hellyer, former deputy prime minister of Canada:

> Globalization is really a code name for corporatization. It's an attempt by the largest corporations in the world, and the largest banks in the world, to re-engineer the world in such a way that they won't have to pay decent wages to their employees, and they won't have to pay taxes to fix potholes and to maintain parks, and to pay pensions to the old and handicapped.[46]

Lowering social and environmental standards is not a good long-term strategy for attracting capital. Investors are also looking for good infrastructure, access to markets, well-trained human resources, and quality of life. While countries are under pressure to lower their production standards and cut down on taxes and public spending, this may also affect their competitiveness in the longer term. Our economic system literally cannot help destroying its own foundations.

As Swedish anthropologist Helena Norberg-Hodge noted:

> Globalization is often portrayed as the product of natural and evolutionary forces beyond anyone's control. The World Bank's website, for example, claims that 'Globalization is an inevitable phenomenon in human history.' Further down the page, however, the Bank acknowledges that globalization is actually not inevitable at all: '[It] occurs when countries lower barriers such as import tariffs and open their economies up to investment and trade with the rest of the world.'

In other words, globalization would not be happening unless governments hadn't changed the rules in order to promote it.[47]

We can undo globalization as we know it and relocalize the economy. Indeed, this movement has already started: the share of international trade in global production had slightly decreased in the years preceding the COVID-19 pandemic, which will likely accelerate this trend.[48] Financial globalization also has shown signs of decline since the 2008 financial crisis, for example with a 35 percent decrease in volume of international loans between banks for the 2008–2019 period and a significant reduction in the share of public debt owned by nonresidents in many countries such as the US or France.[49] By reregulating trade and finance and shifting subsidies, we can regain control over our economic system and make it serve our well-being. In fact, this would reduce pollution and the energy used for transportation, as well as inequalities. It would reaffirm national sovereignties, provide much more autonomy to nations, revive democracy, and allow cultural diversity to flourish.

"There is a structural link between globalization and monoculture: global corporations are successful only if they can market on a massive scale for a huge number of homogenized consumers,"[50] explains Norberg-Hodge. Relocalizing the economy can also strengthen communities, our connection to the landscape, and environmental sustainability (through shorter feedback loops), as well as economic resilience. In general, local economies should provide for our essential needs; whenever conditions are suitable, goods and services should be produced locally. International trade would provide for the rest. If nations recover some degree of autonomy and compete less on the global market, it would become easier to promote both minimum global social and environmental standards (e.g., minimum wage) and international cooperation, in particular between small-scale organizations.

In a world close to collapse and climate chaos, the aim is to build as much as possible, decentralized, self-reliant, human-scale economies, adapted to diverse places and people, which makes localization "not a rigid prescription."[51]

Norberg Hodge has seen how, in a generation, the integration of the global economy has disorganized and negatively affected the Indian Himalayan Ladakhi people. Traditional cultures provide ways of life—integrated cultural, political, social, economic, and environmental practices—that allow people to live sustainably in their particular environment and often enjoy more fulfilled lives. Relocalizing economies and re-embedding them in our societies can help us to regain such balance. Eco-villages and intentional communities are trying to reinvent communitarian practices and widen our sense of community to the natural world, strengthening our connection to the landscape.[52] Their values and practices are generally supportive of the (well-)being paradigm and focus on human, social, and environmental regeneration rather than financial capital. They include a pooled economy, shared work, work-life balance, inclusive decision-making, conflict resolution, limited hierarchy, dimensioned communal group, celebration, physical contact, parent-child proximity, self-development and spiritual practices, inclusiveness, emphasis on arts and culture, healthy food, physical activity, proximity to nature, environmental activism, and ecologically responsible behaviors.[53]

While it seems unlikely that the majority of the population will live in intentional communities and eco-villages (though the development of remote work may considerably facilitate this in the future), they can pilot, experiment, and provide an evidence base for the implementation of the politics of being. Their development should be facilitated, including by establishing a legal status for them associated with specific legal norms and policies.[54] More generally, local communities should be strengthened through numerous policies, including decentralization, participative budgets, local currencies, community-owned companies (in particular for renewable energy production and banking), cohousing, and mandatory community work for all people aged beyond fifteen.

Collaborative (civic tech, crowdfunding, sharing economy, etc.) platforms also have a lot to offer to strengthen community management capacities. Based on cooperation and reciprocity, community management is considered one of the three main types of governance structures, together with markets (based on voluntary exchanges and competition) and hierarchies (systems of command that we can find in companies or the government).[55] From a theoretical perspective, the politics of being stresses the importance of community management and avoiding the concentration of power. It uses governments' capacities to empower communities and better regulate markets.

It takes strong communities to raise responsible individuals and the interbeing paradigm. I have been able to witness this in Plum Village, where the daily coordination and work of all those who live here is not so much based on stringent rules, and even less so on economic incentives. It is much more founded on intrinsic motivation, personal responsibility, self-regulation, and a sense of love and community. It is supported by the spiritual commitments and practices of everyone, as well as specific practices aimed at ensuring healthy communication and solving conflicts ("beginning anew" presented in chapter 11), providing peer feedback ("shining light"), and strengthening community bonds (e.g., parties and games). The coordination is very much flexible and organic, adapting itself continuously to how each individual presently feels to support everyone's freedom, well-being, and growth.

Democratizing the economic system

Relocalization would go along with the democratization of the economic system, which means limiting the size and power of transnational corporations and financial markets. The latter should be much more regulated with measures of capital control. It may become politically more feasible to get tax havens suppressed as economic globalization recedes and they become less relevant. A drastic strengthening of antitrust laws and the abandonment of free-trade agreements (American economist David Korten prefers to call them "international corporate rights agreements"[56]) and subsidies to large corporations could help reduce their size and power.

Intellectual property rights systems need to be reformed to better support the general interest in terms of competition, innovation, access to necessities and human rights, and enact the paradigm of being in which effort, and thus, innovation, is motivated more intrinsically than by the prospect of financial gains. Cooperation can be strengthened in particular by supporting open-source production models and public investments in research.

Instead of transnational companies, relocalization would foster small and place-based economic entities, which can be more accountable to their communities. To that end, David Korten proposes a radical approach, which would not be easy to implement but offers a useful vision: that all companies with more than twenty employees can only operate under the form of cooperatives or public enterprises. Regulation could also favor businesses' contribution to the common good.

As mentioned in the chapter on work and organization, incentives could be also created to favor specific types of companies that pursue public benefit, with or without financial profits. Beyond fostering cooperatives or employees' participation in the capital of companies, decision-making rules within companies (except the smallest ones) could also evolve by giving voting rights to employees. This is, for example, the case in Germany and Sweden, whose successful governance models respectively include a 50 percent and 33 percent allocation of voting rights to employees.[57] These rights could be also extended to other stakeholders.

In the case of companies pursuing a social purpose, such as stakeholders representing intended beneficiaries, these could also be formally associated with decision-making. Countries have the right to decide what types of companies can receive a business license to operate under their jurisdiction and determine the rules of the game. A truly democratic economic system would make good use of this prerogative.

Transforming the monetary system

"Money ... so they say ... is the root of all evil today ..." sang Pink Floyd.[58] In fact, the transformation of our monetary systems at all scales— international, national, and local—is instrumental for the paradigmatic change we are calling for and the establishment of a just and sustainable economic organization that fosters abundance. At the international level, establishing a global currency could have very positive effects (see box 10).

Box 10—A Global Currency

Many famous economists have supported this idea, from John Maynard Keynes to James Tobin or Joseph Stiglitz. A global currency would eliminate currency risk and transaction costs and facilitate fair trade among nations shielded from the manipulation of exchange rates, as well as support global financial stability and prosperity[59] and more harmonious international relations. Nowadays, in practice, the US dollar serves as the main international currency, with 88 percent of international trade[60] and 61 percent of foreign exchange reserves[61] labeled in US dollars. By controlling the issuance of dollars, the US benefits from huge privileges over other nations in terms of access to capital and financing their deficits. However, the US also suffers from corresponding costs as this situation increases the dollar value, eroding US competitiveness and fueling the US trade deficits that are financed by other countries.[62]

Other nations have repeatedly called for a more balanced international monetary system, in particular after the 2008 financial crisis. In 2009, a UN commission of financial experts led by Joseph Stiglitz proposed a world reserve currency issued by the International Monetary Fund that would be used as reserve assets by all national and regional central banks, but not for international trade.[63] This was considered a more politically feasible alternative, but it remained unimplemented as the US opposed it.

Another priority is to transform how money is created. Money creation is nowadays generally carried out through banks in the form of debt. As these debts carry interest, there is always more debt (including interests) to be repaid than the total amount of money available. There begins scarcity. The injection of new money is restricted to financially profitable activities. This fuels economic growth, which at the same time becomes a necessity to reimburse these debts. When economic growth weakens, more debt needs to be created to keep the system afloat. This causes the financial sphere to grow out of proportion with the real economy, with all the associated risks in terms of financial stability, but also inequality, as financial and real asset prices increase.

Many countries, such as Canada, New Zealand, Japan, Germany, the United Kingdom, and the United States, have long relied on a different system, whether as the norm or as an exception.[64] In this alternative system, money creation, a sovereign prerogative, is done debt-free (or interest-free, which has the same effect[65]) by the government to finance all kind of activities for the public benefit[66] and not only financially profitable ones. This idea has been supported by many eminent economists and financial specialists, including John Maynard Keynes, Irving Fisher, Milton Friedman, Paul Krugman, Maurice Allais, and Ben Bernanke (chair of the US Federal Reserve between 2006 and 2014).[67]

In 2012, an IMF study, through a theoretical model, tested the potential effect of replacing the current US financial system organization with one based on public monetary creation, accompanied by the separation of financial institutions between those handling deposits that are required to hold 100 percent reserve backing and those offering credit and investment products. The study found that it "could significantly reduce business cycle volatility caused by rapid changes in banks' attitudes towards credit risk, it would eliminate bank runs, and it would lead to an instantaneous and large reduction in the levels of both government and private debt."[68] It also found that it would result in a production increase of 10 percent and an inflation drop to zero.[69]

The latter is an important result as the fear of such a system being highly inflationary has been a major argument against it. IMF economists assert, "There is nothing in our theoretical framework to support this claim [...], there is very little in the monetary history of ancient societies and Western nations to support it either."[70] The problem is that it would certainly affect the interests of the financial sector, which may explain why most countries have not yet adopted this system. Public money creation is not a silver bullet; it needs to operate within certain limits to avoid inflation, but it has a great potential to contribute to the transformation of our economies. Money creation is a complex, often oversimplified, but important issue, and I invite readers to deepen their understanding of it.[71]

Finally, as mentioned earlier, local currencies can also support the economy's relocalization, strengthen local communities, and favor more socially responsible economic practices as businesses become more accountable to the local community (see box 11). Local currencies usually develop after economic crises, as they support the resilience of local economies by offering protection against the scarcity of national currency. For example, following the 1929 recession, their number doubled in some European countries between 2008 and 2015.[72]

Local currencies' uses are often limited by the global nature of the economy, but they may grow as the range of products and services that can be bought locally increases. Beyond the benefits provided by local currencies, their development may result from the implementation of the proposed policies aimed at relocalizing the economy. It may also naturally develop out of a global economic system becoming less and less inclusive or even collapsing.

Our economic systems have taken many different forms throughout time and space. The current organization will keep evolving. All its institutions will have to be progressively transformed and aligned around the paradigm of being. Many of the objectives, and some of the recommendations stated here, are already widely supported, but the required measures generally oppose the very core of our economic software and meet strong resistance. In a time of disruption and deepening crises, new and unexpected possibilities will certainly manifest to support this evolution.

Box 11—Local Currencies

Local currencies help people, businesses, and local governments who accept them as an exchange for products and services, as well as to pay taxes. There are an estimated five thousand local currencies in the world, but they account for a very limited portion of economic transactions.[73] One of the most famous examples of a complementary currency is the Swiss WIR bank created in 1934, which allows its more than sixty thousand member companies to trade among themselves through a clearinghouse, after having accessed initial credit.

Local currencies can take different forms. Time-based currencies can facilitate services exchange-valued in terms of time spent among people. More classic complementary currencies allow for the exchange of services and goods at a value that usually mirrors the price system of national currencies, with some discounts to incentivize their use.

Three aspects of complementary currencies are particularly significant. First, they can or cannot bear a demurrage rate (designed to progressively lose their value with time) to incentivize money circulation. Second, they can or cannot be convertible, usually with a penalty to incentivize local spending, into the national currency (WIR money is not). Third, they can or cannot be fiat money, that is to say a money created ex-nihilo with no intrinsic value. In that case, instead of replacing one currency with another through conversion, they allow the local money supply to increase, which can provide many benefits.

In difficult economic times, many people have work to offer, and communities have needs to fulfill, but money is just lacking to mediate the transaction. Issuing fiat money can resolve this problem, while fueling local economic activities, as the money received in payment will be spent locally. Local governments are often prohibited from issuing such fiat money, a prohibition that should be lifted to favor decentralization and local autonomy.

19

Governance

"The science of non-violence can alone lead one to pure democracy."

—Mahatma Gandhi,
political and spiritual leader (1869–1948)

FOR DECADES, LIBERAL democracy has been widely considered the best political system. It is founded on free elections, multipartyism, separation of powers, the rule of law, free media, the protection of human rights, civil rights, civil liberties, and political freedoms for all people. However, it is now increasingly being questioned for its current inability to take the long-term and common good into account to solve our problems in pluralistic and fast-changing societies. As noted by a 2020 study from the Berggruen Institute (on which I draw significantly in this chapter): "A vicious cycle of ever-increasing political paralysis has emerged: the inability of democracies to solve increasingly intractable challenges has exacerbated social divides, and these societal cleavages, in turn, inhibit the democratic process from reaching consensus and taking action."[1]

Polarization, crises of representation, corruption, and hijacking by organized special interests have significantly affected citizens' trust and participation in liberal democracies, while the recent cultural backlash and return of survival values highlighted by Inglehart has contributed to the renewed appeal of authoritarian governance as a way to recover effective decision-making capacities. Liberal democracy is under assault: civil liberties and political freedom have been decreasing at a global level since the mid-2000s,[2] and autocratic regimes are increasingly asserting themselves as alternative models to follow.

Populist leaders play on the legitimate desire to "take back control" from the elites for the people but in practice violate bedrock values of democracy: the search for truth, collective deliberation, pluralism, and separation of powers. For liberal democracy to have a future, it quickly needs to reinvent itself in the twenty-first century.

A new paradigm for democracy

"Democracy needs to be reborn every generation," said American philosopher John Dewey (1859–1952). The discontent with democracy has more to do with the way it does not work in practice, rather than the central principle of self-governance behind it, which is supported by the majority. The long-term evolution of values shows a clear trend toward the public demand for more participation in decision-making.[3] The development of the internet and social media have fundamentally changed the distribution of power and opened new possibilities and expectations for this participation. As it has often done throughout history, democracy needs to adapt to this new context, not by compromising its ideals but by deepening its meaning in practice. The way ahead is to democratize democracy, by making it really participatory. The Berggruen Institute affirms:

> We are living through a paradigm shift from a limited notion of democracy to a fundamentally deeper one in which people want and expect more agency and control. [...] The process of selecting political leaders every few years may remain a necessary condition, but it is no longer a sufficient condition for a government to assert that it is by and for the people. Our institutions must respond to this demand by finding ways to both absorb and respond to the various ways citizens want to participate in their own democracy.[4]

Greater citizen participation can revive democracy's effectiveness and legitimacy, in particular by lessening the hold organized special interests tend to have on representative democracy.

This new paradigm aligns with the politics of being, not only by reaffirming important democratic values such as freedom and diversity, but also by empowering citizens, recognizing that our collective self-governance starts at the individual level within each citizen. Indeed, beyond institutional reforms, it highlights the need for more responsible and reasonable citizens, as well as the development of civic virtues— including a sense of ethics, service, and the public good—and key (inter) being skills. These include our capacity to express ourselves, to listen, to keep an open mind and discern the truth, to understand each other and solve conflicts in a respectful and peaceful manner. These skills allow constructive engagement across pluralistic societies and need to be learned and cultivated through practice.

Spiritual wisdom has much to bring to this conversation, and I will refer in particular in this chapter to the Baha'i tradition, which has developed a unique reflection over its own organization, administration, and governance. Its founder, Baha'u'llah, was aware that with time, religious organizations and clergy tend to exert power for their own profit and historically have most often blocked spiritual evolution by failing to recognize the new prophets their own traditions foretold. This was, for example, the case with Jesus or the Bab, Bahais' first prophet, who claimed to be the awaited messiah in Shia Islam and announced the imminent coming of a new prophet who ended up being Baha'u'llah.

Baha'u'llah and his successors have developed an original governance system for the Baha'i religion and community. They believe this system constitutes "an embryonic model to be adopted voluntarily when the world sees its advantages, acknowledging that it is not simply institutions and procedures, but that it depends on the requisite values, norms and commitments."[5]

Competitive democracy and political polarization

The first challenge for democratic systems is to overcome political polarization and rebuild social cohesion, without which nothing is possible. Nordic countries, Switzerland, and the Netherlands, which by many accounts seem to be most successful, have all developed cultures of consensus and constructive conflict-solving mechanisms that permeate their political systems. While social and political polarization has been recently exacerbated by other factors such as economic inequalities and the evolution and development of traditional and social media (in particular through their algorithms, which expose us to the kind of information we are most likely to believe[6]), polarization is built into the very fabric of our liberal democracies, which assumes that democratic governance requires individuals and groups to compete for political power.

Jane Mansbridge, a prestigious American political scientist,[7] called it "adversary democracy."[8] Michael Karlberg from Western Washington University calls this "competitive democracy"[9] and believes it is based on the assumption that individuals are essentially selfish and have conflicting interests, which elections can help arbitrate.

In such a system, political competition can easily turn into a contest in which all means that ensure the victory of one coalition over the other are justified. The general interest can easily get lost as partisanship takes over, civilities break down, mean-spiritedness develops, and the power of money is being harnessed to advance special interests. In this system dominated by political parties, ideological oppositions take the upper hand over reality, and artificial political identities—based on the aggregation within each camp of varied interests—are reified as binary opposition structures in the political field. Views are seen as oppositional rather than complementary; complex issues are reduced to binary alternatives; and political debates boil down to caricaturing one another's positions and gaining political capital at the expense of others.

Long-term commitments become impossible for two reasons. First, political entrepreneurs need to compete for voters with appealing solutions catered to the immediate interests of their constituents and deliver visible results before the term of their mandates, rather than potentially lose political capital in educating voters to adopt more responsible perspectives. Second, the need for parties to oppose whatever is done by their political opponents often leads them to discontinue or dismantle the policies in place in the case of political alternance. Ultimately we see that in competitive democracies, "the pursuit of material interests becomes more important than the cultivation of mutualistic social relationships";[10] politics necessarily divides rather than unites, and cooperation becomes a political trap or even a betrayal, as each election will produce winners and losers.

I always find it naïve when people believe all it takes to improve our societies is to secure a majority of voters for their ideas, especially when they engender polarization. The assumption that it is fine to impose one's agenda on the rest of society does not stand history's test, which shows that it often breaks down social and political cohesion, when it does not end up in civil wars, coups, or despotism. In an age of increased interdependence, the paradigm of competitive democracy has spurred paralysis and definitely reached its limits. We cannot have real and sustainable progress without transforming our governance systems.

The Baha'i governance system

On the contrary, as explained by Karlberg, a Baha'i himself, "The Bahá'í electoral system is entirely non-partisan and non-competitive."[11] Baha'is elect their representatives directly at the local and regional levels, and indirectly through their representatives, at the national, and global levels. Voting is considered a sacred act, essential to the health of the community. Nominations and campaigning are prohibited, and, at all levels, all adult community members are eligible for election.

Voters are urged not to discuss with others who to vote for but to make their decisions guided only by their own consciences and on the basis of the personal qualities of potential delegates. As mentioned by a former leader of the Baha'i faith:

> The elector [...] is called upon to vote for none but those whom prayer and reflection have inspired him to uphold [...]. Hence it is incumbent upon the chosen delegates to consider without

the least trace of passion and prejudice, and irrespective of any material consideration, the names of only those who can best combine the necessary qualities of unquestioned loyalty, of selfless devotion, of a well-trained mind, of recognized ability and mature experience.[12]

Voters write nine names on their votes, and those receiving the most votes have the duty to serve. As the work of the delegates is fundamentally an act of service to the community, there is no incentive for individuals to solicit votes, and whoever does so will automatically disqualify him or herself in the eyes of the community. Power is exerted collectively by the nine elected members of the local, regional, and national "Spiritual Assemblies," and the global "Universal House of Justice," which avoids all the problems and corrupting influence of concentrating power in individual hands. All members are considered to be at-large, which means they represent not a particular constituency but the whole community and make their decisions according to their own consciences for the general interest.

In parallel to these elected institutions where decision-making and authority are exercised collectively, Baha'is have also a set of appointed institutions. Their members act as individuals to propagate and protect the Baha'i faith, as well as to assist in the implementation of the plans adopted by the administrative institutions. At the global level, these "counselors" are appointed by the Universal House of Justice. They support it, as well as the national assemblies. They serve for five years and appoint members of the auxiliary boards, who support regional and local assemblies. These appointed members, who inspire, advise, and encourage Baha'is, have no decision-making power, but they are considered "the learned," and individuals and institutions are morally obliged to consider their opinions. "The result is a wise separation of individual charismatic leadership and power."[13]

The collective search for truth is encouraged through consultations aiming at gaining multiple perspectives and collectively reflecting on spiritual and ethical principles such as justice, collective trusteeship, humility, diversity, and mutual respect. Governance is approached in a learning mode; to be effective, governance systems need to continuously evolve, which requires a spirit of unity to prevail, and not a culture of opposition and sabotage. Education and capacity building are emphasized as Baha'is recognize that "the efficacy of the structures and processes [of governance] depends, ultimately, on the values, qualities, and capabilities of the individuals who participate in them."[14] Their political philosophy of nonpartisanship also applies to the political jurisdictions Baha'is live in. While "Baha'is express loyalty and obedience to whatever governmental systems they live within," they "avoid active participation in partisan politics in order to focus their energy instead on the construction of an alternative system of governance which they offer as a model for others to study."[15]

Integrating all positive values from the whole political spectrum

Our current political contest and cultural war narrow political perspectives and senses of identity, which in turn affect social cohesion and governance. A politics of being values a diversity of perspectives and the integration of all positive values from across the whole political spectrum. For individuals to be complete, balanced, and ultimately fulfilled, they need to learn to respect, value, and embrace all wholesome values and tap into their energizing power.

In *Sacred America, Sacred World*, Stephen Dinan tells his own story as a young and radical liberal, hungry for social change and novelty, who learns to value and integrate the conservative wisdom of discipline, caution, stability, and personal responsibility as he grows in life. His commitment to transpartisan politics has allowed him to recognize that both liberals and conservatives should reclaim some of the values abandoned to the other side. For Democrats, this includes learning to value personal responsibility, the recognition of some forms of hierarchy and skill mastery, as well as of money and strength as potential engines for good. For Republicans, it can mean acknowledging the importance of social causes on individuals' trajectories, the need to balance the power of free enterprise with some regulation, and greater openness to change. Through concrete examples, Dinan shows how both liberals and conservatives can learn to recognize, from their own distinct perspectives the benefits of many pragmatic solutions and agree on common agendas.

In his book *Developmental Politics—How America Can Grow Into a Better Version of Itself*, integral thinker Steve McIntosh affirms that hyperpolarization is fundamentally a cultural problem that can be solved by improving our "cultural intelligence." This means being able to see the bedrock values of different cultural groups behind conflicts and disagreements. Recognizing them allows us to see that, though they seem at first to oppose each other, they can actually be complementary and work together when balanced and cured from their pathologies.

McIntosh distinguishes three major worldviews active in the US (as in most Western countries): traditionalism, modernism, and progressivism, which represent the nation's cultural heritage. Cultural intelligence entails distinguishing their positive from their negative aspects, which are presented in table 5. By acknowledging both its own negative and others' positive tendencies, each cultural group can grow into a more mature, healthy, and enlightened version of itself. Each group can then more constructively dialogue and work together, which makes a country's evolution and development possible.

As political parties are the active agents of a competitive democracy, the new paradigm of participatory or "citizenship democracy"[16] seems particularly well suited to overcome political polarization and populism while revitalizing democracy. Increased citizen participation needs to address the two fundamental elements of the democratic process: deliberation and decision-making.

Table 5—Positive and negative aspects of different worldviews in the United States[17]

	Positive aspects	Negative aspects
Traditionalism	Loyalty to family and country Duty and honor Sacrifice for the greater good	Racism Sexism Homophobia Authoritarianism
Modernism	Individual liberty Human rights Rule of law Economic and scientific progress Achievement and prosperity	Environmental degradation Economic inequality Nuclear proliferation
Progressivism	Environmentalism Diversity and inclusion Social justice	Anti-modernism Reverse patriotism Divisive identity politics Self-righteous scolding Tyrannical demands

Improved deliberation

"Deliberation is the process by which members of a community discuss political issues in order to find solutions that can be accepted by all (or most) reasonable people."[18] Many online and off-line programs have recently emerged to support transpartisan dialogues and actions, such as Braver Angels or Patriots & Pragmatists in the United States and My Country Talks, an international platform for political dialogue, which was initiated in Germany. Indeed, citizens' willingness to deliberate is wider than is often assumed. Deliberative forums have the power to revive political participation as they particularly appeal to the people less likely to participate in traditional partisan politics.[19]

Deliberation in general improves the quality of public opinion and its pro-social orientation, the confidence in the policy process, tolerance and empathy with others' perspectives, reduces political polarization, and often allows people to change their views.[20] Deliberative polling, for example, uses votes at the end of citizens' well-informed and constructive debates on specific issues—involving representatives of the general public selected through sampling—to generate recommendations for the public and improve the quality of voters' opinions.

Crowdlaw is the use of technology to improve the quality of lawmaking through citizens' engagement. The Berggruen Institute estimated more than a hundred local city councils, as well as regional and national parliaments in Iceland, Ireland, India, etc., were using crowdlaw in 2020. Through collective intelligence and increased transparency, crowdlaw seeks to improve the quality and legitimacy of laws and policies. The Berggruen Institute notes:

> The trick [...] is designing the right type of technology platform for the task and in marrying it to offline political institutions. Each stage of decision-making, from identifying to evaluating problems, demands distinct forms of information and action. To identify a problem correctly, it is best to ensure large-scale input from a broad and diverse set of members of society. However, when it comes to solving problems, this requires time and expertise. The best crowdlaw projects offer different ways of participating—including consultations, competitions, and participatory budgeting.[21]

Taiwan currently constitutes the most successful example of how technology can improve political deliberation and democracy, rather than undermining it (see box 12).

Box 12—Taiwan's Digital Democracy

In 2014, the sunflower student protest movement occurred as a response to the Taiwanese government's intent to sign a trade agreement with China, highlighting its lack of dialogue and attention to public demands. In the aftermath, the government invited a Taiwanese civic tech community, which had played a key role during the protests, to create a platform through which it might better communicate with youth.

VTaiwan was created in 2015 to enable citizens, experts, civil society organizations, and government officials to elaborate and propose laws through its website, face-to-face meetings, and hackathons. Contrary to most social media, which polarizes us by appealing to our emotions and highlighting the most controversial positions, the platform is built to favor consensus-seeking. People propose statements that platform users can agree or disagree with (or pass), but to avoid trolling, there is no reply function. Attitude maps, which group people by viewpoints and areas of agreement, are constantly generated. The most consensual statements, especially across diverse groups, are highlighted.

"People compete to bring up the most nuanced statements that can win most people across. Invariably, within three weeks or four, we always find a shape where most people agree on most of the statements,"[22] explains Audrey Tang, Taiwan's current digital minister. Initial opposition is often overcome as the debate is reframed, disagreements are broken down, and solutions are found to honor and satisfy different perspectives. A specific government authority can sponsor each idea, committing to incorporate it or explaining why it is not feasible.

Once the discussion has matured enough online, live-streamed, face-to-face debates with the main stakeholders are organized, with the possibility for other participants to contribute remotely in real time. When a final consensus is reached, a guideline, policy, official statement, or even draft bill is elaborated and submitted to the government authority in charge. In five years, vTaiwan has enabled the discussion of some thirty national issues[23] by two hundred thousand people,[24] which in more than 80 percent of cases led to public decisions,[25] such as Uber or online liquor sale regulations.

The experience has been so successful that in 2016 the government named one of the leading activists behind vTaiwan, Audrey Tang, "digital minister." Aged thirty-five, she became the first transgender member of the top executive cabinet. Without a portfolio, her mission was to help government agencies communicate and collaborate with the population via digital means. She established a platform similar to vTaiwan, but run by the government—"Join"— and established a network of participation officers in each ministry. Join allows for the hosting and debating of online petitions, which can be initiated by any citizen. The relevant ministries must publicly respond once they reach five thousand signatures. It also supports the annual "Presidential Hackathon," through which citizens identify creative solutions to priority problems. The results are binding: the winning projects are put on the national policy agenda with a budget.

Taiwan's nascent democracy (the country held its first presidential election in 1996) has turned digital, a transformation that received overwhelming support from the population, with ten million people having participated on Join.[26] This has been supported by a strong commitment to open government— characterized by high levels of transparency and mechanisms for public scrutiny and oversight—which allowed Taiwan to rank first in the last (2016/2017) measure of the global open data index[27].

This unique collaboration between national and local governments, tech companies, and citizens has supported Taiwan's social and political cohesion and proved essential in making the country a worldwide example in harnessing the COVID-19 pandemic in 2020. Applications were designed to identify shops with masks available or order them online, to help identify cases, infectious risks, and even monitor people in quarantine through their cell phones.[28]

The Taiwanese experience is quickly spreading abroad within civil societies, governments, and even political parties. The Five-Star Movement in Italy, for example, uses the "Lex iscritti" platform to enable its supporters to propose and discuss legislative measures directly with their elected representatives.

In Taiwan we see how social media could work for the greater good, in particular by cultivating civic virtues, instead of encouraging the worst human tendencies just to increase their profits. Indeed, studies have shown these platforms spread fake news,[29] pessimism, anxiety and depression, division and radicalization, while making us less informed, more biased, and unable to think deeply and long term.[30] Social media platforms need greater duty of care.[31] What companies are in a better position to redirect their purpose toward the common good than these ultra-profitable monopolies? Time is ticking, and if they keep failing to do so, external regulations will have to transform their practices for the public good. Moreover, it is urgent to better control the major influence big tech companies can have on votes, such as through their algorithms orienting our research in the case of Google[32] or a simple reminder to go vote in the case of Facebook,[33] which have been put in evidence by some studies.

The development of digital mega-corporations has also led to a decline in the quality of information and public debate, as well as the disappearance of many newspapers. These negative externalities make a clear economic rationale for some sort of taxation, whose revenue could be channeled to revive responsible local media,[34] and/or fund an independent media tasked with providing high-quality, objective, neutral information that informs the public debate.[35]

As the fourth estate essential to democracy, high-quality journalism should be protected. Beyond professional codes of conduct and ethics, which should be promoted, constantly discussed, and updated, the law should also limit concentration of media ownership by large conglomerates, as is the case, for example, in Germany. The rise of digital mega-corporations has severely affected the press's traditional business model. In France, a few large corporations have taken over a good part of the press. Because this industry has low (sometimes negative) profitability, it is clear that what they are buying is political influence. This undermines our democracy, and even international security, as some of these corporations happen to be from the arms industry.

This leads us to the huge problem of corporations' influence on politics. A very strict regulation of political parties' funding needs to complement media reforms to protect our democracy from the influence of money. It needs to be accompanied by strong anticorruption and integrity policies, particularly addressing lobbying practices,[36] conflicts of interests, and the "revolving door" between government and large corporations, which drains our democracies and the public trust government.

In the US, where political corruption is often considered the country's biggest problem,[37] about half of retiring senators and a third of retiring House members—Republicans and Democrats—register as lobbyists. In the 1970s this figure was below 5 percent. Reportedly lobbying is a US\$3.2 billion-a-year business in the US, which might double if we include the nonregistered lobbyists.[38] Lobbying can be useful in facilitating stakeholders' participation and the quality of law-making, but it is nowadays a major source of corruption, undue influence, and regulatory capture from special interests.

In the US, it is estimated that "for every \$1 spent by public interest groups and unions combined, corporations spent \$34"[39] and that "on average, for every dollar spent on influencing politics, the nation's most politically active corporations received \$760 from the government."[40] This may explain why ex-members of Congress earn at least five times as much as lobbyists than they did during their political service. In some cases, their salaries amount to millions of dollars per year.[41] Regaining control over our political systems primarily means freeing them from the corrupting influence of money.

In addition to civic tech platforms, off-line citizen deliberation forums are also developing and are increasingly being integrated into our political systems. In Ireland, for example, between 2016 and 2018, the citizens' assembly played a key role in the legalization and regulation of abortion. This assembly was composed of a government-appointed chairperson and ninety-nine citizens chosen at random from the electoral register and representative of Irish society in terms of age, gender, social class, regional spread, etc. They met twelve times during full weekends from October 2016 to April 2018 (the initially planned timeline was extended twice) to discuss different issues of national interest, in particular the potential modification to the current prohibition of abortion. Their meetings included expert presentations, question and answer sessions, and debates and roundtable discussions, which were live-streamed and prompted a healthy national debate.

Submissions by the public were invited and resulted in seventeen organizations presenting their views to the assembly. While abortion had long been a politically explosive and socially divisive subject in this very religious country, discussions held in the assembly with the support of experts allowed people to overcome ideological claims, clarify the debate, and find pragmatic solutions tailored to a range of potential circumstances that could be embraced by a large majority. In fact, their recommendations, after being examined by a joint committee of politicians from both Houses of the parliament, led to a referendum in May 2018. An unexpectedly large majority—66.4 percent—of voters decided to replace the constitutional prohibition with a provision allowing the parliament to regulate abortion. This was done a couple of months later, in line with the citizens assembly recommendations. The Health (Regulation of Termination of Pregnancy) Act 2018 allows termination of pregnancy under medical supervision, generally up to twelve weeks' gestation, and in case of serious health risks or fatal fetal abnormalities.

Under different names, citizens' assemblies are quickly developing in many countries, such as Canada, Belgium, the Netherlands, or the UK. In France, a "Citizen's Convention on Climate" has been established and ran between October 2019 and June 2020 to propose a series of measures to the government to achieve at least a 40 percent reduction in greenhouse gas emissions (compared to 1990) by 2030 in a spirit of social justice.

Direct democracy

In addition to further participation in deliberation, there has been a renewed interest in direct democracy, in which collective decisions are taken through the direct votes of constituents. It represents an opportunity to reclaim control and address issues of primary concern to the average person, which are neglected or blocked by elected representatives captured by special interests. According to a global Pew Poll conducted in 2017, 66 percent of respondents preferred such a system over representative democracy.[42] The purest form of direct democracy exists in some Swiss cantons, where all citizens regularly meet and vote to make decisions.

Beyond government or legislature-led referendums and recall elections, by which electors can put an end to a representative's term, the emphasis has recently been on popular referendums and citizen-initiated referendums (also called citizens ballot initiative). Both were adopted by Switzerland in the nineteenth century. Popular referendums allow citizens to exert control over their legislators by giving them the power to call, through a successful petition, existing legislation to a vote by citizens. The risk for any law to be vetoed can incentivize due consultation before it is passed. Citizen-initiated referendums open the possibility for citizens to subject their own proposals to referendums when their petitions raise enough support.

The example of Taiwan shows that technology can be a game-changer for direct democracy, for which the size and complexity of modern polities has long been a major barrier. It is possible to imagine that electors in the near future will be frequently consulted on many issues and could vote through their smartphones. As we may not have the time and expertise to make informed votes on all the issues, we may decide to delegate our votes to people or organizations we trust for specific issues while being able, at any time, to change or cancel such delegation and vote directly. This could considerably strengthen the roles of citizen councils and organizations with expertise in specific fields in the functioning of our democracy. We may be able to choose different delegates to represent us for different issues. This delegation would be kept secret, while the delegates' votes would be public to ensure accountability. This is the concept of "liquid"[43] or "delegated"[44] democracy, which lies between direct and representative democracy. It has not yet been thoroughly tested in practice but could well develop in the future to revive democracy.

The effectiveness of direct democracy depends on the quality of deliberation and the institutional checks and balances in place. Institutional mechanisms are required to support a "knowledge democracy"[45] and avoid the pitfalls of populism. They should allow voters access to relevant information and expertise, protection from the sway of special interests, and balance the principle of one-person-one-vote with the work of experienced and informed representatives, which should be accountable but protected from public pressure. "If unmediated, direct democracy in the Digital Age will look a lot like social media itself," warns the Berggruen Institute.[46] "It will encompass the good, the bad and the ugly, a platform not only for the spread of innovative ideas that respond to citizen concerns, but for ill-tempered blogmobs, hateful sentiments, alternative facts, outright lies, utopian delusions, and worse."[47] For example, in California, we see how direct democracy can lead to bad governance, with citizens' ballots often hijacked by special interests, and decisions often taken without taking the long-term common good into account.[48]

Some measures have been recently proposed and implemented to make California's direct democracy work better. In 2014, the state's law on citizens' initiatives was amended to introduce a "second reading" process by which the legislature is informed of any initiative when it has gathered 25 percent of qualifying signatures for a ballot measure. As in Switzerland, this allows for a negotiation process between sponsors and legislators to improve a measure, with mandatory public hearings on the issue. The outcome of the negotiation can either be adopted by the legislature itself or submitted to referendum. This can be helpful in addressing flaws and unintended consequences, and ensuring the legality of proposed measures.

The Berggruen Institute, which has been involved in this political reform, also made several other proposals. For example, the "second reading" process could "further borrow from the Swiss system by enabling the legislature to place a counter-measure on the ballot if they can't reach agreement with a sponsor whose measure they believe to be against the public interest."[49] Furthermore, as in Oregon, review panels composed of randomly selected citizens could be established, and the findings from their informed deliberation communicated as a short report to the voters. This would be similar to Swiss voter pamphlets, which all voters receive prior to any referendums to have access to good, synthesized information.

Direct democracy should not replace but should complement representative democracy. The latter could be improved, not only to balance citizens' demands (as we will also see later with "intelligent governance"[50]), but to better align with them as well. For example, people could be allowed to vote for "none of the candidates." When this category gains the most votes, elections would have to be repeated—which would create a great incentive for better candidates! Voting could be also made mandatory to make sure elections express the will of the whole population.

Political institutions for the politics of being

Ultimately, the politics of being will have to be enacted in our political institutions. National constitutions could recognize the values and principles of the politics of being, in particular the fulfillment of all beings (humans and nonhumans) as the main objective of our states and societies. The responsibility of the state to empower communities, civil societies, and companies to support this pursuit would be emphasized. In each country, a special council—the "wisdom council" or "being council"—would be established to ensure that national efforts are serving this vision and that societies and cultures do evolve toward this goal. Its mission would also be such that the long-term perspectives were well factored into public debates and decision-making. There would be four kinds of council members:

- One quarter would be randomly selected citizens;

- One quarter would be representatives of the outer economic, social, and environmental life of the nation;

- One quarter would be representatives of inner spiritual, cultural, and psychological life of the nation;

- One quarter would be representatives of nonhuman members of the Earth community (ecosystems, plant and animal species, etc.). In countries where they exist, indigenous people would fill that role. As mentioned by Lakota spiritual leader chief Arvol Looking Horse "the original caretakers of mother earth, have no choice but to follow and uphold the original instructions, which sustains the continuity of Life."[51] This generally goes together with a long-term perspective, as with the Native American principle of considering the effects of decisions over seven generations. In other countries, that would be the responsibility of people who are guarding the sacred traditional ecological knowledge (yes, they exist in every country). For the first few decades, these representatives would receive assistance from scientific authorities in the field of ecology. Beyond their traditional ecological knowledge, the particular positions indigenous people occupy within their nations should be recognized through specific quotas for their representatives, not only in the wisdom council but also in parliament.

All these representatives would be indirectly elected or appointed members on the basis of experience, expertise, and spiritual maturity. This council's members would include significant numbers of young people (from ages fifteen or sixteen) to represent future generations, as well as some elderly people, to benefit from their experience.

All young people need to develop the relevant skills and be prepared early on for their future citizen roles. This means that they should progressively be incorporated into the decision-making processes of their families and schools. The wisdom council would have a collective presidency of between seven to ten members that would be representative of its composition.

Like the French Economic Social and Environmental Council, the mandate of this wisdom council would be to review and advise on proposed policies, conduct the necessary research and debates, and inform the public. In addition, it would have the power to veto an adopted law once before it is promulgated, compelling the parliament to rediscuss it, as well as seizing the constitutional court to ensure laws' constitutionality.[52] It would also have the capacity to propose general policies to parliament to turn them into laws, as well as to submit these general policies or those just adopted by government (before their promulgation) to a referendum.[53]

Finally, it would have the responsibility of monitoring the evolution of the nation and evaluating public policies, as well as private initiatives.

Beyond the traditional economic, social, and environmental lens, special attention would be paid to the inner life of the nation through the consideration of self-fulfillment, values, mental health, and social cohesion indicators. The role of the council would mainly be consultative, but with significant resources—in particular a budget for research and expertise, as well as a dedicated administration—and power to steer and orient the political conversation.

Each year, the wisdom council would preside over national discussions with the government and parliament on the nation's evolution. It would present its assessment of the nation, and the government would have to explain how its politics serves the constitutional goal of self-fulfillment and how it intends to address current challenges and opportunities from this perspective. The wisdom council would be integrated with other political institutions, in particular the parliament, with at least a "lower house" inspired by the Baha'i model, that we will now review. In that case, and assuming greater political maturity from this lower house, the council could even play the role of an "upper house," but with no power to vote on laws.

A governance model for the politics of being will share many of the features mentioned in this chapter. It should ideally draw on the wisdom and experience gathered by different civilizations across history, while adjusting to each nation's cultural, historical, and political specificities. The Baha'is' administrative organization, with its nonpartisan and noncompetitive philosophy, which has been designed to serve as a model for the world, can be an important source of inspiration. It has been amazing for me to find out that Berggruen and Gardels, in their search for a template for intelligent governance for the twenty-first century,[54] have come out with a model that displays important similarities with the Baha'i system.

This is particularly striking in their vision of the lower house of parliament at different scales, plus the emphasis on nonpartisan and enlightened decision-making, as well as collective leadership. While they never mention the Baha'is, and there is no trace in their work of any such affiliation, Berggruen and Gardels have sought to combine the wisdom and experience of the United States' democratic and China's meritocratic systems to propose "a middle way between West and East,"[55] toward which each model should move to find or recover its balance. Berggruen and Gardels state:

> The balance might be called "intelligent governance," which devolves power and meaningfully involves citizens in matters of their competence while fostering legitimacy and consent for delegated authority at higher levels of complexity. Devolving, involving and decision-division are the key elements of intelligent governance that will reconcile knowledgeable democracy with accountable democracy.[56]

This search for a balance between democracy and meritocracy has a long history, including in the West, from Plato to America's founding fathers and modern thinkers such as John Rawls.

Building on the work of some of the best Western and Asian scholars—such as political philosopher Bai Tongdong—Berggruen and Gardels have found that both point in the direction of a similar template, which they propose "as an act of political imagination."[57] Very much like the Baha'is' organization, Berggruen and Gardels conceived a pyramidal structure in which elected representatives at one scale elect one delegate to represent them at the next scale. Similar to Baha'is' voting system, they recommend, at the local (district) scale a system, using single transferable voting to ensure representation of the whole community. In such a system, used in places such as Australia or Ireland, people vote for different candidates as their number one, two, three, etc. preference. If a person's preferred candidate has already received enough votes to be elected, the individual's second choice is considered. The same goes for the voter's third choice, etc.

Berggruen and Gardels' system considered four governance scales or levels: district, sector, region, and nation. This "community-based democracy"[58] brings representatives and voters closer at the local level, where it is more relevant, while breaking down the political system into human-scale units, where deliberation can take place. It has the potential to support communities' self-organization, decentralization of decision-making and accountability, diversity, and unity. Moreover, the small communities of elected members formed at every scale allow them to get to know each other and assess their respective skills, maturity, and wisdom. This organization creates favorable conditions to choose the best representatives and hold them accountable, according to Berggruen and Gardels.

This lower house would be complemented by an upper house of parliament, designed as a nonpartisan body protected from undue pressures and focused on the long term and the bigger picture. Hence its members would not be elected but randomly selected citizens (ten), as well as appointed members (forty) on the basis of experience and expertise, in order to match capacities and knowledge with the concerns of the average citizen.[59] The responsibility of the upper house would include proposing legislation, providing a second-reading function with the lower house, negotiating legislative compromises, and overseeing the public administration. The government leader would be elected by the lower house, and its cabinet would be approved by the upper house.

As in the Baha'i model, Berggruen and Gardels stress the importance of the collective exercise of power and propose "a kind of 'council of elders' standing above the operational fray of politics and governance,"[60] whose members are nominated by the executive and approved by the lower house:

> The quadrumvirate, or collective presidency of four members, is a council of distinguished elder statespersons who would represent the unity of the society and the long-term perspective and continuity of the culture. [...] Moral influence would be their main tool and stewardship of the society as a whole their main charge. [...] Their role would be to provide symbolism of the whole and a sense of unity and harmony, especially in ethnically, religiously and culturally diverse societies.[61]

The quadrumvirate would be responsible for selecting twenty of the members of the upper house and for scheduling regular public referenda on key policies of the government. In parallel, the independent Human Resources Agency (HRA) and Government Integrity Office (GIO) would ensure the excellence, honesty, and transparency of the public administration. This could be achieved through regular evaluations (including by the public they serve), meritocratic promotions, and open-government practices, allowing citizens to access all non-security-related government documents. Civil servants would be nonpartisan and have no active business interests.

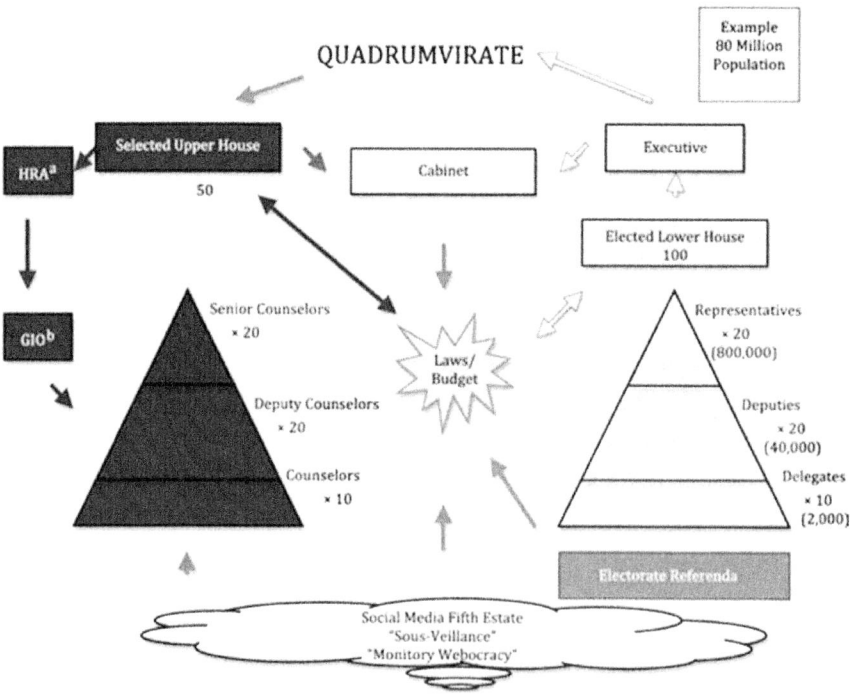

Figure 8. Features of intelligent governance according to Berggruen and Gardels (courtesy of Alexander Gardels).[62]

As Berggruen and Gardels see it, intelligent governance can combine the wisdom of the East and the West "to seek a harmonious equilibrium in human affairs—between responsibility and personal choice, community and the individual, freedom and stability, well-being and well-having, humankind and nature, present and future."[63] They consider that our governance systems have until now lagged behind our technological development, creating multiple imbalances that threaten our future. By improving the quality of decision-making and making our different political operating systems compatible, intelligent governance can enable the emergence of a global civilization. As "the practical application of an evolved worldview,"[64] intelligent governance may be adopted when "our species will graduate from the primitive, competitive mode of human evolution—'survival of the fittest'—to a less conflictive, more intelligent, and more cooperative mode—'survival of the wisest,'"[65] the authors conclude. The purpose of the politics of being is to facilitate this transition.

International governance

Baha'i teachings emphasize one fundamental element in an interdependent world: the need to strengthen international governance and create a global federation of nations with a world's super-state, respecting the autonomy of its state-members and the rights of all individuals. The Baha'i vision includes an elected world parliament as the main power, a binding world tribunal, and a world executive backed by an international force to carry out the decisions of these legislative and judicial bodies. While populist leaders deny this reality, many of our greatest problems—such as climate change, pandemics, terrorism and cybersecurity, tax evasion and financial regulation, immigration, etc.—cannot be managed and solved at the national level.

The idea of a world government can understandably meet with strong resistance considering the dysfunction of our national governance system and the corrupting influence of powerful organized interests. A priority might be to restore national sovereignty before transferring some of it to the international level. Indeed, reviving our democracies would help strengthen international governance, which citizens trust and benefit from.[66] Such a system would operate at all scales under the principle of subsidiarity: functions of government should take place at the lowest possible levels for them to be adequately performed.

The politics of being calls for a transformation of the United Nations, which is the institutional embodiment of humanity's oneness. Its charter is a code of ethics for relations between nations that embodies high ideals such as peace, justice, freedom, nondiscrimination, and human rights. The UN system has all the limitations inherent to large organizations and the current state of international relations, but it has also helped the emergence of an international community and international law, fostered international cooperation to solve many problems, and built one of the longest-lasting times of peace of the last five thousand years.

Some seventy-five years after the foundation of the United Nations, the context, challenges, and priorities have changed. Colonization and the cold war have ended; terrorism has emerged as a major threat; globalization has created a more interdependent world in which many problems are global by nature; and economic development has not only increased standards of living but also threatens the very conditions for human life on Earth. It is now time to review the founding principles, governance, priorities, and operation modalities of the UN system, so that it can be a force for progress in this new era. The UN system needs to go beyond its current intergovernmental nature and become more democratic, more efficient, and more integrated.[67]

- A recent detailed proposal[68] based on reflections accumulated over generations and from multiple backgrounds adapts the Baha'i vision to the current context. Among other things, it suggests:

- A reform of the UN General Assembly introducing weighted representation to enhance its legitimacy and its complement with a second chamber representing global citizenry (a "world parliament"). It would hold legislative power with direct effect on member states for a narrow set of issues, including the maintenance of peace and security and the management of the global environment;

- Replace the Security Council with an executive council elected by the General Assembly operating under its jurisdiction, which would focus on implementation, management, and effective operation of the UN;

- Create a UN International Security (or Peace) Force under the control of the General Assembly via the executive council;

- To foster the peaceful settlement of international disputes and enforcement of international law, give the International Court of Justice (ICJ) compulsory jurisdiction over all substantive matters pertaining to the interpretation and/or enforcement of international law for all UN members.

Turning the Baha'i vision into reality may take some time and could face harsh resistance from the great powers and their veto rights, but possibilities of gradual reforms exist. This will all depend on the political circumstances, which are likely to evolve in the coming decades as the world enters a deepening crisis. A first step will be to organize a world conference on global institutions. At some point, the UN charter will have to be reviewed to pass the above-mentioned reforms. This was initially planned to be done every ten years, or whenever a two-thirds majority in the UN General Assembly or nine members of the council of security requested it, but it never happened.[69]

The revised UN charter, or that of a new organization replacing the UN,[70] will have to be based on a new worldview, as humanity grows from adolescence to adulthood. It needs to recognize that our destinies are tied together, that we share this planet with other species that also have the right to thrive, that environment is not a limit to development but its very condition,[71] that human development is fundamentally about being more, and spiritual values are the foundations of genuine progress. From this perspective, a spiritual advisory body would need to be created, composed of indirectly elected or appointed members chosen for their personal spiritual development and wisdom, and their capacity to apply these qualities to political decision-making. The advisory body's composition would reflect the diversity of cultures and spiritual traditions, including nonreligious ones, but its members would neither be appointed, nor represent specific religious or spiritual organizations—such as clergymen or clergywomen—in order to avoid them being accountable to any of these organizations and to ensure their freedom.

Rather than reacting to each of the many crises the world faces, it is time for governments to sit together and honestly discuss how to proactively address their common roots. Rather than arguing about wars, power, and economic interests, they should discuss how to urgently safeguard the conditions for life to thrive, and how we can help our cultures evolve into a functional and caring human family.

IV

THE POLITICS OF BEING
IN PRACTICE

"[T]hat which has now become the demand of the Time-Spirit on the human race, that it shall find subjectively, not only in the individual, but in the nation and in the unity of the human race itself, its deeper being, its inner law, its real self and live according to that and no longer by artificial standards." [1]

—Sri Aurobindo, Hindu spiritual teacher (1872–1950)

20

One World

"I see a time of seven generations when all the colors of mankind will gather under the sacred Tree of Life and the whole Earth will become one circle again. [...] I salute the light within your eyes where the whole universe dwells. For when you are at that center within you and I am that place within me, we shall be as one."

—Crazy Horse, Lakota leader (1840–1877)

Humanity is one tribe and the Earth our sacred territory. We live in extraordinary times: globalization is bringing back together the human family (Homo genus), which arose 2.3 million years ago in Africa. We spread around the world in small groups, developing into distinct species—Homo Habilis, Homo Erectus, Homo Neanderthalensis, Homo Rhodesiensis, etc.—to adapt to distinct environments. Some two hundred and fifty thousand years ago, our species—Homo Sapiens—appeared again in Africa. Seventy to ninety thousand years ago, these modern humans moved out of Africa, progressively replacing and in some cases interbreeding with archaic humans (e.g., Neanderthals and Denisovans) all over the world.[1] Everywhere, specific cultures developed with their own experience, knowledge, and wisdom that allowed them to thrive in their respective contexts.

As the human family reunifies itself for the first time in history, all this priceless heritage becomes available to us in historical records, as well as living cultures. This opens a unique opportunity for evolution, if the human family can really become functional and cooperate to address our collective challenges from climate change to plastic pollution, from global pandemics to migration.

A civilization of the universal

September 11, 2001, brought with it the fear of a clash of civilizations, a concept formulated by Samuel Huntington.[2] He believed that people's cultural and religious identities were the primary sources of conflict in the post-Cold War world and that this diversity necessarily leads to clashes. This dark view of globalization stands in stark contrast with the one expressed, for example, by poet and first president of Senegal Léopold Sédar Senghor (1906–2001). Inspired by the work of Pierre Teilhard de Chardin and its spiritual vision of history moving toward the "omega point," Senghor called for a "civilization of the universal,"[3] in which all civilizations share their best. He considered this civilization, which puts human beings at its center, "a reconstruction of human unity through its cultural diversity,"[4] as one of Senghor's commentators put it. In fact, Senghor believed that every nation should reconnect to its own roots and cultures, so as to contribute to the civilization of the universal and enrich our common humanity. This is also necessary to be able to positively receive and integrate contributions from other cultures, without being assimilated.[5]

Many prophets of humanity's entrance into adulthood, including Sri Aurobindo and Baha'u'llah, have defended the same idea. Following its founder's proclamation that "the earth is but one country, and mankind its citizens,"[6] the Bahá'í International Community stated:

World citizenship begins with an acceptance of the oneness of the human family and the interconnectedness of the nations of "the earth, our home." While it encourages a sane and legitimate patriotism, it also insists upon a wider loyalty, a love of humanity as a whole. It does not, however, imply abandonment of legitimate loyalties, the suppression of cultural diversity, the abolition of national autonomy, nor the imposition of uniformity. Its hallmark is "unity in diversity."[7]

We see that this vision also opposes the trend of globalization as westernization or Americanization, which has created considerable tensions in many countries, and has incited extremist responses such as Islamic terrorism. Senghor called for a dialogue of civilization, which has been institutionalized at the international level through venues such as the United Nations Alliance of Civilizations (UNAOC) launched in 2005 as a response to rising extremism and tensions, in particular between the Western and Islamic worlds. This dialogue can make our cultural diversity a real source of mutual enrichment, as we have often seen in the past. In the Al-Andalus empire in Spain (eighth to fourteenth century AD), for instance, Muslims, Christians, and Jews coexisted and collaborated relatively peacefully, giving rise to a major cultural center in Europe at this time.

"Unity in diversity" is the key principle to sustain harmonious relationships between individuals, groups, and nations at all scales, as we increasingly actualize our true selves. We can contemplate it in nature (diversity is an indicator of an ecosystem's health and resilience) and evolution, through which organisms become more complex, integrated, and conscious. This perennial wisdom has been adopted by many modern political entities as their founding principle or motto. We can see this in the United States ("E pluribus unum,"[8] usually translated as "out of many, one"), in the European Union ("in varietate concordia"[9]), as well as in Indonesia,[10] Papua New Guinea,[11] Jamaica,[12] and South Africa.[13]

Differences enrich human interactions. Unity should not mean uniformity for all parts of a whole to truly express themselves. Diversity should not signify fragmentation, so every part can truly benefit from the support of the whole. The sense of belonging to strong local and national communities is an important condition for the advent of a truly global civilization.

Interreligious dialogue and a global ethics

Religious roots are central in the characterization of different civilizations, as recognized by Huntington. In 2015, 6.2 billion people were religiously affiliated, while only 1.2 billion (16 percent of the world's population) declared themselves unaffiliated.[14] The largest religious groups are Christians (2.3 billion), Muslims (1.8 billion), Hindus (1.1 billion), and Buddhists (0.5 billion). It may sound surprising, but the world is getting more religious. The process of secularization associated with modernization and economic development is more than offset by the fact that less economically advanced countries have much higher fertility rates (two or three times the replacement rates) than richer countries (below replacement rates).[15] In addition, the world's current turmoil may increase the sense of existential insecurity that is associated with religious affiliation.[16] Sixty-eight percent of human beings consider religion important in their daily lives.[17] While this percentage drops to some 20 percent in high-income countries,[18] these countries' cultures are still very much shaped by their religious and philosophical foundations.

The importance of religions leads to three major conclusions. First, as the main source of meaning and hope for the vast majority of people, religions have a huge capacity to spur and support the changes that are needed and thus should be strongly involved in these efforts. Second, our collective evolution will necessarily go along with religions' transformation, which has been too often a source of conflict and obscurantism. I see this process as a rediscovery of the authentic spiritual wisdoms and messages that lie at religion's core. Third, "There will be no peace among the nations without peace among the religions. There will be no peace among the religions without dialogue among the religions."[19]

The growing interfaith movement responds to this call. While interreligious dialogue has long existed, it has intensified and enriched itself drastically during the last decades. The 1893 Parliament of the World's Religions meeting in Chicago is often considered the birth of the global interfaith movement. While it was not fully inclusive[20] and did not result in any substantial follow-up action, it connected Western and Eastern religions and spurred a new interest in comparative religious studies.[21] The

Parliament of the World's Religions had to wait a century before a second meeting in 1993, and in 2018 celebrated its sixth gathering.

Other international interfaith organizations—such as the United Religions Initiative,[22] Religions for Peace,[23] the Temple of Understanding,[24] the World Congress of Faiths,[25] or the Fellowship of Reconciliation,[26] to name just a few—are now promoting understanding and harmony among religions and bringing them together to work for the good of their communities and the world. Religions have also followed that trend. The Second Vatican Council (1962–1965), for instance, marked a new Catholic commitment to interreligious dialogue. Interfaith organizations are now active in almost all major cities in the world, building a sense of community and friendship among their members, and interfaith ministries have spread. The United Nations also echoed this movement by establishing the World Interfaith Harmony Week in 2010,[27] which occurs during the first week of February. The idea was promoted by King Abdullah II of Jordan and his cousin Prince Ghazi bin Muhammad.

The interfaith movement has played an instrumental role in the development of a global ethics, which has become a necessity for people from different cultures, religions, and nations to live together. The Dalai Lama has been a strong supporter of this global ethic, which he simply considers the promotion of universal human values.[28] I agree with him in that this ethic should be secular and not rely on religious dogma. That does not mean this global ethic opposes religions; on the contrary, religions have major contributions to offer.

"Towards a Global Ethic: An Initial Declaration,"[29] also known as the Global Ethic, mostly drafted by Swiss theologian Hans Küng, became an official declaration of the Parliament of the World's Religions in 1993. In a nonreligious way, it expresses the core principles and values shared by the world's religious, spiritual, and cultural traditions. Based on the foundational tenets of human dignity and the Golden Rule of reciprocity, it calls for a change of consciousness and a commitment to a culture of nonviolence and respect for life, economic justice, truth and compassion, as well as women's rights. As a living document, it was revised in 2018 to include the commitment to care for the Earth. It has inspired numerous other documents, such as the Earth Charter. The interreligious statement at the Rio + 20 Conference recognized this "global ethical consciousness as the foundation of the other three pillars of a sustainable way of life, because it involves the internalization of the values of sustainable human development; it is a source of inspiration and motivation for action, as well as an essential guide regarding the path to genuine sustainability."[30]

Interspirituality

Beyond religion, mystics and contemplatives from all over the world are coming together to frame a new approach to spirituality, a "practical, mystical, universal understanding of spirituality"[31] that can provide the basis for the intended transformation of consciousness and the politics of being. They have realized that at the core of all religions lies the same mystical experience: a profound sense of interconnectedness that is often called unity consciousness, or nondualism. It can be accessed through different practices, take different forms, and be interpreted according to different cultural perspectives, but the experience is the same: the sensation of separateness vanishes, replaced by oneness and unconditional love for all that is.

Wayne Teasdale (1945–2004), an American Catholic monk, was the first to coin the term "interspirituality" in 1999 in his book *The Mystic Heart—Discovering a Universal Spirituality in the World's Religions.* Teasdale states:

> The real religion of humankind can be said to be spirituality itself, because mystical spirituality is the origin of all the world religions. If this is so, and I believe it is, we might also say that interspirituality— the sharing of the ultimate experience across traditions—is the religion of the third millennium. Interspirituality is the foundation that can prepare the way for a planet-wide enlightened culture, and a continuing community among the religions that is substantial, vital and creative.[32] It "will be an enhanced understanding of the inner life through assimilating the psychological, moral, aesthetic, spiritual, and literary treasures of the world's religions."[33]

Twenty years later, the term "interspirituality" is widely recognized, now displaying twenty-eight thousand seven hundred results on Google.[34]

As a mature approach to a spiritual life in the twenty-first century, interspirituality can provide the spiritual foundations for the politics of being. In the words of Teasdale, "Interspirituality [...] seeks the larger understanding of spirituality itself and will not settle for anything else."[35] It recognizes that spiritual life integrates all aspects of ourselves (body, mind, soul, and spirit) and of our lives; it can be nourished not only by contemplative practices, but also by physical disciplines such as hatha yoga or tai-chi-chuan, art, or socially engaged practices. Science is not seen as a threat but as an opportunity to deepen our understanding of our outer and inner worlds. It is necessarily a part of the interspiritual discussion. It can support our comprehension of the active role of the spirit in evolution and history. It can help us to better understand ourselves as human beings and guide our transformation through contemplative practices that are being increasingly studied in terms of their effects on the brain.

While brain studies are now considered a research priority, many leading scientists consider understanding consciousness as the next frontier. Among these scientists are James Watson (Nobel Prize winner and co-discoverer of DNA), David Gross (a leading string theorist), and E.O. Wilson (often called the "father of sociobiology" or the "father of biodiversity").[36] While modern science and spirituality are essentially and methodologically different, they have lots to learn from each other in their search for universal truth. Both "need to relax their narrow, shallow zealotry and open themselves to the good science and the deep spirituality [...] where they both can find a deepening accord," said Ken Wilber.[37]

Over the last centuries, science has developed and, through its focus on the outer world, has enabled a drastic improvement of our material conditions. Turning the lens of science inward, toward the vast and collectively unexplored territories of our psyches, souls, and spirits, now holds the key to human flourishing. This will provide a basis for the development of our collective inner literacy that is needed to sustain a politics of being.

Spiritual traditions enrich and complete each other. Many people engaged in interspirituality have found that engaging with the most enlightening teachings of other traditions has allowed them to reconnect to the essence and deepen their understanding of their own tradition. While being rooted in a tradition can be a good thing, we should avoid being stuck in it. Teasdale explains, "The point is to have roots that nourish, rather than a desperate clinging that chokes off real spirituality vitality. Spirituality is always about what nourishes. Tradition is useful as long as it enhances and serves the inner life. When it becomes an obstacle, we need to rethink the hold our religion has on us."[38]

By bringing traditions' attention back to the mystical experiences that founded them, interspirituality invites all traditions into a profound renewal, which many religious institutions struggle to face. This renewal emphasizes the spiritual dimension of religions over their cultural dimensions and spirit over scriptures. While religions' spiritual dimensions embody unique relationships to the divine, they have the potential to bring humanity together. On the contrary, religions' cultural dimensions, which often provide a rough but comfortable sense of identity and sacralize certain sociocultural institutions, regularly stand in the way of this unification.

Teasdale predicts that the "interspiritual age" we are entering will see the formation of "a universal civilization,"[39] a global culture based on common spiritual values. Echoing Senghor's views, Teasdale values the rich diversity of spiritual traditions as our "common heritage,"[40] believing that each of them is "a living social organism capable of infinite growth"[41] and has its own contribution to make to this "civilization with a heart."[42] He says, "To leave out any spiritual experience is to impoverish humanity. Everything must be included, that is, everything that is authentic and genuine, that springs from contact with the divine, however we know or conceive this."[43]

Interspirituality is allowing the emergence of, or revealing, what I personally like to call the "Earth Wisdom." It includes all the diverse contributions of spiritual traditions: the cosmic, diverse, and universal nature of the Sanātana Dharma (Hinduism); the Buddhist insight of non-self and practice of mindfulness; the nonviolence of Jainism; the Taoist metaphysics and natural wisdom; the indigenous people's sense of Earth sacredness and community; the Jewish attention to God and their law; Jesus's promise of radical individual and social transformation through loving God and the other as oneself; the faith and submission to God's will of the Muslim people; the uncovering of the progressive nature of divine revelation of Baha'u'llah ... [44] They all need to be embraced by the universal civilization as different aspects of the same truth, as the unique multifaceted wisdom of our planet. The recognition and love of the spirit, the divine, or God in all their manifestations is the mark of true global spiritual citizenship.

As all the greatest spiritual teachings are now available to many of us, I have come to consider that an authentic spiritual search naturally leads us to interspirituality. In my case, this search has guided me toward what I needed to grow and heal, to actualize my true being. My Catholic childhood awakened and nurtured my relationship to the divine. Music, literature, poetry, and movies have all contributed to my spiritual journey. They especially inspired me to believe and follow my inspiration when I was a teenager. The contact with native spirituality in Mexico helped me reconnect with the Earth and the spiritual warrior in me. This led me to the practice of martial arts, and then energetic arts (tai-chi-chuan, chi-kong, etc.), which have actualized my energetic potential and my capacities as a healer.

Tai-chi-chuan, which I sometimes teach, is rooted in Taoism. I consider Taoism particularly enlightening to contemplate how reality unfolds and to guide our journey flowing with it. Working for the forest has helped me understand where I come from as a soul. The same is true of my encounter with the work of Sri Aurobindo and his feminine alter-ego, Mirra Alfassa, alias "the Mother,"[45] which a professional assignment in India unexpectedly led me to. Alternative therapists have also helped me to understand myself better and to see how my mind—psychology, emotions, etc.—deeply impact my body.

Finally, I felt the need to be more rooted in one tradition to be able to practice more deeply and systematically. At that time, I found in the teachings of Zen Master Thich Nhat Hanh the medicine for my soul, with their emphasis on joy, ease, and the transformation of suffering.

Once I was in the bookshop in Plum Village; as I turned my head, I noticed a sentence on the cover of the book someone was carrying. It said something like: "If you make your path a struggle then it is not your path." That was a big lesson for someone coming from the warrior path!

I have found the practice of mindfulness very adaptable to my busy life. I can (theoretically!) always practice: while I empty the dishwasher, while I read a book to my daughters in bed, while I walk from one place to another ... As a professional, I have renamed my "to-do list" my "working meditation list." Practicing in Plum Village, I have learned to take care of myself, my mind particularly, which is the main focus of Buddhism. I enjoy the teachings here on engaged or applied Buddhism that have nourished this book.

Some people who come here prefer to consider themselves mindfulness practitioners and are slightly wary of Buddhist teachings. I am not. I very much enjoy and practice Buddhism together with mindfulness. But I prefer not to call myself by any denomination because people tend to perceive this as "exclusive," whereas I feel all the different spiritual traditions that I have been in touch with are alive within and nourishing me. This is what Rabbi Gliberman, an Orthodox rabbi from New York City, explains: "In exploring other traditions and in embracing them, remember, it isn't a question of instead of—Buddhism instead of Christianity, or Christianity instead of Islam—but rather of in addition to, that is, in addition to Buddhism, Christianity, in addition to Christianity, Islam."[46]

Earth wisdom

My interspiritual commitment and its link to the politics of being has recently taken a new form. In November 2019, my wife Emelina almost fainted when she saw Jean Fleury ("Ejna, Jean turned inside out," according to her explanation) serving herself lunch in Plum Village. Emelina could hardly speak but asked me to invite this woman to join us for lunch. Once we were sitting together, Emelina told Ejna, "I saw you in my dreams ... some thirty years ago. I was around ten or eleven years old.

You looked exactly like you do now with this hummingbird tattoo on your face."

Ejna, a Lakota indigenous leader in her seventies, was really surprised and asked Emelina to tell her more about her dreams. Emelina went on:

During the late eighties there was an esoteric Jewish Nicaraguan woman that lived in my house in Costa Rica. One day she told me that it was the time to present me at the council, and she said that I would have a dream about it in the coming days. A couple of days later I had a lucid dream about me entering a room that had a lot of light. There were four people to receive me, and all of them were dressed in white. You were one of them. There was also a female Mongolian shaman, who was holding a large drum, a black man with a beard and white stripes on his face, and another man from southeast Asia. They welcomed me. Nothing more. I just remember a feeling of responsibility toward the planet and humankind.

Emelina was staring at Ejna with tears in her eyes. Ejna was stunned. She started to explain to us why she was in Plum Village. She had been invited to Plum Village as part of the first Earth Week retreat, to make the first public call for the formation of "The Sacred Earth Council," based on a dream she had in 1987–88. We were all amazed. It became clear that the formation of "the Sacred Earth Council"[47] had received a fascinating affirmation, a powerful blessing. The three of us started to work on it. More dreams, visions, and synchronicities followed as more participants joined us. I have come to understand that this council is meant to become what I had envisioned as a necessity for the politics of being: a place where representatives of all spiritual traditions can share their wisdom, and how to apply it for our collective evolution. At the moment, we are focusing on a four-year ceremony cycle for planetary healing (2021–2024).

As we have seen throughout this book, all the rivers of wisdom irrigate the politics of being; all the different cultures have a contribution to make, and their dialogue can be fruitful. They have all developed relevant understandings, philosophies, institutions, models, and practices in that perspective. Western civilization has already offered its vision of democracy, human rights, individual autonomy, and science to the world. Scandinavian cultures of partnership, with their successful family, education, and gender policies, still have a lot to share. However, the many imbalances inherited from the Western worldview are leading us to chaos. As globalization becomes multipolar, it is now time for other civilizations to also share their best and help us find a balance. Provided it is able to abandon foreign Marxism and reconnect more to its Confucian and Taoist roots, Chinese civilization could draw on its millennia of experience and wisdom to offer a nonideological, longer-term, more enlightened and harmonious model of development as it asserts its leadership. We have also mentioned Bhutan's experience with happiness, the buen vivir political philosophy of Andean people, indigenous people's restorative justice models and their recognition of the rights of nature, Costa Rican policies supporting environmental awareness and a sense of community, India's Ayurveda, and Japanese forest bathing practices, to name a few.

We can build on all of that and support globalization based on being rather than having. Spiritual leaders need to reflect on their traditions and dialogue together to weave the vision for the cultural evolution we propose. They should be involved in the conceptualization and development of the politics of being, including concrete policy options, which should be infused with their wisdom. Scientists and experts should lead this endeavor, designing research agendas in line with this vision and monitoring, analyzing and synthesizing research results from all relevant fields and experiences, as well as their implications for the politics of being. All these results should be organized and nourish reference documents on the conceptualization, rationale, and policy options for such politics, which would be available online. Advocacy and communication work would help spread this view, while counseling, consulting, and capacity-building capacities would help implement it.

My deepest aspiration is to help materialize the politics of being by supporting these different works, their coordination and integration into a common framework. Through this book, I am offering a first basis for this framework that should be adapted to the different contexts and evolve based on our collective deliberation. The development of the politics of being could tap into the power of collaborative and civic technologies. Dedicated online platforms could be set up at global, national, and regional levels. They could not only support the design, advocacy, and capacity-building work we have mentioned, but also enable deliberation among citizens and the organization of transpartisan dialogues and coalitions. I hope some of you will bring your unique gifts to this endeavor.

21

Many Nations

> *"The primal law and purpose of the individual life is to seek its own self-development. [...] In the same way the primal law and purpose of a society, community or nation is to seek its own self-fulfillment; it strives rightly to find itself, to become aware within itself of the law and power of its own being and to fulfil it as perfectly as possible, to realise all its potentialities, to live its own self-revealing life."*
>
> —Sri Aurobindo,
> Hindu spiritual teacher (1872–1950)[1]

THE POLITICS OF being aims at facilitating self-actualization, not only for individuals, but also for nations. Whole and part are not separated: individual and collective evolution go hand in hand. Cultures provide the context and color individuals' journeys, while individuals incarnate cultures. Like individuals, when nations flourish and develop higher qualities and values, they contemporaneously express their uniqueness and universal nature.

Evolution rooted in cultural heritage

Ronald Inglehart has shown that "sociocultural change is path dependent and cultural heritages are remarkably enduring."[2] His work highlights two major dimensions of the cultural change associated with modernization and economic development:

> Industrialization brings a shift from traditional to secular-rational values—but with the rise of postindustrial society, cultural change starts to move in another direction. The shift from Traditional to Secular-rational values becomes slower, while another change becomes more powerful—the shift from Survival to Self-expression values, through which people place increasing emphasis on free choice, autonomy and creativity. This change was moving slowly, during the transition from pre-industrial to industrial societies, but it becomes the dominant trend when industrial society gives way to postindustrial society.[3]

Additionally, "these changes are probabilistic and they are not linear."[4] Mapping countries' value systems along these two dimensions reveals clear cultural zones (see figure 9). These persist over time: while modernization tends to move countries in the same direction on this map, the cultural differences between them remain relatively constant over several decades. As explained by Inglehart, "This may seem contradictory, but it is not. If all the world's societies were moving in the same direction at the same rate of speed, the distances between them would remain constant and they would never converge."[5]

While we often tend to imagine that rich and educated people all over the world share common values, this is not really the case. Inglehart's statistical analyses led him to conclude on the contrary that "the cross-national cultural differences are so large that they dwarf the differences within given societies. [...] despite globalization, nations remain an important unit of shared experiences, and the predictive power of nationality is much stronger than that of income, education, region or sex."[6] Values do change, while also continuing to reflect societies' cultural heritage.

Religions, history, and genes are three major dimensions of this cultural heritage. As we can see in figure 9, and in line with the views of many other social scientists such as Samuel Huntington, religious legacies are probably most important. In Inglehart's words: "The fact that a society was historically shaped by a Protestant, or Confucian or Islamic cultural heritage leaves an enduring impact, setting that society on a trajectory that continues to influence subsequent development—even when the direct influence of religious institutions fades away."[7]

Historical experience also shapes cultural evolution. For example, Inglehart has found that Japanese, German, and Italian people, who formed the Axis powers during World War II, display the lowest willingness to fight for their country.[8] History frames our perception of reality and our imagination. It helps explain the appeal of revolution to the French, the German fear of inflation, the American pioneer mentality and attachment to religious freedom, or why contemporary South Africa is still so shaped by racial considerations.

Cross-national genetic variation also seems to explain cultural differences: some studies show a correlation between genetics and values, economic, and political preferences.[9] In fact, cultural values reflect adaptation to the social and physical environments under which genetic selection operates. For example:

Certain populations evolved in environments that were relatively vulnerable to disease, giving a survival advantage to genetic variations linked with avoidance of strangers and strict conformity to social taboos—while other populations evolved in environments that were less vulnerable to disease, which gave a survival advantage to genetic variations linked with greater openness to strangers and different social norms.[10]

Beyond genes, we have also seen that epigenetics can be a source of intergenerational transmission of trauma effects.

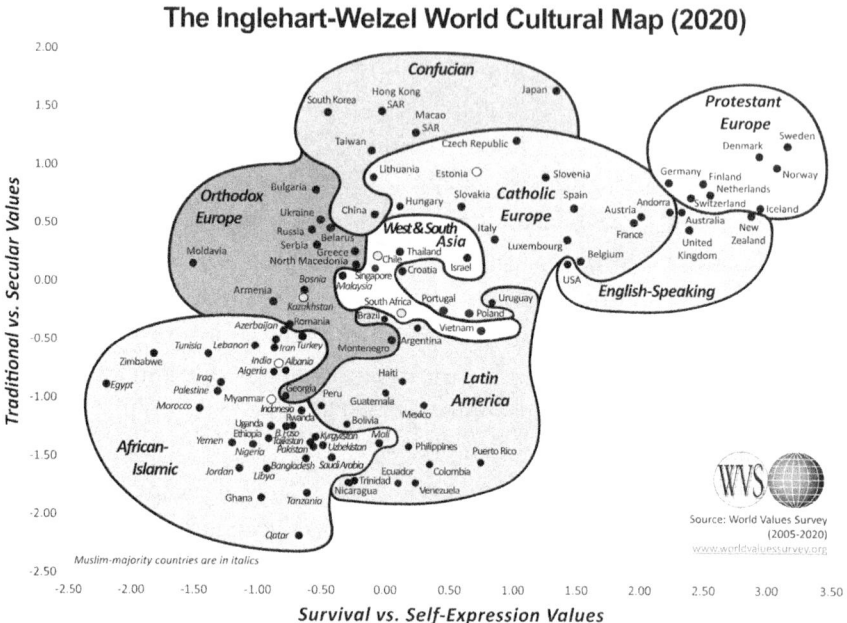

Figure 9. The Inglehart–Welzel world cultural map (2020).[11]

Defining national visions and pathways

As each nation follows its own development path and may be at different stages of evolution, each one needs to define its version of the politics of being. As a nation's cultural heritage shapes its political imaginary, its traditional wisdom is the basis through which each nation can define its vision of the good life. Indeed, while there are important universal aspects, the vision and routes to happiness and the good life seem to significantly vary across cultures. Americans, for example, have a hedonic view of happiness, strongly associated with high arousal positive states such as excitement and enthusiasm[12] in which personal achievements[13] and self-esteem,[14] for example, matter a lot.

The situation is very different in the East. Hong Kong Chinese associate happiness with lower arousal positive states (e.g., calm and relaxation),[15] and Japanese emphasize social harmony more as the source of happiness.[16] The Japanese view of happiness considers individuals as interdependent and understands happiness and unhappiness as ying-yang, both attracting each other.[17] In Andean indigenous cultures, as we have seen, "living well" or "good living" means being in harmony with nature and one another, and various indigenous nations across South America are making explicit and advocating for their visions of the good life along these lines.

Like Andean cultures, many nations have a word or an expression to summarize this vision. In Costa Rica, "pura vida" ("pure life") is the most common answer to the question "How are you?" It depicts the Costa Rican vision of the good life associated with simplicity, humility, nature, abundance, optimism, joy, and one's capacity to just savor life.[18] In most cases, this art of living is inseparable from nations' traditional wisdom or ethics, which, unlike Western emphasis on individuality, tends to emphasize our relational nature, as well as our belonging and responsibilities toward a community. In other words, each nation's traditional wisdom is based on its own version of the story of interbeing. For example, in their RIO + 20 declaration, indigenous peoples presented their cultures as essentially based on the "sacred relationships to each other and Mother Earth."[19] This community often includes ancestors, spiritual beings, and all life forms (including specific animals and plants) in a given territory, something I believe we should include in our definition of a nation.

The words used by many cultures to designate their traditional wisdom carry this meaning, which is so rich that it cannot be easily translated. For example, "Kapwa" is the basis of Philippine ethics. It can be translated as "togetherness" and "is a recognition of a shared identity, an inner self, shared with others," which implies "the moral obligation to treat one another as equal fellow human beings," according to the father of modern Filipino psychology, Virgilio Enriquez.[20] For the Kogis, indigenous people from Colombia, "Zigoneshi"—"I help you and you help me" or "I give you and you give me"—is the key social principle emphasizing exchange, solidarity, and reciprocity. "Fihavanana," which designates the Madagascan traditional wisdom, is often translated as "relationship," "solidarity," or simply "wisdom."

"Botho" or "Ubuntu" is a central concept of Southern African cultures, which is sometimes translated as "humanness."[21] According to some commentators, "The concept of UBUNTU embodies an understanding of what it is to be human and what is necessary for human beings to grow and find fulfilment."[22] Based on the guiding principle of "umuntu ngumuntu ngabantu" ("a person is a person through other people" or "I am because you are"),[23] it affirms that "our deepest moral obligation is to become more fully human and this means entering more and more deeply into community with others. So although the goal is personal fulfilment, selfishness is excluded."[24] "It is an ethical concept and expresses a vision of what is valuable and worthwhile in life."[25]

Like the cultures they emanate from, these notions should not be seen as closed entities with fixed meaning and purely endogenous development but rather as living concepts, offering unique approaches to largely universal values and whose evolution can benefit from intercultural dialogue. The reappropriation of this traditional wisdom and vision of the good life by many nations is an important step in healing the wounds of colonization and the disorientation and cultural alienation it propelled. It is necessary for humanity, and the many nations it is composed of, to overcome our current ethical crisis, find a new balance, and flourish. Unlike the pursuit of economic growth, which provided a single quantitative metric common to all nations—GDP—the politics of being calls for a qualitative, ethical, and culturally appropriate approach to development, which reflects and honors cultural diversity. It is a decolonization process of development theory and practice.

For ages, most philosophers and religions have promoted the virtuous life as the key to individual flourishing and social harmony, though in the last two or three centuries this has been progressively replaced by the gospel of economic growth and its claim of value neutrality. The philosophical basis of this model of development lies in Western enlightenment and liberalism, which is historically an antireligious movement. Liberalism sought to liberate individuals from religious dictates and superstitions, and established a clear separation between the church and the state. While morality was associated with religious paternalism, liberalism argues that the state should not promote any particular vision of the good life. The emphasis is on individual freedom, whereas moral considerations are largely banished from the public sphere: People ought not to be told how to live their lives. In addition, the pluralistic nature of modern societies raises some doubts on the very possibility of ethical consensus.

While it is certainly challenging, it is possible to agree on ethical principles and responsible behaviors that reconcile true individual freedom and social harmony, as we have seen for example with the Global Ethic or with Nordic countries. In order to agree and transcend our differences, whether at the national or global levels, we must be ambitious enough to create an ethical framework that embodies values high enough to be universal. In Swiss philosopher Alain de Botton's words: "Real freedom does not mean being left wholly to one's own devices; it should be compatible with being harnessed and guided,"[26] in particular if that guidance does not come as an imposition of religious dogmas and its acceptance our free choice.

The lack of formal outer freedom is no longer the main problem in most liberal democracies; rather, we lack the wisdom to protect ourselves individually and collectively from the effects of our own character failures, and their manipulation by powerful commercial interests. "In any case, our public spaces are not even remotely neutral. They are—as a quick glance down any high street will reveal—covered with commercial messages. Even in societies theoretically dedicated to leaving us free to make our own choices, our minds are continuously manipulated in directions we hardly consciously recognize,"[27] notes de Botton.

No society is value-neutral. In modern ones, liberalism, individualism, materialism, all imply certain judgments on what is good and bad, and together they created "hyper-commercialism,"[28] which propelled a moral crisis. Each nation needs to redevelop serious discussions, informed by science, intercultural dialogue, and their deepest wisdom, on what authentically good lives are. Wouldn't it be great for states or independent institutions to organize national conversations, articulating different levels (grassroots, experts and social scientists, political representation, etc.) in that perspective?

Nations' souls

Nations' development path toward the good life should allow them to flourish, safeguarding and deepening their specific way of embodying our universal human condition and their most unique qualities; what many thinkers of the past have called "genius" or "spirit." This notion was rediscovered and became particularly popular in Europe along with the development of nation-states in the eighteenth and nineteenth centuries.[29] French political philosopher Montesquieu (1689–1755) notes that "the political and civil laws of each nation [...] should be so well adapted to the people for whom they are made that it is only by extreme chance that the laws of one nation can suit any another."[30]

The concept and idea of "people's spirit" or "people's genius" was particularly developed in Germany under the term of "volksgeist," first coined in 1774 by philosopher Johann Gottfried Von Herder. In the nineteenth century, German national unity was supported by the intense quest of its philosophers, poets, and artists—Hegel, Fichte, Nietzsche, Goethe, Beethoven, Wagner, etc.—for the nation's soul. Hegel considered the divine, which he called "absolute" or "world-spirit,"[31] the fundamental force at work in history, permeating all things and oriented towards its realization. He wrote, "The spirit of the nation is therefore the universal spirit in a particular form [...]. The world spirit transcends this particular form, but it must assume it as so far as it exists, for it takes on a particular aspect as soon as it has actual being or existence."[32]

Unity in diversity—what Hegel calls "identity in difference,"—has a spiritual basis. Hegel considers that the world spirit ("weltgeist") uses nations to express itself, to expand its self-consciousness: each national spirit ("volksgeist") "brings a fruit to maturity, for its activity is directed towards the fulfillment of its principle."[33] When a nation has achieved its end, it becomes satisfied and falls into fixed habits. Its vitality declines as the spirit recedes from it, and finally perishes. "The fruit becomes the seed, but the seed of another nation, which it brings to maturity in turn."[34] Thus "we can observe a progression, growth, and succession from one national principle to another."[35]

National spirits are "themselves only moments of the one universal spirit, which ascends through them in the course of history to its consummation in an all-embracing totality."[36] We can start to see that nations' spirits or souls are not only concepts through which we can understand reality, but, according to some sages, are spiritual realities in themselves. Sri Aurobindo says:

The nation or society, like the individual, has a body, an organic life, a moral and aesthetic temperament, a developing mind and a soul behind all these signs and powers for the sake of which they exist. One may say even that, like the individual, it essentially is a soul rather than has one; it is a group-soul that, once having attained to a separate distinctness, must become more and more self-conscious and find itself more and more fully as it develops its corporate action and mentality and its organic self-expressive life.[37]

Sri Aurobindo believes that a group-soul is of the same nature as an individual soul but "is much more complex because it has a great number of partly self-conscious mental individuals for the constituents of its physical being instead of an association of merely vital subconscious cells. At first, for this very reason, it seems more crude, primitive and artificial in the forms it takes."[38] That is also why its self-consciousness tends to focus at first on its most outward material and objective aspects, such as the land ("only the shell of the [soul's] body, though a very living shell indeed and potent in its influences on the nation"[39]), national idiosyncrasies, habits, prejudices, and marked mental tendencies. This can be the source of great danger for a nation striving for self-realization, as we will see with the example of Germany. As souls in evolution toward self-realization, nations face the same stakes and challenges as individuals and can thus benefit from the same kinds of spiritual teachings.

In the case of France, one of the most notable elements is its great intellectual capacity to convert the light of the spirit into (universal) ideas, a capacity that is particularly suited to the design of new paradigms and ideologies, as shown by its influence on the development of modernity, democracy, human rights, and postmodernism. Unfortunately this is too often expressed in the superficial French tendency for wittiness and disdain for the material, day-to-day implementation of such ideas, which makes actual social evolution less appealing than revolution. France's attachment to its culture, authenticity, and quality of life is as well-known as its conflicting political culture (e.g., strikes), its gloomy mood (which is measured by a subjective well-being well below what material conditions would normally entail), its attachment to a glorious past and difficulties in facing the present (e.g., globalization, which hurts some of its cherished values such as equity).

In the international arena, France's idealistic nature leads it to defend high ideals and virtues—so that it easily comes across as pretentious and righteous—with difficulties in acknowledging its own failures (e.g., colonization). Macron's presidency has been an (so far, relatively failed[40]) attempt to transcend the conflicting and ideological French political culture with his claim to be both left and right, in favor of pragmatically implementing "what works." He has also tried to help France face the present world as it is, by also considering the good sides of globalization and liberalism, and to look to the future with optimism, but his politics that favor a rich minority have disregarded a deep national attachment to equity.

The US is a young and vigorous nation, supported by very high, fresh ideals, such as "the unalienable rights to life, liberty and the pursuit of happiness" enshrined in its Declaration of Independence. It has integrated the genius of some older nations, in particular that of Great Britain, with its passion for freedom. Moved by its pioneering spirit, the United States' great historical role is clearly to pilot and provide the basis for the emergence of a planetary culture. As a young nation, it is geared toward action, but also somehow immature and naive, such as when it seeks to impose its particular values (democracy and capitalism) on others. Though idealistic, it is inclined towards egocentrism. Examples of this are the doctrine of "manifest destiny"— according to which white Americans had a divine mandate to settle the entire continent of North America— its refusal of international law and cooperation on many issues, or its support of many successful attempts to undermine democratic processes, for example in Latin America throughout the twentieth century. Its reconnection to its soul's purpose will lead it to "expand her identity to include the rest of the world and transcend self-interest. [...] The United States needs to grow into the realization that her own needs can be met in honoring the needs of other nations."[41]

President Joe Biden's engagement in "the battle for the soul of America" in 2020 echoed an increasing number of authors who formulated political proposals that explicitly considered the US as a specific soul in evolution.[42] In his book *Sacred America, Sacred World,* Stephen Dinan proposes a new American dream in the age of globalization, one that balances material prosperity with personal fulfillment. Noting that in a 2008 study, 71 percent of Americans agreed with the statement "I see myself as a citizen of Planet Earth as well as an American," Dinan calls his compatriots to fulfill "our mission in service to all."

For the US to evolve toward greatness, Dinan affirms that it first needs to acknowledge its shadow to heal, integrate, and learn from its past, in particular its darkest aspects, something that national pride often resists:

> In psychology, the shadow is the part of ourselves that we exclude from our current identity and thus are literally unable to see.[43] America's shadow side includes a lot of unfinished business of our many previous operating systems, which often thwarts and undermines our larger mission. To do this shadow work, we need to look with clear eyes at some of the ways we've misused power, destroyed lives, and lived in partial truths about ourselves or our world. We need to face and own the ways that we have marginalized and victimized others, as well as to do the work of healing, reparations, and reconciliation. We also need to look at the ways we have used violence as a tool of foreign policy and left behind badly damaged countries from Vietnam to Afghanistan to Iraq. In looking at America's shadow side, it often contains the same qualities that can lead us to noble behaviors, but in immature and self-centered forms. Given the power we wield in the world, these places of immaturity have harmful effects on others and, ultimately, ourselves. Truth telling that is both rigorous and compassionate helps our shadow qualities come to the surface so they can evolve

into their expression and thus alleviate any suffering they are now causing.[44]

Germany, for example, has been able to grow into a wiser, healthier, humbler and more responsible nation by facing its collective responsibility in the two world wars and the Shoah. In the case of the US, Dinan believes this implies facing the fact that America has been founded on Native American genocide, an awareness that is needed to "activate our roots" and open "a deeper connection to the land on which we live."[45] Sacred ceremonies in memory of this mass murder, such as the one carried out in 2015 for the one hundredth and twenty-fifth anniversary of the Wounded Knee massacre, can help heal the intergenerational psychological traumas associated with it. Specific methodologies of group-presencing process, such as the Collective Trauma Integration Process (CTIP) developed by Thomas Hübl, can be leveraged as well.[46] Scaling up these works is critical to "heal the soul of America," for example—an objective that featured prominently in President Biden's 2020 campaign for presidency—and that of every nation.

Healing the legacy of slavery by recognizing America's responsibility and putting an end to African American marginalization is also part of this shadow work. "African culture is our mother culture, quite literally, and we have not honored our mother,"[47] notes Dinan. To fulfill its soul mission, the US needs to honor the heritage of all races and cultures. As a country long dominated by masculine qualities such as self-reliance and competition, the US also needs to balance its masculine and feminine energies in order to express its full potential.

Dinan proposes, for example, to reserve 50 percent of political representation to women to help grow a more compassionate and wiser leadership. He sees Lady Liberty, who has welcomed so many US ancestors who arrived in search of freedom, as the archetype of this feminine power that lies largely untapped deep inside the American psyche. "Give me your tired, your poor, your huddled masses yearning to breathe free ..." she seems to say, according to the poem by Emma Lazarus, now engraved on Lady Liberty. Finally, Dinan, of course, calls for more socioeconomic equity to heal the nation's manifold divisions.

The nationalistic pitfall

For nations, as for individuals, the main spiritual pitfall is to mistake one's ego and its many constituents (body, vital being,[48] and mental) for its soul, and consider ourselves as separate beings. Sri Aurobindo calls it "false subjectivism."[49] In politics, it takes the form of narrow and egoistic nationalism. In the past this has done tremendous harm, as in Germany in the first half of the twentieth century. The deep German quest for the country's soul, which made it one of the most advanced nation on the path toward self-realization, ended in Nazi barbarism. According to Sri Aurobindo, the active expression of Germany's physical/organizational ("the industry, conscientious diligence, the [...]and painstaking spirit of work"[50]), artistic and philosophical genius, combined with "the tremendous sincerity which is the secret of its force,"[51] ended up in abomination. Germany's mistake was to confuse its vital force, the temperament it found in itself, with its real soul.

Internally, this subjected German people to the cult of the state, nation, or community—the collective ego—and externally it led them to subject and even try to exterminate other nations. Germany's error concerned

[W]herein lies the true individuality of man and of the nation. It lies not in its physical, economic, even its cultural life which are only means and adjuncts, but in something deeper whose roots are not in the ego, but in a Self one in difference which relates the good of each, on a footing of equality and not of strife and domination, to the good of the rest of the world.[52]

Being is one in all, expressed in the individual and in the collectivity, and only by admitting and realising our unity with others can we entirely fulfil our true self-being.[53]

Sri Aurobindo was a short-lived Indian nationalistic leader. But like many of the great Indian spiritual leaders who partook in the Indian renaissance in the latter half of the nineteenth century and independentist movements—from Ramakrishna to Gandhi, from Vivekananda to Tagore—he recognized that India needed to be independent not for its own enjoyment but primarily because it had a great spiritual role to fulfill in service of humanity: sharing its spiritual knowledge (that its national motto—"truth alone triumphs"[54] celebrates).

Ironically the current Hindu Nationalistic Modi government, which glorifies Hindu religious heritage, seems to have forgotten this spiritual truth. Nations' natural and healthy aspiration to be themselves can be full of dangers when confused with the national egoistic error "to live solely for and to oneself."[55] It should go along with a sense of belonging to the global community. Sri Aurobindo pointed out:

> It is necessary, if the subjective age of humanity is to produce its best fruits, that the nations should become conscious not only of their own but of each other's souls and learn to respect, to help and to profit, not only economically and intellectually but subjectively and spiritually, by each other.[56]

Cultivating nations' self-awareness

Before nations develop their version of the good life and the pathways for their realization, implementing the politics of being should start by building a nation's awareness of who it truly is in essence and in practice, looking honestly at a country past to better understand its present. In Toltec shamanism, the practice of recapitulating one's path is central toward recovering the parts of oneself, the energy, that we have lost along our personal journey. It can also enable us to access a new and deeper understanding of who we are, our trajectory and the forces at work behind it.

For nations, a starting point could be the organization of a consultation process, backed with the relevant scientific inquiries (including, for example, national value surveys), with well-intentioned, competent people to perform this recapitulation and collective psychological assessment, in order to build a common understanding of:

- The national character and what deeper essence seeks to express itself through it: the distinctive traits, habits, tendencies, principles, values, and passions that have animated a nation lastingly throughout its history. This could serve as the entry point to explore other dimensions;

- A nation's cultural and spiritual roots and the relationships it maintains with them;

- A nation's historical evolution trajectory; the main events, circumstances, and factors that have shaped its evolution; the lessons it has learned or that it has not wanted to look at; the unresolved traumas; the spirit at work throughout its history, etc.;

- The prominent figures through which a nation has more clearly expressed itself and its spiritual dimensions;

- A nation's positive and negative contributions to the world; its role, calling, and mission in the international sphere;

- A nation's relationship to the main spiritual values that have been listed, the current strengths and weaknesses of the national character, their basis and interrelationships, as well as the nation's awareness and recognition of them;

- A nation's current evolutionary potentials and the main challenges associated with them.

As we have seen before with Sri Aurobindo, such a process should avoid the trap of reifying the nation's soul and mistaking it for some of its outward manifestations, which governments would seek to artificially recreate, ending up fossilizing them. On the contrary, by recognizing the essence and evolutionary nature of nations' souls, this process should create the space for the emergence of their ever truer and brighter manifestations.

As a person, there is little chance that I get closer to my authentic being by defining a vision of who I am and trying to actualize it. On the contrary, I can discover who I am by freeing myself from predefined and limiting identities, purifying my intentions, character, and behaviors, and expressing the deepest yearning of my soul. This is a conscious, evolutionary process of emergence, informed but not bounded by the understanding I have of my essence, which is necessarily limited. The same is true for nations.

The outlined consultation process could take the form of a citizen- or state-sponsored initiative. It could articulate local popular debates with more expert discussions and be largely mediatized to have a more profound impact on the collective consciousness. This process could also be supported by online platforms, such as the ones that could be dedicated to the politics of being.

This exercise could be repeated every few years and to some extent be held on a continuous basis for more specific issues, which could be articulated with longer-term research and initiatives. In parallel, political parties from the right and left could also perform such psychological assessments. They could reflect from a wisdom perspective on themselves, their values, and their contemporary expressions, as well as on their vision for the politics of being.[57] Thus nations could start to walk their own paths of conscious evolution.

22

Being Leaders

"If you want to build a ship, don't drum up the men to gather wood, divide the work, and give orders. Instead, teach them to yearn for the vast and endless sea."

—Antoine de Saint-Exupéry,
French writer (1900–1944)

POLITICAL LEADERS PLAY a critical role in the evolution of our societies' values through their example and how they guide our imagination, direct our attention, and frame the debate. Like institutions, they can harness the worst or the best of people to conquer and hold on to power. "Here and now, I give you my word: if you entrust me with the presidency, I will draw on the best of us, not the worst. I will be an ally of the light, not of the darkness,"[1] promised Joe Biden before becoming president. How would the Indian independence movement or South Africa's transition to a postapartheid regime or the civil rights movement have happened had they not been respectively led by Gandhi, Mandela, and Dr. Martin Luther King Jr? What is the responsibility of people such as Trump or Bolsonaro in rousing and liberating anger, hate, and discrimination?

Spiritual intelligence

The politics of being calls for awakened leadership. How can leaders govern their countries or organizations if they can't govern themselves? We need wise leaders, inspired by a spirit of service, that can connect with the soul of their nations or organizations to guide them and activate their evolutionary potentials. The wiser we grow collectively, the less we will tolerate any other type of leadership, and the more we will prepare our future leaders to develop this connection. From this connection springs what is often called "spiritual intelligence."

The concept has been articulated since the late nineties, though so far without a unified framework. Essentially, spiritual intelligence regards the fundamental abilities that individuals need to achieve and help others achieve as the highest level of human thriving. These abilities deepen with spiritual development—understood as a connection to our true selves or the divine—to which they offer a concrete, secular approach. They are neither conditions (e.g., health), nor states (e.g., joy), nor behaviors (e.g., generosity), nor a manifestation of higher states of consciousness (e.g., bliss, powers), nor meta (or aggregated) abilities (e.g., wisdom, communication).

In box 13, I did my best, together with my wife Emelina Corrales, who is an executive coach, to propose the main abilities that characterize spiritual intelligence. Spiritual teachings and exercises from all traditions, enriched by scientific knowledge and secular practices, can help leaders develop these abilities. All our thoughts, words, and actions are impregnated by the quality of our being. The more power we have, the more our qualities and personal flaws tend to be revealed, and the more wisdom we need, the more we ought to cultivate ourselves. While we have already emphasized the need for collective leadership and the institutional arrangements for that, we will look deeply in this chapter into the spiritual abilities each leader, as an individual, needs to develop.

Box 13—Main Abilities Characterizing Spiritual Intelligence

- **Self-awareness:** Being aware of how we function as humans, of who we are as individuals—including our strengths and weaknesses, tendencies and biases—helps us adopt the most adequate behaviors and decisions for our well-being and that of others, as well as better understand the world and others. It also ultimately leads to the awareness of our interbeing nature and our purpose.

- **Acceptance:** Accepting ourselves, others, and situations as they are is important for our individual and collective well-being and is often a necessary condition for transformation.

- **Self-mastery, alignment, and integrity:** This has to do with bringing all parts of our being under the control of our higher self; striving for coherence in our thoughts, words, and deeds; aligning them with our true selves.

- **Presence and authenticity:** We tend to ruminate over the past or worry about the future, but only by being truly present can we adequately live. Having the courage to express the totality of who we truly are, and even recognize our shortcomings, is necessary for our fulfillment. It can also inspire others to do the same and help build trust.

- **Stopping:** Being able to pause, to suspend our internal dialogue, to take a step back helps create the necessary space for the most adequate thinking, words, or actions.

- **Freedom and detachment:** By resisting external pressures, as well as freeing ourselves from our own limiting habits, views, and narrow sense of self, we can express our full potential and learn to flow with grace.

- **Inner peace and equanimity:** By healing our wounds and learning how to take care of strong emotions, and by freeing ourselves from judgments and dualistic notions, we can avoid being carried away and maintain our serenity.

- **Love, empathy, and compassion**: Being able to love and understand others, to experience how they feel and sense the need to alleviate their suffering, is key to our individual and collective wellbeing.

- **Vast mind**: Being aware of the interconnectedness of all things helps us adopt a broader, more adequate perspective and deal with complexity and uncertainty.

- **Deep mind**: Asking fundamental "why" questions, we get to the bottom of things.

- **Creativity:** Expressing our full potential and finding solutions to complex problems both require inventiveness.

- **Capacity to generate joy**: This includes savoring life, cultivating positive attitudes and emotions, such as gratitude for all the good conditions that we have.

- **Sense of purpose**: Finding meaning in life, even in adversity, is crucial for our well-being. The awareness of our life purpose helps us develop clear intentions and priorities and sets us on the path to fulfillment.

- **Inner strength:** The path to fulfillment is long and difficult. It requires willpower, perseverance, and mental resistance against doubt or discouragement.

- **Humility:** Lessening the importance we attribute to ourselves is important to understanding that we are only a tiny part of the great scheme of things.

- **Faith/hope:** Optimism about the future and our profound human nature does not necessarily stem from a religious affiliation.

- **Service and Self-transcendence:** Our sense of interbeing naturally leads us to work in service of the greater good.

- **Intuition and spiritual guidance**: It is our ability to understand things instinctively, without the need for conscious reasoning, and let the spirit guide us.

Implementing the politics of being is not only about adapting the policy recommendations for a nation's objective conditions. A political leader also needs to understand the nation's inner life, its soul's evolutionary trajectory and potentials. Like a spiritual teacher who guides students from where they are or energetic therapists who first need to attend to the surface to allow something deeper to emerge, leaders help deliver the transformations that are knocking at the door of social and political life. They not only need to recognize these evolutionary potentials for what they are; they need the capacity to flow and dance with the life of a nation, which has its own rhythm, melody, and lyrics.

Indeed, the politics of being is not merely about implementing a good plan. "If you want to make God laugh, tell him your plans," says an old Yiddish proverb. Social reality is by nature hyper-complex and, as such, unpredictable. "We may well know that everything that has happened of importance in world history or in our lives was totally unexpected, but we continue to act as if the unexpected will never again appear,"[2] warned Edgar Morin, long before the COVID-19 crisis.

What seems at the surface objectively impossible often occurs because great leaders, through their intimate connection with the inner states and needs of their nation—a sense that goes well beyond the power of reason—are able to develop a greater vision of what they can become. They invoke its manifestation and harness every opportunity to give birth to this vision. This connection to the soul of their nation, in its purest form, is a connection to the spirit itself, which guides and supports awakened leaders.

The inner voice

From our perspective, the most distinctive ability of a great leader is the individual's capacity to receive guidance from the spirit, which lies deep within every one of us. Gandhi considered the real leader of the Indian independence movement "the still small voice within." Many of the decisions he took, including some of the famous fasts he imposed on himself as part of his nonviolent political leadership, emanated from this voice.

For me the Voice of God, of Conscience, of Truth, or the Inner
Voice or 'the Still Small Voice' mean one and the same thing. I saw
no form. I have never tried, for I have always believed God to be
without form. But what I did hear was like a Voice from afar and yet
quite near. It was as unmistakable as some human voice definitely
speaking to me, and irresistible. I was not dreaming at the time I
heard the Voice. The hearing of the Voice was preceded by a terrific
struggle within me. Suddenly the Voice came upon me. I listened,
made certain it was the Voice, and the struggle ceased. I was calm.
The determination was made accordingly, the date and the hour of
the fast were fixed ... [3]

The voice was "the only tyrant that I accept in the world," he said, as he
learned to rely on it in the most difficult situations. "There are moments
in your life when you must act, even though you cannot carry your best
friends with you. The 'still small voice' within you must always be the final
arbiter when there is a conflict of duty."[4]

The voice provided him a clear inner conviction of the path to follow.
"Here come to us moments in life when about some things we need no
proof from without. A little voice within us tells us, 'You are on the right
track, move neither to your left nor right, but keep to the straight and
narrow way,'"[5] he explained.

Gandhi rejoiced in walking this path, "even as the bestirring of true
love necessarily expresses itself in as many (sometimes unconscious and
effortless) ways, so too a person who has heard even a whisper of the inner
voice cannot but follow it."[6]

Gandhi believed "the inner voice does not suppress reason but rather
sanctifies reason"[7] and invited the rationalists to follow what they called the
"dictates of reason." He was well aware that this voice could well have been
the product of his imagination or of some non-divine spiritual influences[8]
as it is often the case. His inquiry honored and went well beyond the
legitimate demand of his reason to encompass the transformation of his
whole person.

Gandhi was fully committed to getting rid of anything within him
that could interfere with the voice. He had no indulgence for himself; his

sincerity was complete. "A humble seeker that I claim to be has need to be most cautious and, to preserve the balance of mind, he has to reduce himself to zero before God will guide him."[9]

The disposition to selfless service is the key enabling condition for leaders to be guided by the spirit. For Gandhi, that was the price to pay not only to access the voice, but also to get the firm and authentic conviction that the voice was truly reliable. Thus he was able to affirm that "not the unanimous verdict of the whole world against me could shake me from the belief that what I heard was the true Voice of God."[10]

Gandhi attributed his "little capacity to hear correctly and clearly the 'still small voice within'" to his "ceaseless effort to attain self-purification."[11] "God's Voice is not heard in the heart of every person. It is no matter of inherent right. You must undergo a course of training, if you want to hear the Voice of God. There are some rules laid down for it. If you follow them, the result would be infallible,"[12] he believed.

Spiritual development connects us with our inner guidance and our life mission. I have often heard people wondering about how to find such guidance. I think the inner voice becomes clearer each time you pay attention to it and walk the path it indicates. It is like listening to your body. The first time you get drunk or you smoke, the body shows discomfort, but if you keep drinking or smoking, little by little, the body gets used to this poisoning and stops manifesting its unease until it really falls sick in the longer term.

Listening to the inner voice and walking its path make things clearer, step after step. People often have difficulties walking the first step: they know the things that are pending but just don't want to address them. Some say they would be eager to do anything but not what lies just in front of them, right in the middle of their way. But that would most often be the best thing for them to do and is sometimes the only way they can really move forward. The voice was the source of Gandhi's willpower and "satyagraha"—or "truth force"—his philosophy of nonviolent resistance. Its extraordinary power, which touched the deeply spiritual Indian soul and shaped the course of history, ultimately remains the best proof of the voice's authenticity.

Instruments of the spirit

"In politics also we have to establish the kingdom of heaven,"[13] believed Gandhi. His power was not only personal and made of wise decisions guided by the voice; he was also harnessing tremendous spiritual forces that are constantly trying to shape, from the invisible world, our destiny.

Hegel, who viewed the spirit's search for its accomplishment as the main force stirring history, considered some historical figures as instruments of the Absolute. For instance, he considered Napoleon a "great man," whose historical function was to bring the modern state and the democratic ideals born out of the French revolution ("this glorious sunrise") to the world through his military conquests. Hegel described Napoleon as the embodiment of the world-spirit, "the world-soul on horseback,"[14] when he saw him parading in Iena (in current Germany) in 1806 after his military victory.

Because heroes know the historical changes that must be accomplished and intend to make these changes, the spirit helps these heroes, or rather uses them (and their ways, which often entail wars) for its own purpose. The historical heroes know "the truth of their times and their worlds because they are aware of the historical necessity: that is why, like Alexander and Caesar, Napoleon is a wise man because he knows the nature of his era," according to Hegel. They know "what is necessary and what to do when the time comes."[15] Their knowledge is largely intuitive and "what they would have learned from others in terms of plans and well-meaning advice would have been, on the contrary, more narrow-minded and more wrong; because they knew best what was at hand."[16] In fact, Prussian general Carl von Clausewitz (1780–1831), whose military theory has been extremely influential until now, considered Napoleon, who flew from victory to victory, "the greatest war leader of modern times."[17]

Among the many aspects of Napoleon's military genius, which included a great attention to many details, were his daring luck and capacity to make the best of unexpected circumstances. In Austerlitz for example, he used an unexpected blanket of fog as camouflage for his soldiers, moving them over the marshes that were reputed to be impassable in order to take the most unprotected flank of the imperial army he was fighting by surprise. Napoleon also pioneered merit-based promotion in his army. Before promoting someone as a general, he would hear the individual's merits, and his famous reaction was: "Very well, but is he lucky?"[18]

His notion of luck was far from superficial. As noted by American historian Jackson Spielvogel:

> Napoleon liked to see himself as a man of destiny and a great man who mastered luck. He once said: "A consecutive series of great actions never is the result of chance and luck. It always is the product of planning and genius. Great men are rarely known to fail in their most perilous enterprises ... Is it because they are lucky that they become great? No, but being great, they have been able to master luck."[19]

Jürgen Habermas and Peter Sloterdijk, the two currently most influential German philosophers, have cited Hegel's view of Napoleon in expressing their hopes that French president Macron will revive the European spirit.[20] While Napoleon did not read Hegel, Macron, who was briefly the assistant of famous French philosopher Paul Ricoeur, did.[21] He referred to Hegel's philosophy of history during an interview for German magazine *der Spiegel*, which used as its title a quote from him: "'We need to develop political heroism."[22]

In fact, Macron's lightning political ascension relied not only on the strong support from the corporate (and thus media) world, but also from his brilliant intuitive understanding of the French current political situation, paralyzed by political parties. Macron awakened my interest during his presidential campaign in 2016–2017, when I started to notice his extraordinary luck.[23] In this campaign that was widely viewed by commentators as unprecedented, he first benefitted from the decision of former socialist president Hollande, to whom Macron had been a close adviser and minister, not to run for a second mandate. Macron's political space grew further when the socialist party chose to turn left with the victory of Benoit Hamon over Manuel Valls during its primary election.

Finally, and most importantly, a former prime minister, Fillon, who, after triumphing in the conservative party's primary elections was running way ahead in the polls, was severely affected by a corruption scandal, which almost forced him to renounce. Macron's political genius, the accuracy of his diagnosis, and his profile as a nonaffiliated politician, to a great extent explain his victory at the age of thirty-nine, which resulted in a profound implosion of the French political system.

Still, I started to sense a spiritual influence, whose subliminal perception was unconsciously expressed in many political comments. This was confirmed by some of Macron's declarations, including a famous interview he gave during his campaign to a French newspaper on the spiritual dimension of his campaign, whose "Christlike dimension" he accepted.[24] In this article Macron recognized that to him "politics is mystical" and involves "transcendence."

The article concluded that "since he set off on his campaign, the path seems to clear and the planets to align in the sky above his head."[25] "That is what I call the guile of History,"[26] confirmed Macron, showing that he is well aware of Hegel's views. The German philosopher believed that to achieve its ends, the spirit, or the history and its reason, often proceed with "guile," that is to say through convoluted means: the spirit uses people's aspirations and passions to produce unexpected results, through which it achieves its own progress.

In May 2016, when he was not yet a candidate and no one would have thought he might run for, or even win the presidential elections, Macron gave a speech in honor of Joan of Arc, during the official national celebration dedicated to her and patriotism. Joan of Arc is one of the nine official secondary patron saints of France, which are regarded as the heavenly advocates of the nation. As a symbol, she has been recently monopolized by the French extreme right. In this speech, Macron shared lessons that Joan of Arc left us.

The life of Joan is first and foremost the power of a destiny, which demonstrates that the order of things doesn't last if it is unjust. [...] She knows that she is not born to live, but to attempt the impossible. Like an arrow, her trajectory cuts through. Joan fends the system.

She overcomes the injustice that tried to imprison her. Joan is a shepherdess who blazes a path to the king. Joan is a woman, but she takes the head of an army, opposing warlords. Joan is nobody, but on her shoulders she carries the will of progress and justice of a nation. She was a crazy dream, she imposes herself as evident.[27]

Macron reminded us. The second lesson is, according to him, "that of the people's energy,"[28] which Joan of Arc awakened to be able to deliver the city of Orléans. It has the capacity to change the course of history "in the darkest moments."[29] Macron, whose leadership was often described as fresh and positive, invoked "this same energy, I can feel it here, among you, today."[30] "Joan's third lesson is that of rallying and unifying France,"[31] according to Macron, who was not affiliated with any political party before founding his own movement and who claimed, during the presidential campaign, to transcend traditional political oppositions and be "both from left and right." During his meetings, he requested his supporters not boo at the names of his opponents.

Not surprisingly, these lessons echo Macron's view of himself and his nascent ascension, but more disconcertingly they retrospectively seem to foreshadow his future victory in the presidential election.

Macron's close relations describe him as "inwardly inhabited,"[32] and his wife has declared, "It is not always easy to live with Joan of Arc."[33] Macron, who came from a lay family but decided to be baptized when he was twelve, is reserved on his own spiritual life and seems to put more emphasis on the most personal dimensions of spirituality. "I am not sure God ever talked. At the end, these are voices that we create ourselves,"[34] he said. Divinely inspired or not, Macron has turned to spirituality to generate some of the forces that have brought him to power. These forces can be emotional, social, and/or spiritual, personal or collective. These categories should not be opposed: they are often the different manifestations of the same reality.

In many cases, in particular when it stands in opposition to reason, the feeling of a spiritual call and its use in politics can be completely erroneous and dangerous. Bolsonaro believes God made him president, while the man who stabbed him said he was acting on "God's orders."[35] But "the misuse of great powers is no argument against their right use,"[36] pointed out Sri Aurobindo. Among the spiritual influences that one can harness, there is a whole range of energies, from the brightest to the darkest, from the most trivial to the most powerful ones. They influence each of us depending on our penchants and receptivity, the latter often characterizing powerful leaders for the better or the worse.

For instance, Sri Aurobindo considered Alexander the Great, Napoléon, Churchill, and De Gaulle as very receptive to spiritual influences, but also Hitler and Stalin, seeing in historical conflicts such as World War II the age-old battle of light against darkness, which is celebrated by so many traditions. People often tend to see God behind all sorts of spiritual influences. Jesus's parable about testing a prophet provides a simple and rational wisdom that one can apply to assess political leaders who, like each of us, channel spiritual energies into the world:

> [F]or a good tree bringeth not forth corrupt fruit; neither doth a corrupt tree bring forth good fruit. For every tree is known by his own fruit. For of thorns men do not gather figs, nor of a bramble bush gather they grapes. A good man out of the good treasure of his heart bringeth forth that which is good; and an evil man out of the evil treasure of his heart bringeth forth that which is evil: for of the abundance of the heart his mouth speaketh.[37]

In any case, because of the dialectical nature of history and its guile, the most abominable political leaders can *in fine* produce political outcomes that support the spirit's progress. Hitler's nationalism and barbarism led to the unification of Europe. Trump or Bolsonaro's leaderships embody, more clearly than ever, the wrongs of the old paradigm and help create the awareness that we need a new story and model of development. As Buddhists practitioners well know, suffering generates awareness, which is the basis for happiness. The real question is, how much suffering do we need to generate awareness and positive changes?

Beyond the reconfiguration of the French political scene and the defense of liberalism's authentic virtues, Macron's inspired leadership is dreadfully missing a strong environmental and social agenda and a politics of being. It is clear that such politics differ widely from that which is currently implemented in France. Macron's strong economic bottom line—which probably reflects his professional immersion in economic and financial worlds—is steeped very much in the old paradigm, in contrast to the vision articulated in this book. Receptivity to spiritual influence does not necessarily translate into good fruits. The spirit also needs to find in the leaders' mind the ideas that enable its proper manifestation in the concrete reality. But cultural evolution is complex, and nations' ways remain to some extent impenetrable.

My own personal and professional experience has brought me the firm conviction of the spirit at work in our private and collective lives, and I try to always pay attention to its manifestations, signs, and indications. When your own experience has made you aware of this possibility and familiarized you with the spirit's ways, it becomes much easier to recognize and even feel its manifestations. You realize that in many cases these manifestations are so obvious but remain unacknowledged because we collectively think that they are just impossible (or because we don't know what to do with them). A limited rationalistic worldview blinds modern people to some possibilities (e.g., synchronicities[38], "déjà vu," basic forms of telepathy like when the person I am thinking about calls me, etc.) that are part of the day-to-day experience in some traditional cultures.

On May 15, 2012, after a successful campaign with the slogan "the change is now," which subliminally echoed the 2012 Mayan prophecy, François Hollande took office as president of France. That same day, it rained so much during the morning ceremony on the Champs Elysées that he later had to change his suit. In the early afternoon, hail fell on Hollande while he was giving another talk. He had to change his suit again. In the evening, he took a private flight to Germany, where he was going to meet Angela Merkel. A few minutes after takeoff, the plane was hit by lightning and had to turn around. The new president took another flight to Germany the same evening.

Hollande's whole five-year term, during which he had to face numerous political storms, became famous for the bad weather that accompanied the president, to the great displeasure of the professionals in charge of his communication. Hollande, whose sense of humor is legendary,[39] said during an official trip to Mayotte:[40] "I come to Mayotte, and it rains. I know that you have been awaiting this moment for four months, and that is why I have organized this trip."[41] In 2013, he concluded that "governing is raining,"[42] using the words of a French colonial governor of the early twentieth century. As an authority in the field, I am sure Hollande appreciated the spirit's sense of humor, but did he get the message?

I have worked for many countries and, when I travel somewhere, I always start by inwardly asking for the support of the spirit of that land, of that nation. I ask to be instructed and guided so that I can become an instrument of service for the country I am in and learn from its wisdom. This has resulted in many surprising experiences! In one country, just by reading newspapers at breakfast, watching some local news, and conducting my interviews, in two weeks I connected the many dots between a corruption scandal in one of the industries I was looking at and political events of the highest significance. Nobody seemed to have made those connections. I spoke about it to two of my local colleagues, who were quite surprised about my explanations. I felt the spirit had directed my mind to this information. Each piece of information seemed to show up as an answer to the questions the previous piece had generated in me.

Knowing that I could easily be killed for making any declaration on this, and that one never knows what can be ultimately of good consequences for the country already prone to political instability, I decided to ask guidance from the spirit. For my final workshop, I invited some people from the kind of organizations that could effectively put that information to work in order to see if the circumstances would be favorable to talk about it in private. They did not show up. My assignment ended, and I did not make any additional use of this explosive information.

I also worked for a country in the Amazonian region on its national strategy for forest conservation. During my different stays, I felt a deep connection to the Amazonian forest, whose presence and breath I could physically feel in the moist air around me and in the land's energy. I put my work into its hands. One of the first days, as I was discovering the difficult situation of the project, I went to bed asking for some support and started receiving so many ideas about what could be done.

Once, we were invited to do a presentation to the council of ministers. My supervisor was coming to do the presentation, but his connecting flight in a small Caribbean island took off some four hours in advance, and he missed his flight! We never understood clearly what happened. I interpreted this as the spirit wanting me to do the presentation.

That morning, I "planted" a crystal in the forest as an offering, something I had planned to do anyway. On the way back, in the car, I concentrated on what I should say in the council of ministers and got some clear ideas. A few hours later, I presented to them. I started with a very solemn tone that was somewhat discordant in the generally relaxed atmosphere, to say something like: "Each country wants to be number one in something. Your forest, which is the main source of national pride and identity, offers you a unique opportunity for that ..." and I explained why it was so important for the future of the country to maintain high forest cover and how that could be done. I felt a bit like I was in a spiritual ceremony, as if something, through me, was speaking to a deeper part of the council members' beings. Retrospectively I would understand this as a call to the soul of the nation, an invitation to connect to it.

The work went on in the following months, but reaching the kind of high-level political support we were looking for proved to be very difficult. Half a year later, the president's cabinet notified us that the country had decided to make an official commitment toward the international community to maintain its forest cover at the existing level. This very ambitious pledge came as a total surprise. I can't say how that presentation influenced the decision, but what I am sure of is that day the spirit used me for its own ends. Tremendous light forces are eager to support humanity's great transition. They are just waiting for each of us to open the door.

Epilogue

"The real question is whether the 'brighter future' is really so distant. What if, on the contrary, it has been here for a long time already, and only our blindness and weakness has prevented us from seeing it around us and within us, and kept us from developing it?"[1]

—Václav Havel, Czech statesman and writer (1938–2011)

A CHANGE OF CONSCIOUSNESS is to believe that a whole different world is possible. It certainly is. The vision outlined in this book is only a first practical sketch of the possibilities that lie in front of us. Will this brighter world emerge in the decades to come? I don't know. The future is not yet written. When we look around at the state of world's affairs, it seems at first blush more probable that we will fail.

There is a moment in the delivery process of a baby that the mother screams, "I won't make it!" It happened with my wife and our second baby. I was standing next to her, overwhelmed. Later I found out that this is indeed very common and a good indication that the birth is near; the mother's surrender just opens the way for the baby to come. Our current form of despair is a normal reaction for those that are able to acknowledge and accept the current reality. It is also a necessary step before its transformation.

The usual feedback I have received on the politics of being is: "Yes, this is definitely the (only) way to go, but I don't think we will be able to make it." People find me optimistic. I don't see myself that way. On the one hand, I try to be as lucid as I can. I feel the suffering all around; I can hear the mother's screams; I am aware of how broken our world is, of how deep and difficult this transformation is. I would not expect it to occur if we were not facing an existential threat.

I also know that the world is so complex, alive, and fast-changing that any probabilistic prediction at this stage is pointless. On the other hand, I recognize that my being is not separate from the world, and my best way to participate in this great transition is to consciously choose hope over despair, joy over sadness, actions over apathy, as long as I am able to. When it is difficult, I just remember that sooner rather than later my life will be over; it is just an experience to be lived fully. Life on Earth will also eventually disappear anyway in some billion years. What do we have other than the possibility to walk a path with heart?

This book is a drop in the ocean, but it is my drop. I have enjoyed writing it, and I am grateful for all the love that I have experienced in this process; it just felt deeply aligned. I wish everyone could hear and respond to their inner calling, finding a way to express their gifts to help deliver this long-awaited birth. I trust one day our societies will be organized to allow people to flourish in service of the whole. Humanity is not stupid; it is just a bit slow!

The clock is ticking. We are just entering the most crucial decade for our future on this planet, that of our children, their children, all the children of Mother Earth. We need visionary leaders, now! This leap of consciousness depends on each of us embodying it. Now is the time for each human being on this planet to assume the responsibility and dare to step in and cocreate this new reality. Are you ready? Our deep, conscious commitment—which is nothing more than the authentic awareness of its truth—has the power to overcome any hindrance and lead us to this new Earth. In one of the Zen centers where I have meditated, I found these words by Scottish mountaineer W.H. Murray (1913–1996), which are equally valid for our collective transformation.

> Until one is committed, there is hesitancy, the chance to draw back, always ineffectiveness. Concerning all acts of initiative (and creation), there is one elementary truth, the ignorance of which kills countless ideas and splendid plans: that the moment one definitely commits oneself, then Providence moves too. All sorts of things occur to help one that would never otherwise have occurred. A whole stream of events issues from the decision, raising in one's favour all manner of unforeseen incidents and meetings and material assistance, which no man could have dreamt would have come his way. I have learned a deep respect for one of Goethe's couplets: 'Whatever you can do, or dream you can, begin it. Boldness has genius, power, and magic in it!'[2]

The world has already changed since I started writing this book. The COVID-19 pandemic has literally stopped our world and its relentless path toward destruction. What we are experiencing is unprecedented.

Humanity is now at a crossroad in its history, and many have intuitively understood that this new crisis is a signal, an opportunity for bifurcation, for a metamorphosis and a new partnership with the Earth community. It is a time to heal our millennial wounds of wars, abuses, and prosecutions, so that a new way of being can inhabit the world. It is a time to think about the future we want, a time to breathe, a time to meditate. Meditate as one Earth family, bound to live together on our beautiful planet, an evolutionary miracle in itself, adrift in the ever-expanding vastness of the universe. Meditate on our history from groups of hunters-gatherers to nation-states structured around megalopolises, from the birth of life as a unicellular being to human beings who can feel, think, and love and are now called to fulfill their destiny. Meditate on our human condition, with its joys and sufferings, its challenges, its eternal impermanence, and its questions that arise from the depth of time: Where do we come from? What are we here for? What do we truly want?

This is a time to choose. The old model is crumbling, carrying away the most vulnerable and those of us that have not yet undone the inner agreements that attach us to it. The new paradigm of being is rising, filling up those who align their lives to it with the vitality, joy, and grace that open its way and attract others. Its emergence is facing strong resistance, but its advent is inexorable. It will necessarily come together with a politics of being, whose basic elements—a simple definition and conceptual framework, a method, and a policy agenda—I have tried to outline in this book (see box 14 below). I believe it is the most reasonable development path; it is idealistic in its goals and horizon, but concrete, pragmatic, and adaptative in how to move forward. I have no doubt that in time it will become self-evident. It is meant to be. More and more people are already sharing this new dream for the Earth. John Lennon said, "A dream you dream alone is only a dream. A dream you dream together is reality."[3]

Box 14—Politics of Being: 10 Core Messages

1. **We need a collective shift of consciousness, a cultural evolution of a spiritual nature, to address our current challenges.** It is already ongoing, and we are currently facing an evolutive crisis, which requires individuals and societies to look inward and transform.

2. **As a wisdom-based, science-informed approach, a politics of being can support this evolution.** Its main goal is to support the fulfillment of all beings, that is to say the realization of our truest and highest being. "Being" is a wiser and more adequate development objective than "having"; it applies to the whole Earth community.

3. **Cultivating our fundamental "interbeing" or relational nature is instrumental to allow us to live in harmony with one another and the Earth community.** Our spiritual nature makes us interconnected at the level of being with everything that is. Only by recognizing their interconnectedness and sustaining the whole can each part thrive.

4. **Societies progress as they increasingly honor the highest values, qualities, and ideals, such as freedom, goodness, beauty, truth, understanding, life, happiness, love, peace, etc.** These are spiritual qualities in the sense that they reflect an awakened human being or divine perfection. Science and practical initiatives shaped around these universal values can help us design a politics of being. Cultural development relates fundamentally to an evolution of our values, which shape our worldviews and institutions.

5. **The focus on being, the highest values, wisdom and science, provides a simple conceptual framework for a politics of being, which can integrate all relevant claims and initiatives.** As such, it can help unify this vision and strengthen this movement.

6. **Our institutions should help cultivate human virtues.** They should acknowledge and facilitate the expression of our potential for goodness, cooperation, and intrinsic motivation.

7. **Concrete and actionable policy recommendations supporting this agenda already exist in many sectors.** A politics of being can bring them together and scale them up, articulating them in a coherent and meaningful narrative.

8. **Spiritual teachings and wisdom traditions, through dialogue among them and with science, have much to bring to inspire, help design, and implement a politics of being.** They are our most valuable common heritage, able to offer a profound understanding of human nature, as well as practical knowledge and tools for inner, and ultimately social, development.

9. **Each nation needs to reconnect to its own soul and wisdom to develop its version of a politics of being** that can support its development and help it bring its unique contribution to the world. Unity in diversity is the key to harmonious coexistence of nations in a globalized world.

10. **Healing trauma is, for individuals and societies, the gateway to being.** It is fundamental in order for new ways of being and living together to be possible, and for the whole Earth community to flourish.

If you feel you are part of this unfolding dream, please connect to:
www.politicsofbeing.com

Endnotes

Introduction

1   "Collective consciousness (sometimes collective conscience or conscious) is a fundamental sociological concept that refers to the set of shared beliefs, ideas, attitudes, and knowledge that are common to a social group or society." https://www.thoughtco.com/collective-consciousness-definition-3026118, accessed July 2, 2020.

2   The Anthropocene is defined as the new geological epoch, following that of the Holocene, which started some twelve thousand years ago, during which human activity has been the dominant influence on climate and the environment. The relevant scientific authorities are now studying the possibility of officially recognizing the Anthropocene as a new epoch of geological time.

3   Harari 2014, 416

4   Harari 2018

5   https://earthcharter.org/about-us/faqs/#ec1, accessed July 22, 2020.

6   Other United Nations declarations explicitly mention the goal of spiritual development, such as Agenda 21, a nonbinding action plan on sustainable development developed for the Earth Summit held in Rio de Janeiro, Brazil, in 1992.

7   His Holiness the Dalai Lama 2013, X

8   His Holiness the Dalai Lama 2013, XIII

9   http://amma.org/, accessed July 22, 2020.

10 Amma 2004

11 Holy Father Francis 2015. The quote is taken from Benedict XVI (Homily for the Solemn Inauguration of the Petrine Ministry, April 24, 2005).

12 Conceição 2020, 412

13 Jaspers 2011

14 Born in 1934, Ronald Inglehart is a professor emeritus of political science at the University of Michigan. Holder of various honorary doctorates, in 2011 he won the Johan Skytte prize in political science, often considered the highest

prize awarded in the field. He is the director of the World Values Survey, a global network of social scientists who have carried out representative national surveys of the public of over eighty societies on all six inhabited continents, containing 90 percent of the world's population.

15   According to Inglehart, the shift from survival to self-expression values that becomes dominant in postindustrial societies is preceded by a shift from traditional to secular-rational values associated with the rise of industrial societies.

16   Inglehart 2018, 75

17   Algan et al. 2019; Rahn and Transue 1998 quoted by Ricard 2014. See chapter 7.

18   Abdu'l-Bahá 1982, "No matter how far the material world advances, it cannot establish the happiness of mankind. Only when material and spiritual civilizations are linked and coordinated will happiness be assured, for in material civilization good and evil advance together and maintain the same pace," said the Baha'i leader.

19   Ray and Anderson 2000

20   Hadot 2002

21   Don Juan Matus, quoted in Castaneda 1991

22   Don Juan Matus, quoted in Castaneda 1985

23   Ostrom 2009

24   King 1967

1. An Obsolete Development Path

1   https://www.un.org/en/development/desa/news/financing/new-paradigm-job-creation.html, accessed July 22, 2020.

2   Roser 2013, with data updated.

3   Boix et al. 2013, with data updated in 2018. Only a handful of countries have continuously experienced democracy for more than one hundred years: Australia, Belgium, Canada, Denmark, Luxembourg, Netherlands, New Zealand, Norway, Sweden, Switzerland, UK, USA.

4   https://www.footprintnetwork.org/, accessed July 22, 2020.

5   Grooten and Almond 2018

6   IPBES 2019.

7   *Reuters* 2018.

8   This is not necessarily reflected in income statistics as people in rural subsistence economies with very low earnings can be better off than slum dwellers who are more dependent on cash.

9   Elliot 2019. These estimates are controversial. According to the World Inequality Report Lab (Alvarado 2018), in China, Europe, and the United States, "the top 1% share of wealth increased from 28% in 1980 to 33% today, while the bottom 75% share hovered around 10%." In terms of income, while

the top 1 percent income share was close to 10 percent in Western Europe and the US in 1980, it has now risen to respectively 12 percent and 20 percent.

10 Morin 2011, 35. Translated from French: "Le développement est complexe, c'est-à-dire ambivalent, à la fois négatif et positif."

11 Inglehart et al. 2008

12 Putnam 2000. Social capital defined as the "collective value of all "social networks" [who people know] and the inclinations that arise from these networks to do things for each other ["norms of reciprocity"]" http:// robertdputnam.com/bowling-alone/social-capital-primer/, accessed July 22, 2020.

13 Sachs 2015, Helliwell et al. 2017a

14 Inglehart 2018

15 Ritchie and Roser 2018

16 Marcus et al. 2012

17 http://www.euro.who.int/fr/health-topics/noncommunicable-diseases/ mental-health/news/news/2012/10/depression-in-europe/depression-in-europe-facts-and-figures accessed July 22, 2020.

18 Nguyen et al. 2017

19 According to the World Health Organization. https://www.who.int/mental_ health/prevention/suicide/evolution/en/, accessed July 22, 2020.

20 Stone et al. 2018

21 Prior 2020

22 Based on Morin 2011

23 According to Albert Einstein, "The horrifying deterioration in the ethical conduct of people today stems from the mechanization and dehumanization of our lives—the disastrous by-product of the scientific and technical mentality. Nostra culpa. Man grows cold faster than the planet he inhabits."

24 Putnam 2000

25 Sachs 2012

26 Sachs 2013, 81

27 Sachs 2012, 3–5

28 Common Cause Foundation 2016, which also provides other references.

29 Kasser and Linn 2016, Schwartz 2007

30 Holtz 2017

2. An Evolutive Crisis

1 Harari 2014, 375

2 Eisenstein 2013, 3–4

3 Eisenstein 2013, 4

4 Adapted from Eisenstein 2013, 4–6

5 As Eisenstein (2013, 6) put it: "The answers to these questions are culturally dependent, yet they immerse us so completely that we have seen them as

reality itself. These answers are changing today, along with everything built atop them—which basically means our entire civilization. That is why we sometimes get the vertiginous feeling that the whole world is falling apart. Seeing the emptiness of what once seemed so real, practical, and enduring, we stand as if at an abyss."

6   Nhat Hanh 2008, 3–5
7   Eisenstein 2013, 15-16
8   Scharmer 2016
9   https://web.archive.org/web/20161120153112/ https://www.britannica.com/topic/religion-Year-In-Review-2010/Worldwide-Adherents-of-All-Religions, accessed October 7, 2019.
10   Universal House of Justice 2002
11   Baha'u'llah (1983, 288) quoted in Hatcher and Martin 1998.
12   https://reference.bahai.org/en/t/c/BWF/bwf-17.html, accessed October 7, 2019.
13   Effendi (1973, 7) quoted in Hatcher and Martin 1998.
14   Effendi (1973, 202) quoted in Hatcher and Martin 1998.
15   Hatcher and Martin 1998, 141-2
16   Effendi (1996, 301-2) quoted in Hatcher and Martin 1998.
17   Aurobindo 2001, 54
18   Aurobindo 1997
19   Each of them is associated with different "energetic centers" called chakras.
20   Aurobindo 1997, 76
21   Aurobindo 1997, 224
22   Aurobindo 1997, 99
23   Aurobindo 1997, 98
24   Aurobindo 1997, 79-80
25   Aurobindo 1997, 13-14
26   Aurobindo 1997, 229
27   Aurobindo 1997, 183
28   Henry Bergson (1859–1941) thought that evolution is motivated by "an élan vital," a "vital impetus" that can also be understood as humanity's natural creative impulse.
29   Teilhard de Chardin 2002b, 258
30   Teilhard de Chardin 2002a, 53
31   In 1962, the Congregation for the Doctrine of the Faith imposed a monitum (warning) on Teilhard's works, which, in 2020, has not yet been officially removed.
32   Ratzinger 2009, Holy Father Francis 2015. In 2009, Vatican spokesman Federico Lombardi estimated that "by now, no one would dream of saying that [Teilhard] is a heterodox author who shouldn't be studied" (Allen, 2009).
33   Hubbard 2015, 67

34 Laloux 2014, 38
35 Adapted from Wilber 2001 and Beck and Cowan 1996.
36 Based on Wilber 2001.
37 Based on Wilber 2001. For some reason, the total is not matching 100%!
38 See chapter 21 for my views on this.
39 http://www.spiral-dynamics.com/faq_overall.htm#08, accessed January 5, 2020.
40 Harari 2014, 410
41 Harari 2014, 413

3. Being as the New Paradigm

1   https://www.un.org/en/development/desa/news/financing/new-paradigm-job-creation.html, accessed July 22, 2020.
2   https://sustainabledevelopment.un.org/?menu=1300, accessed July 22, 2020.
3   Institutions, governance, or culture have been mentioned as the fourth pillar of sustainable development (United Nations 2014).
4   In the political declaration of Indigenous people at the Rio+20 International Conference on Self-determination and Sustainable Development. https://www.forestpeoples.org/sites/default/files/publication/2012/06/final-political-declaration-adopted-rio20-international-conference-indigenous-peoples-self-determina.pdf, accessed July 22, 2020.
5   "Promote sustained, inclusive and sustainable economic growth, full and productive employment and decent work for all."
6   World Commission on Environment and Development 1987
7   Famous quote from *The Leopard,* an Italian movie.
8   https://www.merriam-webster.com/dictionary/paradigm, accessed August 6, 2020.
9   NDP Steering Committee and Secretariat 2013
10 Jacob Soetendorp Institute for Human Values 2012, 1
11 Jacob Soetendorp Institute for Human Values 2012, 3
12 https://www.simplypsychology.org/maslow.html, accessed July 27 2020.
13 http://amma.org/, accessed July 27 2020.
14 Ricard (2014).
15 Henrich and Henrich 2007
16 The values people hold shape to a large extent their behaviors, attitudes, and beliefs. See Schwartz 2006, Inglehart 2018, and also Common Cause Foundation 2016 for a longer list of references in particular in relation to social and environmental attitudes and behaviors.
17 Inglehart 2018
18 Kasser 2002
19 Self-determination theory (SDT) represents a broad framework for the study of human motivation and personality that has developed since the seventies.

It focuses on the interplay between the extrinsic forces acting on persons and the intrinsic motives and needs inherent in human nature. It considers that the most innate needs that motivate us are autonomy, competence, and relatedness, and that can be the basis of human thriving, or the contrary if they are unsupported. https://selfdeterminationtheory.org/theory/, accessed August 6, 2020.

20 Schmuck et al. 2000, 226
21 Kasser et al. 1995
22 Ahuvia and Izberk-Bilgin 2013, 490
23 Thompson et al. 2013
24 Confino 2013
25 Teasdale 1999
26 Aurobindo 1997, 48
27 Maslow highlighted the need for self-rewarding activities and service of self-actualizing persons.
28 See chapter 6.
29 See chapter 5.
30 See chapter 6.
31 Nhat Hanh 2009
32 Ostrom 2009
33 The definition of well-being proposed by O'Toole and Kropf 2012, 75.
34 'Abdu'l-Bahá 1995, 9 quoted in Bahá'i International Community 1998
35 Aurobindo 1997, 224
36 Aurobindo 1997, 225
37 Aurobindo 1997, 265-6
38 Aurobindo 1997, 228
39 Aurobindo 1997, 228-9
40 Aurobindo 1997, 229
41 Sachs 2015
42 Gewirth 2009
43 Morin 2011, 42. Translated from French: "La gigantesque crise planétaire est la crise de l'humanité qui n'arrive pas à accéder à l'humanité."
44 Morin 2002, paragraph 60. Translated from French: "Il y a surtout l'immaturité des Etats-nations, des esprits, des consciences, c'est-à-dire fondamentalement l'immaturité de l'humanité à s'accomplir elle-même."
45 "Pour atteindre l'humanité, il faut le sens d'un au-delà de l'humanité" (Morin, 2011).
46 Morin 1999, 15. Translated from French: "une politique de tout l'être humain."
47 Morin 1999, 15. Translated from French: "de plus en plus, le centre nucléaire de la politique sera l'homme en devenir dans le monde."

48 Morin 1999, 16. Translated from French: "unifier en une politique multidimensionnelle tous les fragments de la politique."
49 Morin 1999, 14. Translated from French: "Ainsi toutes les avenues du vivre (depuis le "survivre jusqu'au" "est-ce ainsi que les hommes vivent?") et toutes les avenues de la politique commencent à s'entre-rencontrer, s'entre-pénétrer, et annoncent une onto-politique, concernant de plus en plus intimement et globalement l'être de l'homme)."
50 Morin 2016. Translated from French "un idéal de consommation, de supermarchés, de gains, de productivité, de PIB ne peut satisfaire les aspirations les plus profondes de l'être humain qui sont de se réaliser comme personne au sein d'une communauté solidaire"
51 Morin 1999, 59. Translated from French: "Il s'agit de continuer la recherche millénaire de conscience, de l'amour, de la science, de continuer ces courants en les faisant confluer ..."
52 Government Office for Science 2008. Foresight Mental Capital and Wellbeing Project.

II. Spiritual Values as the Foundations for the Politics of Being

1 Aurobindo 1997, 226, 239.

4. Understanding

1 Sivaraksa 2016, 45
2 Morin 2008, 3
3 Morin 2008, 6
4 Meadows 2008
5 Wilkinson and Pickett 2010
6 Defined as "the shared idea in the minds of society, the great big unstated assumptions, constitutes that society's paradigm, or deepest set of beliefs about how the world works. These beliefs are unstated because it is unnecessary to state them—everyone already knows them." (Meadows 2008, 162–3)
7 Meadows 2008
8 UNDP/Carlotta Cataldi, inspired by Meadows 1999
9 Scharmer 2016, 251
10 Scharmer 2016, 343
11 Scharmer 2016, 343
12 Scharmer 2016, 7-8
13 Scharmer 2016, 164
14 Scharmer 2016, 187
15 Scharmer 2018
16 Scharmer 2016, 343
17 Figueres and Rivett-Carnac 2020
18 Meadows 2008, 3

19 Adapted from Wilber (2001) and Integral European Conference: https://integraleuropeanconference.com/integral-theory/, accessed August 11, 2020.

20 The "mindfulness training" on "nonattachment from views": "Aware of the suffering created by attachment to views and wrong perceptions, we are determined to avoid being narrow-minded and bound to present views. We shall learn and practice nonattachment from views in order to be open to others' insights and experiences. We are aware that the knowledge we presently possess is not changeless absolute truth. Truth is found in life, and we will observe life within and around us in every moment, ready to learn throughout our lives" (Nhat Hanh 1998, 26).

21 Meadows 2008

22 Farquhar 2021. See also: https://en.wikipedia.org/wiki/History_of_wolves_in_Yellowstone and https://www.youtube.com/watch?v=ysa5OBhXz-Q,a, all accessed July 29, 2020.

23 Chadwick 2011

24 Morin 2008, 30

25 Quoted by Morin 2008, 30

26 Morin 2008, 32

27 https://en.wikipedia.org/wiki/Complex_system, accessed July 29, 2020.

28 Morin 2008, 30

29 Morin 2008, 31

30 Morin 2008, 31

31 Laloux 2014

32 Morin 2005, 10. Translated from French: "traiter avec le réel, de dialoguer avec lui, de négocier avec lui."

33 La Nature de la nature (1977), La Vie de la vie (1980), La Connaissance de la connaissance (1986), Les Idées (1991), L'Humanité de l'humanité (2001), L'Éthique complexe (2004).

34 Morin 2008, 33

35 Morin 2008, 30

36 Morin 2008, 49

37 Morin 2008, 49

38 Morin 2008, 49

39 Bellaimey 2013

40 Morin 2008, 43

41 Morin 2005, 141. Translated from French: "la rencontre entre l'aléa et une potentialité organisatrice."

42 Morin 2008, 44

43 Foucart 2021

44 Morin (2008) talks of undecidability, while referring to Gödel's theorem (p 28).

45 Morin 2008, 28

46 Morin 2008, 6
47 Morin 2008, 45
48 https://en.wikipedia.org/wiki/List_of_cognitive_biases, accessed September 17, 2019.
49 "When we are in touch with the inner truth, the light of our spirit is also able to recognize by an identity principle the truth outward" (Aurobindo 1997).
50 Unknown source but mentioned, for example, by French-Cuban American writer Anaïs Nin (1903–1977).
51 Aurobindo 1997, 214
52 Inspired by Aurobindo 1997, 171

5. Life

1   Des'Ree, "Life" song (1998).
2   See for example Lewis 2013.
3   Descola 2005
4   According to a UNESCO study (Skutnabb-Kangas et al. 2003), "7 out of 9 top countries for linguistic diversity are also among the top 17 countries for biological diversity. In addition, in the top 25 countries for the number of endemic languages (that is, languages spoken only within the borders of the respective countries), we find 13 of the 17 biological megadiversity countries."
5   Teasdale 1999
6   Teasdale 1999, 193
7   Goldsmith 2002
8   Backster 2003. See also Tompkins and Bird (1973) and Mancuso and Viola (2018).
9   Rahmani 2016
10 Yoshiharu Saito, director of the Technical Institute for the Environment and earthquake forecasts.
11 He was shown nine numbers in a specific order. Then the numbers appeared on different parts of the screen for 0.2 seconds. The chimpanzee was able to point in the right order to the different squares on the screen, something the British memory champion was not able to do. (Interview with Frans De Waal, *Le Monde*, October 11, 2016).
12 Translated from French: "Il est temps d'arrêter de courir après le propre de l'homme. Dans ma vie, j'ai dû voir 25 propositions sur le propre de l'homme. Toutes sont tombées" (Herzberg 2016).
13 Translated from French: "C'est une différence de degré, pas de nature" (Herzberg 2016).
14 Jabr 2019
15 Resolution A/RES/63/278 adopted by the UN General Assembly. See: https://undocs.org/A/RES/63/278, accessed July 29, 2020.
16 As the chief of the Suquamish people in the northwestern United States, his

speech was an answer to the American president's proposal to give up their lands and live on a reservation.

17 IPBES 2016. The report states on page 10: "It is estimated that 5–8 percent of current global crop production, with an annual market value of $235 billion–$577 billion (in 2015, United States dollars) worldwide, is directly attributable to animal pollination."

18 See for example: http://www.salud.carlosslim.org/english2/intestinal-bacteria-could-change-our-behavior/, and https://www.youtube.com/watch?v=VzPD009qTN4, both accesseded July 29, 2020.

19 "Une source pure à laquelle on peut boire sans crainte de s'empoisonner" (Apollinaire 1977, 49).

20 Louv 2005

21 Nisbet et al. 2008

22 See https://depts.washington.edu/hhwb/Thm_Community.html, accessed July 29, 2020.

23 https://depts.washington.edu/hhwb/Thm_Crime.html, accessed July 29, 2020.

24 https://depts.washington.edu/hhwb/Thm_SafeStreets.html, accessed July 29, 2020.

25 See https://depts.washington.edu/hhwb/Top_Introduction.html, accessed July 29, 2020.

26 Xi Jinping 2017. Grateful to Lent (2018) for spotting this.

27 *Tao Te Ching of Laozi,* chapter 32

28 Chen 2012

29 Translated from French (Ricard 2014, 765)

30 Ivanhoe 2013

31 This part is in general based on Solon (2018), Gudinas and Acosta (2011), and Beluche (2018).

32 Solon 2018

33 Gudinas and Acosta 2011

34 For example, Teko Kavi and Ñandereko for the Guaraní People, Shiir Waras for the Shuar, and Küme Mongen for the Mapuche (Solon 2018).

35 Such as "ama qhilla, ama llulla, ama suwa" (don't be lazy, don't lie, don't steal), "suma qamaña" (living well), "ñandereko" (harmonious life), "teko kavi" (good life), "ivi maraei" (land without evil), and "qhapaj ñan" (noble path or life).

36 Ministerio de Planificación del Desarrollo 2009, SENPLADES 2017

37 Solon 2018

38 SENPLADES 2009

39 http://www.harmonywithnatureun.org/, accessed July 29, 2020.

40 Vincent et al. 2006

41 Fehrenbacher 2012

42   https://e-rse.net/definitions/biomimetisme-definition-exemples/#gs.ubj96d, accessed July 29, 2020.

43   Schepman 2016

44   In which all matter, energy, or actions produced by an entity are used by another entity in a given system. It is inspired by nature, where nothing is lost and everything is transformed.

45   Industrial ecology "aims at putting in place at the local level an economic system organization, characterized by an optimal use of resources, and a high rate of matter and energy recycling. This calls for incentivizing economic actors to develop synergies in order to reuse locally production wastes and pool some services and equipments." (Legrain 2014, translated from French)

46   In which food production relies on natural principles and the best use of available natural resources and processes.

47   As highlighted by Arthur Nazaret (2019).

48   See the wonderful work initiated by my friends Shelley Ostroff and Yan Golding: https://www.codes.earth/ accessed July 29, 2020.

49   See also Wolfe (2011), Bogatyreva and Shillerov (2015) for example.

50   Ricard 2015

51   Khong 2016

6. Happiness

1   Nhat Hanh 2009

2   GNH Centre Bhutan 2020

3   "The [GNH] index is not intended to be a measurement of happiness" (NDP Steering Committee and Secretariat, 2013), but rather a tool "to orient the people and the nation towards happiness" (Ura et al. 2012).

4   Correa 2017

5   The Bhutanese council of Ministers was initially, in principle, in favor of the country's accession to WTO. However, the official screening of its potential impact on national happiness, which emphasized potential negative impacts in particular from a social, environmental, cultural, and spiritual perspective, noting that it would "probably result in a net increase in feelings of material wellbeing within the population," led to the government's decision not to pursue joining the WTO (Centre for Bhutan Studies 2008).

6   Government of Bhutan 2013

7   NDP Steering Committee and Secretariat 2013. The post-2015 development agenda has finally taken the form of the SDGs.

8   NDP Steering Committee and Secretariat 2013, 37

9   NDP Steering Committee and Secretariat 2013, 35

10   See Tasmania Together at https://tasmaniatogether.com.au/ accessed July 16, 2021.

11   O'Donnel 2013

12   See for example Global Council for Happiness and Wellbeing (2018; 2019), David et al. 2013, the different World Happiness Reports and https://whatworkswellbeing.org/, accessed July 29, 2020.

13   See for example in France the work of the Commission on the Measurement of Economic Performance and Social Progress (CMEPSP) in 2008 that emphasized three areas requiring further attention by statistical offices and policy makers: better measurement of the domestic production of goods and services, the incorporation for sustainability considerations, and the measurement of quality of life. See also the work of the UK's Office for National Statistics (ONS), the Canadian Index of Wellbeing (CIW), the OECD's better life index, the Social Progress Index, the World Happiness Reports, and the World Database of Happiness.

14   Cuming 2019

15   Graham-McLay 2019

16   Chaperon 2015, Optum 2018

17   http://www.actionforhappiness.org/ accessed July 29, 2020.

18   Seligman and Csikszentmihalyi 2000, 5

19   David et al. 2013

20   The Life Satisfaction Approach is an example of an alternative to cost-benefit analyses for public decision-making (Frey et al. 2010). Unemployment is an example of problems that would most probably be less tolerated from a happiness and well-being perspective than from an economic perspective as the loss of subjective happiness and well-being is greater and more permanent than the loss of income associated with unemployment (Clark 2010, Clark et al. 2001).

21   See for example the *World Happiness Report*, Helliwell et al. 2015, 2017, 2019. Each relies on self-reported measures of life satisfaction and affects.

22   Mulgan 2013, Tov and Au 2013, Diener et al. 2010, Helliwell et al. 2015, Rojas 2018

23   Gallup 2019

24   Sachs 2015

25   Sachs 2015, Helliwell et al. 2017a, 2019

26   Indeed, according to Helliwell et al. 2017a, for a given society, the effect on happiness of an extra 10 percent of the population having "someone to count on" is equivalent to that of doubling the GDP per capita.

27   Helliwell et al. 2019

28   The choice of variables is debatable and constrained by available data.

29   While GDP and healthy life expectancy measurements rely on available data, other variables correspond to the answers to the following questions:
- "If you were in trouble, do you have relatives or friends you can count on to help you whenever you need them, or not?"

- "Are you satisfied or dissatisfied with your freedom to choose what you do with your life?"
- "Have you donated money to a charity in the past month?"
- "Is corruption widespread throughout the government or not?" and "Is corruption widespread within businesses or not?"

30 Inglehart 2018

31 Helliwell et al. 2016, 2017a

32 Helliwell et al. 2017a. "These improvements [to the social fabric] not only ensure better responses to the crisis, but also have substantial additional happiness returns, since people place real value on feeling that they belong to a caring and effective community" according to the authors. The results were recorded in 2005–2007 and 2014–2016.

33 Ye et al 2015, 527

34 Ye et al 2015

35 Inglehart 2018, 169

36 Demir 2013

37 Waldinger 2016

38 https://www.adultdevelopmentstudy.org/ accessed July 29, 2020.

39 In particular, the work of US psychologist Tim Kasser (Kasser 2002, Kasser and Sheldon 2002).

40 Inglehart 2018, Myers 2013

41 See for example a poll undertaken in 2005 for the BBC by GfK NOP in the UK. On page 17, among the factors most contributing to their happiness, people have answered "partner/spouse and family relationship" (47.5 percent), health (23.5 percent), followed long after by "a nice place to live in" (8.5 percent), "money and financial situation" (7.5 percent), "religious and spiritual life" (6 percent), "community and friends" (5 percent), and "work fulfillment" (2 percent). In addition, unemployment is known to have a disastrous and long-lasting effect on happiness (Mulgan 2013; De Neve and Ward 2017), probably as it also affects social relationships.

42 Huta 2013, 201

43 Huta 2013

44 Huta 2013, 202

45 Huta 2013, 201

46 Huta 2013, 201

47 Peterson, Park and Seligman (2005) and Vella-Brodrick, Park and Peterson (2009) quoted by Huta (2013).

48 See Keyes 2005, Seligman 2010

49 Keyes 2005, 2007. The main psychological features associated with flourishing are:
- For positive emotions: positive affect and avowed quality;
- For positive psychological functioning: self-acceptance, personal growth, purpose in life, environmental mastery, positive relations with others;

- For positive social functioning: social acceptance, social actualization, social contribution, social coherence, social integration.

50   Keyes 2005
51   Some 40 to 50 percent, according to Pavot and Diener (2013).
52   Keyes 2005, 2007
53   In a program headed by cognitive scientist professor Richard K Davidson, principal of the Laboratory for Affective Neuroscience at the University of Wisconsin-Madison.
54   In particular, levels of gamma waves—those linked to attention, learning, and memory—and excessive activity in his brain's left prefrontal cortex (associated with happiness) compared to its right counterpart (associated with negativity).
55   Bates 2012
56   https://www.actionforhappiness.org/10-keys-to-happier-living, accessed July 29, 2020. Their presentation below includes some additional ideas I have brought in.
57   For example, Keyes 2005, Seligman 2010, or Myers 2013. See also: https://positivepsychology.com/flourishing/, https://selfdeterminationtheory.org/theory/, https://centerhealthyminds.org/about/why-wellbeing, all accessed July 29, 2020.
58   Ricard 2007
59   Ricard 2007, 7-8
60   Ricard 2008
61   Myers 2013
62   However, according to Inglehart (2018), evidence comes mainly from developed democracies.
63   Myers 2013
64   Myers 2013
65   De Neve et al. 2013
66   For this last point, see Brown and al. (2005), Huta (2016), and Ahuvia and Izberk-Bilgin (2013).
67   Huta 2016
68   De Neve et al. 2013
69   While Bhutan is the first country to use happiness as the overall framework guiding its development, it most probably cannot claim paternity of the GNH concept and methodology (GNH index etc.). See GNH Institute (undated) website.   http://gnh.institute/gross-national-happiness-gnh-origin.htm, accessed July 29, 2020.
70   Tho 2016
71   http://www.wearehappyfrom.com/, accessed July 29, 2020.
72   https://en.wikipedia.org/wiki/Happy_%28Pharrell_Williams_song%29, accessed July 29, 2020.
73   Www.Globalhappyparty.com, accessed July 29, 2020.

7. Love

1 His Holiness the Dalai Lama 1998

2 Fredrickson 2013. It is also deactivating the neural pathway responsible for negative emotions, such as fear and social judgment (Edward, undated).

3 See, for example, Khaleque 2018.

4 See, for example, Crocker and Canevello (2008) and Davis (2017). Davis (2017) notes that "dispositional forms of empathy are associated with greater relationship satisfaction, greater popularity, lower levels of conflict and aggression, higher levels of effective support-provision, greater tolerance for partner misbehavior, and greater willingness to forgive." According to her, the cognitive aspect of empathy (perspective taking) has been emphasized as potentially more important than its emotional aspect for the quality of our relationships, to the notable effect of forgiveness (Davis 2017). Note that perspective-taking can also arguably stem from love.

5 1 John 4:8. https://biblehub.com/1_john/4-8.htm, accessed August 1, 2020.

6 https://amma.org/, accessed August 1, 2020.

7 http://www.embracingtheworld.org/, accessed August 1, 2020.

8 Conseil Pontifical Justice et Paix 2005

9 As Ricard 2014, 869 said: "Altruism has been the central concept of my research as it is the most encompassing: yet we won't forget that fundamentally it is about love, a love that extends to all, including oneself." Translated from French: "L'altruisme a été le concept central de mes recherches car il est le plus englobant, mais on n'en oubliera pas pour autant que fondamentalement c'est d'amour qu'il s'agit, d'un amour qui s'étend à tous, y compris soi-même."

10 Ricard 2014

11 Vernant 2007, Plato 2008

12 Rifkin 2009, 24

13 Hobbes 1651

14 Karlberg 2007

15 Dawkins 1976, the favorite book of Jeff Skilling, the former president of Enron, who is now in jail and established extreme competition within his company (Ricard, 2014).

16 Freud (1900/2003, 256) quoted in Ricard (2014, 271).

17 Zarins and Konrath (2017); Twenge et al. (2012). Interesting to note that according to Twenge et al. (2012): "Among the life goals items, some of the largest declines appeared in "developing a meaningful philosophy of life"" and "finding meaning and purpose in my life," but "Millennials still rate finding meaning and purpose as more important than having lots of money."

18 Twenge et al. 2012

19 Twenge and Campbell 2010. The rise of narcissism is not (yet?) such a problem in Europe and Eastern countries.

20 Newsom et al. 2003, quoted by Ricard 2014.

21   Grant et al. 2008, quoted by Ricard 2014.
22   Grant et al. 2008, quoted by Ricard 2014.
23   https://en.wikipedia.org/wiki/Narcissistic_personality_disorder,   accessed
     August 1, 2020.
24   Alicke and Govorun 2005, quoted by Ricard 2014.
25   According to Putnam 2000, social capital has declined in the US since the
     mid-sixties. Putnam defines social capital as the "collective value of all
     'social networks' [who people know] and the inclinations that arise from
     these networks to do things for each other ['norms of reciprocity']" (http://
     robertdputnam.com/bowling-alone/social-capital-primer/, accessed August
     1, 2020).
26   The disappearance of the industrial society organized in classes in which
     work would support socialization. See for example Algan et al. 2019.
27   Rahn and Transue 1998, quoted by Ricard (2014).
28   The expression is from Kenneth Arrow (1921–2017), an American economist
     who won the Nobel Memorial Prize in Economic Sciences.
29   See Algan et al. 2019.
30   Daniel Cohen on France Info, a French Radio Station (Leymarie, 2019).
     Translated from French: "Les électeurs de Marine Le Pen, de Salvini, de
     Trump, mais aussi les électeurs en faveur du Brexit ont une confiance envers
     les autres extrêmement faible (...) Ces électeurs se méfient de tout, des
     immigrés à leurs collègues de bureau et à leurs voisins."
31   Putnam shows strong correlations between the level of social capital in
     certain US states and indicators associated with these variables. He considers
     that social capital seems, in most of these cases, to be the strongest explaining
     factor, beyond interstate variations of these indicators, but he recognizes the
     need to be cautious and better establish the causality direction. He recognizes,
     for example, that in the case of inequality, "The causal arrows are likely to run
     in both directions" (Putnam 2001).
32   Zarins and Konrath (2017), quoting Konrath (2014, 2016), Konrath and
     Brown (2013), as well as Seppala, Rossomando and Doty (2013).
33   Darwin 1859
34   Darwin 1889, 107. In the same book, Darwin estimated that, due to their
     social instinct, it would be natural for humans to extend their "sympathy" to
     members of all nations and races, and finally also to animals.
35   Though helping those that are genetically related to us may also be a good
     reproductive strategy, as shown by William Donald Hamilton (Ricard 2014).
36   Wilson 2012
37   Aggressive behaviors are also common between two and five, while a child's
     natural moral sense develops in interaction with his/her culture and he/she
     learns to regulate his/her emotions (Ricard 2014). Other research has shown
     that children tend to develop aggressive behaviors only when their primary
     need for love is frustrated (Rifkin 2009).

38 Ricard 2014 mentions the work of ethologist Frans de Waal, of ethnologist Irenäus Eibl-Eibesfeldt, and psychologist Alfie Kohn.

39 Ricard 2014

40 "As biology tells us, compassion and its related systems of nurturing and maternal behavior completely align with the organism's interest in self-preservation. As our biology expanded to encompass more sophisticated social interactions, it evolved to reward them through the release of hormones and neurotransmitters and other positive neurological and physiological systems" (Doty 2017).

41 Rilling et al. 2002

42 Aknin et al. 2012; Aknin et al. 2013; Dun et al. 2014, quoted by Spinrad and Eisenberg 2017.

43 For example, participants in an experiment performed a task better when informed that their supervisors' performance would be assessed based on their performance. See Batson (2017) and Ricard (2014) for a synthesis of the experiments of Batson, which have systematically refuted all the main objections to the existence of pure altruism. Denying the evidence tends to lead to a point of nonsense, in which the deniers' position does not seem to fill the scientific criteria of refutability, and they should instead be the ones assuming the charge of proof. This is a good example of the old story of grotesque agony and the inability of some to abandon their views.

44 See the growing research field of behavioral economics.

45 See for example, the Harwood Group 1995, Common Cause Foundation 2016.

46 Common Cause Foundation 2016. "Compassionate values include: 'broadmindedness,' 'a world of beauty,' 'a world at peace,' 'equality,' 'protecting the environment,' 'social justice,' 'helpfulness,' 'forgiveness,' 'honesty,' and 'responsibility.' Values in this group are associated with greater concern about social and environmental issues, and greater motivation to engage in various forms of civic action. These are known to academics as 'self-transcendence' values and encompass some of the 'intrinsic' values" (Common Cause Foundation 2016, 7). "Selfish values include: values of 'wealth,' 'social recognition,' 'social status' and 'prestige,' 'control or dominance over people,' 'authority,' 'conformity,' 'preserving public image,' 'popularity,' 'influence' and 'ambition.' Selfish values are associated with lower concern about social and environmental issues, and lower motivation to engage in various forms of civic action. These are known to academics as 'self-enhancement' values and they are similar to 'extrinsic' values." (Common Cause Foundation 2016, 7).

47 Their assessment of their fellow citizens compassionate value score and selfish value score gives an "adjusted compassionate score" (the difference between the compassionate value score and the selfish value score) that is

some four times smaller than reality. Potential biases in the answers have been controlled for. Liberals' perceptions are in general less accurate than conservative ones.

48   Miller 1999
49   Miller 1999
50   Deci et al. 1999
51   Gneezy and Rustichini 2000a
52   Gneezy and Rustichini 2000b
53   Frey and Götte 1999
54   Common Cause Foundation 2016, 1
55   UNICEF 2019
56   Doty 2017, xxii
57   See Seppälä et al. 2017; Ricard 2014
58   http://ccare.stanford.edu/education/about-compassion-cultivation-training-cct/, accessed August 1, 2020.
59   Brito-Pons et al. 2018 ; Scarlet et al. 2017; Goldin and Jazaieri 2017
60   Ricard 2014
61   https://charterforcompassion.org/, accessed August 1, 2020.
62   This type of organization seems to be more sustainable than a governmental initiative that can change its priorities over time following elections.
63   Mehring 2013
64   Compassionate Games International. http://compassiongames.org/about-us/, accessed August 1, 2020.
65   http://compassiongames.org/about-us/, accessed August 1, 2020.
66   Morin 1999, 38. Translated from French, "Il faut oser prononcer le mot qui nous a tant fait honte que jamais, politiquement, nous n'avons osé l'employer."
67   Williamson 2019, 10
68   Williamson 2019, 28
69   Teilhard de Chardin 1973, 86

8. Peace

1   UNESCO 2018
2   It can also mean harmony, wholeness, completeness, prosperity, welfare, and tranquility.
3   These concepts have been particularly developed by Johan Galtung. He considers cooperation and empathy the pillars of positive peace, while reconciliation efforts to heal past traumas, and our capacity to solve present conflicts in a nonviolent way, are the foundations of negative peace (Galtung 2017).
4   Resolution 53/243.
5   Resolution 52/15 of the UN General Assembly.

6 Resolution 53/25 of the UN General Assembly.
7 Marchand 2020. Translated from French: "Ce qui fonde la dignité des êtres humains, ce ne sont pas leurs 'droits' mais leur « devoirs » volontairement consenti et appliqué."
8 https://plumvillage.org/mindfulness-practice/the-5-mindfulness-trainings/, accessed August 10, 2020.
9 Nhat Hanh 2009
10 Eisler and Fry 2019
11 The Masai traditional culture is also mentioned as an example.
12 Eisler and Fry 2019, 100
13 Eisler and Fry 2019, 100
14 Eisler and Fry 2019, 271
15 See Møller and Skaaning 2013 for the most recent advances (over the last decades).
16 Eisner 2003
17 UNODC 2019
18 Pinker 2011b
19 See Eisler and Fry 2019 for a full list.
20 Frenkel-Brunswik 1958, 669-70, quoted by Eisler and Fry 2019, 184.
21 Niehoff 1999, 185 and 187
22 Norway, Sweden, and Denmark were in the top five countries in the UNDP 2018 gender inequality index (UNDP 2019).
23 Norway, Sweden, and Denmark were in the top five countries in *The Economist's* Democracy Index 2018 (*Economist* Intelligence Unit 2019).
24 Through the creation of peace studies programs and institutes early on, Nordic countries pioneered legal measures and attitude changes against the physical punishment and abuse of children, as well as nonviolent conflict resolution.
25 Nordic countries arguably have among the most environmentally aware people in the world, though the nations' ecological footprints are high.
26 Eisler and Fry 2019, 147
27 Pietilä 2007
28 Even succumbing to romantic love is condemned in many cultures as a potential weakness in men, which could interfere with using violence against their wives when necessary to maintain domination.
29 Eisler and Fry 2019, 144
30 Central Asia Institute 2020; Hodge 2017
31 Common Cause Foundation 2016; Eisenberg and Lennon 1983
32 Finucane and Hidalgo 2018
33 Ye et al. 2015
34 Eisler and Fry 2019
35 Abdu'l-Bahá. https://www.bahai.org/documents/nsa-usa/two-wings-bird, accessed August 3, 2020.

36   Eisler and Fry 2019, 144
37   Eisler and Fry 2019, 189, based on analysis by Milburn and Conrad 1996, 2018.
38   Eisler and Fry 2019, 188, based on analysis by Milburn and Conrad 1996, 2018.
39   Wilkinson and Pickett 2010
40   Mainly data availability and the need to control statistically for the effects of per capita income increase that is still important in poorer countries.
41   Wilkinson and Pickett 2010
42   They quote the work of philosopher and evolutionary psychologist Helena Cronin (1991).
43   Gilligan 1996, 110
44   See for example Wilson and Daily 1988
45   Percentage of people agreeing that "most people can be trusted."
46   Justice Policy Institute 2002
47   Quote on the 2010 edition book cover.
48   See for example Sahlins 2003
49   They quote Henrich et al. 2007
50   Wilkinson and Pickett 2010, 239
51   Wilkinson and Pickett 2010, 239
52   The GPI is based on three broad themes: the level of societal safety and security, the extent of ongoing domestic and international conflict, and the degree of militarization.
53   You and Khagram 2005
54   Kawachi and Kennedy 1997 and Uslaner 2002
55   Geysa 2006
56   Wilkinson and Pickett 2010, 233
57   Chenoweth 2017; Chenoweth and Gallagher Cunningham 2013; Schock 2013
58   Christian Peacemaker Teams undated
59   Sweet 2020
60   After the death of Franco in 1975, both leftist and rightist parties decided to avoid dealing with the legacy of Francoism, put the past behind them, and concentrate on the future of Spain. This was called the Pact of Forgetting (Pacto del Olvido in Spanish), which was given a legal basis in the 1977 Amnesty Law. In 2007, the socialist government, led by prime minister Jose Luis Rodriguez Zapatero, instituted the Historical Memory Law. The law recognized and broadened rights and established measures in favor of those who suffered persecution or violence during the Civil War and the dictatorship. In 2010, Spanish judge Baltasar Garzón challenged the Pact of Forgetting on the basis that international law amnesties do not apply to crimes against humanity, something the United Nations reminded Spain of several times. His investigations into Francoist crimes were eventually discontinued,

as was the exhumation of victims of Francoist repression, which followed the passing of the Historical Memory Law.

61 Catalan independentists often refer to the Franco legacy of domination and violence to justify their independency claim. The Republican Left of Catalonia (ERC), the main independentist party, voted against passage of the 2007 Historical Memory Law on the basis that it did not go far enough. Spanish philosopher Reyes Mate sees in the Catalan national construction, based on the exclusion of others, an expression of Francoism. Quoting the work of Spanish cultural historian Américo Castro (1885–1972), Mate says this type of national construction predates the Franco era and is rooted in how Spanish identity developed through the exclusion of Jewish people in the fifteenth century and the expulsion of the Moors in the seventeenth century. According to Reyes Mate: "Spanish democracy has not settled the score with [Franco's] dictatorship" ("La democracia española no ha arreglado las cuentas con la dictadura") (Munárriz 2017).

62 CNN 2020

63 *Walking Eagle News* 2017

64 Fletcher 2019

65 Canada at first did not include forests in its GHG emissions accounting because of the important amount of emissions linked to forest fires and insect infestations, so its forests have represented a net source of emission (and not a carbon sink) since 2001. Then it decided to include only the "managed forests," that is to say the ones under direct human influence, which represent 65 percent of the country's forests. In these "managed forests," natural disturbances in 2016, such as fires and insect infestations, accounted for about 98 Mt CO2e emissions, while human activities such as reforestation or "sustainable forest management" accounted for the removal of about 20 Mt CO2e, resulting in net emissions of 78 Mt CO2e (Fletcher 2019; Government of Canada 2020).

66 For example, in the Greco-Roman philosophical tradition, it is a central value referred to as the *Tranquilitas Animi* (the title of a book by Seneca and Plutarch) or *ataraxia*.

9. Mindfulness

1 Grateful for this information to Brother Phap Lin and William Addey's presentation in Plum Village "Know your Brain to Practice Well" (2019).

2 Pickert 2014

3 This is an observation. The numbers you find on the internet, such as twelve thousand to sixty thousand to eight thousand thoughts per day, of which some 95 percent would be repetitive (same as the day before) and 80 percent would be negative, do not seem scientifically backed. They refer to a 2005 study from the National Science Foundation that has never been found.

4   Accessed from Brainy Quote.
5   Dashti 2011, 248
6   Mindfulness Initiative 2015
7   Joshi 2017
8   See for example:
  • De Vibe et al. (2012), a meta-study on the benefits of Mindfulness-Based Stress Reduction (MBSR) for improving mental and somatic health, quality of life, resilience, and empathy.

  • For the effects of mindfulness on physical health: Levine et al. (2017) for heart disease, Creswell et al. (2009) for immunity, Schutte and Malouff (2014) and Alda et al. (2016) for aging, Hilton et al. (2017) for chronic pain.

  • For the effects of mindfulness on mental health and happiness, Keng et al. (2011), a meta-study that found trait mindfulness (how "mindful" a person generally is in their approach to life) to be positively associated with well-being indicators such as life satisfaction, conscientiousness, vitality, self-esteem, empathy, sense of autonomy, competence, and optimism, and negatively correlated with depression, neuroticism, absent-mindedness, rumination, cognitive reactivity, social anxiety, emotion regulation difficulties, and general psychological symptoms. See also Khoury et al. (2013), a meta-analysis of 209 studies with a total of 12,145 participants, which concluded that mindfulness-based interventions (MBIs) showed "large and clinically significant effects in treating anxiety and depression, and the gains were maintained at follow-up."

  • For the effects of mindfulness on social skills, pro-social attitudes and behaviors: Bristow et al. (2020), Chiesa et al. (2011) on improving emotion-regulation capacity, Condon et al. (2013) on compassionate responses, Brown et al. (2007) on personal relationships and environmentally responsible decisions, Lueke and Gibson (2016) on discriminatory behavior reduction, Baer (2015) and Shapiro et al. (2006) on values clarification and alignment.

  • For mindfulness's cognitive benefits (attention, decision-making, memory): Bristow et al. (2020), Chiesa et al. (2011) and Ostafin and Kassman (2012), Kudesia (2015) for creativity, Moore and Malinowski (2009) for cognitive flexibility, Bihari and Mullan (2012), as well as Allen et al. (2009) on perspective-taking and meta-cognition awareness.

9   Baer 2015
10   Bristow et al. 2020
11   https://www.umassmed.edu/cfm/mindfulness-based-programs/mbsr-courses/about-mbsr/history-of-mbsr/, accessed August 3, 2020.

12   Pickert 2014
13   https://umassmed.edu/cfm/About-Us/people/2-Meet-Our-Faculty/Kabat-Zinn-Profile/, accessed August 3, 2020.
14   On the impact of mindfulness and quality of care, including through improved empathy, see Martin Asuero et al. 2014.
15   Taylor 2016
16   Snel 2013; Chahine 2017
17   Mindfulness Initiative 2015
18   https://www.themindfulnessinitiative.org/mindfulness-all-party-parliamentary-group, accessed August 3, 2020.
19   Mindfulness Initiative 2015, 5
20   Mindfulness Initiative 2015, 5
21   Mindfulness Initiative 2015, 13
22   Mindfulness Initiative 2015, 4
23   Mindfulness Initiative 2015, 39
24   Piet and Hougaart 2011
25   Mindfulness Initiative 2015
26   Sachs 2012 in chapter 9, 161-83
27   Sachs 2012, 164
28   Sachs 2012, 165
29   Ericson et al. 2014; Fischer et al. 2017
30   According to IBISWorld (Scott 2017).
31   Wieczner 2016
32   According to Headspace website.
33   Confino 2014

10. Light

1   Lao Tzu 2006
2   This is expressed in many traditions, for example in the Buddhist Heart Sutra: "This Body itself is Emptiness and Emptiness itself is this Body. This Body is not other than Emptiness and Emptiness is not other than this Body," translated by Zen Master Thich Nhat Hanh. https://plumvillage.org/about/thich-nhat-hanh/letters/thich-nhat-hanh-new-heart-sutra-translation/, accessed March 9, 2021.
3   The soul is often presented as a lower dimension than the spirit (Wilber, 2000).
4   Where E means energy, c is the speed of light, and m is matter.
5   Einstein and Infeld 1938
6   https://plato.stanford.edu/entries/panpsychism/, accessed August 3, 2020.
7   Electromagnetic force, the strong nuclear force, the weak nuclear force, and gravity
8   The size of the Planck length through "some recent versions of string theory

have predicted that the strings could have a longer length, up to nearly a millimeter in size, which would mean they're in the realm that experiments could detect them" (Jones 2019).

9   News Heads Bureau 2018

10 Sunim 2017

11 NASA undated

12 Gosseries et al. 2020

13 Brasey 1996, 13. Translated from French: "Mais qu'est-ce que la science sinon une magie dont a su expliquer, en partie, les mystères ? Et qu'est-ce que la magie, sinon l'esquisse de la science de demain?"

14 That is the case, for example, of Russian professor Konstantin Korotkov.

15 Reiki is a Japanese energetic healing technique.

16 Castaneda 1991

17 Some people consider Quetzalcoatl to have been a real spiritual and political leader.

18 The "magic village" is a touristic label assigned by the Mexican government.

19 A famous example, which was subject to scientific observations (fifteen days in a hospital), was German Catholic mystic Thèrèse Neumann, who said she did not consume any food or water, with the exception of the Holy Eucharist, from 1926 until her death in 1962 (Fahsel 2013).

20 https://www.lightdocumentary.com/prahlad-jani.html,   https://www.leparisien.fr/societe/inde-mort-de-prahlad-jani-un-yogi-affirmant-n-avoir-pas-mange-ou-bu-pendant-80-ans-26-05-2020-8323626.php, both accessed August 3, 2020.

21 Emoto's work is often associated with that of Nobel Prize recipient Luc Montanier on water memory and also the work of Gerard Pollack of Washington University.

22 Unity is also sometimes considered.

23 Paragraph 41 in part one, section 1, chapter 1. IV. https://www.vatican.va/archive/ENG0015/__PC.HTML, accessed August 6, 2020.

24 Translated from Spanish: "Los preceptos no son mandamientos morales enviados por un ser divino o que lo sabe todo. Ellos más bien revelan como se comportaría una persona que está profundamente iluminada, completamente perfecta, sin sentido de yo y del otro. Esta persona no imita los preceptos sino que ellos la imitan a ella."

25 Horton 2015

26 John 8:32

27 Though the economics of climate change hold many methodological challenges and is uncertain by nature. See for example the Stern review (Stern 2007) or Burke et al. (2018) on the important economic returns associated with climate change mitigation. The investments necessary to address climate change have been often estimated, for example by McKinsey or the

Stern review, to be around 1 percent of global GDP. The Intergovernmental Panel on Climate Change concluded that the actions necessary to have a 66 percent chance of avoiding global warming of more than 2°C, will entail a global consumption reduction of 1–4 percent in 2030, 2–6 percent in 2050, and 3–11 percent in 2100. This is very small in comparison to the benefits of avoiding climate change and the many cobenefits associated with that avoidance, especially if we consider the underlying growth that the global economy is likely to experience at the same time.

28 Repucci 2020
29 We demain 2015
30 Baer 2015
31 In *Young India*, published on March 5, 1925.

III. An Agenda for Action

1 Ostrom 2009

11. Childhood and Family

1 *Lancet* 2016; Government Office for Science 2008
2 Government Office for Science 2008
3 Gilbert and Mascaro 2017, 405
4 Lynch and Vaghul 2015
5 Petronzio 2018
6 *Lancet* 2016
7 Wilkinson and Pickett 2009
8 Lundberg et al. 2007
9 Griggs and Walker 2008
10 *Lancet* 2016
11 *Lancet* 2016
12 *Lancet* 2016
13 Sarakatsannis and Winn 2018
14 *Lancet* 2016
15 Cherry 2019
16 Kasser et al. 1995; Cohen and Cohen 1996
17 See European Commission 2018
18 https://en.wikipedia.org/wiki/Parental_leave, accessed August 4, 2020.
19 Bonus days of parental leaves are added for twins. The days don't expire until the child is eight years old (Kane 2018).
20 *Lancet* 2016. Among the most widely implemented of programs in low- and middle-income country settings are the WHO/UNICEF Care for Child Development and Reach Up and Learn, a parenting program tested in trials in Jamaica over the past 20 years and now expanding to other regions.

21 https://www.who.int/mental_health/maternal-child/en/, accessed August 4, 2020.
22 Layard et al. 2013; Johnston et al. 2011
23 Gray et al. 2018; Barlow and Coren 2018
24 Kirby 2017
25 Huta 2012
26 Kirby 2017; Mindfulness Initiative 2015
27 Gibbs et al. 2018
28 https://www.who.int/features/factfiles/breastfeeding/en/, accessed August 4, 2020.
29 Burke 2015
30 Cordier 2021
31 Center for Youth Wellness (undated), which serves as the main basis for this part.
32 Burke et al. 2011; Felitti et al. 1998
33 Center for Youth Wellness undated
34 Johnson et al. 2013
35 https://centerforyouthwellness.org/the-science/, accessed August 3, 2020.
36 Center for Youth Wellness undated
37 Wilkinson and Picket 2010
38 Burke 2015
39 Jackson et al. 1999
40 Regalado et al. 2004
41 Michelet 1962, 154. Translated from French: "Deux âmes harmonisées, c'est déjà une cité. C'est déjà un monde. L'accord trouvé une fois, c'est le même d'ici aux étoiles, le même pour la voie lactée."
42 Khong 2014

12. Education

1 Dalin and Rust 1996
2 Laininen 2019
3 "WISE is the premier international platform dedicated to innovation and creative action in education, where top decision-makers share insights and ideas with on-the-ground practitioners" (WISE, 2014). https://www.wise-qatar.org/, accessed August 3, 2020.
4 Salovey and Mayer 1990
5 Goleman 1996
6 Boniwell 2013; White 2013
7 https://www.who.int/mental_health/maternal-child/en/, accessed August 4, 2020.
8 European Network of Ombudspersons for Children 2018; Boniwell 2013
9 Mental Health America 2017

10 Gillham et al. 2013; Noble and McGrath 2013
11 Gilham et al. 2013; Seligman and Adler 2018; Moore 2020
12 Helliwell 2018; Mc Inerney 2013; Chodkiewicz and Boyle 2017
13 Rosier 2017
14 Rosier 2017
15 Mindfulness Initiative 2015. For a complete bibliography, see also: https://www.mindfulschools.org/about-mindfulness/research-on-mindfulness/, accessed August, 4, 2020.
16 https://mindfulnessinschools.org/, accessed August, 4, 2020.
17 https://mindup.org/, accessed August, 4, 2020.
18 https://wakeupschools.org/, accessed August, 4, 2020.
19 Mindfulness Initiative 2015
20 Berkowitz 2011; Johnson et al. 2008
21 Johnson et al. 2006; Slavin et al. 2003
22 Johnson et al. 2000
23 Ricard 2014
24 Lovat et al. 2010
25 Berkowitz 1985
26 Maradan 2017
27 http://www.occe.coop/~ad86/IMG/pdf Le conseil de cooperation.pdf, accessed August 4, 2020.
28 Berkowitz 2011
29 Berkowitz and Bier 2005; Billig 2002
30 Piff and Moskowitz 2017
31 Elbert et al. 1995 ; Lin et al. 2013; Münte et al. 2002 ; Schlegel et al. 2015
32 UNESCO 2006
33 Scheuler 2010 ; Rinne et al. 2011 ; Peppler et al. 2014 ; Robinson 2013 ; Scripps and Paradis 2014 ; Hardiman et al. 2019
34 Hardiman et al. 2019; Robinson 2013
35 Scheuler 2010; Roege and Kim 2013. See also: https://www.americansforthearts.org/sites/default/files/pdf/2014/by program/research studies and publications/one pagers/15.%20ArtsEducation Drop%20Out.pdf, accessed August 4, 2020.
36 Guthold et al. 2019
37 UNESCO 2015; Bangsbo et al. 2016; Sattelmair and Ratey 2009
38 Morin 2016
39 Fadel and Groff 2019
40 Garner 2015
41 Riordan and Caillier 2019
42 Riordan and Caillier 2019, 151
43 White 2013; Morris 2013
44 Helliwell 2019, 11

45   Berkowitz 2011
46   Lähdemäki 2019; Korpela 2017
47   Korpela 2017; Varlas 2011
48   Sabel et al. 2011
49   Korpela 2017
50   https://www.educationfinland.fi/why-finland, accessed August, 4, 2020.
51   Korpela 2017
52   https://web.archive.org/web/20120109164034/http:/www.minedu.fi/pisa/taustaa.html?lang=en, accessed August 4, 2020.
53   Finish National Agency for Education (undated).
54   Lähdemäki 2019
55   Colagrossi 2018
56   Korpela 2017
57   Korpela 2017
58   https://www.educationfinland.fi/why-finland, accessed August 4, 2020.
59   https://web.archive.org/web/20120109164034/http:/www.minedu.fi/pisa/taustaa.html?lang=en, accessed August 4, 2020.
60   Korpela 2017
61   Andersen and Björkman 2017; Björkman 2018

13. Work and Organization

1   The quote is often, and probably erroneously, attributed to Confucius (551–479 BC). https://quoteinvestigator.com/2014/09/02/job-love/, accessed August 4, 2020.
2   A psychological disorder causing physical illness, due to a lack of stimulation at work.
3   A stage before burnout when employees feel overworked, demotivated, and disengaged.
4   Keller and Schaninger 2019
5   Sisodia et al. 2007; Cameron et al. 2004; Laloux 2014
6   Laloux 2014, 8
7   Carney and Getz 2016
8   Laloux 2014, 63-4
9   Adapted from Laloux 2014
10 Laloux 2014, 117
11 Zobrist 2018
12 Laloux 2014, 108-9, quoting Zobrist 2018.
13 Laloux 2014, 109-10
14 Laloux refers to the conclusions of a 2012 Tower Watson study on global workforce.
15 Laloux 2014, 144
16 Laloux 2014, 189

17 Laloux 2014, 175

18 Resources for Human Development (RHD), a US nonprofit with four thousand employees serving people suffering from disabilities, addiction recovery, and homelessness.

19 Laloux 2014, 189

20 Laloux 2014, 189

21 Laloux 2014, 199

22 Laloux 2014, 56

23 Laloux 2014, 171

24 Laloux 2014, 285

25 Laloux 2014, 290

26 Laloux 2014, 290

27 https://basicincome.org/basic-income/, accessed August 4, 2020. Much information in this chapter is drawn from the Basic Income Earth Network's website.

28 Other information in this chapter is also drawn from the Basic Income Lab at Stanford University. https://basicincome.stanford.edu/, accessed August 4, 2020.

29 Under the form of a negative income tax.

30 In France, it is called the "Active Solidarity Income" ("Revenu de Solidarité Active").

31 Gentilini et al. 2020

32 https://basicincome.org/basic-income/history/, accessed April 30, 2020.

33 https://www.undp.org/content/undp/en/home/news-centre/news/2020/ Temporary_Basic_Income_to_protect_the_worlds_poorest_people_slow_ COVID19.html, accessed February 11, 2021.

34 Sixty-four to 96 percent rate of return on grants to male entrepreneurs after five years in Sri Lanka (de Mel et al. 2008); 30 to 49 percent rate of return on grants to poor, unemployed youth in Uganda (Blattman et al. 2013). For more references, see https://www.givedirectly.org/research-on-cash-transfers/, accessed April 30, 2020.

35 For references, see https://www.givedirectly.org/research-on-cash-transfers/, accessed April 30, 2020.

36 For example, see experiments in the US and Canada in the 1960s–80s, in Iran, and in many cash transfer programs in low-income countries (Gentilini et al. 2020). See also (Hivert 2019) for Finland 2017–2018.

37 Hum and Simpson 2001

38 Belik 2011

39 Cholet and Lemahieu (2010) quote a German film on UBI *Grundeinkommen— Ein Kulturimpuls*. According to this poll, while 80 percent of respondents think people would stop working, only 40 percent of them think they themselves would stop or work less.

40 Hivert 2019

41   Evans and Popova 201

42   The recognition of this right has led to concepts similar to UBI, such as citizens' dividend and global resources dividend.

43   https://www.bloomberg.com/billionaires/profiles/mark-e-zuckerberg/, accessed April 29, 2020.

44   https://basicincome.org/basic-income/faq/#expensiveincome-unconditional, accessed April 29, 2020.

45   See for more explanations https://basicincome.org/basic-income/faq/#expensiveincome-unconditional, accessed April 29, 2020.

14. Health

1   Prentice 2008, https://data.worldbank.org/indicator/SP.DYN.LE00.IN, accessed August 12, 2020.

2   World Economic Forum 2019

3   World Economic Forum 2019

4   World Economic Forum 2019

5   https://www.who.int/news-room/fact-sheets/detail/obesity-and-overweight, accessed August 4, 2020..

6   https://www.who.int/dietphysicalactivity/factsheet_adults/en/, accessed August 4, 2020.

7   Also referred to Disability-Adjusted Life Years (DALY) (Rehm et al. 2006).

8   https://www.who.int/mental_health/who_urges_investment/en/, accessed August 10, 2020.

9   Gallup 2019

10   Vitteta et al. 2005

11   https://www.who.int/mental_health/who_urges_investment/en/, accessed August 4, 2020.

12   Keyes 2005; Seligman 2010

13   Ginn et al. 2012; Still et al. 2014

14   Vos et al. 2012

15   Vigo et al. 2016

16   Layard et al. 2013

17   Wahlbeck et al. 2011

18   Layard et al. 2013

19   OECD 2012. Another study (Bloom et al. 2011) estimated the cumulative global impact of mental disorders in terms of lost economic output to some US$16 trillion over twenty years—equivalent to 25 percent of the 2010 global GDP. Layard et al. (2013, 45) wrote that "in most high-income countries, mental illness accounts for at least a third of those on disability benefits—and more if psychosomatic conditions are included. Finance ministries in high-income countries are typically losing at least 1.5% of Gross Domestic Product (GDP) in disability benefits and lost taxes due to mental illness."

20 CDC 2012; Lando et al. 2006
21 CDC 2012; World Health Organization and Calouste Gulbenkian Foundation 2014
22 World Health Organization and Calouste Gulbenkian Foundation 2014
23 Layard et al. 2013
24 Vigo et al. 2016
25 Layard et al. 2013
26 Vigo et al. 2016. Mental health is now included in the SDGs, within objective 3.
27 Layard et al. 2013
28 Hoffman and Gomez 2017
29 Pfeffer and Williams 2020
30 Insel et al. 2015
31 Kessler et al. 2017
32 This can include past-life trauma, which I can personally attest to.
33 Horsthemke 2018
34 Costa et al. 2018
35 Kaati et al. 2002
36 Hübl 2020
37 Benazzo and Benazzo 2021
38 Brown and Courtois 2019
39 Fischer 2014. Neurofeedback is a type of biofeedback that measures brain waves to produce a signal that can be used as feedback to teach self-regulation of brain function.
40 Health Europa 2020
41 Marglin 2020
42 O'Brien 2020
43 World Health Organization 2013
44 Kelley et al. 2014
45 Turabian 2018
46 National Academies of Sciences, Engineering, and Medicine 2019. The range for medical students and residents is between 45 percent and 60 percent.
47 CSDH. 2008.
48 Prüss-Ustün et al. 2016
49 Buguet-Degletagne 2018. The estimate only takes into account air and sound pollution, as well as a limited proportion of quantifiable damages associated with endocrine disruptors.
50 Wilcox and Ellis 2006; United Nations Environment Programme and International Livestock Research Institute 2020
51 Sage and Carpenter 2012
52 Balmori 2009; Belyaev et al. 2016; Sage and Carpenter 2012; Nittby et al. 2011; Waldmann-Selsam et al. 2016; Wyde et al. 2018

53 The 5G spectrum is a range of radio frequencies in the sub-6 GHz range and the millimeter-wave frequency range that is 24.25 GHz and above. In France, the first allocation of frequency licenses is for an average frequency of 3.5 GHz for which there is very limited date available on health effects (ANSES 2009).

54 Netscribes 2019

55 "The interconnection via the Internet of computing devices embedded in everyday objects, enabling them to send and receive data" (Oxford Languages).

56 The precautionary principle holds that "when human activities may lead to morally unacceptable harm that is scientifically plausible but uncertain, actions shall be taken to avoid or diminish that harm" (UNESCO 2005, 14).

57 Fagot 2020. This agency has already mentioned in a preliminary report the lack of enough scientific studies for the frequencies to be used by 5G (ANSES 2009).

58 French experts Jancovici and Ferreboeuf have estimated that 5G deployment would multiply the electricity consumption of operators by 2.5 or 3 in the next five years, which would represent a 2 percent increase of the country's electricity consumption. This does not consider the energy used for building the networks' infrastructure and the new connected devices that will be required (Ferreboeuf and Jancovici 2020).

59 https://smombiegate.org/list-of-cities-towns-councils-and-countries-that-have-banned-5g/ accessed July 8, 2020.

60 See the 5G appeal in Europe. http://www.5gappeal.eu/scientists-and-doctors-warn-of-potential-serious-health-effects-of-5g/ accessed July 8, 2020.

61 Sage and Carpenter 2012

62 In Europe, critics have denounced situations of conflicts of interests from the forty-two members of the International Commission on Non-Ionizing Radiation Protection (ICNIRP) that informs European Union decisions on that matter, as well as the relative absence of medical experts (only two members) within that commission (Mandard 2020).

63 Wilkinson and Pickett 2009, which includes a large bibliography on this matter.

64 World Economic Forum 2010

65 https://integrativemedicine.arizona.edu/about/definition.html, accessed July 22, 2020._

66 Herman et al. 2005

15. Food and Agriculture

1   Seward and Kelly 2016

2   Jacka et al. 2013

3   Bellisle 2004

4 Jacka et al. 2013; O'Neil et al. 2014

5 Bellisle 2004; Jacka et al. 2015; Psaltopoulou 2013

6 Between 21 and 37 percent according to the Intergovernmental Panel on Climate Change's Special Report on Climate Change and Land (IPPC 2019).

7 IPCC 2019, 754

8 Heller and Keoleian 2015

9 Poore and Nemecek 2018

10 Cut by 53 percent according to calculations based on IPCC 2019 numbers (750, 766).

11 Hallström et al. 2017

12 Snowdon 2017

13 EAT-Lancet Commission 2019

14 Weekly: 100 grams of beef, lamb, or pork; 200 grams of fish; and 200 grams of chicken.

15 Rogissart et al. 2019

16 Rogissart et al. 2019

17 Jacka et al. 2013 ; O'Neil et al. 2014

18 Bellisle 2004

19 Jacka et al. (2010, 2011, 2014). Studies comparing "traditional" diets like the Mediterranean diet and the traditional Japanese diet to a typical "Western" diet have shown that the risk of depression is 25 percent to 5 percent lower in those who eat a traditional diet (Selhub 2015).

20 Brown 2020

21 Psaltopoulou 2013

22 Jacka et al. 2015

23 Torres and Nowson 2007

24 Beshara et al. 2013; Kristeller et al. 2014

25 Ricard 2014. For fish, crustaceans, and seafoods, the estimated number is a trillion.

26 After controlling for the effects of other potential explanatory variables (Fitzgerald et al. 2009).

27 IPPC 2019

28 Union of Concerned Scientists undated

29 Norberg-Hodge 2016

30 High Level Panel of Experts on Food Security and Nutrition 2019

31 Graham et al. 2011; Pottenger 1983; Price 2009

32 Behere and Bhise 2009

33 Schaller 2013; Altieri 2018

34 Poux et Aubert 2018, 3

35 Schaller 2013, 2

36 Valenzuela 2016

37 Call for action for agroecological transition of agri-food systems (https://

www.cirad.fr/en/media/documents/news/call-for-action-for-agroecological-transition-of-agri-food-systems, accessed August 4, 2020), High Level Panel of Experts on Food Security and Nutrition (2019), International Panel of Experts on Sustainable Food Systems (2016), McIntyre et al. (2009), UNCTAD (2013).

38 Schaller 2013
39 Hathaway 2015; Holmgren 2002
40 Willer and Lernoud 2019
41 Stratistics 2019 estimates that this market will grow on average 10.4 percent annually between 2017 and 2026.
42 Valenzuela 2016
43 Poux et Aubert 2018
44 Hedges, trees, ponds, stony habitats favorable to insects.
45 International Panel of Experts on Sustainable Food Systems 2016
46 Avetisyan et al. 2014
47 Rogissart et al. 2019
48 Federations of City Farms & Community Gardens (undated).
49 Federations of City Farms & Community Gardens (undated).

16. Nature

1 In Ecuador, Bolivia, and in Mexico City's constitution and numerous municipalities in the US (Pecharroman 2018).
2 This includes the Yarra river in Australia; the Ganges and its main tributary, the Yamuna, in India (a decision that was stayed later by the Supreme Court of India); the Vilcabamba River in Ecuador; and the Atrato River in Colombia (Pecharroman 2018). See also Gleeson-White 2018.
3 New Zealand granted legal personhood to the Te Urewera forest in New Zealand in 2014, for example (UN Secretary General 2016).
4 New Zealand granted legal personhood to Mount Taranaki in 2017 (Roy 2017).
5 Germany guaranteed rights to animals in a 2002 amendment to its constitution, becoming the first European Union member to do so. The Uttarakhand High Court in India declared the entire animal kingdom to be a legal entity, with the corresponding rights, duties, and liabilities of a living person (Chapron et al. 2019).
6 In New Zealand, great apes have been recognized as "human beings" since 1999 (Cabanes 2017).
7 In India, dolphins have gained "nonhuman person" status, and all dolphinariums are prohibited (Cabanes 2017).
8 Pecharroman 2018; Chapron et al. 2019
9 Stone 1972; Pecharroman 2018
10 Stone 1972, 6

11 UN Secretary General 2016

12 World People's Conference on Climate Change 2010

13 Chapron et al. 2019

14 Bétaille 2019

15 In Bolivia, an ombudsman for Mother Earth (Defensoría de la Madre Tierra) has been created to look after compliance and enforcement of those rights, but it has not yet been put in place in Bolivia. In Ecuador, the constitution doesn't include mechanisms for enforcing these rights, but gives the state the flexibility to interpret these regulations for national interests (Solon 2014).

16 Through a 2012 resolution on the "incorporation of the Rights of Nature as the organizational focal point in IUCN's decision making." See: https://portals.iucn.org/library/sites/library/files/resrecfiles/WCC_2012_RES_100_EN.pdf, accessed August 4, 2020.

17 Goldenberg and Kirchgaessner 2015

18 Chapron et al. 2019

19 This notion has been defined as "the extensive damage to, destruction of or loss of ecosystems of a given territory, whether by human agency or by any other causes, to such an extent that peaceful enjoyment by the inhabitants of that territory has been severely diminished" (Higgins et al., 2013).

20 "Pagamentos" in Spanish. I am grateful to my friends Mindahi Bastida from the Otomi-Toltec peoples (Mexico) and Jorge Dibs, who works with the Kogis (Colombia), for having shared with me relevant information.

21 Translated from French (Tchendukua 2020): "Shikwa est un fil invisible, créé dans le monde spirituel, qui entoure complètement la terre d'est en ouest, formant un tissu de connexion de la terre avec le soleil et le reste de l'Univers. [...] C'est ça que nous appelons Shikwakala. Ce sont tous les fils qui, connectés, aident à soutenir l'Univers et qui, sous forme de chemins, sillonnent la terre," quoted as an extract of Rawitscher and Mestre 2018.

22 Tchendukua (2020). A similar exercise is planned for the watershed of Geneva in 2021.

23 Perez Barreto 2012. The use of cosmo-telluric energies creates an electromagnetic field thanks to large metal discs buried in the ground connected to aboveground antennas. Don José Carmen said he uses this very powerful image to attract attention to his clean farming techniques, which are less difficult to implement.

24 Both documentary films can be bought at http://www.magique-trotter.com/Mexico.html, accessed August 4, 2020.

25 Perez Barreto 2011

26 Perez Barreto 2012

27 See an extract (Perez Barreto 2016).

28 See https://www.hortalizas-gigantes.com/anexos, accessed August 4, 2020.

29 Articles from Spanish newspaper El Pais in its January 7, 1996 edition "Agua

en el grifo"—"water in the tap," "La naturaleza más valiosa del sur español se recobra con el agua, tras agontzar seis años"—"the most valuable nature of Southern Spain is covering with water, after being near death" tells the importance of the rain and its important ecological, economic, and social effects.

30   Evans 2012; Wright et al. 2017; Loomis 2017; Kilvert 2018
31   Kirkby et al. 2016. For a more accessible explanation, see Skolnick 2016 and also Norbe 2014.
32   Other concrete examples include cultural burning used to prevent wildfires, such as by Aboriginal Australian, or the construction of artificial glaciers in the Himalayas.
33   Solon 2018
34   According to Don José Carmen, trees' role is even more significant as the function of the Earth in the cosmos is essentially to bring "tree-essence" in exchange for "water-essence." See: https://www.hortalizas-gigantes.com/lluvia-como-provocarla, accessed August 4, 2020.
35   Other categories are climate change, climate neutral community, animal well-being, embassies, and consulates.
36   Also animal well-being and food waste management.
37   Comisión Nacional – Programa Bandera Azul Ecológica 2018
38   Blackman et al. 2014

17. Justice

1   Nhat Hanh 2016
2   Cayley 1998; Penal Reform International 2016
3   3.6 million of those peple were on probation and eight hundred and forty thousand were on parole (Sawyer and Wagner 2019).
4   http://worldpopulationreview.com/countries/incarceration-rates-by-country/, accessed August 4, 2020.
5   Blumstein and Beck 1999
6   There is no clear relationship between crime rates and imprisonment rates. Imprisonment does not decrease reoffending rates (Gendreau et al. 1999; Harding et al. 2019), which are higher in more punitive systems (Wilkinson and Picket 2010).
7   Wilkinson and Picket 2010
8   Gilligan 2001
9   At least half of prisoners have some mental health concerns. About 10–25 percent of US prisoners suffer from serious mental illnesses, such as major affective disorders or schizophrenia, compared to some 5 percent in the US population in general. https://www.apa.org/monitor/2014/10/incarceration, accessed August 13, 2020.
10   Haney 2002

11 Eisler and Fry 2019
12 Brookes and McDonough 2006
13 Mammarella 2016
14 We have already mentioned that childhood violence is the best predictor of adult violence (Wilkinson and Pickett 2010).
15 Mindfulness Initiative 2015
16 In the US, 72 percent of juvenile murderers, 70 percent of long-term prisoners, and 60 percent of rapists grew up in fatherless homes (Popenoe 1996).
17 Looney and Turner 2008
18 In the US, black Americans make up 40 percent of the incarcerated population while representing only 13 percent of US residents (Sawyer and Wagner 2019).
19 See for example Walgrave 2011, quoting Mc Cold 2006.
20 http://restorativejustice.org/world-map/#sthash.FcPfFmfr.dpbs,   accessed August 4, 2020.
21 Hadley 2001b.
22 Huculak 2001, 219-20
23 Walgrave 2011
24 According to Walgrave 2011, 98: "The meta-analyses in the 'what works' research tradition, for example, list a number of methodological shortcomings in many evaluations, including unclear indication of measurable program objectives, invalid instruments, absence of or inadequate control groups, doubtful external validity, problematic measurement of reoffending, overoptimistic interpretations by committed believers, and lack of attention to undesirable side effects. In general, overconfidence in—evidence-based work may be naïve."
25 Walgrave 2011; See also UNODC 2006.
26 Aertsen 2004, quoted by Walgrave 2011.
27 See Walgrave 2011 for references.
28 Walgrave 2011, 106-7
29 Bonta et al. 2006
30 UNODC 2006, 88
31 UNODC 2006; Walgrave 2011
32 UNODC 2006
33 UNODC 2006
34 UNODC 2006; Walgrave 2011; Bonta et al. 2006
35 Maxwell et al. 2004
36 Walgrave 2011
37 Walgrave 2011
38 Maples 2017
39 See Hadley 2001a
40 Quoted in Hadley 2001b, 10

41 Resolution 2000/14.
42 Paragraph 20.
43 In traditional indigenous systems, specific attention must be given to the rights and interests of vulnerable groups, including women and children (UNODC 2006).
44 UNODC 2006, 66
45 Lindh and Stark 2017
46 Carlin 2015
47 See https://mindfuljustice.org/, accessed August 4, 2020. The initiative was formed as a collaboration between two organizations, Prison Mindfulness Institute and Transforming Justice. See also Prison Mindfulness Institute and Transforming Justice: The Center for Mindfulness And Criminal Justice 2016.
48 Carlin 2015
49 Mindfulness Initiative 2015, 28
50 Mindfulness Initiative 2015
51 Mindfulness Initiative 2015
52 Maples 2017
53 This included a nondenominational retreat in 2003 with Thich Nhat Hạnh and criminal justice professionals, which led to a book (Nhat Hanh 2005).

18. Economy

1 Williamson 2019, 20-1
2 Sahlins 2017
3 Military expenditures represent more than 2 percent of global GDP. https://data.worldbank.org/indicator/MS.MIL.XPND.GD.ZS, accessed August 4, 2020.
4 Social Progress Imperative 2019
5 Diamandis and Kotler 2012
6 Patents cover broader characteristics of an invention while copyright focuses on exact or close to exact duplication. Trademarks distinguish the goods or services of one enterprise from those of other enterprises.
7 Stratistics 2020
8 Hoffower 2020
9 Pollock 2018, 14
10 Handke et al. 2016
11 Pollock 2018, p 64
12 Thankful for this insight into the vitality code from my friend Dr. Shelley Ostroff. See: https://www.7days-of-rest.org/the-vitality-code, accessed August 4, 2020.
13 Social Progress Imperative 2019. However, a politics of being would call for indicators monitoring not only the evolution of positive conditions for

individuals to achieve their full potential but also their actual fulfillment (see next chapter).

14 United Nations Environment Programme 2019

15 Greenhouse gases remain in the atmosphere for decades, hundreds, or thousands of years, depending on the gases and the different natural processes at work.

16 Birol 2020

17 IPCC 2018

18 UNCTAD 2014

19 The Global Commission on the Economy and Climate 2016

20 The Global Commission on the Economy and Climate 2016

21 According to Richard Kozul-Wright, head of the UN trade, investment, and development agency (UNCTAD)'s globalisation and development strategies division, considering an annual investment of 2 percent of global output.

22 Taylor 2020

23 Ferron and Morel 2014

24 AFP 2019

25 UNCTAD 2019

26 The concept of "uneconomic growth" is from American ecological economist Herman Daly and designates economic growth that reflects or creates a decline in the quality of life.

27 Raworth 2012

28 Raworth 2017

29 Raworth 2017

30 Michel et al. 2019; Ahuvia and Izberk-Bilgin 2013

31 Oxfam 2015

32 https://www.parisschoolofeconomics.eu/en/news/thomas-piketty-every-human-society-must-justify-its-inequalities/, accessed August 4, 2020. This would raise potential issues related to privacy and liberties that would need to be addressed.

33 I am not suggesting that debts are always wrong but that their recent growth is the symptom of a major problem: wealth concentration.

34 Piketty 2019

35 Kahloon 2020

36 Piketty 2019

37 Even if it is used for the public good, wealth concentration is not healthy and should ideally be reduced. That may advocate for a partial deduction of these resources from the wealth tax basis.

38 Gandhi 1969, 137

39 Kahloon 2020; Clifford 2019

40 Korten 2016; Norberg-Hodge 2016

41 New York Times 2012

42 UNCTAD 2019, 42

43   Ostry et al. 2016
44   Tucker and Daskin 2020
45   Babic et al. 2017
46   Quoted in Norberg-Hodge 2016, 11
47   Norberg-Hodge 2016, 11
48   World Trade Organization 2020
49   Chavagneux 2020. From 70 percent in 2010 to 54 percent in 2019 in France; from close to 50 percent in 2008 in the US to 40 percent in 2019. Foreign direct investments as a percentage of GDP have also decreased between 2015 and 2019 to reach their lowest level in twenty years (World Bank data). https://data.worldbank.org/indicator/BX.KLT.DINV.WD.GD.ZS, accessed July 14, 2020.
50   Norberg-Hodge 2016, 25
51   Norberg-Hodge 2016, 8
52   Kasser 2008
53   Hall 2015
54   For example, in terms of building, land-use, and energy.
55   Vatn 2009
56   Korten 2016, 52
57   Pikettty made this proposal based on what already exists in Germany and Sweden (Normand 2019).
58   "Money" by Pink Floyd (1973).
59   See for example United Nations (2009), UNDP (1994). Some potential negative effects are also mentioned in the literature, such as the loss of national monetary policies and the fact that an international monetary policy cannot be adequate with all heterogenous national economic situations.
60   https://data.imf.org/?sk=E6A5F467-C14B-4AA8-9F6D-5A09EC4E62A4, accessed August 4, 2020.
61   D'Antona, Jr. 2020
62   Bunker 2014
63   United Nations 2009
64   Van Lerven 2016. Private monetary creation has also often been accompanied by the obligation for private banks to use this money to buy public debt, which puts into perspective the private nature of monetary creation in those cases.
65   In practice, provided that the debt is interest-free and the government can refinance it as long as it wishes, it is similar to equity. Hence it does not matter whether public money creation is done debt-free or interest-free (Benes and Kumhof, 2012).
66   The production of non-tradable goods and services creates more risk of inflation.
67   Van Lerven 2016
68   Benes and Kumhof 2012

69 "Output gains approach 10 percent, and steady state inflation can drop to zero without posing problems for the conduct of monetary policy" (Benes and Kumhof 2012, 1).
70 Benes and Kumhof 2012, 57
71 See also Sharafeddine 2015 and http://www.fullreservebanking.com/ accessed August 4, 2020, including a list of different organizations supporting this view.
72 Magnen and Fourel 2015
73 Magnen and Fourel 2015

19. Governance

1   Berggruen Institute (2020, 3). The report is a result of a three-year research program on the future of democracy involving renowned experts and multi-stakeholder consultations in many Western countries. See https://www.berggruen.org/work/the-future-of-democracy/future-of-democracy-project/, accessed August 5, 2020.
2   Repucci 2020
3   Berggruen Institute 2020; Inglehart 2018
4   Berggruen Institute 2020, 5
5   Dahl 2017
6   Birkett 2020
7   She was the Charles F. Adams Professor of Political Leadership and Democratic Values in the Kennedy School of Government at Harvard University and earned the Johan Skytte Prize in Political Science (often nicknamed "the Nobel Prize for Political Science").
8   Mansbridge 1980
9   Karlberg 2007
10 Karlberg 2007, 106
11 Karlberg 2007, 147
12 Effendi 1973, 24
13 Dahl 2017, 6
14 Institute for Studies in Global Prosperity 2012, 6
15 Karlberg 2007, 152
16 Berggruen Institute 2020, 5
17 McIntosh 2020
18 Susskind 2020
19 Neblo et al. 2020
20 See references in Quick et al. (2015) and on: https://www.involve.org.uk/resources/knowledge-base/what-are-effects-deliberation, accessed August 4, 2020. See in particular the work of James Fishkin on deliberative polling for the change in views and reduced polarization and Gastil et al. (2010) on impacts on pro-social orientation.

21 Berggruen Institute 2020, 23
22 Miller 2019
23 Chang 2019
24 Berggruen Institute 2020
25 Berggruen Institute 2020
26 Berggruen Institute 2020
27 https://index.okfn.org/place/, accessed August 4, 2020. See also the work of the Open Government Partnership: https://www.opengovpartnership.org/, accessed August 4, 2020.
28 Jaffe 2020
29 Vosoughi et al. 2018
30 Berggruen Institute 2020, 3, 13.
31 "A duty of care is the legal responsibility of a person or organization to avoid any behaviors or omissions that could reasonably be foreseen to cause harm to others." https://legaldictionary.net/duty-of-care/, accessed August 4, 2020.
32 Epstein 2016
33 Bond et al. 2012
34 Berggruen Institute 2020
35 Berggruen and Gardels 2013
36 The OECD has developed recommendations for anticorruption and integrity in the public sector. See https://www.oecd.org/gov/ethics/, accessed August 4, 2020.
37 ALG Research and GS Strategy Group 2019
38 Drutman 2016
39 Drutman 2016. The figure is from Drutman 2015.
40 Allison and Harkins 2014
41 Fang 2012
42 Berggruen Institute 2020
43 Berggruen Institute 2020
44 Ford 2002
45 Berggruen and Gardels 2013
46 Berggruen Institute 2020, 41
47 Berggruen Institute 2020, 41
48 Berggruen and Gardels 2013; Berggruen Institute 2020
49 Berggruen Institute 2020, 52
50 Berggruen and Gardels 2013
51 Looking Horse 2014
52 Like the long-term assembly proposed by Bourg 2011
53 Like the long-term assembly proposed by Bourg (2011) and the quadrumvirate proposed by Berggruen and Gardels (2013).
54 Berggruen and Gardels 2013
55 The subtitle of their book.

56 Berggruen and Gardels 2013, 13
57 Berggruen and Gardels 2013, 73
58 Berggruen and Gardels 2013, 109
59 Appointed members would be nominated by the "quadrumvirate," the executive and the lower house leadership and approved by the lower house.
60 Berggruen and Gardels 2013, 118
61 Berggruen and Gardels 2013, 118
62 Berggruen and Gardels 2013, 109
63 Berggruen and Gardels 2013, 183
64 Berggruen and Gardels 2013, 184
65 Berggruen and Gardels 2013, 183-4
66 Berggruen Institute 2020
67 Weiss 2012
68 Lopez-Claros et al. 2020
69 Article 109(3) and 109(1) of the UN Charter (Lopez-Claros et al. 2020).
70 If a revised UN charter is adopted but vetoed by one of the five permanent members of the UN security council, members will have the legal right to withdraw from the UN and could well found a parallel organization that the remaining countries could join in the future. Lopez-Claros et al. (2020) refer to it as the United World Organization.
71 Currently the environment stands under the "development" pillar of the UN, while it should stand on its own.

IV. The Politics of Being in Practice

1 Aurobindo 1997, 39

20. One World

1 See for example Harari 2014
2 Huntington 1993. He considered eight main civilizations: Western civilization, Latin American civilization, the Orthodox world, the Muslim world, the civilization of Sub-Saharan Africa, the Buddhist, Sinic, Hindu, and Japanese worlds.
3 "civilisation de l'universel" in French.
4 Diop (undated).
5 Mabana 2011; Njoh-Mouelle (undated).
6 Baha'u'llah 1983, 288 quoted in Hatcher and Martin 1998.
7 Bahá'í International Community 2013
8 Traditional motto included on its seal.
9 Official motto.
10 Based on an Old Javanese phrase, "Bhinneka Tunggal Ika."
11 Official motto.
12 Official motto.

13   Mentioned in the preamble of the 1996 Constitution of South Africa.
14   Hackett and Mcclendon 2017
15   Inglehart 2018
16   Inglehart 2018
17   Diener et al. 2011
18   Inglehart 2018
19   As formulated by Hans Küng, a Swiss theologian and honorary president of the Global Ethic Foundation. https://www.global-ethic.org/, accessed August 5, 2020.
20   According to Teasdale (1999, 7): "Native Americans, other indigenous people, and African Americans were excluded, and only one Muslim, an American Convert, was present as a delegate."
21   Teasdale 1999
22   https://uri.org/, accessed August 5, 2020.
23   https://rfp.org/, accessed August 5, 2020.
24   https://templeofunderstanding.org/, accessed August 5, 2020.
25   http://www.worldfaiths.org/, accessed August 5, 2020.
26   http://www.ifor.org/#mission, accessed August 5, 2020.
27   UNGA Resolution A/65/PV.34.
28   His Holiness the Dalai Lama 2013
29   Parliament of the World's Religions 1993. See: https://parliamentofreligions.org/program/global-ethic, accessed August 5, 2020.
30   Jacob Soetendorp Institute for Human Values 2012, 2
31   Teasdale 1999, 4
32   Teasdale 1999, 26
33   Teasdale 1999, 238
34   On January 24, 2020.
35   Teasdale 1999, 238
36   Johnson and Ord 2012
37   Wilber 2001, 82
38   Teasdale 1999, 20
39   Teasdale 1999, 5
40   Teasdale 1999, 19
41   Teasdale 1999, 241
42   Teasdale 1999, 5. "In the long run, each tradition of the spiritual life will come to the service of the whole humanity" (Teasdale 1999, 241).
43   Teasdale 1999, 236
44   Grateful to Hubbard (2015) for some of these formulations.
45   She is also the founder of Auroville, a famous community of some three thousand residents in Tamil Nadu, India. https://www.auroville.org/, accessed August 5, 2020.
46   Quoted by Teasdale 1999, 49
47   https://sacredearthcouncil.com/, accessed August 5, 2020.

21. Many Nations

1   Aurobindo 1997, 35
2   Inglehart 2018, 11
3   Inglehart 2018, 43. For more information on these values and the methodology of the World Value Survey, see https://www.worldvaluessurvey.org/WVSContents.jsp, accessed February, 27, 2021.
4   Inglehart 2018, 43
5   Inglehart 2018, 42
6   Inglehart 2018, 48
7   Inglehart 2018, 44
8   Among the countries for which data is available (Inglehart 2018, 44).
9   See for example Inglehart 2018; Gelfand et al. 2011; Thornhill et al. 2009; Thornhill et al. 2010; and Chiao and Blizinsky 2009.
10 Inglehart 2018, 53. He mentions that this is suggested by Chia and Blizinsky (2009) study, which found "linkages between genetic factors and collectivist attitudes" (Inglehart 2018, 53).
11 The Inglehart-Welzel World Cultural Map - World Values Survey 7 (2020) [Provisional version]. Source: http://www.worldvaluessurvey.org/, accessed February 27, 2021.
12 Tsai and Park 2014
13 Uchida and Kitayama 2009
14 Diener and Diener 1995 showed a stronger association between self-esteem and life satisfaction in individualistic compared to collectivist cultures.
15 Tsai and Park 2014
16 Uchida and Kitayama 2009
17 Happiness attracts unhappiness, for example through envy or jealousy of others, whereas negative events may attract sympathy from others and prove to be an opportunity for self-improvement.
18 Apéstegui 2012
19 https://www.forestpeoples.org/sites/default/files/publication/2012/06/final-political-declaration-adopted-rio20-international-conference-indigenous-peoples-self-determina.pdf, accessed July 22, 2020.
20 Lagdameo-Santillan 2018
21 Dolamo 2013
22 Shutte 2001, 2, quoted in Dolamo 2013, 2.
23 Brooddryk 2008, quoted in Dolamo 2013.
24 Shutte 2001, 30, quoted in Dolamo 2013, 1.
25 Shutte 2001, 2, quoted in Dolamo 2013, 2.
26 De Botton 2012, 78
27 De Botton 2012, 87
28 I borrow the term from Sachs 2013.

29 In France, see for example Voltaire's *Essay on the Manners and Spirit of Nations* or François-Ignace d' Espiard's *Spirit of Nations* (1753).
30 Montesquieu 1993, Book I, Chapter III.
31 A concept that, as we have seen, is present in many cultures with different nuances and goes back in Western history at least to Greek philosophers such as Socrates, Plato, and Aristotle.
32 Hegel 1998, 53 quoted in Tibebu 2011, 151.
33 Hegel 1998, 62-3 quoted in Tibebu 2011, 152.
34 Hegel 1998, 62-3 quoted in Tibebu 2011, 152.
35 Hegel 1998, 56 quoted in Tibebu 2011, 152.
36 Hegel 1998, 65 quoted in Tibebu 2011, 152.
37 Aurobindo 1997, 35
38 Aurobindo 1997, 35-6
39 Aurobindo 1997, 36
40 While Macron's voter base initially occupied the center (left) of the political spectrum, with supporters coming from both left and right wings, it has progressively evolved into a more conventional right-wing political force.
41 Mac Laughlin and Davidson 1994, 295
42 For example, Marianne Williamson's *Healing the Soul of America: Reclaiming Our Voices as Spiritual Citizens,* published in 2000. Has it inspired Joe Biden's campaign?
43 Dinan 2016, 51
44 Dinan 2016, 51-2
45 Dinan 2016, 57
46 Hübl 2020
47 Dinan 2016, 64
48 Life force made of emotions, passions, desires, likes, and dislikes ... that other systems would call the emotional being.
49 Aurobindo 1997
50 Aurobindo 1997, 41
51 Aurobindo 1997, 51
52 Aurobindo 1997, 54
53 Aurobindo 1997, 48
54 In Sanskrit "Satyameva Jayate."
55 Aurobindo 1997, 40
56 Aurobindo 1997, 40
57 See for example Dinan 2016.

22. Being Leaders

1 Joe Biden's speech at the 2020 Democratic National Convention.
2 Morin 2008, 56
3 In Harijan, July 8, 1933, 4.

4   *Young India*, August 4, 1920, 3.
5   *The Leader*, December 25, 1916.
6   Morrison 2006
7   Morrison 2006
8   "There are occasions when the devil's voice speak as God's voice," he recognized, quoted in Kamath 2007, 118.
9   In Harijan, July 8, 1933, 4.
10   In Harijan, July 8, 1933, 4.
11   Pyarelal 1932, 34
12   Quoted in Kamath 2007, 118
13   In *Young India*, June 18, 1925, 214
14   "Die Weltseele zu Pferde." The expression was part of a letter, dated October 13, 1806, which Hegel addressed to his friend Niethammer.
15   Quoted in Broussard 1995
16   Quoted in Broussard 1995
17   Quoted in Broussard 1995
18   Tulard 2012
19   Spielvogel 2018, 583
20   Zizek 2018
21   Brinkbäumer et al. 2017
22   Brinkbäumer et al. 2017
23   The night of the first round of the election, one of the most important French newspapers, *Liberation,* titled its editorial by Laurent Joffrin: "Macron's baraka." Baraka means luck in French, but its Arabic original meaning is "blessing."
24   *Le journal du dimanche* 2017.
25   Translated from French: "Depuis qu'il s'est mis en marche, la voie semble se dégager et les planètes s'aligner dans le ciel au-dessus de sa tête."
26   Translated from French: "C'est ce que j'appelle la ruse de l'Histoire."
27   Translated from French: "La vie de Jeanne, c'est avant tout la puissance d'un destin, qui démontre que l'ordre des choses ne tient pas si cet ordre est injuste. [...] Elle sait qu'elle n'est pas née pour vivre, mais pour tenter l'impossible. Comme une flèche, sa trajectoire fut nette. Jeanne fend le système. Elle brusque l'injustice qui devait l'enfermer. Jeanne est bergère mais elle se fraye un chemin jusqu'au roi. Jeanne est une femme, mais elle prend la tête d'un groupe armé et s'oppose aux chefs de guerre. Jeanne n'est personne, mais elle porte sur ses épaules la volonté de progrès et de justice de tout un peuple. Elle était un rêve fou, elle s'impose comme une évidence. "
28   Translated from French: "celle de l'énergie du people."
29   Translated from French: "aux moments les plus sombres."
30   Translated from French: "Cette même énergie, je la sens là, parmi vous, aujourd'hui."

31 Translated from French: "La troisième leçon de Jeanne, c'est celle du rassemblement et de l'unité de la France."

32 Bonnefous and De Royer 2017

33 Translated from French: « Ce n'est pas toujours facile de vive avec Jeanne d'Arc » (Gala Politique 2017).

34 *Le journal du dimanche* 2017

35 BBC news 2018

36 Aurobindo 1997, 42

37 Luke 6:43–45.

38 First introduced by Swiss psychiatrist Carl Jung (1875–1961), the term "synchronicity" refers to "meaningful coincidences" when some events occur simultaneously and seem to be meaningfully related but no causal relationship between them is discernible.

39 He even earned the grand prize of political humor (*Le Monde* 2017).

40 A French department in the Indian Ocean.

41 Translated from French: "Je viens un jour à Mayotte et il pleut. Je sais que ça fait quatre mois que vous attendiez ce moment et j'ai donc organisé ce déplacement à cette fin" (*Le Figaro* 2017).

42 Translated from French: "Gouverner c'est pleuvoir." The catchphrase is from Théodore Steeg, General resident in Morocco from 1925 to 1929 (*Le Figaro* 2017).

Epilogue

1 Havel 1985, 96

2 Murray 1951

3 Sheff 2000, 16

References

Abdu'l-Bahá. 1982. *The Promulgation of Universal Peace*. Wilmette, IL: Baha'I Publishing Trust.

Abdu'l-Bahá. 1995. *Paris Talks* (twelfth edition). London: Baha'I Publishing Trust.

Aertsen, Ivo. 2004. *Rebuilding community connections - mediation and restorative justice in Europe*. Strasbourg: Council of Europe Publishing.

Ahuvia, Aaron, and Elif Izberk-Bilgin. 2013. "Well-Being in Consumer Societies." In *The Oxford Handbook of Happiness*. Edited by Susan David, Ilona Boniwell, and Amanda Conley Ayers, 482-98. Oxford, UK: Oxford University Press.

Aknin, Lara B., Christopher Barrington-Leigh, Elizabeth W. Dunn, John F. Helliwell, Justine Burns, Robert Biswas-Diener, Imelda Kemeza, Paul Nyende, Claire E. Ashton-James, and Michael I. Norton. 2013. "Prosocial Spending and Well-Being: Cross-Cultural Evidence for a Psychological Universe." *Journal of Personality and Social Psychology* 104 (4): 635-52.

Aknin, Lara. B., J. Kiley Hamlin, and Elizabeth W Dunn. 2012. "Giving Leads to Happiness in Young Children." *PLOS ONE* 7, no. 6. https://doi.org/10.1371/journal.pone.0039211.

Alda, Marta, Marta Puebla-Guedea, Baltasar Rodero, Marcelo Demarzo, Jesus Montero-Marin, Miquel Roca, and Javier Garcia-Campayo. 2016. "Zen Meditation, Length of Telomeres, and the Role of Experiential Avoidance and Compassion." *Mindfulness* 7:651-59. https://doi.org/ 10.1007/s12671-016-0500-5.

Algan, Yann, Elizabeth Beasley, Daniel Cohen, and Martial Foucault. 2019. *Les Origines du Populisme*. Paris: Le Seuil.

ALG Research and GS Strategy Group. 2019. "Poll Finds Overwhelming Support for a more active Federal Election Commission." Survey results, November 8, 2019. Accessed June 2, 2020. https://campaignlegal.org/sites/default/files/2019-11/CLC%20FEC%20MEMO.pdf.

Alicke, Mark D., and Oleysa Govorun. 2005. "The Better-than-Average-Effect." In *The Self in Social Judgment.* Edited by Mark D. Alicke, David A. Dunning, and Joachim I. Krueger, 85-106. New York: Psychology Press. https://doi.org/10.4324/9780203943250

Allen, John L., Jr. 2009. "Pope Cites Teilhardian Vision of the Cosmos as a 'Living Host.'" *National Catholic Reporter,* July 28, 2009. https://www.ncronline.org/news/pope-cites-teilhardian-vision-cosmos-living-host.

Allen, Mark, Andrew Bromley, Willem Kuyken, and Stefanie J. Sonnenberg. 2009. "Participants' Experiences of Mindfulness-Based Cognitive Therapy: 'It Changed Me in Just about Every Way Possible.'" *Behavioural and Cognitive Psychotherapy* 37 (4): 413-30. https://doi.org/10.1017/S135246580999004X

Allison, Bill, and Sarah Harkins. 2014. "Fixed Fortunes: Biggest corporate political interests spend billions, get trillions." Sunlight Foundation (website). November 17, 2014. Accessed August 4, 2020. https://sunlightfoundation.com/2014/11/17/fixed-fortunes-biggest-corporate-political-interests-spend-billions-get-trillions/.

Altieri, Miguel. 2018. *Agroecology. The Science of Sustainable Agriculture.* Boca Raton: CRC Press.

Alvaredo, Facundo, Lucas Chancel, Thomas Piketty, Emmanuel Saez, and Gabriel Zucman. 2018. *World Inequality Report 2018.* https://wir2018.wid.world/

Amma. 2004. "The Greatest Tragedy Takes Place When Our Talents and Capabilities are Underutilized." Keynote address at the Parliament of the World's Religions on July 13, 2004, Barcelona, Spain.

Andersen, Lene Rachel, Tomas Björkman. 2017. *The Nordic Secret: A European story of beauty and freedom.* Sweden: Fri Tanke.

ANSES. 2019. « Exposition de la population aux champs électromagnétiques liée au déploiement de la technologie de communication '5G' et effets sanitaires associés. » Rapport préliminaire. Agence Nationale De Sécurité Sanitaire. November 29, 2019.

Apéstegui, F. 2012. "La muerte del 'pura vida.'" *La Nación,* November 11, 2012. https://www.nacion.com/opinion/foros/la-muerte-del-pura-vida/NVPE3C45DVFFZGKOBKEA3EI6TE/story/

Apollinaire, Guillaume. 1977. *Oeuvres en Prose Complètes.* Paris: Gallimard.

Aristotle. 2001. "Nichomachean Ethics." In *The Basic Works of Aristotle.* Edited by Richard McKeeon, 928-1112. New York, NY: The Modern Library.

Aurobindo, Sri. 1997. *The Human Cycle.* Pondicherry, India: Sri Aurobindo Ashram.

Aurobindo, Sri. 2001. *The Essential Aurobindo: Writings of Sri Aurobindo*. N.p.: Lindisfarne Books.

Avetisyan, Misak, Thomas Hertel, and Gregory Sampson. 2014. "Is Local Food More Environmentally Friendly? The GHG Emissions Impacts of Consuming Imported versus Domestically Produced Food." *Environmental and Resource Economics* 58, (3): 415-62.

Babic, Milan, Jan Fichtner, and Eelke M. Heemskerk. 2017. "States versus Corporations: Rethinking the Power of Business in International Politics." *The International Spectator* 52 (4): 20-43.

Backster, Cleve. 2003. *Primary Perception: Biocommunication with Plants, Foods, and Human Cells*. Anza, CA: White Rose Millennium Press.

Baer, Ruth. 2015. "Ethics, Values, Virtues, and Character Strengths in Mindfulness-Based Interventions: A Psychological Science Perspective." *Mindfulness* 6 (4): 956-69.

Bahá'i International Community. 1998. "Valuing Spirituality in Development." A concept paper presented to the "World Faiths and Development Dialogue" in London, England February 18, 1998. https://www.bic.org/statements/valuing-spirituality-development

Bahá'i International Community. 2013. "World Citizenship: A Global Ethic for Sustainable Development." Statement to the first session of the United Nations Commission on Sustainable Development, New York, June 14-25, 1993.

Baha'u'llah. 1983. Gleanings from the Writings of Baha'u'llah. Translated by Shoghi Effendi. Wilmette, Illinois: Baha'i Publishing Trust.

Ballet, Jérôme. 2010. *Sri Aurobindo: Une Philosophie Politique Spiritualiste*. Paris: L'Harmattan.

Balmori, Alfonso. 2009. "Electromagnetic pollution from phone masts. Effects on wildlife." *Pathophysiology* 16 (2-3): 191-99. https://doi.org/10.1016/j.pathophys.2009.01.007

Bangsbo, Jens, Peter Krustrup, Joan Duda, Charles Hillman, Lars Bo Andersen, Maureen Weiss, Craig A. Williams, et al. 2016. "The Copenhagen Consensus Conference 2016: Children, Youth, and Physical Activity in Schools and during Leisure Time." *British Journal of Sports Medicine* 50 (19): 1177-78.

Bates, Claire. 2012. "Is This the World's Happiest Man? Brain Scans Reveal French Monk has 'Abnormally Large Capacity' for Joy—Thanks to Meditation." *Daily Mail*, October 31, 2012. https://www.dailymail.co.uk/health/article-2225634/Is-worlds-happiest-man-Brain-scans-reveal-French-monk-abnormally-large-capacity-joy-meditation.html

BBC news. 2018. "Bolsonaro: Brazil politician's health 'improving' after stabbing." *BBC.com*, September 10, 2018. https://www.bbc.com/news/world-latin-america-45470986

Behere Prakash B., and Manik C. Bhise. 2009. "Farmers' suicide: Across culture." *Indian Journal of Psychiatry*, 51(4): 242–243.

Belik, Vivian. 2011. "A Town Without Poverty?" *The Dominion*, September 5, 2011. http://www.dominionpaper.ca/articles/4100

Bellaimey, John. 2013. "The Hidden Meanings of Yin and Yang." YouTube video. Accessed July 29, 2020. https://www.youtube.com/watch?v=ezmR9Attpyc

Bellisle, France. 2004. "Effects of diet on behaviour and cognition in children". *British Journal of Nutrition* 92, Suppl. 2: S227–S232.

Beluche, G. 2018. Personal Communication.

Belyaev, Igor, Amy Dean, Horst Eger, Gerhard Hubmann, Reinhold Jandrisovits, Markus Kern, Michael Kundi, et al. 2016. "EUROPAEM EMF Guideline 2016 for the prevention, diagnosis and treatment of EMF-related health problems and illnesses." *Reviews on Environmental Health* 31 (3): 363-97.

Benes, Jaromir, and Michael Kumhof. 2012. "The Chicago Plan Revisited." International Monetary Fund Working Paper.

Benazzo, Zaya and Mauricio Benazzo, directors. 2021. The wisdom of trauma.

Berggruen Institute. 2020. "Renewing Democracy in the Digital Age." Report on the future of democracy. March 9, 2020. https://www.berggruen.org/activity/renewing-democracy-in-the-digital-age/

Berggruen, Nicholas, and Nathan Gardels. 2013. *Intelligent Governance for the 21st Century: A Middle Way Between West and East.* Cambridge: Polity Press.

Berkowitz, Marvin W. 1985. "The Role of Discussion in Moral Education." In *Moral Education: Theory and Applications.* Edited by Marvin W. Berkowitz and Fritz Oser, 197-218. Hillsdale, NJ: Lawrence Erlbaum and Associates.

Berkowitz, Marvin W., and Melinda C. Bier. 2005. "What Works in Character Education: A Research-Driven Guide for Educators." Washington, DC: Character Education Partnership.

Berkowitz, Marvin. 2011. "What Works in Value Education." *International Journal of Educational Research* 50 (3): 153-58.

Beshara, Monica, Amanda D. Hutchinson, Carlene Wilson. 2013. "Does mindfulness matter? Everyday mindfulness, mindful eating and self-reported serving size of energy dense foods among a sample of South Australian adults." *Appetite*, 67:25-9.

Bétaille, Julien. 2019. "Rights of Nature: Why it Might Not Save the Entire World." *Journal for European Environmental & Planning Law* 6 (1).

Bihari, Joanne L. N., and Eugene G. Mullan. 2012. "Relating Mindfully: A Qualitative Exploration of Changes in Relationships Through Mindfulness-Based Cognitive Therapy." *Mindfulness* 5 (1): 46–59.

Billig, Shelley H. 2002. "Support for K-12 Service-Learning Practice: A Brief Review of the Research." *Educational Horizons* 80, 4 (Summer): 184-89.

Birkett, Alex. 2020. "Online Manipulation: All The Ways You're Currently Being Deceived." *CXL*, last updated September 25, 2020. Accessed August 5, 2020. https://cxl.com/blog/online-manipulation-all-the-ways-youre-currently-being-deceived/

Birol, Fatih. 2020. "What the 2008 financial crisis can teach us about designing stimulus packages today." International Energy Agency, April 19, 2020. https://www.iea.org/commentaries/what-the-2008-financial-crisis-can-teach-us-about-designing-stimulus-packages-today

Björkman, Tomas. 2018. "How to Use Personal, Inner Development to Build Strong Democracies." TedXBerlin Talk, August 20, 2018. Accessed February 17, 2021. https://www.youtube.com/watch?v=b4dFsHgd1rQ&t=1s&ab_channel=TEDxTalks

Blackman, Allen, Maria Angelica Naranjo, Juan Robalino, R. Francisco Alpizar, and Jorge Rivera Cayupi. 2014. "Does Tourism Eco-Certification Pay? Costa Rica's Blue Flag Program." *World Development* 58:41-52.

Blattman, Christopher, Nathan Fiala, and Sebastian Martinez. 2013. "The Economic and Social Returns to Cash Transfers: Evidence from a Ugandan Aid Program." CEGA Working Paper. April 2013. http://cega.berkeley.edu/assets/cega_events/53/WGAPE_Sp2013_Blattman.pdf

Bloom, David E., Elizabeth T. Cafiero, Eva Jané-Llopis, Shafika Abrahams-Gessel, Lakshmi Reddy Bloom, Sana Fathima, Andrea B. Feigl, et al. 2011. "The global economic burden of non-communicable diseases: a report by the World Economic Forum and the Harvard School of Public Health." World Economic Forum and the Harvard School of Public Health. http://www3.weforum.org/docs/WEF_Harvard_HE_GlobalEconomicBurdenNonCommunicableDiseases_2011.pdf

Blumstein, Alfred, and Allen J. Beck. 1999. "Population growth in US prisons, 1980-1996." *Crime in Justice* 26 (Prisons): 17-61. http://www.jstor.org/stable/1147683.

Bogatyreva, Olga A., and Alexandr E. Shillerov. 2015. *Biomimetic Management: Building a Bridge between People and Nature.* N.p.: CreateSpace Independent Publishing Platform.

Boix, Carles., Michael Miller, and Sebastian Rosato. 2013. "A Complete Data Set of Political Regimes, 1800–2007." *Comparative Political Studies* 46 (12): 1523-54. https://doi.org/10.1177%2F0010414012463905

Bond, Robert M., Christopher J. Fariss, Jason J. Jones, Adam D I Kramer, Cameron Marlow, Jaime E Settle, James H Fowler. 2012. "A 61-million-person experiment in social influence and political mobilization." *Nature* 489:295-98. https://doi.org/10.1038/nature11421

Boniwell, Ilona. 2013. "Introduction to Positive Education." In *The Oxford Handbook of Happiness*. Edited by Susan David, Ilona Boniwell, and Amanda Conley Ayres, 535-39. Oxford, UK: Oxford University Press.

Bonta, James, Rebecca Jesseman, Tanya Rugge, and Robert Cormier. 2006. "Restorative Justice and Recidivism: Promises Made, Promises Kept?" In *Handbook of Restorative Justice: A Global Perspective*. Edited by Dennis Sullivan and Larry Tifft, 108-18. London: Routledge.

Bourg, Dominique, editor. 2011. *Pour une 6ème République écologique*. Odile Jacob edition.

Brasey, Edouard. 1996. *Enquête Sur L'existence des Fées et des Esprits de la Nature*. N.p. : Editions Filipacchi.

Brinkbäumer, von Klaus, Julia Amalia Heyer, and Britta Sandberg. 2017. "Interview with Emmanuel Macron:UK: 'We Need to Develop Political Heroism.'" *Der Spiegel,* October 13. https://www.spiegel.de/international/europe/interview-with-french-president-emmanuel-macron-a-1172745.html

Bristow, Jamie, Rosie Bell, and Dan Nixon. 2020. *Mindfulness: Developing Agency in Urgent Times*. Sheffield, UK: The Mindfulness Initiative.

Brito-Pons, Gonzalo, Daniel Campos, and Ausiàs Cebolla. 2018. "Implicit or Explicit Compassion? Effects of Compassion Cultivation Training and Comparison with Mindfulness-Based Stress Reduction." *Mindfulness* 9 (5), 1494-1508.

Brooddryk, Johann. 2008. *Understanding South Africa: the Ubuntu way of Living*. Pretoria: Ubuntu School of Philosophy.

Brookes, Derek, and Ian McDonough. 2006. "The Differences between Mediation and Restorative Justice/Practice." Unpublished paper.

Brown, Benjamin I. 2020. "Violence, Aggression and Our Food". *International Society for Orthomolecular Medicine* 35 (1).

Brown, Laura S., Kirk Warren, and Tim Kasser. 2005. "Are Psychological and Ecological Wellbeing Compatible? The Role of Values, Mindfulness, and Lifestyle." *Social Indicators Research* 74:349-68.

Brown, Laura S. Kirk Warren, Richard M. Ryan, and J. David Creswell. 2007. "Mindfulness: Theoretical Foundations and Evidence for its Salutary Effects." *Psychological Inquiry* 18 (4): 211-37.

Brown, Laura S. and Christine A. Courtois. 2019. "Trauma Treatment: The Need for Ongoing Innovation." *Practice Innovations* 4 (3): 133-38.

Broussard, Nicholas. 1995. "Napoleon, Hegelian hero." *Revue du Souvenir Napoléonien.* Review number 400. https://www.napoleon.org/en/history-of-the-two-empires/articles/napoleon-hegelian-hero/

Brunk, Conrad G. 2001. "Restorative justice and the philosophical theories of criminal punishment." In *The spiritual roots of restorative justice.* Edited by Michael L. Hadley, 31-56. Albany, NY: State University of New York Press.

Buguet-Degletagne, Beatrice. 2018. « Evaluation du troisième plan national santé environnement et préparation de l'élaboration du plan suivant. » Edited by Inspection Générale des Affaires Sociales. Inspection report.

Bunker, Nick. 2014. "Being the reserve currency has its privileges and costs." Washington Center for Economic Growth, July 7. https://equitablegrowth.org/reserve-currency-privileges-costs/

Burke, Marshall, W. Matthew Davis, and Noah Diffenbaugh. 2018. "Large Potential Reduction in Economic Damages under UN Mitigation Targets." *Nature* 557, 549-53.

Cabanes, Valerie. 2017. « Reconnaissons la nature comme sujet de droit. » *Le Monde,* March 13. https://www.lemonde.fr/idees/article/2017/03/30/reconnaissons-la-nature-comme-sujet-de-droit_5102997_3232.html

Cameron, Kim S., David Bright, Arran Caza. 2004. "Exploring the Relationships between Organizational Virtuousness and Performance." *American Behavioral Scientist* 47 (6): 766–790. https://doi.org/10.1177/0002764203260209

Carlin, Dan. 2015. "Mindful Justice. Creating a Criminal Justice System Grounded in Mindfulness, Compassion and Human Dignity." Conference Summary Paper written in preparation for a conference titled Mindful Justice: Creating a Criminal Justice System Grounded in Mindfulness, Compassion, and Human Dignity, hosted in September 2015 by the Fetzer Institute in Kalamazoo, Michigan. https://afc724b7-5fdd-4ef2-92bf-6d2ad2de05d4.filesusr.com/ugd/8ea141_f2bcdc8df77b40d495379542d9ea94b7.pdf

Carney, Brian M., and Isaac Getz. 2016. *Freedom, Inc: How Corporate Liberation Unleashes Employee Potential and Business Performance.* 2nd edition. Somme Valley House.

Castaneda, Carlos. 1985a. *Journey to Ixtlan: The Lessons of Don Juan.* New York: Washington Square Press.

Castaneda, Carlos. 1985b. *The Teachings of Don Juan: A Yaqui Way of Knowledge.* New York: Washington Square Press. First published in 1968 by University of California Press (Berkeley, CA).

Castaneda, Carlos. 1991. *A Separate Reality.* Washington Square Press; Reissue edition.

Cayley, David. 1998. *The Expanding Prison: The Crisis in Crime and Punishment and the Search for Alternatives.* Toronto: House of Anansi Press.

Center for Disease Control and Prevention. 2012. "Mental Health and Chronic Diseases." Issue Brief No. 2. 6p.

Center for Youth Wellness. Undated. "The Landmark Adverse Childhood Experiences Study." Accessed August 3, 2020. https://centerforyouthwellness. org/the-science/

Central Asia Institute. 2020. "The Top 10 Reasons To Support Girls' Education." Website content. July 8, 2020. Accessed August 3, 2020. https://centralasia institute.org/top-10-reasons-to-support-girls-education/

Centre for Bhutan Studies and GNH. 2008. "GNH Policy and Project Selection Tools." Website content. Accessed August 11, 2020. http://www. grossnationalhappiness.com/gnh-policy-and-project-screening-tools/

Chadwick, Douglas H. "Keystone Species: How Predators Create Abundance and Stability" *Mother Earth News.* Originally published June/July 2011. Accessed July 29, 2020. https://www.motherearthnews.com/nature-and-environment/ wildlife/keystone-species-zm0z11zrog#ixzz1clbGyAwq,

Chahine, Vicky. 2017. « Méditer, un jeu d'enfant. » *Le Monde*, November 26. https://www.lemonde.fr/m-perso/article/2017/11/26/mediter-un-jeu-d-enfant_5220501_4497916.html

Chang, I-wei Jennfer. 2019. "Taiwan's 'Warm Power': Sharing Lessons on Digital Governance." *Global Taiwan Brief* 4 (23): 4. Accessed May 21, 2020. http:// globaltaiwan.org/wp-content/uploads/2020/02/4.23-PDF-GTB.pdf

Chaperon, Isabelle. 2015. « La Qualité de Vie au Travail, un Critère qui Prend du Galon. » *Le Monde*, Updated September 1, 2020. https://www.lemonde. fr/economie/article/2015/09/01/la-qualite-de-vie-au-travail-un-critere-qui-prend-du-galon_4742406_3234.html

Chapron, Gillaume, Yaffa Epstein, and José Vicente López-Bao. 2019. "A rights revolution for nature." *Science* 363 (6434): 1392-93. https://www.doi.org/ 10.1126/science.aav5601.

Chavagneux, Christian. 2020. « Une mondialisation de moindre intensité. » *Alternatives économiques* N°402. https://www.alternatives-economiques.fr/ une-mondialisation-mode-mineur/00092863

Chen, Yin-Ching. 2012. "The Idea of Nature in the Daoist Classic of Liezi." Dissertation submitted in partial fulfillment of the requirements for the degree of Doctor of Philosophy in East Asian Languages & Cultures in the Graduate College of the University of Illinois at Urbana-Champaign.

Chenoweth E. 2017. It May Only Take 3.5% of the Population to Topple a Dictator—with Civil Resistance. In The Guardian, February, 1st.

Chenoweth, Erica, and Kathleen Gallagher Cunningham. 2013. "Understanding Non-Violent Resistance." *Journal of Peace Research* 50 (3): 271–276.

Cherry, Kendra. 2019. "What Is Attachment Theory? The Importance of Early Emotional Bonds." *Very Well Mind*, July 17. https://www.verywellmind.com/what-is-attachment-theory-2795337

Chiao, Joan Y., and Katherine Blizinsky. 2009. "Culture-gene coevolution of individualism—collectivism and the serotonin transporter gene." *Proceedings of the Royal Society B* 277 (1681): 529-53. https://doi.org/10.1098/rspb.2009.1650

Chiesa, Alberto, Rafaella Calati, and Alessandro Serretti. 2011. "Does Mindfulness Training Improve Cognitive Abilities? A Systematic Review of Neuropsychological Findings." *Clinical Psychology Review* 31 (3):449-64. https://doi.org/10.1016/j.cpr.2010.11.003

Chodkiewicz, Alicia R., and Christopher Boyle. 2017. "Positive Psychology School-Based Interventions: A Reflection on Current Success and Future Directions." *Review of Education* 5 (1): 87-90. https://doi.org/10.1002/rev3.3080

Cholet, Mona, and Thomas Lemahieu. 2010. « Et Vous, Quel Travail Feriez-Vous si Votre Revenu Était Assuré »? *Périphéries*, December. https://www.peripheries.net/article326.html

Christian Peacemaker Teams. Undated. "Martin Luther King, Jr.'s Principle of Nonviolence." Accessed August 3, 2020. PDF file available at https://www.cpt.org/files/PW%20-%20Principles%20-%20King.pdf

Clark, Andrew E. 2010. "Works, Jobs and Wellbeing across the Millennium." In *International Differences in Wellbeing*. Edited by Ed Diener, John Helliwell, and Daniel Kahneman: 436-64. New York, NY: Oxford University Press. https://doi.org/10.1093/acprof:oso/9780199732739.003.0014

Clark, Andrew E., Yannis Georgellis, and Peter Sanfey. 2001. "Scarring: The Psychological Impact of Past Unemployment." *Economica* 68 (270): 221–41. https://doi.org/10.1111/1468-0335.00243

Clark, Andrew E., Paul Frijters, and Michael A. Shields. 2006. "Income and Happiness: Evidence, Explanation and Economic Implications." Paris-Jourdan Sciences Economiques Discussion paper N° 2006-24.

Clifford, Catherine. 2019. "Famous economist: Government should give all French citizens $132,000 in cash when they turn 25." *CNBC Money*, September 13. https://www.cnbc.com/2019/09/13/economist-piketty-french-citizens-should-get-6-figures-in-cash-at-25.html

CNN. 2020. "Transcript of Trump's Call with Governors: 'Dominate … or You'll Look Like a Bunch of Jerks.'" June 2. https://www.mercurynews.com/2020/06/02/transcript-of-trumps-call-with-governors-dominate-or-youll-look-like-a-bunch-of-jerks/

Cohen, Patricia, and Jacob Cohen. 1996. *Life Values and Adolescent Mental Health*. Mahwah, NJ: Lawrence Erlbaum Associates.

Colagrossi, Mike. 2018. "10 Reasons why Finland's Education System is the Best." *Big Think*, September 9. https://bigthink.com/mike-colagrossi/no-standardized-tests-no-private-schools-no-stress-10-reasons-why-finlands-education-system-in-the-best-in-the-world

Comisión Nacional—Programa Bandera Azul Ecológica. 2018. Informe Galardonados 2018. https://www.banderaazulecologica.org/user/pages/05.galardonados/Informe%20Ganadores%202018%20PBAE%20Versi%C3%B3n%202.pdf?cache

Commission on Social Determinants of Health (CDSH). 2008. "Closing the gap in a generation: Health equity through action on the social determinants of health." Final Report of the Commission on Social Determinants of Health. Geneva: World Health Organization. https://www.who.int/social_determinants/final_report/csdh_finalreport_2008.pdf

Conceição, Pedro. 2020. *The Human Development Report: The Next Frontier; Human Development and the Anthropocene*. United Nations Development Programme. https://report.hdr.undp.org/

Condon, Paul, Gaëlle Desbordes, Willa B. Miller, and David DeSteno. 2013. "Meditation increases compassionate responses to suffering." *Psychological Science* 24 (10): 2125-27.

Confino, Jo. 2013. "Zen Master Thich Nhat Hanh: Only Love Can Save Us from Climate Change." *The Guardian*, January 21. http://www.theguardian.com/sustainable-business/zen-master-thich-nhat-hanh-love-climate-change

Confino, Jo. 2014. "Thich Nhat Hanh: Is Mindfulness Being corrupted by Business and Finance?" *The Guardian*, March 28. https://www.theguardian.com/sustainable-business/thich-nhat-hanh-mindfulness-google-tech

Conseil Pontifical Justice et Paix. 2005. « Compendium de la Doctrine Sociale de L'église. » Les Éditions du Cerf.

Cordier, Solène. 2021. « L'inceste, un Phénomène Tabou à L'ampleur Méconnue. » *Le Monde*, January 5.

Correa, Mónica. 2017. "The History of Gross National Happiness." Working Paper. Accessed August 11, 2020. https://doi.org/10.13140/RG.2.2.18737.38243

Costa, Dora L., Noelle Yetter, and Heather DeSomer. 2018. "Intergenerational transmission of paternal trauma among US Civil War ex-POWs." *Proceedings of the National Academy of Sciences*, 115 (44): 11215-220.

Creswell, J. David, Hector F. Myers, Steven W. Cole, Michael R. Irwin. 2009. "Mindfulness Meditation Training Effects on CD4+ T Lymphocytes in HIV-1 Infected Adults: A Small Randomized Controlled Trial." *Brain, Behavior and Immunity* 23 (2):184-8.

Crocker, Jennifer, and Amy Canevello. 2012. "Creating and Undermining Social Support in Communal Relationships: The Role of Compassionate and Self-Image Goals." *Journal of Personality and Social Psychology* 95 (3): 555-75.

Crompton, Tom, Rebecca Sanderson, Mike Prentice, Netta Weinstein, Oliver Smith, and Tim Kasser. 2016. *Perceptions Matter: The Common Cause UK Values Survey.* London: Common Cause Foundation.

Cronin, Helena. 1991. *The Ant and the Peacock: Altruism and Sexual Selection from Darwin to Today.* Cambridge: Cambridge University Press.

Cuming, Angela. 2019. "This Country is Basing its Entire Budget on the Happiness of its People."*HuffPost*, May 6, 2019. https://www.huffingtonpost.com.au/entry/new-zealand-well-being-budget-happiness-economy_n_5cf4f7e1e4b0e8085e3cf4b0D

Dalin, Per, and Val Dean Rust. 1996. *Towards Schooling for the 21st Century.* New York: Bloomsbury Publication.

D'Antona, John Jr. 2020. "88% of All 2019 Forex Transactions Are in US Dollars." *Traders Magazine*, January 24, 2020. https://www.tradersmagazine.com/am/88-of-all-2019-forex-transactions-are-in-us-dollars/

Darwin, Charles. 1859. *On the Origin of Species by Means of Natural Selection.* New York: D. Appleton and Company. http://darwin-online.org.uk/converted/pdf/1861_OriginNY_F382.pdf

Darwin, Charles. 1889. *The Descent of Man and Selection in Relation to Sex.* New York: D. Appleton and Company. http://darwin-online.org.uk/converted/pdf/1889_Descent_F969.pdf

Dashti, Ali. 2011. *In Search of Omar Khayyam.* Iran: Routledge.

David, Susan, Ilona Boniwell, and Amanda Conley Ayers, eds. 2013. *The Oxford Handbook of Happiness.* Oxford, Great Britain: Oxford University Press. https://doi.org/10.1093/oxfordhb/9780199557257.001.0001

David, Susan, Ilona Boniwell, and Amanda Conley Ayers. 2013. "Introduction." In David et al. 2013, 1-8.

Davidson, Richard J., and Brianna S. Schuyler. 2015. "Neuroscience of Happiness." In *World Happiness Report*. Edited by John Helliwell, Richard Layard, and Jeffrey Sachs, 88-105.

Davis, Mark H. 2017. "Empathy, Compassion and Social Relationships." In *The Oxford Handbook of Compassion Science*. Edited by Emma M. Seppälä, Emiliana Simon-Thomas, Stephanie L. Brown, Monica C. Worline, C. Daryl Cameron, and James R. Doty, 299-315. New York, NY: Oxford University Press.

Dawkins, Richard. 1976. *The Selfish Gene*. Oxford: Oxford University Press.

Deci, Edward L., Richard Koestner, and Richard M. Ryan. 1999. "A Meta-Analytic Review of Experiments Examining the Effects of Extrinsic Rewards on Intrinsic Motivation." *Psychological Bulletin* 125 (6): 627-68. https://doi.org/10.1037/0033-2909.125.6.627.

De Mel, Suresh, David McKenzie, and Christopher Woodruff. 2008. "Returns to Capital in Microenterprises: Evidence from a Field Experiment." *The Quarterly Journal of Economics* 12 (4): 1329-72. https://doi.org/10.1162/qjec.2009.124.1.423

Demir, Meliksah. 2013. "Introduction to Relationships and Happiness." In David et al. 2013, 817-20.

De Neve, Jan-Emmanuel, Ed Diener, Louis Tay, and Cody Xuereb. 2013. "The Objective Benefits of Subjective Wellbeing." In *World Happiness Report*. Edited by John Helliwell, Richard Layard, and Jeffrey Sachs, 54-79. New York: Sustainable Development Solutions Network.

De Neve, Jan-Emmanuel, and George Ward. 2017. "Happiness at Work." In *World Happiness Report*. Edited by John Helliwell, Richard Layard, and Jeffrey Sachs, 144-77.

De Royer, Solenn, and Bastien Bonnefous. 2017. « Emmanuel Macron, un président très spirituel. » *Le Monde*, September 24. https://www.lemonde.fr/politique/article/2017/09/23/macron-un-president-tres-spirituel_5190170_823448.html

Descola, Philippe. 2005. *Par-delà Nature et Culture*. Paris: Gallimard, collection Folio Essais.

De Vibe, Michael, Arild Bjørndall, Elizabeth Tipton, Karianne Hammerstrøm, and Krystyna Kowalski. 2012. "Mindfulness-Based Stress Reduction (MBSR) for Improving Health, Quality of Life and Social Functioning in Adults." *Campbell Systematic Reviews* 2012, no. 3. https://doi.org/10.4073/csr.2012.3

Diamandis, Peter and Steven Kotler. 2012. *Abundance: The Future Is Better Than You Think*. New York: Free Press.

Diener, Ed, and Robert Biswas-Diener. 2002. "Will Money Increase Subjective Wellbeing? A Literature Review and Guide to Needed Research." *Social Indicators Research* 57 (2): 119-69.

Diener, Ed, and Marissa Diener. 1995. "Cross-cultural correlates of life satisfaction and self-esteem." *Journal of Personality and Social Psychology* 68 (4): 653-63. https://doi.org/10.1037//0022-3514.68.4.653

Diener, Ed, and Shigehiro Oishi. 2000. "Money and Happiness: Income and Subjective Wellbeing across Nations." In *Culture and Subjective Wellbeing*. Edited by Ed Diener and Eunkook M. Suh, 185-218. Cambridge, MA: MIT Press.

Diener, Ed, Weitang Ng, James Harter, and Raksha Arora. 2010. "Wealth and happiness across the world: material prosperity predicts life evaluation, whereas psychosocial prosperity predicts positive feeling." *Journal of Personality and Social Psychology* 99 (1): 52-61. https://doi.org/10.1037/a0018066

Diener Ed, Louis Tay, and David G. Myers. 2011. "The religion paradox: if religion makes people happy, why are so many dropping out?" *Journal of Personality and Social Psychology* 101 (6): 1278-90.

Dinan, Stephen. 2016. *Sacred America, Sacred World: Fulfilling Our Mission in Service to All*. Charlottesville, VA: Hampton Roads Publishing.

Diop, Doudou. Undated. « Mondialisation et civilisation de l'Universel chez Léopold Sédar Senghor. » Accessed August 5, 2020. https://www.cercle-richelieu-senghor.org/mondialisation-et-civilisation-de-luniversel-chez-leopold-sedar-senghor/

Dittmer, Kristofer. 2014. "Alternative to money-as-usual in ecological economics: a study of alternative local currencies and 100 percent reserve banking." PhD thesis.

Dolamo, Ramathate. 2013. "Botho/ubuntu: the heart of african ethics." *Scriptura* 112 (1): 1-10.

Doty, James R. 2017. "Preface." In *The Oxford Handbook of Compassion Science*. Edited by Emma M. Seppälä, Emiliana Simon-Thomas, Stephanie L. Brown, Monica C. Worline, C. Daryl Cameron, and James R. Doty, xxi–xxii. New York, NY: Oxford University Press.

Drutman, Lee. 2015. *The Business of America is Lobbying: How Corporations Became Politicized and Politics Became More Corporate* (Studies in Postwar American Political Development). New York: Oxford University Press.

Drutman, Lee. 2016. "About half of retiring senators and a third of retiring House members register as lobbyists." *Vox*, January 15, 2016. https://www.vox.com/2016/1/15/10775788/revolving-door-lobbying

Dunn, Elizabeth W., Lara B. Aknin, and Michael I. Norton. 2014. "Prosocial Spending and Happiness: Using Money to Benefit Others Pays Off." *Current Directions in Psychological Science* 23 (1): 41-7.

EAT-Lancet Commission. 2019. Summary report. This report was prepared by EAT and is an adapted summary of the Commission Food in The Anthropocene: the EAT-Lancet Commission on Healthy Diets From Sustainable Food Systems.

Economist Intelligence Unit, *The*. 2018. "Democracy Index 2018: Me Too? Political Participation, Protest and Democracy." A Report by *The Economist* Intelligence Unit. http://enperspectiva.uy/wp-content/uploads/2019/01/Democracy_Index_2018.pdf

Edwards, Scott. 2015. "Love and the Brain." *On The Brain*. Web content published by the Harvard Mahoney Neuroscience Institute. https://hms.harvard.edu/news-events/publications-archive/brain/love-brain

Effendi, Shoghi. 1973. *Directives from the Guardian*. Wilmette: Bahá'í Publishing Trust.

Eisenstein, Charles. 2011. *Sacred Economics. Money, Gift and Society in the Age of Transition*. Berkeley, CA: Evolver Editions.

Eisenstein, Charles. 2013. The more beautiful world our heart knows is possible. North Atlantic Books.

Einsentein, Charles. 2018. "Our New, Happy Life? The Ideology of Development by Charles Eisenstein." Accessed August 11, 2020. https://charleseisenstein.org/essays/7061-2/

Einstein, Albert, and Leopold Infeld. 1938. *The Evolution of Physics: The Growth of Ideas from Early Concepts to Relativity and Quanta*. Cambridge: Cambridge University Press.

Eisenberg, Nancy, and Randy Lennon. 1983. "Sex Differences in Empathy and Related Capacities." *Psychological Bulletin* 94 (1): 100-31. https://doi.org/10.1037/0033-2909.94.1.100

Eisler, Riane, and Douglas P. Fry. 2019. *Nurturing our Humanity: How Domination and Partnership Shape Our Brains, Lives, and Future*. New York: Oxford University Press.

Eisner, Manuel. 2003. "Long-term Historical Trends in Violent Crime." *Crime and Justice* no. 30, 83-142. https://www.jstor.org/stable/1147697

Elbert, Thomas, Christo Pantev, Christian Wienbruch, Brigitte Rockstroh, and Edward Taub. 1995. "Increased Cortical Representation of the Fingers of the Left Hand in String Players." *Science* 270 (5234): 305-7. https://doi.org/10.1126/science.270.5234.305

Elliot, Larry. 2019. "World's 26 Richest People Own as much as Poorest 50%, says Oxfam." *The Guardian,* January 20, 2019. https://www.theguardian.com/business/2019/jan/21/world-26-richest-people-own-as-much-as-poorest-50-per-cent-oxfam-report

El País. 1996. "Agua en el grifo." Opinion article published January 7, 1996. https://elpais.com/diario/1996/01/07/opinion/820969210_850215.html

Epstein, Robert. 2016. "The new mind control." *Aeon,* February 18, 2016.

Ericson, Torgier, Bjørn Gunaketu Kjønstad, and Anders Barstad. 2014. "Mindfulness and Sustainability." *Ecological Economics* 104 (C): 73-9. https://doi.org/10.1016/j.ecolecon.2014.04.007

European Commission. 2018. "Paternity and Parental Leave Policies across the European Union." Luxembourg: Publications Office of the European Union.

European Network of Ombudspersons for Children. 2018. "Child and Adolescent Mental Health in Europe". http://enoc.eu/wp-content/uploads/2019/06/Rapport-ENOC-ENG-NUM-17.06.19.pdf

Evans, David K., and Anna Popova. 2014. "Cash Transfers and Temptation Goods: A Review of Global Evidence." World Bank Policy Research Working Paper 6886.

Evans, Kate. 2012. "Make it rain: Planting forests could help drought-stricken regions." *Forests News,* July 23,2012. https://forestsnews.cifor.org/10316/make-it-rain-planting-forests-to-help-drought-stricken-regions?fnl=en

Fagot, Vincent. 2020. « Le déploiement de la 5G en France se heurte de plus en plus à des préoccupations écologiques. » *Le Monde,* July 2, 2020. https://www.lemonde.fr/economie/article/2020/07/02/le-deploiement-de-la-5g-se-heurte-a-la-poussee-des-preoccupations-ecologiques_6044908_3234.html

Fahsel H. 2013. *Thérèse Neumann: L'extraordinaire Mystique de Konnersreuth.* Paris: Editions Le Jardin des Livres.

Fehrenbacher, Jill. 2012. "Biomimetic Architecture: Green Building in Zimbabwe Modeled After Termite Mounds." *InHabitat,* November 29, 2012. https://inhabitat.com/building-modelled-on-termites-eastgate-centre-in-zimbabwe/

Fadel, Charles, and Jennifer S. Goff. 2019. "Four-Dimensional Education for Sustainable Societies." In *Sustainabilty, Human Well-Being and the Future of Education.* Edited by Justin W. Cook, 269-82. N.p.: Palgrave Mac Millan. https://doi.org/10.1007/978-3-319-78580-6

Fang, Lee. 2012. "When a Congressman Becomes a Lobbyist, He Gets a 1,452 Percent Raise (On Average)." *The Nation*, March 14, 2012. First published by *Republic Reports.org*.

FAO. 2018. "The 10 elements of agroecology guiding the transition to sustainable food and agricultural systems." Food and Agriculture Organization of United Nations. Rome: FAO

Farquhar, Brodie. 2021. "Wolf Reintroduction Changes Ecosystem in Yellowstone." *Outside+*. June 30, 2021. https://www.yellowstonepark.com/things-to-do/wolf-reintroduction-changes-ecosystem

Federations of City Farms & Community Gardens. Undated. "Benefits of community growing, green spaces and outdoor education."

Felitti, Vincent J., Robert F. Anda, Dale Nordenberg, David F. Williamson, Alison M. Spitz, Valerie Edwards, Mary P Koss, and James S. Marks. 1998. "Relationship of Childhood Abuse and Household Dysfunction to Many of the Leading Causes of Death in Adults: The Adverse Childhood Experiences (ACE) Study." *American Journal of Preventive Medicine* 14 (4): 245-57. https://doi.org/10.1016/S0749-3797(98)00017-8

Ferreboeuf, Huges, and Jean-Marc Jancovici. 2020. « La 5G est-elle vraiment utile ? » *Le Monde*, January 10, 2020.

Ferron, Camille, and Romain Morel. 2014. "Smart Unconventional MOnetary (SUMO) policies: giving impetus to green investment." Appendix of CDC Climat Research's 46th Climate Report.

Figueres, Christiana, and Tom Rivett-Carnac. 2020. *The Future we Choose. Surviving the Climate Crisis*. New York: Knopf Doubleday Publishing.

Finnish National Agency for Education. Undated. Finnish Education in a Nutshell.

Finucane, Anne, and Anne Hidalgo. 2018. "Climate Change Is Everyone's Problem. Women Are Ready to Solve It." *Fortune*, September 12, 2018. https://fortune.com/2018/09/12/climate-change-sustainability-women-leaders/

Fischer, Daniel, Laura Stanszus, Sonja Geiger, Paul Grossman, and Ulf Schrader. 2017. "Mindfulness and Sustainable Consumption: A Systematic Literature Review of Research Approaches and Findings." *Journal of Cleaner Production* 162:544-58. https://doi.org/10.1016/j.jclepro.2017.06.007

Fisher, Sebern F. 2014. *Neurofeedback in the Treatment of Developmental Trauma: Calming the Fear-Driven Brain*. New York: W. W. Norton & Company.

Fitzgerald, Amy J., Linda Kalof, and Thomas Dietz. 2009. "Slaughterhouses and Increased Crime Rates: An Empirical Analysis of the Spillover From 'The Jungle' Into the Surrounding Community." *Organization & Environment* 22 (2).

Fletcher, Robson. 2019. "Canada's Forests Actually Emit More Carbon Than They Absorb—Despite What You've Heard on Facebook." *CBC News*, February 12, 2019. https://www.cbc.ca/news/canada/calgary/canada-forests-carbon-sink-or-source-1.5011490

Ford, Bryan. 2002. "Delegative democracy." Accessed May 21, 2020. https://bford.info/deleg/deleg.pdf.

Foucart, Stéphane. 2021. « L'environnement est le Grand Impensé du Plan Cancer. » *Le Monde*, February 28, 2021. https://www.lemonde.fr/idees/article/2021/02/28/l-environnement-est-le-grand-impense-du-plan-cancer_6071451_3232.html

Fredrickson, Barbara L. 2013. *Love 2.0: Finding Happiness and Health in Moments of Connection*. New York, NY: Plume.

Frenkel-Brunswik, Else. 1958. "Intolerance of Ambiguity as a Personality Variable." In *Readings in Perception*. Edited by David Cromwell Beardsley and Michael Wertheimer. Princeton, NJ: Van Nostrand.

Freud, Sigmund. 2003. « Gesammelte Werke: II/III » In *L'interprétation du Rêve. Œuvres complètes, vol. 4*, 290. Paris: Presses Universitaires de France.

Frey, Bruno S., and Lorenz Götte. 1999. *Does Pay Motivate Volunteers?* Working Paper 7. Zurich: Institute for Empirical Economic Research, University of Zurich.

Frey, Bruno S., and Alois Stutzer. 2013. "Economics and the Study of Individual Happiness." In David et al. 2013, 431-47.

Frey, Bruno S., Simon Luechinger, and Alois Stutzer. 2010. "The Life Satisfaction Approach to Environmental Valuation." *Annual Review of Resource Economics* 2 (1): 139-60.

Gala Politique. 2017. La drôle de confidence de Brigitte Macron sur la fidélité de son mari. Published on June 14, 2017. https://www.gala.fr/l_actu/news_de_stars/la_drole_de_confidence_de_brigitte_macron_sur_la_fidelite_de_son_mari_396692

Gallup. 2019. 2019 Global Emotions Report. https://www.gallup.com/analytics/248906/gallup-global-emotions-report-2019.aspx

Galtung, Johan. 2017. "Peace: A Peace Practitioner's Guide." *Ideas for Peace* 13, July 2017.

Gandhi, Mahatma. 1969. *All Men Are Brothers*. India: UNESCO.

Garner, Richard. 2015. "Finland Schools: Subjects Scrapped and Replaced with 'Topics' as Country Reforms its Education System." *Independent*, March 20, 2015.

Gastil, John., Chiara Bacci, and Michael Dollinger. 2010. "Is Deliberation Neutral? Patterns of Attitude Change During 'The Deliberative Polls.'" *Journal of Public Deliberation* 6 (2): Article 3.

Gelfand, Michael, Jana L. Raver, Lisa Nishii, Lisa M. Leslie, Janetta Lun, Beng Chong Lim, Lili Duan, et al. 2011. "Differences between tight and loose cultures: a 33-nation study." *Science* 332 (6033): 1100-4. https://doi.org/10.1126/science.1197754.

Gendreau, Paul, Claire Goggin, and Francis T. Cullen. 1999. *The Effects of Prison Sentences on Recidivism.* Ottawa, ON: Solicitor General Canada

Gentilini, Ugo, Margaret Grosh, Jamele Rigolini, and Ruslan Yemtsov, eds. 2020. *Exploring Universal Basic Income: A Guide to Navigating Concepts, Evidence, and Practices.* Washington, DC: World Bank. https://openknowledge.worldbank.org/handle/10986/32677

Gewirth, Alan. 2009. *Self-Fulfillment.* NJ: Princeton University Press.

Geys, Benny. 2006. "Explaining Voter Turnout: A Review of Aggregate Level Research" *Electoral Studies* 25 (4): 637-63.

Gibbs, Benjamin G., Renata Forste, and Emily Lybbert. 2018. "Breastfeeding, Parenting, and Infant Attachment Behaviors." *Maternal and Child Health Journal* 22 (1): 579-88.

Gilbert, Paul, and Jennifer Mascaro. 2017. "Compassion Fears, Blocks and Resistances: An Evolutionary Investigation." In *The Oxford Handbook of Compassion Science.* Edited by Emma M. Seppälä, Emiliana Simon-Thomas, Stephanie L. Brown, Monica C. Worline, C. Daryl Cameron, and James R. Doty, 399-418. New Yok, NY: Oxford University Press.

Gilham, Jane, Rachel M. Abenavoli, Steven M. Brunwasser, Mark Linkins, Karen J. Reivich, and Martin E. P. Seligman. 2013. "Resilience Education." In David et al. 2013, 609-30. https://doi.org/ 10.1093/oxfordhb/9780199557257.013.0046

Gilligan, James. 1996. *Violence: Our Deadly Epidemic and its Causes.* New York: G. P. Putnam.

Gilligan, James. 2001. *Preventing violence.* New York: Thames & Hudson.

Ginn, Stephen, and Jamie Horder. 2012. "'One in four' with a mental health problem: the anatomy of a statistic." *BMJ* 344 (7845). https://doi.org/10.1136/bmj.e1302

Gleeson-White, Jane. 2018. "It's only natural: the push to give rivers, mountains and forests legal rights." *The Guardian*, April 1, 2018.

Global Commission on the Economy and Climate, The. 2016. *The sustainable infrastructure imperative. financing for better growth and development.* The 2016 New Climate Economy Report. Washington, DC: NCE

Gneezy, Uri, and Aldo Rustichini. 2000a. "A Fine is a Price." *The Journal of Legal Studies* 29 (1): 1–17.

Gneezy, Uri, and Aldo Rustichini. 2000b. "Pay Enough or Don't Pay at All." *Quarterly Journal of Economics* 115 (3): 791-810.

GNH Centre Bhutan. Undated. "History of GNH." Website content. http://www. gnhcentrebhutan.org/what-is-gnh/history-of-gnh/, accessed July 29, 2020.

GNH Institute. Undated. "The Gross National Happiness Origin." Web content. Accessed August 11, 2020. http://gnh.institute/gross-national-happiness-gnh-origin.htm

Goldenberg, Suzanne, and Stephanie Kirchgaessner. 2015. "Pope Francis demands UN respect rights of environment over 'thirst for power.'" *The Guardian*, September 25, 2015. https://www.theguardian.com/world/2015/sep/25/pope-francis-asserts-right-environment-un

Goldin, Philippe, and Hooria Jazaieri. 2017. "The Compassion Cultivation Training (CCT) Program." In *The Oxford Handbook of Compassion Science*. Edited by Emma M. Seppälä, Emiliana Simon-Thomas, Stephanie L. Brown, Monica C. Worline, C. Daryl Cameron, and James R. Doty, 237-45. New York, NY: Oxford University Press.

Goldsmith, Edouard. 2002. *Le Tao de L'écologie: Une Vision Écologique du Monde*. Trans. Agnes Bertrand and Thierry Pielat. Monaco: Editions du Rocher

Goleman, Daniel. 1996. *Emotional Intelligence: Why it Can Matter More than IQ*. New York: Bantam.

Gosseries, Olivia, Matteo Fecchio, Audrey Wolff, Leandro R. D. Sanz, Corine Sombrun, Audrey Vanhaudenhuyse, and Steven Laureys. 2020. "Behavioural and Brain Responses in Cognitive Trance: A TMS-EEG Case Study." Letter to the Editor. *Clinical Neurophysiology* 131 (2): 586-88. https://doi.org/10.1016/j.clinph.2019.11.011

Government of Bhutan. 2013. "Readiness Preparation Proposal (R-PP)." Accessed August 11, 2020. https://www.forestcarbonpartnership.org/sites/fcp/files/2014/July/R-PP%20Bhutan%20_rev_January%2012%2C%202014.pdf

Government of Canada. 2020. "Indicator: Carbon Emissions and Removals." Accessed August 3, 2020. https://www.nrcan.gc.ca/our-natural-resources/forests-forestry/state-canadas-forests-report/how-does-disturbance-shape-canad/indicator-carbon-emissions-removals/16552

Government Office for Science, The. 2008. Final Project Report. Foresight Mental Capital and Wellbeing Project. London: The Government Office for Science.

Graham, Gray, Deborah Kesten, and Larry Scherwitz. 2011. *Pottenger's Prophecy: How Food Resets Genes for Wellness or Illness.* Amherst, MA: White River Press.

Graham-McLay, Charlotte. 2019. "New Zealand's Next Liberal Milestone: A Budget Guided by 'Well-Being.'" *New York Times,* May 22, 2019. Accessed July 29, 2020. https://www.nytimes.com/2019/05/22/world/asia/new-zealand-wellbeing-budget.html

Grant, Bridget F., S, Patrica Chou, Risë B. Goldstein, Boji Huang, Frederick S. Stinson, Tulshi D. Saha, Roger P. Pickering, et al. 2008. "Prevalence, Correlates, Disability, and Comorbidity of DSM-IV Borderline Personality Disorder: Results from the Wave 2 National Epidemiologic Survey on Alcohol and Related Conditions." *The Journal of Clinical Psychiatry* 69 (4): 533. https://doi.org/10.4088/jcp.v69n0404

Gray, Gemma R., Vasiliki Totsika, and Geoff Lindsay. 2018. "Sustained Effectiveness of Evidence-Based Parenting Programs After the Research Trial Ends." *Frontiers in Psychology.* https://doi.org/10.3389/fpsyg.2018.02035

Griggs, Julia, and Robert Walker. 2008. "The Costs of Child Poverty for Individuals and Society." A literature review. Joseph Rowntree Foundation. Accessed August 10, 2020. https://www.jrf.org.uk/sites/default/files/jrf/migrated/files/2301-child-poverty-costs.pdf

Grooten, Monique, and Rosamunde Almond, eds. 2018. *Living Planet Report—2018: Aiming Higher.* Gland, Switzerland: WWF.

Gudynas, Eduardo, and Alberto Acosta. 2011. "La Renovación de la Crítica al Desarrollo y el Buen Vivir Como Alternativa." *Utopía y Praxis Latinoamericana* 16, no. 53 (April-June, 2011). http://www.gudynas.com/publicaciones/GudynasAcostaCriticaDesarrolloBVivirUtopia11.pdf

Guthold, Regina, Gretchen A. Stevens, Leanne M. Riley, and Fiona C. Bull. 2019. "WorldwideTrends in Insufficient Physical Activity Among Adolescents: A Pooled Analysis of 298 Population-Based Surveys with 1.6 Million Participants." *The Lancet Child & Adolescent Health* 6: e1077-86.

Hackett, Conrad, and David McClendon. 2017. "Christians remain world's largest religious group, but they are declining in Europe." *Pew Research Center.* Web content published April 5, 2017. Accessed August 5, 2020._https://www.pewresearch.org/fact-tank/2017/04/05/christians-remain-worlds-largest-religious-group-but-they-are-declining-in-europe/

Hadley, Michael L., editor. 2001a. *The Spiritual Roots of Restorative Justice.* State University of New York Press.

Hadley, Michael L. 2001b. "Introduction: Multifaith Reflection on Criminal Justice." In *The Spiritual Roots of Restorative Justice.* Edited by Michael L. Hadley, 1-29. New York: State University of New York Press.

Hadot, Pierre. 2002. *Exercices Spirituels et Philosophie Antique*. Paris: Editions Albin Michel.

Hall, Robert. 2015. "The ecovillage experience as an evidence base for national wellbeing strategies." *Intellectual Economics*, 9 (1): 30-42.

Hallström, Elinor, Quentin Gee, Peter Scarborough, and David A. Cleveland. 2017. "A healthier US diet could reduce greenhouse gas emissions from both the food and health care systems." *Climate Change* 142:199-212.

Handke C., Balazs B., Vallbé J-J. 2016. "Going means trouble and staying makes it double: the value of licensing recorded music online". *Journal of Cultural Economics* 40:227-259.

Haney, Craig. 2001. "The Psychological Impact of Incarceration: Implications for Post-Prison Adjustment." ASPE, U.S. Department of Health and Human Services.

Harari, Yuval Noah. 2014. *Sapiens: A Brief History of Humankind*. Toronto: McClelland & Stewart.

Harari, Yuval Noah. 2018. *21 Lessons for the 21st Century*. London: Penguin Random House.

Harding D., Morenoff J., Nguyen A., Bushway S., Binswanger I. 2019. A natural experiment study of the effects of imprisonment on violence in the community. *Nature Human Behaviour* 3:671-77.

Harwood Group, The. 1995. *Yearning for Balance Views of Americans on Consumption, Materialism, and the Environment*. Takoma Park, MD: Merck Family Fund.

Hatcher, William, and Douglas Martin. 1998. *The Baha'i Faith: The Emerging Global Religion*. Wilmette, Illinois: Baha'i Publishing.

Hathaway, Mark D. 2015. "Agroecology and permaculture: Addressing key ecological problems by rethinking and redesigning agricultural systems." *Journal of Environmental Studies and Sciences* 6:239-50.

Havel, Václav. 1985. *The Power of the Powerless: Citizens Against the State in Central Eastern Europe*. Routledge.

Health Europa. 2020. "MDMA-assisted psychotherapy for PTSD approved by FDA." Published January 27, 2020.

Hegel, Georg. 1998. *Lectures on the Philosophy of World History*. Introduction: Reason in History. Translated by Hugh B. Nisbet, with an introduction by Duncan Forbes. New York: Cambridge University Press.

Heller, Martin C., and Gregory A. Keoleian. 2015. "Greenhouse Gas Emission Estimates of U.S. Dietary Choices and Food Loss." *Journal of Industrial Ecology* 19 (3): 391–401.

Helliwell, John. 2019. "How To Open Doors To Happiness." In *Global Happiness and Wellbeing Policy Report 2019*, 9-26.

Helliwell, John, Haifang Huang, and Shun Wang. 2015. "The Geography of World Happiness." In *World Happiness Report 2015*. Edited by John Helliwell, Richard Layard, and Jeffrey Sachs, 12-41. New York: Sustainable Development Solutions Network. http://worldhappiness.report/ed/2015/

Helliwell, John, Richard Layard, and Jeffrey Sachs, eds. 2015. *World Happiness Report 2015*. New York: Sustainable Development Solutions Network. http://worldhappiness.report/ed/2015/

Helliwell, John, Haifang Huang, and Shun Wang. 2016. "Distribution of World Happiness." In *World Happiness Report 2016*. Edited by John Helliwell, Richard Layard, and Jeffrey Sachs, 8-9. New York: Sustainable Development Solutions Network. https://s3.amazonaws.com/happiness-report/2016/HR-V1_web.pdf

Helliwell, John, Richard Layard, and Jeffrey Sachs, eds. 2016. *World Happiness Report 2016*. New York: Sustainable Development Solutions Network. https://s3.amazonaws.com/happiness-report/2016/HR-V1_web.pdf

Helliwell, John, Haifang Huang, and Shun Wang. 2017a. "Social Foundations of World Happiness." In *World Happiness Report 2017*. Edited by John Helliwell, Richard Layard, and Jeffrey Sachs, 8–47. New York: Sustainable Development Solutions Network. https://worldhappiness.report/ed/2017/

Helliwell, John, Richard Layard, and Jeffrey Sachs, eds. 2017b. *World Happiness Report 2017*. New York: Sustainable Development Solutions Network. https://worldhappiness.report/ed/2017/

Helliwell, John, Richard Layard, and Jeffrey Sachs, eds. 2018. *World Happiness Report 2018*. New York: Sustainable Development Solutions Network. https://worldhappiness.report/ed/2018/

Helliwell, John, Haifang Huang, and Shun Wang. 2019. "Changing World Happiness." In *World Happiness Report 2019*. Edited by John Helliwell, Richard Layard, and Jeffrey Sachs, 11–46. New York: Sustainable Development Solutions Network. https://worldhappiness.report/ed/2019/

Henrich, Joseph, Robert Boyd, Samuel Bowles, Colin F. Camerer, Ernst Fehr, Herbert Gintis, and Richard Mc Elreath. 2004. "Overview and Synthesis." In *Foundations of Human Sociality: Economic Experiments and Ethnographic Evidence from Fifteen Small-Scale Societies*. Edited by Joseph Henrich, Robert Boyd, Samuel Bowles, Colin Camerer, Ernst Fehr, and Herbert Gintis. Oxford: Oxford Humanity Press.

Henrich, Joseph, and Natalie Henrich. 2007. *Why Humans Cooperate: A Cultural and Evolutionary Explanation*. New York: Oxford University Press.

Herman, Patricia, Benjamin M. Craig, and Opher Caspi. 2005. "Is complementary and alternative medicine (CAM) cost-effective? A systematic review." *BMC Complement Altern Med* 5, (11). https://doi.org/10.1186/1472-6882-5-11

Herzberg, Nathaniel. 2016. « Frans de Waal: Il est Temps d'arrêter de Courir Après le Propre de L'homme. » *Le Monde*, October 11, 2016. https://www.lemonde.fr/sciences/article/2016/10/10/frans-de-waal-il-est-temps-d-arreter-de-courir-apres-le-propre-de-l-homme_5011270_1650684.html

Higgins, Polly, Damien Short, and Nigel South. 2013. "Protecting the planet: a proposal for a law of ecocide." *Crime Law and Social Change* 59:257. DOI 10.1007/s10611-013-9413-6

High Level Panel of Experts on Food Security and Nutrition (HLPE). 2019. "Agroecological and other innovative approaches." Executive summary.

Hilton Shapiro Lara, Susanne Hempel, Brett A. Ewing, Eric Apaydin, Lea Xenakis, Sydne Newberry, Ben Colaiaco, et al. 2017. "Mindfulness Meditation for Chronic Pain: Systematic Review and Meta-Analysis." *Annals of Behavioral Medicine* 51 (2): 199-213.

His Holiness the Dalai Lama. 1998. *The Art of Happiness.* New York, NY: Riverhead.

His Holiness the Dalai Lama. 2012. *Beyond Religion: Ethics for a Whole World.* Boston, MA: Houghton Mifflin Harcourt.

Hivert, Anne-Françoise. 2019. « En Finlande, le Revenu de Base est une Source de Bien-être Pour Ses Bénéficiaires. » *Le Monde*, February 9, 2019.

Hobbes, Thomas. 1651. *Leviathan.* Available at: https://socialsciences.mcmaster.ca/econ/ugcm/3ll3/hobbes/Leviathan.pdf

Hodge, Shannon. 2017. "Six Ways in Which Educating Girls Benefits Their Wider Community." *The Circle,* published August 30, 2017. Accessed August 3, 2020. https://thecircle.ngo/six-positive-impacts-educating-girls/

Hofmann, Stefan G., and Angelina F. Gómez. 2017. "Mindfulness-Based Interventions for Anxiety and Depression." *Psychiatric Clinics of North America* 40 (4): 739-49.

Hoffower, Hillary. 2020. "These are the 15 richest people in the world right now". *Business Insider,* April 7, 2020.

Holmgren, David. 2002. *Permaculture—Principles and Pathways beyond Sustainability.* Holmgren Design Services: Victoria, Australia.

Holtz, Joshua. 2017. "Poverty Is Caused By A Failure Of Ethics, Not Economy, Sachs Says." *The Heights,* March 26, 2017. Updated June 3, 2020. https://www.bcheights.com/2017/03/26/poverty-caused-ethical-failure-not-economical-one-sachs-says/

Holy Father Francis. 2015. *Laudato Si': Encyclical Letter of the Holy Father on Care for our Common Home.* https://www.vatican.va/content/francesco/en/encyclicals/documents/papa-francesco_20150524_enciclica-laudato-si.html

Horsthemke, Bernard. 2018. "A critical view on transgenerational epigenetic inheritance in humans." *Nature Communications* 9, Article number: 2973.

Horton, Chris. 2018. "The simple but ingenious system Taiwan uses to crowdsource its laws." *MIT Technology Review*, August 21,2018. Accessed May 21, 2020. https://www.technologyreview.com/2018/08/21/240284/the-simple-but-ingenious-system-taiwan-uses-to-crowdsource-its-laws/

Horton, Richard. 2015. "Offline: What is Medicine's 5 Sigma?" *The Lancet* 385 (9976): 1380. https://doi.org/10.1016/S0140-6736(15)60696-1

Hubbard, Barbara Marx. 2015. *Conscious Evolution. Awakening the Power of our Social Potential.* Novato, CA: New World Library.

Hübl, Thomas, and Julie Jordan Avritt. 2020. *Healing Collective Trauma. A process for integrating our intergenerational and cultural wounds.* Boulder, Colorado: Sounds True.

Huculak, Bria. 2001. "Epilogue: justice as hope." In *The Spiritual Roots of Restorative Justice.* Edited by Michael L. Hadley, 217-23. New York: State University of New York Press.

Hum, Derek, and Wayne Simpson. 2001. "A Guaranteed Annual Income? From MINCOME to the Millennium." *Policy Options Politiques*, January-February 2001.

Huntington, Samuel. 1993. "The Clash of Civilizations?" *Foreign Affairs* 72 (3): 22-49.

Huta, Veronika. 2012. "Linking People's Pursuit of Eudaimonia and Hedonia with Characteristics of Their Parents: Parenting Styles, Verbally Endorsed Values, and Role Modeling." *Journal of Happiness Studies* 13, 47-61. https://doi.org/10.1007/s10902-011-9249-7

Huta, Veronika. 2013. "Eudaimonia." In David et al. 2013, 201-13.

Huta, Veronika. 2016. Eudaimonia Versus Hedonia: What's the Difference? And is it Real? Accessed August 11, 2020. https://cppa.ca/resources/Documents/Minutes/CPPA%202016%20Huta%20invited%20talk%20-%20revised.pdf

Inglehart, Ronald F. 2018. *Cultural Evolution: People's Motivations are Changing, and Reshaping the World.* Cambridge: Cambridge University Press.

Inglehart, Ronald F., Roberto Foa, Christopher Peterson, and Christian Welzel. 2008. "Development, Freedom, and Rising Happiness: A Global Perspective (1981-2007)." In *Perspectives on Psychological Science* 3 (4): 264–285. https://doi.org/10.1111%2Fj.1745-6924.2008.00078.x

Insel, Thomas R., Pamela Y. Collins, and Steven E. Hyman. 2015. "Darkness invisible: the hidden global costs of mental illness." *Foreign Affairs* 94 (1): 127-35.

Intergovernmental Science-Policy Platform on Biodiversity and Ecosystem Services (IPBES). 2019. "Summary for Policymakers of the Global Assessment Report on Biodiversity and Ecosystem Services." Zenodo. https://doi.org/10.5281/zenodo.3553579

International Panel of Experts on Sustainable Food Systems. 2016. "From uniformity to diversity. A paradigm shift from industrial agriculture to diversified agroecological systems." Executive summary.

IPBES. 2016. "Summary for Policymakers of the Assessment Report of the Intergovernmental Science-policy Platform on Biodiversity and Ecosystem Services on Pollinators, Pollination and Food Production." Zenodo. https://doi.org/10.5281/zenodo.2616458.

IPCC. 2018. "Summary for Policymakers." In *Global Warming of 1.5°C*. An IPCC Special Report on the impacts of global warming of 1.5°C above pre-industrial levels and related global greenhouse gas emission pathways, in the context of strengthening the global response to the threat of climate change, sustainable development, and efforts to eradicate poverty. Edited by Valerie Masson-Delmotte, Panmao Zhai, Hans Otto Pörtner, Debra Roberts, Jim Skea, Priadarshi R. Shukla, Anna Pirani, et al. Geneva: World Meteorological Organization.

IPCC. 2019. "IPCC Special Report on Climate Change, Desertification, Land Degradation, Sustainable Land Management, Food Security, and Greenhouse gas fluxes in Terrestrial Ecosystems." Edited by Priyadarshi R. Shukla, Jim Skea, Eduardo Calvo Buendia, Valérie Masson-Delmotte, Hans-Otto Pörtner, Debra C. Roberts, Panmao Zhai, et al. Geneva: World Meteorological Organization.

ISGP. 2012. *Reflections on Governance*. Institute for Studies in Global Prosperity, Bahá'í International Community. Bahá'í World Centre, Haifa, Israel.

Ivanhoe, Philip J. 2013. "Happiness in Early Chinese Thought." In *The Oxford Handbook of Happiness*. Edited by Susan David, Ilona Boniwell, and Amanda Conley Ayers, 431-47. Oxford, Great Britain: Oxford University Press.

Jabr, Ferris. 2019. "The Earth Is Just as Alive as You Are. Scientists Once Ridiculed the Idea of a Living Planet. Not anymore." *The New York Times*, April 20, 2019.

Jacob Soetendorp Institute for Human Values. 2012. "Towards RIO + 20 and Beyond—a Turning Point in Earth History." Interreligious statement to the Rio+20 Conference. Access date February 4, 2020. http://www.soetendorpinstitute.org/images/stories/pdf/towards_rio__20_and_beyond_-_carrying_document.pdf,

Jacka, Felice N., Julie A. Pasco, Arnstein Mykletun, Lana J. Williams, Allison M. Hodge, Sharleen Linette O'Reilly, Geoffrey C. Nicholson, Mark A. Kotowicz, and Michael Berk. 2010. Association of Western and traditional diets with depression and anxiety in women. *American Journal of Psychiatry* 167:305-11.

Jacka, Felice N., Arnstein Mykletun, Michael Berk, Ingvar Bjelland, and Gretha S. Tell. 2011. "The association between habitual diet quality and the common mental disorders in community-dwelling adults: the Hordaland Health study." *Psychosomatic Medicine* 73 (6): 483-90.

Jacka, Felice N., Nicolas Cherbuin, Karin J. Anstey, and Peter Butterworth. 2014. "Dietary patterns and depressive symptoms over time: examining the relationships with socioeconomic position, health behaviours and cardiovascular risk." *PLoS One* 9 (1): e87657. https://doi.org/ 10.1371/journal. pone.0087657

Jacka, Felice N., Eivid Ystrom, Anne Lise Brantsaeter, Evalill Karevold, Christine Roth, Margaretha Haugen, Helle Margrete Meltzer, Synnve Schjolberg, and Michael Berk. 2013. "Maternal and early postnatal nutrition and mental health of offspring by age 5 years: a prospective cohort study." *Journal of the American Academy of Child and Adolescent Psychiatry* 52 (10): 1038-47

Jacka, Felice N., Nicolas Cherbuin, Karin J. Anstey, Sachdev Perminder, and Peter Butterworth. 2015. "Western diet is associated with a smaller hippocampus: a longitudinal investigation." *BMC Medicine* 13: 215.

Jackson, Shelly, Ross A. Thompson, Elaine H. Christiansen, Rebecca A. Colman, Jennifer Wyatt, Chad W. Buckendahl, et al. 1999. "Predicting Abuse-Prone Parental Attitudes and Discipline Practices in a Nationally Representative Sample." *Child Abuse & Neglect 23*, 15–29.

Jaffe, Eric. 2020. "How open data and civic participation helped Taiwan slow Covid." *Medium*, March 27, 2020.

Jaspers, Karl. 2011. *The Origin and Goal of History*. London: Routledge Revivals.

Johnson, David, Roger T. Johnson, and Mary Beth Stanne. 2000. *Cooperative Learning Method: A Meta-Analysis*. Minneapolis. University of Minnesota.

Johnson, David W., Roger T. Johnson, and Edythe Johnson Holubec. 2008. *Cooperation in the Classroom* 7th edition. Edina, MN: Interaction Book Company.

Johnson, David W., Roger T. Johnson, and Karl A. Smith. 2006. *Cooperation in the College Classroom*, 4th edition. Edina, MN: Interaction.

Johnson, Sara B., Anne W. Riley, Douglas A. Granger, and Jenna Riis. 2013. "The Science of Early Life Toxic Stress for Pediatric Practice and Advocacy." *Pediatrics* 131 (2): 319-27.

Johnston, David W., Stefanie Schurer, and Michael Shields. 2011. "Evidence on the Long Shadow of Poor Mental Health across Three Generations." IZA Discussion Paper Series No. 6014. https://ssrn.com/abstract=1944717

Jones, Andrew Zimmerman. 2019. "The Basics of String Theory." ThoughtCo, March 2, 2019. https://www.thoughtco.com/what-is-string-theory-2699363

Joshi, Meera. 2017. "How Does Mindfulness Affect the Brain?" Bupa, November 10, 2017. Accessed August 3, 2020. https://www.bupa.co.uk/newsroom/ourviews/mindfulness-my-brain

Justice Policy Institute. 2002. "Cellblocks or Classrooms? The Funding of Higher Education and Corrections and Its Impact on African American Men." Washington, DC: Justice Policy Institute.

Kaati, Gunnar, Lars Olov Bygren, and Sören Edvinsson. 2002. "Cardiovascular and diabetes mortality determined by nutrition during parents' and grandparents' slow growth period." European Journal of Human Genetics 10, 682-88.

Kahloon, Idrees. 2020. "Thomas Piketty Goes Global." The New Yorker, March 9, 2020. https://www.newyorker.com/magazine/2020/03/09/thomas-piketty-goes-global

Kamath, M. V. 2007. Gandhi: A Spiritual Journey. Mumbai, India: Indus Source Books.

Kane, Libby. 2018. "Sweden is Apparently Full of 'Latte Dads' Carrying Toddlers—and it's a Sign of Critical Social Change." Business Insider France, April 4, 2018.

Karlberg, Michael. 2007. "Western Liberal Democracy as New World Order?" In The Baha'i World 2005-2006: An International Record. Edited by Robert Weinberg. Haifa, Israel: World Centre Publications.

Kasper, Debbie 2008. "Redefining community in the ecovillage." Human Ecology Review 15 (1): 12-24.

Kasser, Tim. 2002. The High Price of Materialism. Boston, MA: MIT Press.

Kasser, Tim, and Kennon M. Sheldon. 2002. "What Makes for a Merry Christmas?" Journal of Happiness Studies 3, 313-29.

Kasser, Tim, and Susan Linn. 2016. "Growing Up Under Corporate Capitalism: The Problem of Marketing to Children, with Suggestions for Policy Solutions." Social Issues and Policy Review 10, 122-50. https://doi.org/10.1111/sipr.12020

Kasser, Tim, Richard M. Ryan, Melvin Zax, and Arnold J. Sameroff. 1995. "The Relations of Maternal and Social Environments to Late Adolescents' Materialistic and Prosocial Values." Developmental Psychology 31 (6): 907-14. https://psycnet.apa.org/doi/10.1037/0012-1649.31.6.907

Kawachi, Ichiro, and Bruce P. Kennedy. 1997. "Socioeconomic Determinants of Health: Health and Social Cohesions: Why Care About Income Inequality?" *BMJ: British Medical Journal* 314 (7086): 1037-40. https://www.jstor.org/stable/25174195

Keng, Shian-Ling, Moria J. Smoski, and Clive J. Robins. 2011. "Effects of Mindfulness on Psychological Health: A Review of Empirical Studies." *Clinical Psychology Review* 31 (6): 1041-56. https://doi.org/10.1016/j.cpr.2011.04.006

Keller, Scott, and Bill Schaninger. 2019. "Getting Personal about Change." *McKinsey Quarterly*, April 21, 2019.

Kelley J., Kraft-Todd G., Schapira L., Kossowsky J., Riess H. 2014. The Influence of the Patient-Clinician Relationship on Healthcare Outcomes: A Systematic Review and Meta-Analysis of Randomized Controlled Trials. *PLoS One*; 9(4): e94207.

Keniger, Lucy, Kevin J. Gaston, Katherine N. Irvine, and Richard A. Fuller. 2013. "What are the Benefits of Interacting with Nature?" *International Journal of Environmental Research and Public Health* 10 (3): 913-35. https://doi.org/10.3390/ijerph10030913

Kessler, Roland C., Sergio Aguilar-Gaxiola, Jordi Alonso, Corina Benjet, Evelyn J. Bromet, Graça Cardoso, Louisa Degenhardt, et al. 2017. "Trauma and PTSD in the WHO World Mental Health Surveys." *European Journal of Psychotraumatology* 8 (5): 1353383. https://doi.org/10.1080/20008198.2017.1353383. eCollection 2017.

Keyes, Corey L. M. 2005. "Mental Illness and/or Mental Health? Investigating Axioms of the Complete State Model of Health." *Journal of Consulting and Clinical Psychology* 73 (3): 539-48.

Keyes, Corey L. M. 2007. "Promoting and Protecting Mental Health as Flourishing. A Complementary Strategy for Improving National Mental Health." *American Psychologist* 62 (2): 95-108.

Khaleque, Abdul. 2018. "Worldwide Implications of Parental Love and Lack of Love on Children's and Adults' Psychological Adjustment and Maladjustment: Meta-Analytic Evidence." *Journal of Mental Disorders and Treatment* 3 (2): 1-2. https://doi.org/10.4172/2471-271X.1000150

Khong, Chan. 2014. *Beginning Anew. Four Steps to Restoring Communication.* Berkeley, CA: Parralax Press.

Khong, Chan. 2016. "Can You Hear Mother Earth?" Website content accessed July 26, 2020. https://plumvillage.org/news/can-you-hear-mother-earth/

Khoury, Bassam, Tania Lecomte, Gillaume Fortin, Marjolaine Masse, Phillip Therien, Vanessa Bouchard, Marie-Andrée, et al. 2013. "Mindfulness-Based

Therapy: A Comprehensive Meta-Analysis." *Clinical Psychology Review* 33 (6): 763-71. https://doi.org/10.1016/j.cpr.2013.05.005.

Kilvert, Nick. 2018. "When trees make rain: Could restoring forests help ease drought in Australia?" *ABC Science*, September 14, 2018. https://www.abc.net.au/news/science/2018-09-15/trees-make-rain-ease-drought/10236572

King, Martin Luther, Jr. 1967. Nomination of Thich Nhat Hanh for the Nobel Peace Prize. Letter to the Nobel Institute. https://plumvillage.org/letter-from-dr-martin-luther-king-jr-nominating-thich-nhat-hanh-for-the-nobel-peace-prize-in-1967/

Kirby, James N. 2017. "Compassion-Focused Parenting." In *The Oxford Handbook of Compassion Science.* Edited by Emma M. Seppälä, Emiliana Simon-Thomas, Stephanie L. Brown, Monica C. Worline, C. Daryl Cameron, and James R. Doty, 91-105. New York, NY: Oxford University Press.

Kirkby, Jasper, Jonathan Duplissy, Kamalika Sengupta, Carla Frege, Hamish Gordon, Christina Williamson, Martin Heinritzi, et al. 2016. "Ion-induced nucleation of pure biogenic particles." *Nature* 533:521-26.

Konrath, Sara. 2014. "The Power of Philanthropy and Volunteering." In *Wellbeing: A Complete Reference Guide Volume VI.* Edited by Felicia A. Huppert and Cary L. Cooper, 387-427. Hoboken: John Wiley & Sons, Inc.

Konrath, Sara. 2016. "The Joy of Giving." In *Achieving Excellence in Fundraising.* Edited by Eugene R. Tempel, Timothy L. Seiler, and Dwight F. Burlingame, 11-25. New York: Wiley.

Konrath, Sara, and Stephanie Brown. 2013. "The Effects of Giving on Givers." In *Handbook of Health and Social Relationships.* Edited by Matthew L. Newman and Nicole A. Roberts, 39-64. Washington, D.C.: American Psychological Association

Korpela, Salla. 2017. "Education in Finland: Key to the Nation's Success." Ministry for Foreign Affairs. Otavamedia OMA.

Korten, David. 2016. "The New Economy: A Living Earth System Model." A report prepared for and published the Next System Project, August 10, 2016. https://davidkorten.org/new-economy-system-model/

Kristeller, Jean, Ruth Q. Wolever, and Virgil Sheets. 2014. "Mindfulness-Based Eating Awareness 912 Training (MB-EAT) for Binge Eating: A Randomized Clinical Trial." *Mindfulness* 5 (3): 282-97.

Kudesia, Ravi S. 2015. "Mindfulness and Creativity in the Workplace." In *Mindfulness in Organisations.* Edited by Jochen Reb and Paul W. B. Atkins, 190-212. Cambridge Companions to Management. Cambridge: Cambridge University Press. https://doi.org/10.1017/CBO9781107587793.010.

Lagdameo-Santillan, Karina. 2018. "Roots of Filipino Humanism (1) 'Kapwa.'" Website content. Pressenza International Press Agency, July 24, 2018. https://www.pressenza.com/2018/07/roots-of-filipino-humanism-1kapwa/

Lähdemäki, Jenna. 2019. "Case Study: The Finnish National Curriculum 2016—A Co-Created National Education Policy." In *Sustainabilty, Human Well-Being and the Future of Education*. Edited by Justin W. Cook, 397-422. N.p.: Palgrave Mac Millan.

Laininen, Erkka. 2019. "Transforming Our Worldview Towards a Sustainable Future." In *Sustainabilty, Human Well-Being and the Future of Education*. Edited by Justin W. Cook, 161-200. N.p.: Palgrave Mac Millan.

Laloux, Frederic. 2014. *Reinventing Organizations: A Guide to Creating Organizations Inspired by the Next Stage of Human Consciousness*. Mills, MA: Nelson Parker.

The Lancet. 2016. "Advancing Early Childhood Development: from Science to Scale." An Executive Summary for *The Lancet*'s Series. https://www.thelancet.com/pb-assets/Lancet/stories/series/ecd/Lancet_ECD_Executive_Summary.pdf

Lando, James, Sheree Marshall Williams, Stephanie Sturgis, and Branalyn Williams. 2006. "A Logic Model for the Integration of Mental Health Into Chronic Disease Prevention and Health Promotion." *Prevention Chronic Disease* 3 (2): A61.

Lao Tzu. 2006. *Tao te Ching*. Translated by D. Lin. SkyLight Paths.

Larson, Nina. 2019. "UN calls for 'Global Green New Deal' to boost world economy." *AFP News,* September 25, 2019.

Layard, Richard, Dan Chisholm, Vikram Patel, and Shekhar Saxena. 2013. "Mental illness and unhappiness." In *World Happiness Report*. Edited by John Helliwell, Richard Layard, and Jeffrey Sachs, 38-53. New York: Sustainable Development Solutions Network.

Layard, Richard, Andrew E. Clark, Francesca Cornaglia, Nattavudh Powdthavee, and James Vernoit. 2014. "What Predicts a Successful Life? A Life-Course Model of Wellbeing." *The Economic Journal* 124 (580): F720-F738. https://doi.org/10.1111/ecoj.12170

Le Figaro. 2017. « François Hollande: un quinquennat ... sous la pluie ou presque. » Published on May, 8, 2017.

Legrain, Yves. 2014. « Transitions vers une Industrie Économe en Matières Premières. » Rapport et Avis du Conseil Économique, Social et Environnement. Les Éditions des Journaux Officiels.

Le journal du dimanche. 2017. « Macron, confidences sacrées. » Published on February 12, 2017.

Le Monde. 2017. « L'humour de François Hollande récompensé par un prix. » Published on November 29, 2017.

Lent, Jeremy. 2018. "What Does China's "Ecological Civilization" Mean for Humanity's Future?" Website content accessed July 29, 2020. https://patternsofmeaning.com/2018/02/08/what-does-chinas-ecological-civilization-mean-for-humanitys-future/.

Lester, Simon, and Bryan Mercurio. 2020. "We Need a Coronavirus Vaccine. Patents Might Slow the Process." Blog post. *The National Interest,* April 7, 2020.

Levine, Glenn N., Richard A. Lange, C. Noel Bairey-Merz, Richard J. Davidson, Kenneth Jamerson, Puja K Mehta, Erin D. Michos, et al. 2017. "Meditation and Cardiovascular Risk Reduction. A Scientific Statement From the American Heart Association." *Journal of the American Heart Association* 6 (10): 28.

Lewis, Tanya. 2013. "The Singularity Is Near: Mind Uploading by 2045?" *LiveScience* June 13, 2013. https://www.livescience.com/37499-immortality-by-2045-conference.html

Leymarie, Jean. 2019. « L'économiste Daniel Cohen: De "la Solitude Sociale" au Vote Populiste. » *France Info,* September 5, 2019. Accessed August 1, 2020. https://www.francetvinfo.fr/replay-radio/l-interview-eco/leconomiste-daniel-cohen-de-la-solitude-sociale-au-vote-populiste_3585379.html.

Li, Qing. 2018. *Shinrin-Yoku: The Art and Science of Forest Bathing.* London: Penguin Life.

Lin, Chia-Shu, Yong Liu, Wei-Yuan Huang, Chia-Feng Lu, Shin Teng, Tzong-Ching Ju, Yong He, et al. 2013. "Sculpting the Intrinsic Modular Organization of Spontaneous Brain Activity by Art." *PloS One* 8 (6): e66761. https://doi.org/10.1371/journal.pone.0066761

Lindh, Thomas and John Stark, directors. 2017. "Breaking the cycle." Accessed July 4, 2021 https://www.youtube.com/watch?v=GgclCm5IAEE&ab_channel=Jo%C3%A3oSilva

Looking Horse, Arvol. 2014. "Earth Day Message From Chief Arvol Looking Horse." Statement for Earth Day. Culture Collective.org. Accessed August 5, 2020. https://www.culturecollective.org/message-chief-arvol-lookinghorse-earth-day/

Loomis, Ilima. 2017. "Trees in the Amazon make their own rain." *ScienceMag. org,* August 4, 2017. Accessed August 20, 2020. https://www.sciencemag.org/news/2017/08/trees-amazon-make-their-own-rain

Looney, Adam, and Nicholas Turner. 2008. "Work and opportunity before and after incarceration." Report. The Brookings Institution. March 14, 2018. https://www.brookings.edu/research/work-and-opportunity-before-and-after-incarceration/

Lopez-Claros, Augusto, Arthur L. Dahl, and Maja Groff. 2020. *Global Governance and the Emergence of Global Institutions for the 21st Century*. Cambridge: Cambridge University Press.

Lorenz, Konrad. 2002. *On Aggression*. London: Psychology Press.

Louv, Richard. 2005. *Last Child in the Woods: Saving Our Children From Nature-Deficit Disorder*. New York: Algonquin Books.

Lueke, Adam, and Bryan Gibson. 2016. "Brief Mindfulness Meditation Reduces Discrimination." *Psychology of Consciousness: Theory, Research, and Practice* 3 (1): 34-44.

Lundberg, Olle, Monica Åberg Yngwe, Kölegård Stjärne, Lisa Björk, et al. 2007. "The Nordic Experience: Welfare States and Public Health (NEWS)." Report for the Commission on Social Determinants of Health. Stockholm, Centre for Health Equity Studies (CHESS).

Lynch, Robert, and Kavya Vaghul. 2015. "The Benefits and Costs of Investing in Early Childhood Education." Washington Center for Equitable Growth. www.equitablegrowth.org.

Mabana, Kahiudi Claver. 2011. « Léopold Sédar Senghor et la civilisation de l'universel.» *Diogènes* 3 (235-236): 3-13.

Magallanes, Iorns, and J. Catherine. 2016. "Maori cultural rights in aotearoa New Zealand: protecting the cosmology that protects the environment." Victoria University of Wellington Legal Research Papers. Paper No 6/2016. Volume 6, Issue No 2.

Magnen, Jean-Philippe, and Christophe Fourel. 2015. « D'autres monnaies pour une nouvelle prospérité. » Mission d'étude sur les monnaies locales complémentaires et les systèmes d'échange locaux.

Mammarella, Brian T. 2016. "An Evidence-Based Objection to Retributive Justice." *Yale Journal of Health Policy, Law, and Ethics* 16 (2): 289-326.

Mancuso, Stefano, and Alessandra Viola A. 2018. *L'intelligence des Plantes*. London: Editions Albin Michel.

Mandard, Stéphanie. 2020. « 5G: l'impartialité du comité qui guide l'Europe pour protéger la population des ondes en question. » *Le Monde*, June 19, 2020.

Mansbridge, Jane J. 1980. *Beyond Adversary Democracy*. Chicago: The University of Chicago Press.

Maples, Cheri. 2017. "Mindfulness and the Police". *The Mindfulness Bell mindfulnessbell.org*, Winter/spring 2017. 7p.

Maradan, Isabelle. 2017. « Education: Et si on Arrêtait la Compétition ? » *Le Monde*, November 15, 2017.

Marchand, P. 2020. "L'histoire du Manifeste 2000."

Marcus, Marina, M. Taghi Yasamy, Mark van Ommeren, Dan Chisholm, and Shekhar Saxena. 2012. "Depression: a global public health concern." WHO Department of Mental Health and Substance Abuse.

Marglin, Elizabeth. 2020. "'Magic Mushrooms' for PTSD: Why Psychedelics May Help Heal Trauma." *The Healthy*, January 22, 2020.

Martin Asuero, Andrés, Jenny Moix Queralto, Enriqueta Pujol-Ribera, Anna Berenguera, Teresa Rodriquez-Blanco, and Ronald M. Epstein. "Effectiveness of a Mindfulness Education Program in Primary Health Care Professionals: A pragmatic Controlled Trial." *Journal of Continuing Education in the Health Professions* 34 (1): 4-12. https://doi.org/10.1002/chp.21211.

Maxwell, Gabrielle, Venezia Kingi, Jeremy Robertson, Allison Morris, Chris Cunningham. 2004. "Achieving Effective Outcomes in Youth Justice." Final report. Crime and Justice Research Centre, Victoria University of Wellington.

Mc Cold, Paul. 2006. "The Recent History of Restorative Justice: Mediation, Circles and Conferencing." In *Handbook of Restorative Justice: A Global Perspective*. Edited by Dennis Sullivan and Larry Tifft, 23-51. London: Routledge.

McInerney, Laura. 2013. "Applying Happiness and Well-Being Research to the Teaching and Learning Process." In David et al. 2013, 592-608.

McIntosh, Steve. 2020a. *Developmental Politics: How America Can Grow Into a Better Version of Itself*. Paragon House.

McIntosh, Steve. 2020b. *Developmental Politics Simplified in 5-Minutes*. Video. Accessed August 5, 2020. https://www.youtube.com/watch?time_continue=355&v=nAvMcui3_y0&feature=emb_logo

McIntyre, Beverly D., Hans R. Herre, Judi Wakhungu, and Robert Watson. 2009. "Agriculture at a crossroad: International Assessment of Agricultural Knowledge, Science and Technology for Development." Washington, DC: Island Press.

McLaughlin, Corinne, and Gordon Davidson. 1994. *Spiritual politics. Changing the world from the inside out*. NY: Ballantine Books.

Meadows, Donella H. 1999. *Leverage Points: Places to Intervene in a System*. N.p.: The Sustainability Institute.

Meadows, Donella H. 2008. *Thinking in Systems: A Primer.* White River Junction, VT: Chelsea Green Publishing.

Mehring, Liana. 2013. "Botho: A Dual-Purpose in Botswana." *Georgetown Journal of International Affairs*, online edition. Accessed August 1, 2020. https://www. georgetownjournalofinternationalaffairs.org/online-edition/botho-a-dual-purpose-in-botswana-by-liana-mehring

Mestre Pacheco, Yanelia. 2018. *Shikwakala.* Santa Marta, Colombia: Resguardo Kogui-Malayo-Arhuaco.

Michel, Chloe, Michelle Sovinsky, Eugenio Proto, and Andrew J. Oswald. 2019. "Advertising as a Major Source of Human Dissatisfaction: Cross-National Evidence on One Million Europeans." In *The Economics of Happiness.* Edited by Mariano Rojas, 217-39. Springer, Cham. https://doi.org/10.1007/978-3-030-15835-4_10

Michelet, Jules. 1962. *Journal, tome II : 1849-1860.* Paul Viallaneix edition. Paris: Gallimard.

Milburn, Michael A., and Sheree D. Conrad. 1996. *The Politics of Denial.* Cambridge, MA: MIT Press.

Milburn, Michael A., and Sheree D. Conrad. 2018. *Raised to Rage: The Politics of Anger and the Roots of Authoritarianism.* Cambridge, MA: MIT Press.

Miles-Yepez, Netanel. 2006. *The Common Heart: An Experience of Interreligious Dialogue.* New York, NY: Lantern Books.

Miller, Carl. 2019. "Taiwan is making democracy work again. It's time we paid attention." *Wired*, November 26, 2019.

Miller, Dale T. (1999). "The Norm of Self-Interest." *American Psychologist* 54 (12): 1053-60. https://doi.org/10.1037/0003-066X.54.12.1053

Mindfulness Initiative. 2015. "Mindful Nation UK." Report by the Mindfulness All-Party Parliamentary Group (MAPPG).

Ministerio de Planificación del Desarrollo. 2009. Plan Nacional de Desarrollo "Bolivia Digna, Soberana, Productiva y Democrática para Vivir Bien" for Bolivia (2009–2014).

Møller, Jørgen, and Svend-Erik Skaaning. 2013. "The Third Wave: Inside the Numbers." Journal of Democracy 24 (4): 97-109.

Montesquieu. 1993. « De l'esprit des lois, tome I. » N.p. : Flammarion.

Moore, Adam W., and Peter Malinowski. 2009. "Meditation, Mindfulness and Cognitive Flexibility." *Consciousness and Cognition* 18 (1): 176-86.

Moore, Catherine. 2020. "What is Positive Education, and How Can We Apply It?" Web content. PositivePsychology.com. Accessed August 4, 2020. https://positivepsychology.com/what-is-positive-education/

Morin, Edgar. 1999. *Introduction à Une Politique de L'homme*. Paris: Editions du Seuil.

Morin, Edgar. 2002. « Au-delà de la Globalisation et du Développement, Société-monde ou Empire-monde? » *Revue Mauss,* no. 20, 43-53.

Morin, Edgar. 2005. *Introduction à la Pensée Complexe*. Paris: Editions du Seuil.

Morin, Edgar. 2008. *On Complexity*. New York: Hampton Press.

Morin, Edgar. 2011. *La Voie: Pour L'avenir de L'humanité*. Paris: Fayard.

Morin, Edgar. 2016. « Eduquer à la Paix Pour Résister à L'esprit de Guerre.» *Le Monde*, February 5, 2016. Updated on February 9, 2016.

Morris, Ian. 2013. "Going Beyond the Accidental: Happiness, Education, and the Wellington College Experience." In David et al. 2013, 644-56.

Morisson, Deborah. 2006. "A Gandhian Commentary on the Inner Voice." In *Nexus: A Neo Novel*, September 23. Blog entry. https://nexusnovel.wordpress.com/2006/09/23/a-gandhian-commentary-on-the-inner-voice/

Mulgan, Geoff. 2013. "Wellbeing and Public Policy." In David et al. 2013, 517-32.

Munárriz, Angel. 2017. "Reyes Mate: 'En la Construcción Nacional Catalana Hay una Expresión del Franquismo.'" *Infolibre*, November 20, 2017.

Münte, Thomas F., Eckart Altenmüller, and Lutz Jäncke. 2002. "The Musician's Brain as a Model of Neuroplasticity." *Nature Reviews Neuroscience* 3 (6): 473-78.

Murray, W. H. 1951. *The Scottish Himalayan Expedition*. London & Toronto: J.M. Dent & Sons.

Myers, David G. 2013. "Religious Engagement and Wellbeing." In David et al. 2013, 88-100.

NASA. Undated. "Dark Energy, Dark Matter." Web content. Accessed August 3, 2020. https://www.ncronline.org/news/pope-cites-teilhardian-vision-cosmos-living-host.

National Academies of Sciences, Engineering, and Medicine. 2019. Taking Action Against Clinician Burnout: A Systems Approach to Professional Well-Being. Washington, DC: The National Academies Press

Nazaret, Arthur. 2019. *Une Histoire de L'écologie Politique*. Editions La Tengo.

NDP Steering Committee and Secretariat, 2013. *Happiness: Towards a New Development Paradigm. Report of the Kingdom of Bhutan*. Access date February 4, 2020. http://www.penseesdemonrecif.org/images/inspirations/NDP_Report_Bhutan_2013.pdf

Neblo, Michael A., Kevin M. Esterling, Ryan Kennedy, David Lazer, and Anand E. Sokhey. 2010. Who Wants To Deliberate—And Why? *American Political Science Review* 104 (3): 566-83.

Netscribes. 2019. "Global 5G Market (2019–2025)." Report published March 2019. India: Netscribes

New York Times, The. 2012. "Race to the bottom." December 5, 2012. Accessed August 12, 2020. https://www.nytimes.com/2012/12/06/opinion/race-to-the-bottom.html

News Heads Bureau. 2018. "Stephen Hawking's Final Paper May Discover Parallel Universes." Published May 3, 2018.

Newsom, Cassandra Rutledge, Robert P. Archer, Susan Trumbetta, and Irving I. Gottesman. 2003. Changes in Adolescence Response Patterns on the MMPI/MMPI-A across Four Decades. *Journal of Personality Assessment* 81 (1): 74-84.

Nhat Hanh, Thich. 1998. *Interbeing: Fourteen Guidelines for Engaged Buddhism.* Berkeley: Parallax Press.

Nhat Hanh, Thich. 2005. *Keeping the Peace: Mindfulness and Public Service.* Parallax Press.

Nhat Hanh, Thich. 2008. *The Heart of Understanding: Commentaries on the Prajñaparamita Sutra.* Berkeley: Parallax Press.

Nhat Hanh, Thich. 2009. Dharma Talk to the 2009 Parliament of World's Religions.

Nhat Hanh, Thich. 2009. *Happiness. Essential Mindfulness Practices.* Berkeley: Parallax Press.

Nhat Hanh, Thich. 2016. *At home in the world.* Penguin Random House UK.

Niehoff, Debra. 1999. *The Biology of Violence: How Understanding the Brain, Behavior, and Environment Can Break the Vicious Circle of Aggression.* New York: The Free Press.

Nisbet, Elizabeth K., John M. Zelenski, and Steven A. Murphy. 2009. "The Nature Relatedness Scale: Linking Individuals' Connection With Nature to Environmental Concern and Behavior." *Environment and Behavior* 41 (5): 715-40. https://doi.org/10.1177%2F0013916508318748

Nittby, Henrietta, Arne Brun, Susanne Strömblad, Mehri Kaviani Moghadam, Wenjun Sun, Lars Malmgren, Jacob Eberhardt, Bertil R. Persson, and Leif G. Salford L. 2011. Nonthermal GSM RF and ELF EMF effects upon rat BBB permeability. *The Environmentalist* 31:140-48. https://doi.org/10.1007/s10669-011-9307-z

Njoh-Mouelle, Ebénézer. undated. « Léopold Sedar Senghor et le thème du metissage culturel. » Exposé présenté lors de la table ronde du 16 mars à l'Institut des Relations Internationales (IRIC) de l'université de Yaoundé II, à l'occasion de la célébration de la 36eme Journée Mondiale de la Francophonie.

Noble, Toni, and McGrath, Helen. 2013. "Well-Being and Resilience in Education." In David et al. 2013, 563-78.

Nobre, Antonio Donato. 2014. "The Future Climate of Amazonia, Scientific Assessment Report." Sponsored by CCST-INPE, INPA and ARA. São José dos Campos, Brazil.

Norberg-Hodge, Helena. 2016. *Localization: Essential Steps to an Economics of Happiness*. eBook published by Local Futures.

Normand, Grégoire. 2019. « Piketty: 'Tant qu'il n'y aura pas plus de justice fiscale, ce gouvernement aura du mal à réformer.' » *La Tribune*, November 15, 2019.

Nguyen, Theresa, Michele Hellebuyck, Madeline Halpern, and Danielle Fritze. 2017. "The State of Mental Health in America 2018." Report. Mental Health America. https://www.mhanational.org/issues/state-mental-health-america-2018

O'Brien, Jeffrey M. 2020. "Business gets ready to trip: How psychedelic drugs may revolutionize mental health care." *Fortune*. February 17, 2020. https://fortune.com/longform/psychedelic-drugs-business-mental-health/

O'Donnel, Gus. (2013). "Using Wellbeing as a Guide to Policy." In *World Happiness Report*. Edited by John Helliwell, Richard Layard, and Jeffrey Sachs, 96-111. New York: Sustainable Development Solutions Network.

OECD. 2012. *Sick on the Job? Myths and Realities about Mental Health and Work*. Mental Health and Work Series. Paris: OECD Publishing. https://doi.org/10.1787/9789264124523-en

O'Neil, Adriene, Shae E. Quirk, Siobhan Housden, Sharon L. Brennan, Lana J. Williams, Julie Pasco, Michael Berk, and Felice N. Jacka. 2014. "Relationship Between Diet and Mental Health in Children and Adolescents: A Systematic Review." *American Journal of Public Health* 104 (10): e31–e42.

Optum. 2018. "Boost Employee Net Promoter Score with Health and Well-Being Programs." White paper.

Ostafin, Brian D., and Kyle T. Kassman. 2012. "Stepping Out of History: Mindfulness Improves Insight, Problem-Solving." *Consciousness and Cognition* 21 (2):1031-6.

Ostrom, Elinor. 2009. "Beyond Markets and States: Polycentric Governance of Complex Economic Systems." Nobel Prize Lecture, December 8, 2009. https://www.nobelprize.org/uploads/2018/06/ostrom_lecture.pdf

Ostry, Jonathan D., Prakash Loungani, and Davide Furceri. 2016. "Neoliberalism: Oversold ?" International Monetary Fund Finance and Development. https://www.imf.org/external/pubs/ft/fandd/2016/06/ostry.htm

O'Toole, Linda, and Daniel Kropf. 2012. *Changing Paradigms, Sharing our Hearts, Beginning a Dialogue.* Learning for Well-being Foundation. Brussels: Universal Education Foundation

Oxfam. 2015. Extreme carbon inequality.

Parliament of the World's Religions. 1993. Towards A Global Ethic: An Initial Declaration.

Pecharroman, Lidia. 2018. "Rights of Nature: Rivers That Can Stand in Court." *Resources* 7 (13).

Penal Reform International. 2016. "Why criminal justice reform is essential to the UN Agenda for Sustainable Development." May 2016.

Peppler, Kylie A., Christy Wessel Powell, Naomi Thompson, and James Catterall. 2014. "Positive Impact of Arts Integration on Student Academic Achievement in English Language Arts." *Education Forum* 78 (4): 364-77. https://doi.org/10.1080/00131725.2014.941124

Perez Barreto, Yvo. 2011. *The Man Who Speaks To The Plants.* Video. Accessed August 4, 2020. https://www.youtube.com/watch?v=qohNxer3mkY

Perez Barreto, Yvo. 2012. *L'homme qui parle avec les plantes.* Editions Clair de Terre.

Perez Barreto, Yvo. 2016. *Maya Rain.* Video. Accessed August 4, 2020. https://www.youtube.com/watch?v=ZSR5vC-lm6A&t=354s

Peterson, Christopher, Nansook Park, and Martin P. Seligman. 2005. "Orientations to Happiness and Life Satisfaction: The Full Life Versus the Empty Life." *Journal of Happiness Studies* 6, 25-41. https://doi.org/10.1007/s10902-004-1278-z

Petronzio, Matt. 2018. "Jacinda Ardern Wants to Make New Zealand the 'Best Place in the World to Be a Child.'" *Global Citizen*, September 23, 2018. https://www.globalcitizen.org/en/content/jacinda-ardern-social-good-summit-2018/

Pfeffer, Jeffrey, and Leanne Williams. 2020. "Mental health in the workplace: The coming revolution." *McKinsey Quarterly.* December 8, 2020. https://www.mckinsey.com/industries/healthcare-systems-and-services/our-insights/mental-health-in-the-workplace-the-coming-revolution

Pickert, Kate. 2014. "The Mindful Revolution." *Time* magazine. January 23, 2014. https://time.com/1556/the-mindful-revolution/

Piet, Jacob, and Espen Hougaard. 2011. "The Effect of Mindfulness-Based Cognitive Therapy for Prevention of Relapse in Recurrent Major Depressive Disorder:

A Systematic Review and Meta-Analysis." *Clinical Psychology Review* 31 (6): 1032-40. https://doi.org/ 10.1016/j.cpr.2011.05.002

Pietilä, Hilkka. 2007. "Nordic Welfare Society: Welfare in Finland built by the people and the State." A case study. Revised in 2007, original 2001. Available at http://www.hilkkapietila.net/en/

Piketty, Thomas. 2019. « La création, pour la première fois, d'un impôt sur la fortune aux Etats-Unis. » *Le Monde,* February 9, 2019.

Pinker, Steve. 2011a. *The Better Angels of Our Nature: The Decline of Violence in History and its Causes.* New York: Viking Books.

Pinker, Steve. 2011b. "A History of Violence: Edge Master Class 2011." *Edge,* September 27, 2011.

Plato. 2008. *The Symposium.* Cambridge: Cambridge University Press.

Pollock, Rufus. 2018. *The Open Revolution. Rewriting the rules of the information age.* N.p.: A/E/T Press.

Poore, Joseph, and Thomas Nemecek. 2018. "Reducing food's environmental impacts through producers and consumers." *Science* 360, 6392: 987-92.

Popenoe, David. 1996. *Life Without Father: Compelling new evidence that fatherhood and marriage are indispensable for the good of children and society.* New York: Free Press.

Pottenger, Francis M. 1983. *Pottenger's Cats: A Study in Nutrition.* N.p.: The Price-Pottenger Nutrition Foundation.

Poux, Xavier, Pierre-Marie Aubert. 2018. "An agroecological Europe in 2050: multifunctional agriculture for healthy eating." Findings from the Ten Years For Agroecology (TYFA) modelling exercise. Paris: Institute for Sustainable Development and International Relations (IDDRI). 74p.

Powers, John, ed. 2017. *The Buddhist World.* London: Routledge.

Prentice, Thomson. 2008. Health, History, and Hard Choices: Funding Dilemmas in a Fast-Changing World. *Non Profit and Voluntary Sector Quarterly* 37 (1).

Price, Weston A. 2009. *Nutrition and Physical Degeneration. A Comparison of Primitive and Modern Diets and Their Effects, 8th edition.* Lemon Grove, CA: Price-Pottenger Nutrition Foundation.

Prior, Ryan. 2020. "1 in 4 Young People are Reporting Suicidal Thoughts. Here's How to Help." In CNN *Health,* August 15, 2020. https://www.cnn.com/2020/08/14/health/young-people-suicidal-ideation-wellness/index.html

Prison Mindfulness Institute and Transforming Justice: The Center for Mindfulness And Criminal Justice. 2016. The Mindful Justice Initiative Report September 2016.

Prüss-Ustün, Annette, J. Wolf, Carlos F. Corvalán., R. Bos, and Maria Neira. 2016. "A global assessment of the burden of disease from environmental risks." Paris: World Health Organization. https://doi.org/ 10.1093/pubmed/fdw085

Psaltopoulou, Theodora, Theodoros Sergentanis, Demosthenes B. Panagiotakos, Ioannis N. Sergentanis, Rena Kosti, Nikolaos Scarmeas. 2013. "Mediterranean diet, stroke, cognitive impairment, and depression: A meta-analysis." *Annals of Neurology* 74 (4): 580–91

Putnam, Robert D. 2000. *Bowling Alone: The Collapse and Revival of American Community*. New York: Simon and Schuster.

Putnam, Robert D. 2001. Social Capital: Measurement and Consequences. *Isuma: Canadian Journal of Policy Research* [Internet] 2:41-51.

Pyarelal. 1932. *The Epic Fast*. Mohanlal Maganlal Bhatt; Ahmedabad.

Quick, Kathy, Guillermo Narváez, and Emily Saunoi-Sandgren. 2015. "Changing Minds through Deliberation: Participants' Accounts of their Learning." Public Management Research Conference.

Rahmani, Sabah. 2016. « Les Plantes, ces Grandes Communicantes. » *Le Monde*, February 29, 2016. https://www.lemonde.fr/sciences/article/2016/02/29/les-plantes-ces-grandes-communicantes_4873936_1650684.html

Rahn, Wendy M., and John E. Transue. 1998. "Social Trust and Value Change: The Decline of Social Capital in American Youth, 1976–1995." *Political Psychology* 19 (3): 545-65.

Ratzinger, John. 2009. *The Spirit of the Liturgy*. Ignatius Press.

Raworth, Kate. 2012. "A safe and just space for humanity. Can we live within the doughnut?" Oxfam Discussion Papers.

Raworth, Kate. 2017. *Doughnut Economics: Seven Ways to Think Like a 21st-Century Economist*. VT: Chelsea Green Publishing.

Ray, Paul H., and Sherry Ruth Anderson. 2000. *The Cultural Creatives: How 50 Million People Are Changing the World*. New York: Harmony Books.

Regalado, Michael, Harvinder Sareen, Moira Inkelas, Lawrence S. Wissow, and Neal Halfon. 2004. "Parents' Discipline of Young Children: Results from the National Survey of Early Childhood Health." *Pediatrics* 113 (6): 1952-58.

Rehm, Jürgen. Benjamin Taylor, and Robin Room. 2006. "Global burden of disease from alcohol, illicit drugs and tobacco." *Drug and Alcohol Review* 25 (6): 503-13.

Repucci, Sarah. 2020. "A Leaderless Struggle for Democracy." Freedom in the World series. Freedom House (website). https://freedomhouse.org/report/freedom-world/2020/leaderless-struggle-democracy

Reuters Staff. 2018. "Global Temperatures on Track for 3–5 Degree Rise by 2100: U.N." *Reuters,* November 29, 2018. https://www.reuters.com/article/us-climate-change-un-idUSKCN1NY186

Ricard, Matthieu. 2007. *Happiness, A Guide to Developing Life's Most Important Skill.* New York City: Little Brown.

Ricard, Matthieu. 2008. The Habits of Happiness. Video. Accessed July 31, 2020. https://www.youtube.com/watch?v=vbLEf4HR74E&t=32s

Ricard, Matthieu. 2014. *Plaidoyer pour L'altruisme.* Paris: Éditions Nil, Pocket.

Ricard, Patricia. 2015. *Le Biomimétisme: S'inspirer de la Nature pour Innover Durablement.* Avis du Conseil Économique, Social et Environnemental. Les Éditions des Journaux Officiels. Accessed July 29, 2020. https://www.lecese.fr/sites/default/files/pdf/Rapports/2015/2015_23_biomimetisme.pdf.

Rifkin, Jeremy. 2009. *The Empathic Civilization: The Race to Global Consciousness in a World in Crisis.* New York, NY: Penguin Books.

Rilling, James K., David A. Gutman, Torsten R. Zeh, Giuseppe Pagnoni, Gregory S. Berns, and Clinton D. Kilts. 2002. "A Neural Basis for Social Cooperation," *Neuron* 35 (2): 395-405. https://doi.org/10.1016/S0896-6273(02)00755-9

Rinne, Luke, Emma Gregory, Julia Yarmolinskaya, and Mariale Hardiman. (2011). "Why Arts Integration Improves Long-Term Retention of Content." *Mind, Brain, and Education* 5 (2): 89-96.

Riordan, Robert, and Stacey Caillier. 2019. "Schools as Equitable Communities of Inquiry." In *Sustainabilty, Human Well-Being and the Future of Education.* Edited by Justin W. Cook, 121-60. N.p.: Palgrave Mac Millan

Ritchie, Hannah, and Max Roser. 2018. "Mental Health." Published online in *OurWorldinData.org.* https://ourworldindata.org/mental-health.

Robinson, A. Helene. 2013. "Arts Integration and the Success of Disadvantaged Students: A Research Evaluation." *Arts Education Policy Review.* 114 (4): 191-204. https://doi.org/10.1080/10632913.2013.826050

Rodriguez, Tori. 2015. "Descendants of Holocaust Survivors Have Altered Stress Hormones. *Scientific American,* March 1, 2015.

Roege, Gayle B., and Kyung Hee Kim. 2013. "Why We Need Arts Education." *Empirical Studies of the Arts* 31 (2): 121-130.

Rogissart, Lucile, Claudine Foucherot, and Valentin Bellassen. 2019. "Food policies and climate: a literature review." Institute For Climate Economics.

Rojas, Mariano. 2018. "Happiness in Latin America Has Social Foundations." In *World Happiness Report 2018.* Edited by John Helliwell, Richard Layard, and Jeffrey Sachs, 115-45. New York: Sustainable Development Solutions Network.

Roser, Max. 2013. "Economic Growth." Published online at *OurWorldInData.org*. https://ourworldindata.org/economic-growth.

Rosier, Florence. 2017. « Quand L'école de la Vie S'invite en Classe. » *Le Monde*, January 31, 2017.

Roy, Eleanor Ainge. 2017. "New Zealand gives Mount Taranaki same legal rights as a person." *The Guardian*, December 22, 2017. https://www.theguardian.com/world/2017/dec/22/new-zealand-gives-mount-taranaki-same-legal-rights-as-a-person

Ryan, Tim. 2012. *A Mindful Nation: How a Simple Practice Can Help Us Reduce Stress, Improve Performance, and Recapture the American Spirit.* Carlsbad, CA: Hay House Inc.

Sabel, Charles, AnnaLee Saxenian, Reijo Miettinen, Peer Hull Kristensen, and Jarkko Hautamäki. 2011. "Individualized Service Provision in the New Welfare State. Lessons from Special Education in Finland." Working Paper. Department of Business and Politics. Copenhagen Business School.

Sachs, Jeffrey. 2012. *The Price of Civilization.* New York: Vintage.

Sachs, Jeffrey. 2015. "Investing in Social Capital." In *World Happiness Report 2015*. Edited by Helliwell, John, Richard Layard and Jeffrey Sachs, 152-166.

Sachs, Jeffrey. 2013. "Restoring virtue ethics in the quest for happiness." In *World Happiness Report 2013*. Edited by John Helliwell, Richard Layard and Jeffrey Sachs, 81-97.

Sage, Cindy, and David O. Carpenter, eds. 2012. "BioInitiative Report: A Rationale for a Biologically-based Public Exposure Standard for Electromagnetic Radiation." Bioinitiative Working Group.

Sahlins, Marshall. 2003. *Stone Age Economics.* London: Routledge.

Salovey, Peter, and John D. Mayer. 1990. "Emotional Intelligence." *Imagination, Cognition, and Personality* 9 (3): 185-211. https://doi.org/10.2190%2FDUGG-P24E-52WK-6CDG

Sanger, Toby. 2016. "How Progressive is a Basic income?" Left and Labour Perspectives.

Sarakatsannis, Jimmy, and Bryony Winn. 2018. "How States Can Improve Well-Being for all Children, from Birth to Age Five." Web content. McKinsey & Company, published October 16, 2018.

Sattelmair, Jacob, and John J. Ratey. 2009. "Physically Active Play and Cognition An Academic Matter?" *American Journal of Play* 1, (3): 365-74.

Sawyer, Wendy, and Peter Wagner. 2019. "Mass Incarceration: The Whole Pie 2019." Report. Prison Policy Initiative. https://www.prisonpolicy.org/reports/pie2019.html

Scarlet, Janina, Nathaniel Altmeyer, Susan Knier, and R. Edward Harpin. 2017. "The Effects of Compassion Cultivation Training (CCT) on Health-Care Workers." *Clinical Psychologist* 21 (2): 116-24.

Schaller, Noémie. 2013. "Agro-ecology: different definitions, common principles." *Analysis: Center for Studies and Strategic Foresight* 59, July 2013: 1-4.

Scharmer, C. Otto. 2016. *Theory U: Leading from the Future as it Emerges.* Oakland, CA: Berrett-Koehler.

Scharmer, C. Otto. 2018. *The Essentials of Theory U: Core Principles and Applications.* Oakland, CA: Berrett-Koehler Publishers.

Schepman, T. 2016. « Biomimétisme: Cinq inventions Géniales Inspirées par la Nature. » *L'Obs*, November 17, 2016. Accessed July 29, 2020. https://www.nouvelobs.com/rue89/rue89planete/20120324.RUE8759/biomimetisme-cinq-inventions-geniales-inspirees-par-la-nature.html

Scheuler, Leslie. 2010. "Arts Education Makes a Difference in Missouri Schools." Missouri Alliance for Arts Education.

Schlegel, Alexander, Prescott Alexander, Sergey V. Fogelson, Xueting Li, Zhengang Lu, Peter J. Kohler, Enrico Riley, et al. 2015. "The artist emerges: Visual art learning alters neural structure and function." *NeuroImage* 105:440-51.

Schmuck, Peter, Tim Kasser, Richard M. Ryan. 2000. "Intrinsic and Extrinsic Goals." *Social Indicators Research* 50 (2): 225-41.

Schock, Kurt. 2013. "The Practice and Study of Civil Resistance." *Journal of peace research* 50 (3): 277-90. https://doi.org/10.1177/0022343313476530

Schutte, Nicola S., and John M. Malouff. 2014. "A Meta-Analytic Review of the Effects of Mindfulness Meditation on Telomerase Activity." *Psychoneuroendocrinology* 42, 45-8. https://doi.org/10.1016/j.psyneuen.2013.12.017

Schwartz, Shalom H. 2006. *Basic Human Values: An Overview.* Jerusalem: The Hebrew University of Jerusalem.

Schwartz, Shalom H. 2007. "Cultural and Individual Value Correlates of Capitalism: A Comparative Analysis." *Psychological Inquiry* 18 (1): 52–57.

Scott, Bartie. 2017. "Why Meditation and Mindfulness Training is One of the Best Industries for Starting a Business in 2017." *Inc.,* March 1, 2017.

Scripp, Lawrence, and Laura Paradis. 2014. "Embracing the Burden of Proof: New Strategies for Determining Predictive Links between Arts Integration Teacher Professional Development, Student Arts Learning, and Student Academic Achievement Outcomes." *Journal of Learning Arts* 10: 1-18. https://doi.org/10.21977/D910119293

Selhub, Eva. 2020. "Nutritional psychiatry: Your brain on food." *Harvard Health Blog*, November 16, 2015. Updated March 26, 2020.

Seligman, Martin. 2010. "Flourish: Positive Psychology and Positive Interventions." The Tanner Lectures on Human Values. Delivered at University of Michigan on October 7, 2010. Accessed August 11, 2020. https://tannerlectures.utah. edu/_documents/a-to-z/s/Seligman_10.pdf

Seligman, Martin, and Alejandro Adler. 2018. "Positive Education." Chapter. In *Global Happiness Policy Report 2018*. Global Happiness Council, 53-74.

Seligman, Martin, and Mihaly Csikszebtmihalyi. 2000. "Positive Psychology: an Introduction." *American Psychologist* 55 (1): 5-14.

Sen, Amartya. 1999. *Development as Freedom*. New York: Oxford University Press.

SENPLADES. 2009. Plan Nacional para el Buen Vivir, 2009–2013.SENPLADES (Secretaría Nacional de Planificación), Quito.

Seppälä, Emma M., Timothy Rossomando, and James R. Doty. 2013. "Social Connection and Compassion: Important Predictors of Health and Well-Being." *Social Research* 80 2: 411.

Seppälä, Emma M., Emiliana Simon-Thomas, Stephanie L. Brown, Monica C. Worline, C. Daryl Cameron, and James R. Doty, eds. 2017. *The Oxford Handbook of Compassion Science*. New York, NY: Oxford University Press.

Seward, Emily A., and Steven Kelly. 2016. "Dietary nitrogen alters codon bias and genome composition in parasitic microorganisms." *Genome Biology* 17:226.

Shapiro, Shauna L., Linda E. Carlson, John A. Astin, and Benedict Freedman. 2006. "Mechanisms of Mindfulness." *Journal of Clinical Psychology* 62 (3): 373-86. https://doi.org/10.1002/jclp.20237

Sharafeddine, Randa. 2015. "The Economic Power of Money Creation." In *Microeconomics and Macroeconomics 2015* 3 (3): 67-81. https://doi. org/10.5923/j.m2economics.20150303.03.

Sheff, David. 2000. *All We Are Saying: The Last Major Interview with John Lennon and Yoko Ono*. New York: St. Martin's Griffin

Shutte, Augustine. 2001. Ubuntu: An Ethic for a New South Africa. Pietermaritzburg: Cluster Publications

Sisodia, Rajendra, Jagdish N. Sheth, and David B. Wolfe. 2007. *Firms of Endearment: How World-Class Companies Profit from Passion and Purpose*. Harlow Essex, UK: Financial Times/ Prentice Hall.

Sivaraksa, Sulak. 2016. *The Wisdom of Sustainability. Buddhist Economics for the 21st Century*. Asheville, NC: Chiron Publications.

Skolnick, Stephen. 2016. "Trees May Tell it When to Rain." *Physics Central*, June 8, 2016. Accessed August 4, 2020. https://www.physicscentral.com/explore/plus/trees-make-rain.cfm

Skutnabb-Kangas, Tove, Luisa Maffi, and Dave Harmon. 2003. "Sharing a World of Difference: The Earth's Linguistic, Cultural, and Biological Diversity." Paris: UNESCO.

Slavin, Robert E., Eric A. Hurley, and Anne Chamberlain. 2003. *Cooperative Learning and Achievement: Theory and Research*. Wiley Online Library. https://doi.org/10.1002/0471264385.wei0709

Snel, Eline. 2013. *Sitting Still Like a Frog*. Boston, MA: Shambhala.

Snowdon, Christopher. 2017. "Cheap as chips. Is a healthy diet affordable?" IEA Discussion Paper No.82. Institute of Economic Affairs.

Social Progress Imperative. 2019. "2019 Social Progress Index." Accessed June 4, 2020. Available at https://www.socialprogress.org/assets/downloads/resources/2019/2019-Global-SPI-findings-9.12.19.pdf

Solon, Olivia. 2018. "'Rain dancing 2.0': Should humans be using tech to control the weather?" *The Guardian*, August 26, 2018.

Solon, Pablo. 2014. Notes for the debate. *Systemic Alternatives*.

Solon, Pablo. 2018. "Vivir Bien: Old Cosmovisions and New Paradigms." Accessed July 29, 2020. https://greattransition.org/publication/vivir-bien.

Spielvogel, Jackson J. 2018. *Western civilization, Tenth edition*. N.p.: Cengage learning.

Spinrad, Tracy L. and Nancy Eisenberg. 2017. "Compassion in Children." In *The Oxford Handbook of Compassion Science*. Edited by Emma M. Seppälä, Emiliana Simon-Thomas, Stephanie L. Brown, Monica C. Worline, C. Daryl Cameron, and James R. Doty, 53-63. New York, NY: Oxford University Press.

Steel, Zachary, Claire Marnane, Changiz Iranpour, Tien Chey, John W. Jackson, Vikram Patel, and Derrick Silove. 2014. "The global prevalence of common mental disorders: a systematic review and meta-analysis 1980–2013." *International Journal of Epidemiology* 43 (2): 476-93.

Stern, Nicholas. 2007. *The Economics of Climate Change: The Stern Review*. Cambridge: Cambridge University Press.

Stiglitz, Joseph E., Amartya Sen, and Jean-Paul Fitoussi. 2008. Report by the Commission on the Measurement of Economic Performance and Social Progress. Accessed August 11, 2020. https://ec.europa.eu/eurostat/documents/8131721/8131772/Stiglitz-Sen-Fitoussi-Commission-report.pdf

Stone, Christopher D. 1972. "Should Trees Have Standing? Towards Legal Rights for Natural Objects." *Southern California Law Review* 45:450-501.

Stone, Deborah M., Thomas R. Simon, Katherine A. Fowler, Scott R. Kegler, Kening Yuan, Kristin M. Holland, Asha Z. Ivey-Stephenson, et al. 2018. "Vital Signs: Trends in State Suicide Rates—United States, 1999–2016 and Circumstances Contributing to Suicide—27 States, 2015." *Centers for Disease Control and Prevention MMWR* 67 (22): 617-24.

Stratistics MRC. 2019. *Organic Farming - Global Market Outlook (2017–2026)*. Digital PDF report. Published by Stratistics Market Research Consulting.

Sunim, Hwansan. 2017. "A Quantum Theory of Consciousness." *Huffington Post*, July 19, 2017.

Susskind, Jamie. 2020. "Digital technology and government." In *Renewing Democracy in the Digital Age*. Bergrruen Institute, 56-9.

Sweet, Lynn. 2020. "Trump Invokes Iran Hostages after Soleimani Attack; Outrageous They are Still Owed Compensation." *Chicago Sun-Times*, January 13, 2020.

Taylor, Tess. 2016. "22% of Companies Now Offering Mindfulness Training." *HRdive*, August 16, 2020. https://www.hrdive.com/news/22-of-companies-now-offering-mindfulness-training/424530/

Taylor, Michael. 2020. *Energy subsidies: Evolution in the global energy transformation to 2050*. Staff Technical Paper. International Renewable Energy Agency, Abu Dhabi.

Tchendukua. 2020. *Ici & ailleurs* N°25.

Teasdale, Wayne. 1999. *The Mystic Heart: Discovering a Universal Spirituality in the World's Religions*. Novato, CA: New World Library.

Teilhard de Chardin, Pierre. 1973. *Toward the Future*. San Diego, CA: Harcourt Brace Jovanovich.

Teilhard de Chardin, Pierre. 2002a. *The Heart of Matter*. Fort Washington, PA: Harvest Book.

Teilhard de Chardin, Pierre. 2002b. *The Phenomenon of Man*. Trans. B. Wall. New York: Harper Collins.

Tho, Ha Vinh. 2016. Personal Communication with Dr. Ha Vinh Tho, former Program Director of the Gross National Happiness Centre in Bhutan.

Thompson, Sam, Nic Marks, and Tim Jackson. 2013. "Well-Being and Sustainable Development." In *The Oxford Handbook of Happiness*. Edited by Susan David, Ilona Boniwell, and Amanda Conley Ayer, 498-516. Oxford, Great Britain: Oxford University Press.

Thornhill, Randy, Corey L. Fincher, and Devaraj Araan. 2009. "Parasites, democratization, and the liberalization of values across contemporary countries." *Biological reviews* 84 (1): 113-31.

Thornhill, Randy, Corey L. Fincher, Damian R. Murray, Mark Schaller. 2010. "Zoonotic and non-zoonotic diseases in relation to human personality and societal values." *Evolutionary psychology* 8:151-55.

Tibebu, Teshale. 2011. *Hegel and the Third World: The Making of Eurocentrism in World History*. Syracuse University Press.

Tompkins, Peter, and Christopher Bird. 1973. *The Secret Life of Plants*. New York: Harper & Row.

Torres, Susan J., and Caryl A. Nowson. 2007. "Relationship between stress, eating behavior, and obesity." *Nutrition* 23 (11-12): 887-94.

Tov, William, and Evelyn Au. 2013. "Comparing Wellbeing Across Nations: Conceptual and Empirical Issues." In David et al. 2013, 448-64.

Tower Watson. 2012. Global Workforce Study. Accessed June 2, 2020. https://employeeengagement.com/wp-content/uploads/2012/11/2012-Towers-Watson-Global-Workforce-Study.pdf

Tsai, Jeanne, and BoKyung Park. 2014. "The cultural shaping of happiness: The role of ideal affect." In *Positive Emotion: Integrating the Light and Dark Sides*. Edited by Judith Tedlie Moskowitz and June Gruber, 345-62. New York, NY: Oxford University Press.

Tucker, Emily, and Mark Daskin. 2020. "Medical supply chains are fragile in the best of times and COVID-19 will test their strength." *The Conversation*, March 25, 2020. https://theconversation.com/medical-supply-chains-are-fragile-in-the-best-of-times-and-covid-19-will-test-their-strength-133688

Tulard, Jean. 2012. *Napoléon chef de guerre*. Paris: Tallandier.

Turabian, Jose Luis. 2018. "The enormous potential of the doctor-patient relationship." *Trends in General Practice, Volume 1* 3: 1-2. https://doi.org/10.15761/TGP.1000115

Twenge, Jean M., and W. Keith Campbell. 2010. *The Narcissism Epidemic: Living in the Age of Entitlement*. Free Press.

Twenge, Jean M., W. Keith Campbell, and Elise C. Freeman. 2012. "Generational Differences in Young adults' life Goals, Concern for Others, and Civic Orientation, 1966–2009." *Journal of Personality and Social Psychology* 102 (5): 1045-62.

Uchida, Yukika, and Shinobu Kitayama. 2009. "Happiness and unhappiness in east and west: Themes and variations." *Emotion* 9 (4): 441-56. https://doi.org/10.1037/a0015634

UNCTAD. 2013. *Trade and Environment Review 2013: Wake-up before it is too late. Make agriculture truly sustainable now for food security in a changing climate.*

UNCTAD. 2014. World Investment Report.

UNCTAD. 2019. *Trade and Development Report 2019.* Financing a global green new deal.

UNDP. 2019. Human Development Report 2019. UNESCO. 2018. Basic texts.

UNESCO. 2005. The precautionary principle.

UNESCO. 2006. Road Map for Arts Education. 26p.

UNESCO. 2015. Quality physical education. 88p.

UNICEF (2019). The State of the World's Children 2019. Children, Food and Nutrition: Growing Well in a Changing World. UNICEF, New York.

Union of Concerned Scientists (UCS). Undated. "Counting on agroecology. Why we should invest more in the transition to sustainable agriculture." https://www.ucsusa.org/sites/default/files/attach/2015/11/ucs-counting-on-agroecology-2015.pdf

United Nations. 2009. Report of the Commission of Experts of the President of the United Nations General Assembly on Reforms of the International Monetary and Financial System.

United Nations. 2009. Resolution adopted by the General Assembly on 22 April 2009. https://undocs.org/A/RES/63/278, accessed July 29, 2020.

United Nations. 2014. *Prototype Global Sustainable Development Report.* New York: United Nations Department of Economic and Social Affairs, Division for Sustainable Development, July 2014. https://sustainabledevelopment.un.org/globalsdreport/2014

United Nations Development Programme. *Human Development Report 1994. A Tax on International Currency Transactions.* New York: Oxford University Press.

United Nations Environment Programme. 2019. *Emissions Gap Report 2019.* Nairobi: UNEP.

United Nations Environment Programme and International Livestock Research Institute. 2020. *Preventing the Next Pandemic: Zoonotic diseases and how to break the chain of transmission.* Nairobi: UNEP.

United Nations Office on Drugs and Crime. 2019. Global Study on Homicide. Executive Summary.

Universal House of Justice. 2002. *To The World's Religious Leaders.* Haifa: Bahá'í World Centre.

UNODC. 2006. Handbook on Restorative justice programmes.

UN Secretary General. 2016. "Harmony with Nature." Note by the Secretary General. A/71/266.

Ura, Karma, Sabina Alkire, Tsoki Zangmo, and Karma Wangdi. 2012. *A Short Guide to Gross National Happiness Index*. Thimphu: Centre for Bhutan Studies.

Uslaner, Eric M. 2002. *The Moral Foundations of Trust*. Cambridge: Cambridge University Press.

Valenzuela, Hector. 2016. "Agroecology: A Global Paradigm to Challenge Mainstream Industrial Agriculture." *Horticulturae* 2 (1): 2. https://doi. org/10.3390/horticulturae2010002

2Van Lerven, Frank. 2016a. "A Guide to Public Money Creation. Outlining the Alternatives to Quantitative Easing." Positive Money.org. https:// positivemoney.org/2016/04/our-new-guide-to-public-money-creation/

Van Lerven, Frank. 2016b. "A history of public money creation—summary." Positive Money.org. https://positivemoney.org/2016/06/a-history-of-qe-for-people-summary/

Varlas, Laura. 2011. "Five Elements of Personalized Learning in Finland." *ASCD Newsletters & Publications*, February 2, 2011. https://inservice.ascd.org/mary-forte-hayes/

Vatn, Arild. 2010. "An institutional analysis of payments for environmental services." *Ecological Economics* 69 (6): 1245-52. https://doi.org/10.1016/j. ecolecon.2009.11.018

Vernant, Jean-Pierre. 2007. *Les Origines de la pensée grecque*. Paris: Presses Universitaires de France - collection Quadrige.

Vella-Brodrick, Dianne A., Nansook Park, and Christopher Peterson. 2009. "Three Ways to be Happy: Pleasure, Engagement, and Meaning—Findings from Australian and US Samples." *Social Indicators Research* 90, 165-179. https:// doi.org/10.1007/s11205-008-9251-6

Vigo, Daniel, Graham Thornicroft, and Rifat Atun. 2016. "Estimating the true global burden of mental illness." *Lancet Psychiatry* 3 (2): 171-78. https://doi. org/10.1016/S2215-0366(15)00505-2

Villacorta, Mark, Richard Koestner, and Natasha Lekes. 2003. Further Validation of the Motivation toward the Environment Scale. *Environment and Behavior* 35 (4): 486-505. https://doi.org/10.1177/0013916503035004003

Vincent, Julian F. V., Olga A. Bogatyreva, Nikolaj R. Bogatyrev, Adrian Bowyer, and Anja-Karina Pahl. 2006. "Biomimetics: its Practice and Theory." *Journal of the Royal Society Interface* 3 (9): 471-82. https://doi.org/10.1098/rsif.2006.0127

Vitteta, Luis, Anton B., Cortizo F., and Sali A. 2005. Mind-body medicine: stress and its impact on overall health and longevity," *Annals of the New York Academy of Sciences* no. 1057, 492-505. https://doi.org/10.1196/annals.1322.038.

Vos, Theo, Abraham D. Flaxman, Mohsen Naghavi, Rafael Lozano, Catherine Michaud, Majid Ezzati, Kenji Shibuya, et al. 2012. "Years lived with disability (YLDs) for 1160 sequelae of 289 diseases and injuries 1990–2010: A systematic analysis for the Global Burden of Disease Study 2010." *Lancet* 380 (9859): 2163-96.

Vosoughi, Soroush, Deb Roy, and Sinan Aral. 2018. "The spread of true and false news online." *Science* 359 (6380): 1146-51. https://science.sciencemag.org/content/sci/359/6380/1146.full.pdf

Wahlbeck, Kristian, Jeanette Westman, Merete Nordentoft, Mika Gissler, and Thomas Munk Laursen. 2011. "Outcomes of Nordic mental health systems: life expectancy of patients with mental disorders." *British Journal of Psychiatry* 199 (6): 453-58.

Waldinger, Robert. 2016. "What Makes a Good Life? Lessons from the Longest Study on Happiness." Video. Accessed July 29, 2020. https://www.youtube.com/watch?v=8KkKuTCFvzI

Waldmann-Selsam, Cornelia, Alfonso Balmori-de la Puente, Helmut Breunig, and Alfonso Balmori. 2016. "Radiofrequency Radiation Injures Trees Around Mobile Phone Base Stations." *Science of the Total Environment* 572 (1): 554-69. https://doi.org/10.1016/j.scitotenv.2016.08.045

Walgrave, Lode. 2011. "Investigating the Potentials of Restorative Justice Practice." *Washington University Journal of Law & Policy* 36 (1): 91-139.

Walking Eagle News. 2017. "Trudeau Speech Almost Entirely of Word 'Reconciliation.'" December 1, 2017.

Waterman, Alan S. 1993. "Two Conceptions of Happiness: Contrasts of Personal Expressiveness (Eudaimonia) and Hedonic Enjoyment." *Journal of Personality and Social Psychology* 64 (4): 678-91. https://doi.org/10.1037/0022-3514.64.4.678

We Demain. 2015. « Au Mexique, du Street-art Contre la Délinquance. » December 8, 2015. Accessed August 4, 2020. https://www.wedemain.fr/Au-Mexique-du-street-art-contre-la-delinquance_a1185.html

Weiss, Thomas G. 2012. *What's Wrong with the United Nations and How to Fix it.* Cambridge: Polity.

White, Matthew A. 2013. "Positive Education at Geelong Grammar School." In David et al. 2013, 657-68.

Wieczner, Jan. 2016. "Meditation Has Become A Billion-Dollar Business." *Fortune,* March 12, 2016. https://fortune.com/2016/03/12/meditation-mindfulness-apps/

Wilber, Ken. 2001. *A Theory of Everything. An Integral Vision for Business, Politics, Science and Spirituality.* Boston, MA: Shambhala Publications.

Wilcox, Bruce A., and Brett Ellis. 2006. "Forests and emerging infectious diseases of humans." *Unasylva* 224 (57): 11-18. http://www.fao.org/3/a0789e/a0789e03.html

Wilkinson, Richard G., and Kate Pickett. 2010. *The Spirit Level—Why Equality is Better for Everyone.* London, England: Penguin Books.

Willer, Helga, and Julia Lernoud, eds. 2019. *The World of Organic Agriculture. Statistics and Emerging Trends 2019.* Research Institute of Organic Agriculture (FiBL), Frick, and IFOAM – Organics International, Bonn.

Wilson, Edward Osborne. 2012. *The Social Conquest of Earth.* New York: Liveright.

Williamson, Marianne. 2000. *Healing the Soul of America: Reclaiming Our Voices as Spiritual Citizens.* New York: Simon & Schuster.

Wilson, Margo, and Martin Daily. 1988. *Homicide.* Piscataway, NJ: Aldine Transaction.

Wirsching, Elisa Maria. 2018. "The Revolving Door for Political Elites: An Empirical Analysis of the Linkages between Government Officials' Professional Background and Financial Regulation." Report. 2018 OECD Global Anti-Corruption & Integrity Forum. Accessed June 2, 2020. https://www.oecd.org/corruption/integrity-forum/academic-papers/Wirsching.pdf

Wohlleben, Peter. 2016. *The Hidden Life of Trees: What They Feel, How They Communicate—Discoveries from A Secret World.* Vancouver: Greystone Books.

Wolf, Kathleen L. 2012. "The Nature and Health Connection: Social Capital and Urban Greening Ecosystems." Proceedings of the 2012 International Society of Arboriculture Conference August 11–15, 2012; Portland, Oregon. Accessed July 29, 2020. https://www.naturewithin.info/New/ISA_prcdngs.Ecosystem_Social_Capital_Wolf.pdf

Wolfe, Norman. 2011. *The Living Organization: Transforming Business To Create Extraordinary Results.* N.p.: Quantum Leaders Publishing.

World Commission on Environment and Development. 1987. *Our Common Future.* Oxford: Oxford University Press.

World Economic Forum. 2019. Health and Healthcare in the Fourth Industrial Revolution.

World Health Organization. 2001. *Strengthening Mental Health Promotion*. Geneva: World Health Organization (Fact sheet, No. 220).

World Health Organization. 2013. *Strengthening the doctor–patient relationship*. A framework for action. Geneva: World Health Organization.

World Health Organization and Calouste Gulbenkian Foundation. 2014. *Integrating the response to mental disorders and other chronic diseases in health care systems*. Geneva: World Health Organization.

World People's Conference on Climate Change and the Rights of Mother Earth. 2010. Universal declaration of the rights of mother Earth. https://pwccc. wordpress.com/

World Trade Organization. 2020. "Trade set to plunge as COVID-19 pandemic upends global economy." Press release. https://www.wto.org/english/news_e/ pres20_e/pr855_e.htm

Wright, Jonathon S., Rong Fu, John R. Worden, Sudip Chakraborty, Nicholas Clinton, Camille Risi, Ying Sun, and Lei Yin. 2017. "Rainforest-initiated wet season onset over the southern Amazon." *Proceedings of the National Academy of Sciences* 114 (32): 8481-86. https://doi.org/10.1073/pnas.1621516114

Wyde, Michael, Mark Cesta, Chad Blystone, Susan Elmore, Paul Foster, Michelle Hooth, Grace Kissling, et al.2018. "Report of Partial findings from the National Toxicology Program Carcinogenesis Studies of Cell Phone Radiofrequency Radiation in Hsd: Sprague Dawley® SD rats (Whole Body Exposures)." *bioRxiv. The Preprint Server for Biology*. Posted February 1, 2018. https://doi. org/10.1101/055699;

Xi Jinping. 2017. Report at 19th CPC National Congress on October 18. Accessed July 29, 2020. http://www.chinadaily.com.cn/china/19thcpcnationalcongress/ 2017-11/04/content_34115212.htm

Ye, Dezhu, Yew-Kwang Ng, and Yujun Lian. 2015. "Culture and Happiness." *Social Indicators Research* 123 (2): 519-47. https://www.jstor.org/stable/24721617

Yehuda, Rachel, Nikolaos P. Daskalakis, Linda M. Bierer, Heather N. Bader, Torsten Klengel, Florian Holsboer, and Elisabeth B. Binder. 2016. "Holocaust Exposure Induced Intergenerational Effects on FKBP5 Methylation." *Biological Psychiatry* 80 (5): 372-80. https://doi.org/10.1016/j.biopsych.2015.08.005

You, Jong-Sung, and Sanjeev Khagram. 2005. "Comparative Study of Inequality and Corruption." *American Sociological Review* 70 (1): 136-57. https://www. jstor.org/stable/4145353

Zarins, Sasha, and Sara Konrath. 2017. "Changes over Time in Compassion-Related Variables in the United States." In *The Oxford Handbook of Compassion Science*. Edited by Emma M. Seppälä, Emiliana Simon-Thomas, Stephanie L.

Brown, Monica C. Worline, C. Daryl Cameron, and James R. Doty, 331-52. New York, NY: Oxford University Press.

Zizek, Slavoj. 2018. *Like a Thief in Broad Daylight: Power in the Era of Post-Human Capitalism*. New York: Seven Stories Press.

Zobrist, Jean-François. 2018. *La Belle Histoire de Favi:* L'entreprise Qui Croit Que L'homme est Bon. Paris: Humanisme & Organisations.

Index

About the Author

BORN IN 1979 in Paris, France, Thomas Legrand is a wisdom seeker, a social scientist, and a sustainability practitioner.

He holds a PhD in economics and has studied international development, political science, and management. Anchored in ecological and institutional economics, his PhD thesis was on the Costa Rican program of Payment for Environmental Services, which aims at conserving tropical forests.

Thomas works in the field of sustainability for UN agencies, private companies, and NGOs. His focus is on forest conservation, climate change, sustainable finance, organizational transformation, and leadership.

His spiritual journey began at the age of twenty-three with an encounter with native spirituality in Mexico, before embracing the wisdom of a wide range of traditions and practices, including meditation, energetic healing, and Tai-chi-chuan. He lives with his wife and their two young daughters near Plum Village, the monastery of Zen Master Thich Nhat Hanh in the southwest of France.

Thomas's spiritual search, his thoughts as a social scientist, and his professional experience have gradually converged on the importance of spiritual wisdom in humanity's ongoing transition. Searching for a way to mainstream this understanding in the political and sustainability conversation, he has dedicated much of the last ten years to researching and reflecting how we can radically rethink our model of development. The result is this book.